Kaplan Publishing are constantly finding ways to make a difference to your studies exciting online resources really do offer something different to students looking for exam success.

D0347575

This book comes with free MyKaplan online resources so that you can study anytime, anywhere. This free online resource is not sold separately and is included in the price of the book.

Having purchased this book, you have access to the following online study materials:

CONTENT	ACCA (including FFA,FAB,FMA)		FIA (excluding FFA,FAB,FMA)	
	Text	Kit	Text	Kit
iPaper version of the book	✓	✓	✓	✓
Interactive electronic version of the book	✓			
Check Your Understanding Test with instant answers	✓			
Material updates	✓	✓	✓	✓
Latest official ACCA exam questions*		✓		
Extra question assistance using the signpost icon**		✓		
Timed questions with an online tutor debrief using clock icon*		✓		
Interim assessment including questions and answers	✓		✓	
Technical answers	✓	✓	✓	✓

* Excludes F1, F2, F3, F4, FAB, FMA and FFA; for all other papers includes a selection of questions, as released by ACCA

** For ACCA P1-P7 only

How to access your online resources

Kaplan Financial students will already have a MyKaplan account and these extra resources will be available to you online. You do not need to register again, as this process was completed when you enrolled. If you are having problems accessing online materials, please ask your course administrator.

If you are already a registered MyKaplan user go to www.MyKaplan.co.uk and log in. Select the 'add a book' feature and enter the ISBN number of this book and the unique pass key at the bottom of this card. Then click 'finished' or 'add another book'. You may add as many books as you have purchased from this screen.

If you purchased through Kaplan Flexible Learning or via the Kaplan Publishing website you will automatically receive an e-mail invitation to MyKaplan. Please register your details using this email to gain access to your content. If you do not receive the e-mail or book content, please contact Kaplan Flexible Learning.

If you are a new MyKaplan user register at www.MyKaplan.co.uk and click on the link contained in the email we sent you to activate your account. Then select the 'add a book' feature, enter the ISBN number of this book and the unique pass key at the bottom of this card. Then click 'finished' or 'add another book'.

Your Code and Information

This code can only be used once for the registration of one book online. This registration and your online content will expire when the final sittings for the examinations covered by this book have taken place. Please allow one hour from the time you submit your book details for us to process your request.

Please scratch the film to access your MyKaplan code.

Please be aware that this code is case-sensitive and you will need to include the dashes within the passcode, but not when entering the ISBN. For further technical support, please visit www.MyKaplan.co.uk

110000019724

Paper F6

Taxation
(Finance Act 2016)

EXAM KIT

For June 2017 to March 2018 examination sittings

British Library Cataloguing-in-Publication Data

A catalogue record for this book is available from the British Library.

Published by:

Kaplan Publishing UK

Unit 2 The Business Centre

Molly Millar's Lane

Wokingham

Berkshire

RG41 2QZ

ISBN: 978-1-78415-695-4

Acknowledgements

The past ACCA examination questions are the copyright of the Association of Chartered Certified Accountants. The original answers to the questions from June 1994 onwards were produced by the examiners themselves and have been adapted by Kaplan Publishing.

We are grateful to the Chartered Institute of Management Accountants and the Institute of Chartered Accountants in England and Wales for permission to reproduce past examination questions. The answers have been prepared by Kaplan Publishing.

CONTENTS

Key features in this edition

In addition to providing a wide ranging bank of real past exam questions, we have also included in this edition:

- An analysis of all of the recent examination papers.

- Paper specific information and advice on exam technique.

- Our recommended approach to make your revision for this particular subject as effective as possible. This includes step by step guidance on how best to use our Kaplan material (complete text, pocket notes and exam kit) at this stage in your studies.

- A wealth of past real examination questions adapted to the new examination style with enhanced tutorial answers and packed with specific key answer tips, technical tutorial notes and exam technique tips from our experienced tutors.

- Complementary online resources including full tutor debriefs and question assistance to point you in the right direction when you get stuck.

You will find a wealth of other resources to help you with your studies on the following sites:

www.mykaplan.co.uk

www.accaglobal.com/en/student.html

Quality and accuracy are of the utmost importance to us so if you spot an error in any of our products, please send an email to mykaplanreporting@kaplan.com with full details, or follow the link to the feedback form in MyKaplan.

Our Quality Coordinator will work with our technical team to verify the error and take action to ensure it is corrected in future editions.

INDEX TO QUESTIONS AND ANSWERS

INTRODUCTION

A new examination format has been introduced with effect from September 2016.

The main change to the format of the examination was the introduction, in a new section B, of three objective test (OT) case questions, each involving five OT questions, based around a common scenario. To compensate, section C only includes three long form questions (instead of five) for 40 marks in total (see Paper Specific Information).

In addition, computer-based exams (CBEs) are available in certain locations in respect of the ACCA Fundamental Skills Level papers (F5–F9) during the examination sittings covered by this exam kit. A paper-based examination will still be available.

If you would like further information on sitting a CBE F6 examination please contact either Kaplan or the ACCA.

In the paper-based examination, all of the objective test questions in sections A and B will be of multiple choice style. However, CBEs will contain different styles of OT questions in sections A and B as well as multiple choice questions. This exam kit contains some OT question styles which will only appear in a CBE. However, they still provide valuable practice for all students, whichever version of the examination they are entered for.

As a result of these changes to the F6 exam format, the majority of past exam questions in their original format are not representative of current F6 examination questions. The questions contained in this exam kit are therefore based on past exam questions but it has been necessary to adapt them to ensure that they are representative of questions in the examinations from September 2016 onwards. The adaptations have been made to reflect the new style of paper, new legislative changes in recent Finance Acts, Tax law changes and IFRS® Standards terminology. We have also included new topics brought into the syllabus in some questions.

Many of the questions within the kit are past ACCA exam questions, and the more recent questions (from 2005) are labelled as such in the index. Note that if a question within this kit has been adapted or changed in any way from the original version, this is indicated in the end column of the index below with the mark *(A)*.

Also included are the marking schemes for past ACCA examination questions to assist you in understanding where marks are earned and the amount of time to spend on particular tasks. Note that if a question has been changed from the original version, it will have also been necessary to change the original ACCA marking scheme. Therefore, if a question is marked as 'ADAPTED' you should assume that this also applies to the marking scheme.

The new section B OT case questions, and the majority of the section A OT questions included in this kit have been generated based on the style of questions in the ACCA specimen papers and to provide as broad coverage of the syllabus as possible. The sections A and B questions in the real exam will be two marks each, but some will be slightly longer and some slightly shorter. The questions should take approximately 3.6 minutes each and this will average out over the OT questions in the exam. The majority of the questions in this kit are worth 2 marks. However, some are longer than that for tutorial purposes in order to maximise the syllabus coverage.

A number of questions included in the exam kit are referenced to two examination sittings e.g. March/June 2016. This is as a result of a change in policy made by the ACCA regarding the release of examination questions. Previously, examination papers were released in their entirety. The ACCA now release a selection of questions from the March/June and September/December examinations. Therefore, questions referenced as such are taken from the sample released by the ACCA.

KEY TO THE INDEX

PAPER ENHANCEMENTS

We have added the following enhancements to the answers in this exam kit:

Key answer tips

All answers include key answer tips to help your understanding of each question.

Tutorial note

All answers include tutorial notes to explain some of the technical points in more detail.

Tutor's top tips

For selected questions, we 'walk through the answer' giving guidance on how to approach the questions with helpful 'tips from a top tutor', together with technical tutor notes.

These answers are indicated with the 'footsteps' icon in the index.

ONLINE ENHANCEMENTS

 Timed question with Online tutor debrief

For selected questions, we recommend that they are to be completed in full exam conditions (i.e. properly timed in a closed book environment).

In addition to the examining team's technical answer, enhanced with key answer tips and tutorial notes in this exam kit, online you can find an answer debrief by a top tutor that:

- works through the question in full

- points out how to approach the question

- advises you how to ensure that the easy marks are obtained as quickly as possible, and

- emphasises how to tackle exam questions and exam technique.

These questions are indicated with the 'clock' icon in the index.

Online question enhancements and answer debriefs will be available from Spring 2017 on **My**Kaplan at:

www.mykaplan.co.uk

PRACTICE INCOME TAX AND NATIONAL INSURANCE QUESTIONS

KAPLAN PUBLISHING

PRACTICE CHARGEABLE GAINS QUESTIONS

PRACTICE INHERITANCE TAX QUESTIONS

PRACTICE CORPORATION TAX QUESTIONS

PRACTICE VALUE ADDED TAX QUESTIONS

ANALYSIS OF PAST EXAM PAPERS

The table below summarises the key topics that have been tested in recent exams.

Key:

Q   The question references are to the number of the question in this edition of the exam kit.

✓   Refers to questions which have not been included in the kit due to similarity to other recent questions.

*   Refers to topics that were included in the question when originally set, but with the adaptation of the question to the new style exam, this topic element has been removed from this question in the exam kit.

	Dec 2012	June 2013	Dec 2013	June 2014	Dec 2014	June 2015	Sept/ Dec 2015	Mar/ Jun 2016
Principles of taxation/Ethics								
Revenue/capital taxes							Q64	
Ethics of non-disclosure			Q268					
Money laundering			Q268					
Tax evasion/avoidance						Q65		
Income tax								
Exempt income	✓						Q4	
Basic income tax computation	✓ Q93	Q112 Q191 *		Q87 Q102		Q94	Q89	Q84 Q92
Savings income				Q87			Q88	
Dividend income				Q87	Q101			
Child benefit tax charge				Q87*		Q7		
Gift Aid donation	✓				Q101		Q88	
Reduction of personal allowance	✓							
Property income	✓	Q112 * Q191 *		Q87			Q17	Q84
Furnished holiday lettings	✓	Q112 *						
ISAs	Q190 *				Q101			
Residence						Q10		
Employed individual								
Employed vs. self-employed								Q92
Salary and bonus				Q87	Q101	Q94	Q88	Q84
Exempt benefits								Q84
Car and fuel benefit		Q112 *	Q100	Q87		✓	Q88	
Living accommodation				Q87		✓		

	Dec 2012	June 2013	Dec 2013	June 2014	Dec 2014	June 2015	Sept/ Dec 2015	Mar/ Jun 2016
Payroll giving					Q101 *		Q88	
Beneficial loan		Q112					Q111	Q84
Use/gift of assets				Q87*	Q101 *	✓		
Mileage allowance		Q112			Q101 *	✓		
Professional subscriptions					Q101 *		Q88	
Overnight expenses						✓		
PAYE forms						✓		
Self-employed individual								
Adjustment to profits			Q100	Q102				
Capital allowances	✓	✓	Q100	Q87*	Q101		Q31	Q84 Q92
Basis of assessment rules	✓	✓	Q96	Q87*	Q101		Q88 Q111	Q84
Partnerships – allocation					Q101		Q88 Q111	
Cash basis				Q102				
Pre-trading expenditure			Q96					
Pensions								
Pension income		Q112 *						
Occupational pension		Q112			Q101 *			Q84
Personal pension contributions	Q190	Q112		Q87*	✓			Q84
Annual allowance	Q190	Q112		Q87*				
Income tax losses								
Relief against income			Q96			Q41	Q111	
Opening year loss relief								
Terminal loss relief								
Tax savings								
Ongoing losses			Q96					
Relief against gains			Q96				Q111	
National Insurance contributions								
Class 1	Q93	Q112	Q100		Q101	Q50 Q94	Q48	Q92
Class 1A		Q112	Q100		Q101 *	Q50		
Class 2				Q102			Q48	Q92
Class 4				Q102	Q101		Q48	Q92

	Dec 2012	June 2013	Dec 2013	June 2014	Dec 2014	June 2015	Sept/ Dec 2015	Mar/ Jun 2016
Capital gains								
Chargeable person								
Residence					✓			
Basic CGT computation		Q160 Q191	Q154	Q161	✓		Q162	Q84 Q159
Enhancement	Q156			Q161				
Part disposal	Q156			Q161	✓			Q159
Shares	Q156	Q160	Q154			Q165	Q162	
Takeover						Q165		
Wasting asset							Q126	
Insurance for damaged assets	Q156						Q129	
Husband and wife			Q154	Q161 *				Q159
Capital losses	Q93*					Q125		
Planning re disposal date			Q154 *					
Reliefs								
Entrepreneurs' relief		Q160	Q154 *	Q161	✓		Q162	
Principal private residence relief			Q154					
Gift relief		Q160	Q154 *	Q161 *				Q159
Rollover relief		Q160 *		Q161		Q141		
Self-assessment – individual								
Payments on account	✓				Q101	Q72		
Filing dates			Q100		Q101 *		Q69	
Amendments to returns						Q70		
Compliance checks			Q100					
Interest and penalties						Q73		
Record retention					Q101 *			
Inheritance tax								
PETs	Q190	Q191	Q188	Q192	✓	✓	Q195	Q193
CLTs	Q190		Q188	Q192	✓	✓ Q172	Q195	Q193
Exemptions		Q191	Q188	Q192	✓		Q195	Q193
Diminution in value			Q188		✓		Q195	
Estate computation		Q191			✓	Q175		
After tax inheritance			Q188 *	Q192 *	✓		Q176	

	Dec 2012	June 2013	Dec 2013	June 2014	Dec 2014	June 2015	Sept/ Dec 2015	Mar/ Jun 2016
Reduction of tax							Q170	Q193
Due dates		Q191 *	Q188 *			Q172		
Transfer of nil rate band					✓			
Corporation tax								
Residence							Q197	
Definition of accounting periods							Q238	
Adjustment to profits	Q245	Q226	Q236	Q246	Q237	Q241	Q238	Q243
Capital allowances	Q245	Q226	Q236	Q246	Q237	Q241	Q238	Q243
Lease premiums			Q236 *	Q246	Q237			
Basic TTP computation	Q245 Q93	Q228 *	Q236	Q246	Q237	✓	Q238	
Property income			Q236		Q237			
Interest income	Q245		Q236	Q246	Q237		Q238	
Chargeable gains	✓			Q246		Q165		
Long period of account		✓						
Qualifying donations				Q246				
Corporation tax losses								
Capital losses	Q156 *							
Trading losses				Q246		Q241		Q243
Groups								
Group relief		Q228		Q246	✓	Q210		Q243
Capital gains group			Q236 *		✓	Q210		
Group structure planning					✓			
Self-assessment – companies								
Due dates and interest	Q245		Q236				Q225	
Quarterly instalments					Q237		Q223	
iXBRL	Q245			Q246				
Retention of records							Q238	
Value added tax								
Registration			Q268				Q280	
VAT return computation		Q273		Q246 *		Q255 Q281	Q250	Q274
Tax point		Q273		Q246 *			Q280	
Due dates			Q268 *				Q280	
VAT invoices			Q268					
Default surcharge		Q273			Q278			

	Dec 2012	June 2013	Dec 2013	June 2014	Dec 2014	June 2015	Sept/ Dec 2015	Mar/ Jun 2016
Errors in a VAT return					Q278			
Overseas supplies	Q277				Q278			
VAT Groups		Q273						
Annual accounting scheme	Q277							
Cash accounting scheme	Q277						Q280	Q274
Flat rate scheme						Q281		
Net after tax cost comparison	Q93							

EXAM TECHNIQUE

GENERAL COMMENTS

- We recommend that you spend **15 minutes reading the paper** at the beginning of the exam:

    - read the questions and examination requirements carefully, and

    - begin planning your answers.

    See the Paper Specific Information for advice on how to use this time for this paper.

- If 15 minutes are spent reading the examination paper, this leaves three hours to attempt the questions.

- **Divide the time** you spend on questions in proportion to the marks on offer:

    - one suggestion for this examination is to allocate 1.8 minutes to each mark available (180 minutes/100 marks), so a 10 mark question should be completed in approximately 18 minutes. If you plan to spend more or less time than 15 minutes reading the paper, your time allocation per mark will be different.

    - within that, try to allow time at the end of each question to review your answer and address any obvious issues.

- If you **get completely stuck** with a question:

    - leave space in your answer book (or leave it blank on your OT answer sheet), and **return to it later.**

- Spend the last **five minutes** of the examination:

    - reading through your answers, and

    - **making any additions or corrections**.

SECTION A OBJECTIVE TEST QUESTIONS

- Decide whether you want to attempt these at the start of the examination or at the end.

- Stick to the timing principle of 1.8 minutes per mark. This means that the 15 OT questions in section A (30 marks) should take 54 minutes.

- No credit for workings will be given in these questions; the answers will either be correct (2 marks) or incorrect (0 marks).

- Work steadily. Rushing leads to careless mistakes and questions are designed to include answers which result from careless mistakes.

- If you don't know the answer, eliminate those options you know are incorrect and see if the answer becomes more obvious.

- Remember that there is no negative marking for an incorrect answer. After you have eliminated the options that you know to be wrong, if you are still unsure, guess.

SECTION B OT CASE QUESTIONS

- There is likely to be a significant amount of information to read through for each case. You should begin by reading the OT questions that relate to the case, so that when you read through the information for the first time, you know what it is that you are required to do.

- Each OT question is worth two marks. Therefore you have 18 minutes (1.8 minutes per mark) to answer the five OT questions relating to each case. It is likely that all of the cases will take the same length of time to answer, although some of the OT questions within a case may be quicker than other OT questions within that same case.

- Once you have read through the information, you should first answer any of the OT questions that do not require workings and can be quickly answered. You should then attempt the OT questions that require workings utilising the remaining time for that case.

- All of the tips for section A are equally applicable to each section B question.

SECTION C CONSTRUCTED RESPONSE (LONG) QUESTIONS

- The constructed response questions in section C will require a written response rather than being OT questions. Therefore, different techniques need to be used to score well.

- Unless you know exactly how to answer the question, spend some time planning your answer. Stick to the question and tailor your answer to what you are asked. Pay particular attention to the verbs in the question e.g. 'Calculate', 'State', 'Explain'.

- If you do not understand what a question is asking, state your assumptions. Even if you do not answer in precisely the way the examining team hoped, you should be given some credit, if your assumptions are reasonable.

- You should do everything you can to make things easy for the marker. Your answer should:
  - be legible
  - have a clear structure
  - be concise.

  It is better to write a little about a lot of different points than a great deal about one or two points.

- **Section C Computations:**
  - It is essential to include all your workings in your answers. Many computational questions require the use of a standard format e.g. income tax computations, corporation tax computations and capital gains.
  - Be sure you know these formats thoroughly before the examination and use the layouts that you see in the answers given in this book and in model answers.
  - Adopt a logical approach and cross reference workings to the main computation to keep your answers tidy.
  - If you are entered for a CBE, you may be presented with either a blank response area, or a pre-formatted area (a template) to enter your answer.
  - A number of standard spreadsheet functions are available via the menu and tool bar for you to use when responding to the question.

- **Section C Reports, memos and other documents:**

  - Some questions ask you to present your answer in the form of a report, a memo, a letter or other document.

  - If you are entered for a CBE you may either be presented with a blank response area, or a pre-formatted area (a template) to enter your answer.

  - A number of standard word processing functions are available via the tool bar for students to use when responding to the question.

COMPUTER-BASED EXAMS – ADDITIONAL TIPS

- Do not attempt a CBE until you have completed all study material relating to it.

- On the ACCA website there is a CBE demonstration. It is ESSENTIAL that you attempt this before your real CBE. You will become familiar with how to move around the CBE screens and the way that questions are formatted, increasing your confidence and speed in the actual examination.

- Be sure you understand how to use the software before you start the examination. If in doubt, ask the assessment centre staff to explain it to you.

- Questions are displayed on the screen and answers are entered using keyboard and mouse.

- In addition to multiple choice type questions, CBEs will also contain other types of questions. You need to be sure you know how to answer questions of these types before you sit the examination, through practice. The types of objective test questions you could see in your CBE are as follows:

Question type	Description	Example exam kit question
Multiple choice	Select one correct answer from a choice of four	2
Multiple choice – multiple correct answers	Select a given number of correct answers	31
Pull down list	Select one correct answer from a drop down list	141
Fill in box	Input a numerical answer	16
Hot area	Select one or more areas in an image as a correct answer (e.g. true or false)	1
Enhanced matching	Match chosen answer to chosen areas of the screen	80 (5)

PAPER SPECIFIC INFORMATION

THE EXAM

FORMAT OF THE EXAM

The exam will be in **THREE sections**, and will be predominantly computational.

Section A will consist of 15 multiple choice questions, each worth 2 marks.

Section B will consist of three 10 mark questions which each comprise five objective test questions of 2 marks each.

Section C will consist of one 10 mark question and two 15 mark questions.

All questions are compulsory.

		Number of marks
Section A:	15 multiple choice questions of 2 marks each	30
Section B:	Three 10 mark questions covering any area of the syllabus	30
Section C:	One 10 mark questions covering any area of the syllabus	10
	Two 15 mark questions, one focusing on income tax and one on corporation tax	30
Total:		100

Total time allowed for paper-based exam: 3 hours 15 minutes.

Note that:

- The CBE will be 3 hours and 20 minutes long, due to the inclusion of 'seeded content'. These are questions that do not contribute towards a student's mark, but are used to ensure that results are fair and reliable.

  Students will have up to 10 minutes to familiarise themselves with the CBE system before starting the exam.

- Section A and section B questions can be drawn from any area of the syllabus.

- The two 15 mark section C questions could include a small number of marks in respect of other taxes.

- There is no set order for the section C questions. In the specimen paper the 10 mark question appeared before the 15 mark questions, but the examining team could change the order.

PASS MARK

The pass mark for all ACCA Qualification examination papers is 50%.

SUGGESTED APPROACH TO THIS PAPER

Decide in advance whether you will attempt section A, B or C first so that you are not wasting time on this decision in the real examination.

- This is a personal choice and you have time on the revision phase to try out different approaches, for example, if you sit mock examinations.

- A common approach is to tackle the short section A questions first, so they are out of the way, then section B and finally the longer constructed response questions in section C.

- Others may prefer to tackle the longer section B and C questions first, as they will take longer than the individual questions in section A.

You should complete at least one mock examination under examination conditions to try out your chosen approach in advance.

Whatever your approach though, you must make sure that you leave enough time to attempt all questions fully and be very strict with yourself in timing each question.

READING AND PLANNING

The F6 examination will be 3 hours 15 minutes long, with no separate time allocated for reading and planning. However, reading and planning remain crucial elements of your examination technique and is important that you allocate time in the examination to this.

Spend time reading the examination paper carefully. As stated earlier, we recommend that 15 minutes should be spent reading the paper, paying particular attention to sections B and C, where questions will be based on longer scenarios than the 2 mark OTs in section A .

Whatever happens, always keep your eye on the clock and do not over run on any part of any question!

As all questions are compulsory, there are no decisions to be made about choice of questions, other than in which order you would like to tackle them.

Therefore, in relation to F6, we recommend that you take the following approach with your reading and planning:

- There is very little information to consider for each section A question and there should be no need to plan your answers so don't waste your reading and planning time on section A – go straight to sections B and C.

- **Skim through sections B and C** of the paper, assessing the level of difficulty of each question.

- **Write down** on the question paper next to the mark allocation **the amount of time you should spend on each part.** Do this for each part of every question or part of question.

- **Decide the order** in which you think you will attempt each question in sections B and C:

  A common approach is to tackle the question you think is the easiest and you are most comfortable with first.

  Others may prefer to tackle the longest questions first, or conversely leave them to the last.

  It is usual however for students to tackle their least favourite topic and/or the most difficult question in their opinion last.

  Whatever your approach, you must make sure that you leave enough time to attempt all questions fully and be very strict with yourself in timing each question.

- The remainder of your planning time should be allocated to the longer constructed questions in section C.

- **For each section C question** in turn, read the requirements and then the detail of the question carefully.

  Always read the requirement first as this enables you to **focus on the detail of the question with the specific task in mind**.

  For section C computational questions:

  Highlight key numbers/information and key words in the question, scribble notes to yourself on the question paper to remember key points in your answer.

  Jot down pro formas required if applicable.

  For section C written questions:

  Take notice of the format required (e.g. letter, memo, notes) and identify the recipient of the answer. You need to do this to judge the level of financial sophistication required in your answer and whether the use of a formal reply or informal bullet points would be satisfactory.

  Plan your beginning, middle and end and the key areas to be addressed and your use of titles and sub-titles to enhance your answer.

  For all section C questions:

  Spot the easy marks to be gained in a question and parts which can be performed independently of the rest of the question. For example, writing down due dates of payment of tax, due dates for making elections, laying out basic pro formas correctly.

  Make sure that you do these parts first when you tackle the question.

  Don't go overboard in terms of planning time on any one question – you need a good measure of the whole paper and a plan for all of the section C questions at the end of the 15 minutes.

  By covering all questions you can often help yourself as you may find that facts in one question may remind you of things you should put into your answer relating to a different question.

- With your plan of attack in mind, **start answering your chosen question** with your plan to hand, as soon as you are ready to start.

- As mentioned in the 'Exam Technique' section earlier, you should decide in advance of the real examination whether to attempt section A, B or C first.

 Always keep your eye on the clock and do not over run on any part of any question!

DETAILED SYLLABUS

The detailed syllabus and study guide written by the ACCA can be found at:

www.**acca**global.com/en/student.html

KAPLAN'S RECOMMENDED REVISION APPROACH

QUESTION PRACTICE IS THE KEY TO SUCCESS

Success in professional examinations relies upon you acquiring a firm grasp of the required knowledge at the tuition phase. In order to be able to do the questions, knowledge is essential.

However, the difference between success and failure often hinges on your examination technique on the day and making the most of the revision phase of your studies.

The **Kaplan complete text** is the starting point, designed to provide the underpinning knowledge to tackle all questions. However, in the revision phase, pouring over text books is not the answer.

Kaplan Online knowledge checks help you consolidate your knowledge and understanding and are a useful tool to check whether you can remember key topic areas.

Kaplan pocket notes are designed to help you quickly revise a topic area, however you then need to practice questions. There is a need to progress to full examination standard questions as soon as possible, and to tie your examination technique and technical knowledge together.

The importance of question practice cannot be over-emphasised.

The recommended approach below is designed by expert tutors in the field, in conjunction with their knowledge of the examining team and the recent real examinations.

The approach taken for the fundamental papers is to revise by topic area. However, with the professional stage papers, a multi topic approach is required to answer the scenario based questions.

You need to practice as many questions as possible in the time you have left.

OUR AIM

Our aim is to get you to the stage where you can attempt examination standard questions confidently, to time, in a closed book environment, with no supplementary help (i.e. to simulate the real examination experience).

Practising your examination technique on real past examination questions, in timed conditions, is also vitally important for you to assess your progress and identify areas of weakness that may need more attention in the final run up to the examination.

In order to achieve this we recognise that initially you may feel the need to practice some questions with open book help and exceed the required time.

The approach below shows you which questions you should use to build up to coping with examination standard question practice, and references to the sources of information available should you need to revisit a topic area in more detail.

Remember that in the real examination, all you have to do is:

- attempt all questions required by the examination

- only spend the allotted time on each question, and

- get them at least 50% right!

Try and practice this approach on every question you attempt from now to the real examination.

EXAMINER COMMENTS

We have included the examining team's comments to the examination questions in this kit for you to see the main pitfalls that students fall into with regard to technical content.

However, too many times in the general section of the report, the examining team comment that students had failed due to:

- 'misallocation of time'

- 'running out of time' and

- showing signs of 'spending too much time on an earlier question and clearly rushing the answer to a subsequent question'.

Good examination technique is vital.

KAPLAN'S F6 EXAMINATION REVISION PLAN

Stage 1: Assess areas of strengths and weaknesses

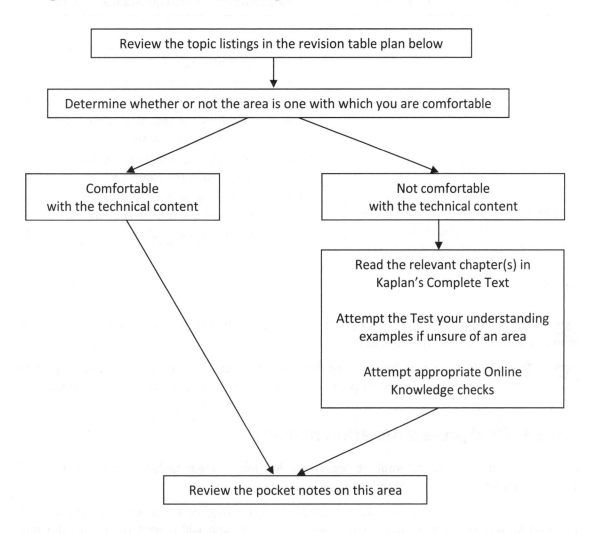

Review the topic listings in the revision table plan below

Determine whether or not the area is one with which you are comfortable

Comfortable
with the technical content

Not comfortable
with the technical content

Read the relevant chapter(s) in
Kaplan's Complete Text

Attempt the Test your understanding
examples if unsure of an area

Attempt appropriate Online
Knowledge checks

Review the pocket notes on this area

Stage 2: Practice questions

Follow the order of revision of topics as recommended in the revision table plan below and attempt the questions in the order suggested. Note that although the plan is organised into different subject areas, the real examination questions will cover more than one topic, and therefore some parts of the examination questions set below will be on topics covered later in the revision plan.

For each topic listed below you must also practice a selection of multiple choice questions covering that topic. Do bear in mind that some of the questions in this kit will take longer than 3.6 minutes each.

Try to avoid referring to text books and notes and the model answer until you have completed your attempt.

Try to answer the question in the allotted time.

Review your attempt with the model answer and assess how much of the answer you achieved in the allocated examination time.

Fill in the self-assessment box below and decide on your best course of action.

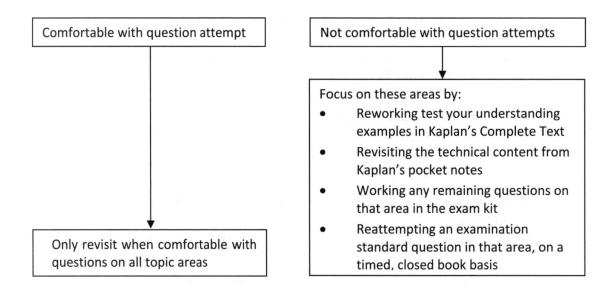

Comfortable with question attempt		Not comfortable with question attempts
		Focus on these areas by: • Reworking test your understanding examples in Kaplan's Complete Text • Revisiting the technical content from Kaplan's pocket notes • Working any remaining questions on that area in the exam kit • Reattempting an examination standard question in that area, on a timed, closed book basis
Only revisit when comfortable with questions on all topic areas		

Note that:

 The 'footsteps questions' give guidance on examination techniques and how you should have approached the question.

 The 'clock questions' have an online debrief where a tutor talks you through the examination technique and approach to that question and works the question in full.

Stage 3: Final pre-examination revision

We recommend that you **attempt at least one full mock examination** containing a set of previously unseen examination standard questions.

It is important that you get a feel for the breadth of coverage of a real examination without advanced knowledge of the topic areas covered – just as you will expect to see on the real examination day.

Ideally this mock should be sat in timed, closed book, real examination conditions and could be:

• a mock examination offered by your tuition provider and/or

• the specimen paper in the back of this exam kit and/or

• the last released examination paper (available shortly afterwards on **My**Kaplan with 'enhanced walk through answers').

THE DETAILED REVISION PLAN

Topic	Complete Text Chapter	Pocket note Chapter	Questions to attempt	Tutor guidance	Date attempted	Self-assessment
			Section B/C			
Personal income tax computation	2	1		Review the layout of an income tax computation and rates of tax.		
				Section C in the examination will include at least one question focusing on income tax, and it is crucial that you are comfortable with the pro forma.		
				Various aspects of income tax will also inevitably be tested in section A and possibly section B as well, and it is important to practice a cross-section of these questions.		
– Residence	2	1	110(a) 150(1)	The rules to determine whether an individual is resident in the UK are relatively complex. Revise the rules from the pocket notes and practice these two questions.		
– Employment income and assessable benefits	4	2	81 82 83 92 79	A popular exam topic, almost guaranteed to form part of the exam.		
				There are many questions on this area.		
				Start with Q81 which is a basic warm up question covering a number of employment benefits.		
				Build up to Q82,Q83 and Q92 which are more demanding past exam questions on this area.		
				Q92 tests the rules for determining whether an individual is employed or self-employed and the consequences of this decision.		

Topic	Complete Text Chapter	Pocket note Chapter	Questions to attempt	Tutor guidance	Date attempted	Self-assessment
			Section B/C			
				Q79 is an example of a section B case OT question. It is important that you practice these before your examination as you are likely to find it takes practice to isolate the information that you need for each individual question from the case information.		
– Property income	3	1	86	This is a detailed question solely on property income which is an excellent test of your retention of these rules. However, be aware that this topic often appears as part of an income tax computation, where property is just one of a few sources of income for an individual.		
– Badges of trade	5	3	98	Revise the badges of trade rules from the pocket notes, before attempting this question. Note that although you are not required to apply the rules to a particular scenario in this question, you may be asked to do so in the exam. The consequences of the decision are however covered and this question demonstrates the importance of the badges of trade and how an individual is taxed as a consequence.		
– Adjusted trading profit, including capital allowances and cash basis	5 & 6	3 & 4	91 90 100	An adjustment of profits calculation is almost certain to be tested in the exam, although it may form part of a sole trader/partnership or corporation tax question. Q91 tests many of the typical adjustments you may see, and having practiced this question you can then attempt Q100 to time. Q90 tests the cash basis of assessment.		

Topic	Complete Text Chapter	Pocket note Chapter	Questions to attempt	Tutor guidance	Date attempted	Self-assessment
			Section B/C			
– Basis of assessment	7	5	95 96(a)(i) 97(a)	You may benefit from practising the test your under-standings from the complete text before attempting these questions. The opening year rules are commonly tested and these questions provide good practice.		
– National insurance	11	8	114(b)	National insurance may form part of a section B or C question and can provide easy marks to a well-prepared student. It is also likely to be tested in Section A. This question covers NICs for both an employee and a self-employed individual.		
– Trading losses for individuals	9	7	106 105 104	These questions cover the range of ways losses can be tested – in an ongoing business, losses in the opening years and losses on cessation. Q106 also tests the cap on income tax reliefs. Losses are a popular examination topic and it is important to be familiar with each of the reliefs.		
– Partnerships	8	6	110(b) 111(a)	The allocation of profits between partners is a relatively straightforward computation, but does require practice.		
– Pensions	10	8	113 115	Like National Insurance, pensions is a topic which is likely to form a small part of a longer question, however the two questions listed here provide excellent practice of the various ways this topic could be tested.		

Topic	Complete Text Chapter	Pocket note Chapter	Questions to attempt	Tutor guidance	Date attempted	Self-assessment
			Section B/C			
− Tax admin for individuals	12	9	116 118	Administration is highly likely to be tested in sections A and B as an OT question. It is vital to learn the dates for submission and payment as well as the potential penalties and interest.		
Consolidation of income tax			84 89 108	Having revised all of the above topics, attempt Q84 and Q89, these questions incorporate many aspects of the taxation of individuals. Don't forget to practice a number of section A questions on income tax if you haven't already done so.		
Inheritance tax (IHT)	17	13	189 191 195	IHT can be tested in all three sections of the examination and therefore it is important to study this area. Use your pocket notes to revise the key facts and techniques. Warm up with Q189 then practice questions 191 and 195.		
Corporation tax computation	18	14	–	Review the layout of a corporation tax computation and the rates of tax. One of the 15 mark section C questions will focus on CT, and it is crucial that you are comfortable with the pro forma. There may also be a section B question and certainly some section A questions as well.		

KAPLAN PUBLISHING

Topic	Complete Text Chapter	Pocket note Chapter	Questions to attempt	Tutor guidance	Date attempted	Self-assessment
			Section B/C			
– Adjustment of profits and capital allowances	19	14	229 237 226	It is important to be comfortable with the differences between sole traders and companies for adjustments to profits and capital allowances. Use Q229 to check that you are clear about these differences, then attempt Q237, which is classic example of this type of question. Q226 is an example of a section B OT case question on corporation tax.		
– Property income	19	14	236	There are minor but important differences between taxing property income for individuals and companies. This question covers property income for a company.		
– Long periods of account	19	14	230 233	In order to deal with a long period of account, you need to learn the rules regarding apportioning different types of income between the two periods. Having revised these rules from the pocket notes, practice them using these questions.		
– Corporation tax losses	21	16	234 239 241	Many students are daunted by loss questions, however a systematic approach is all that is required and practice is key. Remind yourself of the layout required using the pocket notes, and practice the test your understandings from the complete text if you are not confident, before attempting these questions.		

Topic	Complete Text Chapter	Pocket note Chapter	Questions to attempt	Tutor guidance	Date attempted	Self-assessment
			Section B/C			
– Groups	22	17	242 243 228	Groups are often tested as part of a Corporation tax question. Q243 tests group relief and Q242 tests the rules for determining a capital gains group. Q228 is an example of a section B case OT question.		
– Tax admin for a company	23	18	231	Administration could make up part of a constructed response question so you need to be prepared for this. It is also highly likely to be tested in sections A and B as an OT question. It is vital to learn the dates for submission and payment as well as the potential penalties and interest.		
Chargeable gains for individuals	13	10	–	Chargeable gains could appear in section B or C and these questions will usually test a wide variety of the topics below. They are also likely to be tested in Section A. Revise the basic computation using the pocket notes before looking at the detailed areas.		
Chattels, shares, PPR, Entrepreneurs relief	14 & 16	11 & 12	154 158 162	These questions demonstrate how various aspects of capital gains will be tested in one question. Few of these areas are technically challenging, however, it is important that you can tackle them all.		
– Deferral reliefs	16	12	159 160	Recognising which deferral reliefs apply and whether they are available in full is important These questions cover all these reliefs and provide excellent practice.		
Chargeable gains for companies	20	15	164	Remind yourself of the different gains rules for companies, and test your understanding using Q164.		
– Quoted shares	15 & 20	11 & 15	165	A brief revision of the share pool and matching rules from the pocket notes may be useful.		

Topic	Complete Text Chapter	Pocket note Chapter	Questions to attempt	Tutor guidance	Date attempted	Self-assessment
			Section B/C			
				Then attempt Q165 which tests the capital gains rules for companies, including share pooling.		
Value added tax	24 & 25	19	268 270 276 278	Start by reviewing the examiner's VAT article. VAT could be tested in any of the three sections so it is important that you practise VAT questions from both sections.		
Scenario style exam questions	N/A	20	87 93 161 192	These questions test a range of subjects and the tax rules covered are not complex, however, the style of questions differs from the others in the kit. Look at the different styles of question using the chapter in the pocket notes, and then ensure you are comfortable with the different question styles by practicing each of these questions.		

Note that not all of the Sections B and C questions in the exam kit are referred to in the programme above.

We have recommended an approach to build up from the basics to examination standard Section B and C questions using a selection of the exam kit questions. The remaining questions are available in the kit for additional practice for those who require more questions on some areas.

It is also vital that you practice Section A questions on all topics.

TAX RATES AND ALLOWANCES

Throughout this exam kit:

1   **Calculations and workings need only to be made to the nearest £.**

2   **All apportionments should be made to the nearest month.**

3   **All workings should be shown in Section C.**

The tax rates and allowances below will be reproduced in the examination paper for Paper F6 in the year 1 April 2017 to 31 March 2018. In addition, other specific information necessary for candidates to answer individual questions will be given as part of the question.

INCOME TAX

		Normal rates	Dividend rates
Basic rate	£1 – £32,000	20%	7.5%
Higher rate	£32,001 – £150,000	40%	32.5%
Additional rate	£150,001 and above	45%	38.1%
Savings income nil rate band	– Basic rate taxpayers		£1,000
	– Higher rate taxpayers		£500
Dividend nil rate band			£5,000

A starting rate of 0% applies to savings income where it falls within the first £5,000 of taxable income.

Personal allowance

Personal allowance	£11,000
Transferable amount	£1,100
Income limit	£100,000

Residence status

Days in UK	Previously resident	Not previously resident
Less than 16	Automatically not resident	Automatically not resident
16 to 45	Resident if 4 UK ties (or more)	Automatically not resident
46 to 90	Resident if 3 UK ties (or more)	Resident if 4 UK ties
91 to 120	Resident if 2 UK ties (or more)	Resident if 3 UK ties (or more)
121 to 182	Resident if 1 UK tie (or more)	Resident if 2 UK ties (or more)
183 or more	Automatically resident	Automatically resident

Child benefit income tax charge

Where income is between £50,000 and £60,000, the charge is 1% of the amount of child benefit received for every £100 of income over £50,000.

Car benefit percentage

The relevant base level of CO_2 emissions is 95 grams per kilometre.

The percentage rates applying to petrol cars with CO_2 emissions up to this level are:

50 grams per kilometre or less	7%
51 grams to 75 grams per kilometre	11%
76 grams to 94 grams per kilometre	15%
95 grams per kilometre	16%

Car fuel benefit

The base figure for calculating the car fuel benefit is £22,200.

Individual Savings Accounts (ISAs)

The overall investment limit is £15,240.

Pension scheme limits

Annual allowance	– 2014/15 to 2016/17	£40,000
	– 2013/14	£50,000
Minimum allowance		£10,000
Income limit		£150,000

The maximum contribution that can qualify for tax relief without any earnings is £3,600.

Authorised mileage allowances: cars

Up to 10,000 miles	45p
Over 10,000 miles	25p

Capital allowances: rates of allowance

Plant and machinery

Main pool	18%
Special rate pool	8%

Motor cars

New cars with CO_2 emissions up to 75 grams per kilometre	100%
CO_2 emissions between 76 and 130 grams per kilometre	18%
CO_2 emissions above 130 grams per kilometre	8%

Annual investment allowance

Rate of allowance	100%
Expenditure limit	£200,000

Cap on income tax reliefs

Unless otherwise restricted, reliefs are capped at the higher of £50,000 or 25% of income.

CORPORATION TAX

Rate of tax	20%
Profit threshold	£1,500,000

VALUE ADDED TAX

Standard rate	20%
Registration limit	£83,000
Deregistration limit	£81,000

INHERITANCE TAX: Tax rates

£1 – £325,000	Nil
Excess – Death rate	40%
– Lifetime rate	20%

Inheritance tax: Taper relief

Years before death:	Percentage reduction
Over 3 but less than 4 years	20%
Over 4 but less than 5 years	40%
Over 5 but less than 6 years	60%
Over 6 but less than 7 years	80%

CAPITAL GAINS TAX

		Normal rates	Residential property
Rates of tax	– Lower rate	10%	18%
	– Higher rate	20%	28%
Annual exempt amount		£11,100	
Entrepreneurs' relief –	Lifetime limit	£10,000,000	
	– Rate of tax	10%	

NATIONAL INSURANCE CONTRIBUTIONS

Class 1	Employee	£1 – £8,060 per year	Nil
		£8,061 – £43,000 per year	12%
		£43,001 and above per year	2%
Class 1	Employer	£1 – £8,112 per year	Nil
		£8,113 and above per year	13.8%
		Employment allowance	£3,000
Class 1A			13.8%
Class 2		£2.80 per week	
		Small profits threshold	£5,965
Class 4		£1 – £8,060 per year	Nil
		£8,061 – £43,000 per year	9%
		£43,001 and above per year	2%

RATES OF INTEREST (assumed)

Official rate of interest	3%
Rate of interest on underpaid tax	3%
Rate of interest on overpaid tax	0.50%

TIME LIMITS AND ELECTION DATES

Income tax

Election/claim	Time limit	For 2016/17
Agree the amount of trading losses to carry forward	4 years from the end of the tax year in which the loss arose	5 April 2021
Current and prior year set-off of trading losses against total income (and chargeable gains)	12 months from 31 January following the end of the tax year in which the loss arose	31 January 2019
Three year carry back of trading losses in the opening years	12 months from 31 January following the end of the tax year in which the loss arose	31 January 2019
Three year carry back of terminal trading losses in the closing years	4 years from the end of the last tax year of trading	5 April 2021

National Insurance Contributions

Class 1 employee and employer's – pay days	17 days after the end of each tax month under PAYE system (14 days if not paid electronically)	22nd of each month
Class 1 A NIC – pay day	22 July following end of tax year (19 July if not paid electronically)	22 July 2017
Class 2 NICs – pay day	Paid under self-assessment with balancing payment	31 January 2018
Class 4 NICs – pay days	Paid under self-assessment with income tax	See self-assessment

Capital gains tax

Replacement of business asset relief for individuals (Rollover relief)	4 years from the end of the tax year: – in which the disposal occurred or – the replacement asset was acquired whichever is later	5 April 2021 for 2015/16 sale and 2016/17 acquisition
Holdover relief of gain on the gift of a business asset (Gift relief)	4 years from the end of the tax year in which the disposal occurred	5 April 2021
Entrepreneurs' relief	12 months from 31 January following the end of the tax year in which the disposal occurred	31 January 2019
Determination of principal private residence	2 years from the acquisition of the second property	

Self-assessment – individuals

Election/claim	Time limit	For 2016/17
Pay days for income tax and class 4 NIC	1st instalment: 31 January in the tax year	31 January 2017
	2nd instalment: 31 July following the end of tax year	31 July 2017
	Balancing payment: 31 January following the end of tax year	31 January 2018
Pay day for CGT and class 2 NIC	31 January following the end of tax year	31 January 2018
Filing dates If return issued by 31 October in the tax year	Paper return: 31 October following end of tax year	31 October 2017
	Electronic return: 31 January following end of tax year	31 January 2018
If return issued after 31 October in the tax year	3 months from the date of issue of the return	
Retention of records Business records	5 years from 31 January following end of the tax year	31 January 2023
Personal records	12 months from 31 January following end of the tax year	31 January 2019
HMRC right of repair	9 months from date the return was filed	
Taxpayer's right to amend a return	12 months from 31 January following end of the tax year	31 January 2019
Taxpayer's claim for overpayment relief	4 years from the end of the tax year	5 April 2021
HMRC can open an enquiry	12 months from submission of the return	
HMRC can raise a discovery assessment		
– No careless or deliberate behaviour	4 years from the end of the tax year	5 April 2021
– Tax lost due to careless behaviour	6 years from the end of the tax year	5 April 2023
– Tax lost due to deliberate behaviour	20 years from the end of the tax year	5 April 2037
Taxpayer's right of appeal against an assessment	30 days from the assessment – appeal in writing	

Corporation tax

Election/claim	Time limit
Replacement of business asset relief for companies (Rollover relief)	4 years from the end of the chargeable accounting period: – in which the disposal occurred or – the replacement asset was acquired whichever is later
Agree the amount of trading losses to carry forward	4 years from the end of the chargeable accounting period in which the loss arose
Current year set-off of trading losses against total profits (income and gains), and 12 month carry back of trading losses against total profits (income and gains)	2 years from the end of the chargeable accounting period in which the loss arose
Surrender of current period trading losses to other group companies (Group relief)	2 years after the claimant company's chargeable accounting period
Election for transfer of capital gain or loss to another company within the gains group	2 years from the end of the chargeable accounting period in which the disposal occurred by the company actually making the disposal

Self-assessment – companies

Election/claim	Time limit
Pay day for small and medium companies	9 months and one day after the end of the chargeable accounting period
Pay day for large companies	Instalments due on 14th day of: – Seventh, Tenth, Thirteenth, and Sixteenth month **after the start** of the chargeable accounting period
Filing dates	Later of: – 12 months from the end of the chargeable accounting period – 3 months from the issue of a notice to deliver a corporation tax return
Company's claim for overpayment relief	4 years from the end of the chargeable accounting period
HMRC can open an enquiry	12 months from the actual submission of the return
Retention of records	6 years from the end of the chargeable accounting period

Value added tax

Election/claim	Time limit
Compulsory registration Historic test: – Notify HMRC – Charge VAT	 30 days from end of the month in which the threshold was exceeded First day of second month after the month when taxable supplies exceeded the threshold
Future test: – Notify HMRC – Charge VAT	30 days from the date it is anticipated that the threshold will be exceeded The date it is anticipated that the threshold will be exceeded (i.e. the beginning of the 30 day period)
Compulsory deregistration	30 days from cessation
Filing of VAT return and payment of VAT	One month and seven days after the end of the return period

Section 1

PRACTICE INCOME TAX AND NATIONAL INSURANCE QUESTIONS

PRACTICE SECTION A OBJECTIVE TEST QUESTIONS

INCOME TAX BASICS AND EMPLOYMENT INCOME

1 Said has made a number of investments during the tax year 2016/17.

Which of the following investments will generate taxable income and which will generate exempt income?

	Taxable	Exempt
£400 in shares in the company he works for		
£1,000 in an Individual Savings Account		
£800 in a NS&I investment account		
£500 purchasing a NS&I certificate		

2 *Specimen paper June 2015 OT question*

Martin is self-employed, and for the year ended 5 April 2017 his trading profit was £110,200. During the tax year 2016/17, Martin made a gift aid donation of £800 (gross) to a national charity.

What amount of personal allowance will Martin be entitled to for the tax year 2016/17?

A   £11,000

B   £6,300

C   £5,900

D   £1,600

3   Fiona is a sole trader. During the tax year 2016/17 she had taxable trading income of £105,800 and received dividend income of £1,500. Fiona made a gift aid donation of £2,000 (gross) during the tax year 2016/17.

What amount of personal allowance is Fiona entitled to for the tax year 2016/17?

A   £8,350

B   £9,100

C   £8,600

D   £7,350

4   *September 2015 OT question*

Which TWO of the following items of expenditure are deductible in the calculation of an individual's taxable income?

(1)   A contribution into a personal pension scheme

(2)   A charitable gift aid donation

(3)   A contribution into an employer's HM Revenue and Customs' registered occupational pension scheme

(4)   A charitable donation made under the payroll deduction scheme

A   (3) and (4)

B   (1) and (2)

C   (2) and (3)

D   (1) and (4)

5   Genna and Wayne are a married couple. In the tax year 2016/17 Genna has a salary of £5,000 and Wayne has property income of £40,000. They have made an election to transfer the fixed amount of personal allowance from Genna to Wayne.

What is Wayne's income tax liability for the tax year 2016/17?

A   £4,700

B   £9,380

C   £4,600

D   £5,580

6   Ifram has been employed for many years and has also recently become a partner in a partnership. He is in the process of completing his tax return for the tax year 2016/17 and has asked your advice regarding the interest payments he has made during the tax year.

Identify whether his interest payments represent qualifying interest and are deductible from his total income or are not qualifying.

	Qualifying interest	**Not qualifying**
Interest paid on a loan he incurred to purchase a laptop for use in his employment		
Interest paid on the mortgage for his principal private residence		
Interest paid on an amount he borrowed to finance the acquisition of 2,000 shares in a quoted company		
Interest paid on a loan he took to invest capital in a partnership in order to become a partner		

7   *June 2015 OT question*

For the tax year 2016/17, Chi has a salary of £53,000. She received child benefit of £1,789 during this tax year.

What is Chi's child benefit income tax charge for the tax year 2016/17?

A   £1,789

B   £0

C   £1,253

D   £536

8   During the tax year 2016/17 Petra had trading income of £56,500 and she paid an annual charitable donation of £400 under the gift aid scheme. She received child benefit of £1,076 during the tax year 2016/17 in respect of her son, Kostas. Petra had no other income for the tax year 2016/17.

What child benefit income tax charge, if any, will be added to Petra's income tax liability for 2016/17?

A   £699

B   £645

C   £656

D   £1,076

9   Amber is in employment earning an annual salary of £55,000. Her only other income is bank interest of £3,000. She received child benefit of £1,789 during the tax year 2016/17.

Select Amber's child benefit tax charge and method of collection for the tax year 2016/17, by selecting the appropriate box in the table below.

		Method of collection	
		Self-assessment	PAYE
Child benefit tax charge	£1,431	A	B
	£894	C	D

10   *June 2015 OT question*

Samuel is planning to leave the UK to live overseas, having always previously been resident in the UK. He will not automatically be treated as either resident in the UK or not resident in the UK. Samuel has several ties with the UK and will need to visit the UK for 60 days each tax year. However, he wants to be not resident after he leaves the UK.

For the first two tax years after leaving the UK, what is the maximum number of ties which Samuel could keep with the UK without being treated as resident in the UK?

A   One

B   Four

C   Two

D   Three

11   Bao spent 37 days travelling in the UK during the tax year 2016/17. He has never been resident in the UK prior to the tax year 2016/17.

Minh arrived in the UK from Vietnam on 10 November 2016 to work full time in the UK. Minh did not work full-time in Vietnam before arriving in the UK.

Identify who is treated as UK resident in the tax year 2016/17:

	Resident	Not resident
Bao		
Min		

12   **Identify the treatment of each of the following forms of savings income:**

	Taxable	Exempt
NS&I investment account interest		
Gilt edged security interest		
NS&I savings certificate interest		

13 Ahmed purchased £10,000 (nominal value) gilts, paying interest at 2%, for £11,000 on 1 June 2016. Interest is payable half yearly on 31 March and 30 September.

He sold the gilts on 28 February 2017 for £11,400 (including accrued interest).

How much will Ahmed include in savings income in respect of the gilts in the tax year 2016/17?

A   £150

B   £165

C   £100

D   £183

14 Matthew purchased £200,000 (nominal value) gilts, paying interest at 1%, for £211,000 on 1 September 2015. Interest is payable half yearly on 30 June and 31 December.

He sold the gilts on 1 December 2016 for £213,000 (including accrued interest).

How much will Matthew include in savings income in respect of the gilts in the tax year 2016/17?

A   £833

B   £2,000

C   £1,000

D   £1,833

15 James had taxable income the tax year 2016/17 of £13,075 which comprised non-savings income of £1,200 and savings income of £11,875.

What is James's income tax liability for the tax year 2016/17?

A   £1,655

B   £2,615

C   £1,855

D   £2,415

16 Harrison's only income in the tax year 2016/17 was dividend income of £43,600.

What is Harrison's income tax liability for the tax year 2016/17?

£ [   ]

17 *September 2015 OT question*

Since 6 April 2016, Nicolas has let out an unfurnished freehold office building. On that date, the tenant paid Nicolas a premium of £82,000 for the grant of a 15-year lease.

How much of the premium of £82,000 will Nicolas include when calculating his property income for the tax year 2016/17?

A   £59,040

B   £22,960

C   £82,000

D   £5,467

18   Maisy has a cottage which she lets out furnished for an annual rent of £9,600, payable monthly in advance.

She incurred the following expenditure, which was paid for on the dates shown:

		£
6 April 2016	Council tax (for the year to 31 March 2017)	900
6 October 2016	Insurance for the year ended 30 September 2017 (previous year £480)	540
9 December 2016	Replaced the refrigerator with a similar model	870

What is Maisy's property income for the tax year 2016/17?

A   £8,220

B   £7,290

C   £7,320

D   £8,190

19   Hannah grants a 23 year lease on a warehouse to Mandy for £42,000 on 1 September 2016.

What is the property income assessable on Hannah for the tax year 2016/17?

£

20   Sanjay is employed. As well as his annual salary he is also paid a bonus in April each year. The amount of the bonus is based upon his performance to the end of the previous calendar year.

On 6 April 2016 he received a bonus of £2,800 in respect of the year to 31 December 2015 and on 3 April 2017 he received a bonus of £3,300 in respect of the year to 31 December 2016.

What amount of bonus is taxed in the tax year 2016/17?

A   £2,800

B   £3,300

C   £2,475

D   £6,100

21 Katie earned an annual salary of £55,000 throughout the 2016/17 tax year. She used her own car for business travel, and she travelled 14,500 business miles during the 2016/17 tax year.

What is Katie's assessable employment income assuming her employer paid her 43p per business mile?

A £55,610

B £54,390

C £54,710

D £55,290

22 Christos, a higher rate taxpayer, is provided with the following benefits in the tax year 2016/17 by his employer:

(1) Free use of the staff canteen at lunchtime for 200 days during the tax year. The canteen is available to all staff and the average cost of preparing a meal is £4.

(2) £40 per week of childcare vouchers which he uses with an approved childcare provider.

(3) £3 per week for the additional household costs incurred when he works from home.

What is the assessable value of his benefits in the tax year 2016/17?

£ ☐

23 Jo is provided with accommodation by her employer, which the employer purchased 35 years ago at a cost of £72,000. The property has an annual value of £2,600, and had a market value of £245,000 when first made available to Jo 8 years ago. Jo pays £250 per month to her employer to live in the property.

The accommodation does not qualify as job-related.

What is the assessable benefit for Jo in the tax year 2016/17?

A £0

B £4,700

C £4,790

D £2,600

24 Thiago is provided with a new diesel company car on 6 May 2016 which he used for both business and private purposes during the tax year 2016/17. The car has a list price of £28,000 and CO_2 emissions of 188 grams per kilometre.

What is Thiago's car benefit for the tax year 2016/17?

A £8,727

B £9,520

C £10,360

D £9,497

25 Woojin is provided with a loan, on which he pays interest at 1% per annum, by his employer. The loan was £100,000 when it was taken out on 6 April 2016 and he repaid £40,000 of the loan on 6 August 2016.

What is Woojin's beneficial loan benefit for the tax year 2016/17 assuming the average method of calculation is used?

A   £2,400

B   £1,667

C   £1,467

D   £1,600

26 On 6 April 2014 Ritvik was provided, by his employer, with the use of a home cinema system which cost £8,500. On 6 April 2016 he purchased the home cinema system from his employer for £1,500 even though the market value was £2,400

What is Ritvik's benefit in respect of the cinema system for the tax year 2016/17?

A   £900

B   £5,300

C   £5,100

D   £3,600

27 On 6 June 2016 Albert, a marketing manager employed Generous Ltd, was reimbursed £500 in respect of subscriptions fees he had paid to The Chartered Institute of Marketing.

Which of the following statements concerning the tax treatment of the reimbursed subscription fees for tax purposes, is correct?

A   The reimbursed fees must be added to taxable pay and taxed through the PAYE system

B   No action is required for tax purposes as the reimbursement is exempt income

C   Generous Ltd must include the reimbursed fees on Albert's P11D

D   Albert Ltd must include the reimbursed fees on his tax return

INCOME TAX BASICS AND INCOME FROM SELF-EMPLOYMENT

28   Wilson is a sole trader. When calculating his trading profits for the year ended 31 March 2017 Wilson has deducted the following expenses:

(1)   Gifts of food hampers for 10 customers costing £450 in total

(2)   Christmas party for 3 staff members costing £630 in total

(3)   Legal fees of £150 in respect of the acquisition of a 20 year lease of a property

(4)   Employee parking fine whilst on business of £30

What amount must be added back when calculating Wilson's tax adjusted trading profits for the year ended 31 March 2017?

£ [   ]

29   Haniful has taken goods from his business for personal use. The goods cost £850 and have a selling price of £1,100. He has made no entry in his business accounts in respect of the goods except to record their original purchase by the business.

Haniful's trading profits prior to any adjustment required for the goods taken for own use were £247,500.

What is Haniful's tax adjusted trading profit after making any necessary adjustments in respect of the goods taken for personal use?

A   £248,350

B   £248,600

C   £246,400

D   £247,750

30   Fleur runs a sole trader business and on 1 January 2016 she paid a £25,000 premium for a 20 year lease on an office from which she will run her business.

What amount can be deducted in respect of the lease premium when calculating Fleur's tax adjusted trading profits for the year ended 31 December 2016?

A   £25,000

B   £15,500

C   £1,250

D   £775

31   *September 2015 OT question*

Wan ceased trading on 31 December 2016, having been self-employed since 1 January 2004. On 1 January 2016, the tax written down value of her plant and machinery main pool was £6,200. On 10 November 2016, Wan purchased a computer for £1,600. All of the items included in the main pool were sold for £9,800 on 31 December 2016.

What is the balancing charge which will arise upon the cessation of Wan's trade?

A   £4,716

B   £3,404

C   £2,000

D   £3,600

32   **Which TWO of the following assets bought by a sole trader will be allocated to the main pool for capital allowance purposes?**

A   Delivery van costing £12,500 with 25% private use by the owner of the business

B   Laptop computer costing £4,500 with 15% private use by the owner of the business

C   Motor car with CO_2 emissions of 115 g/km costing £17,500 with 25% private use by an employee of the business

D   Motor car with CO_2 emissions of 135 g/km costing £16,500 used solely for business purposes by the owner of the business

E   Factory air-conditioning system costing £110,000 with a 27 year expected life

F   Packing machine costing £105,000 and with a 24 year expected life

33   Andrew prepares accounts for the eight months to 31 March 2017. The tax written down value of the main pool on 1 August 2016 was £18,000.

On 15 January 2017 he purchased a new motor car with CO_2 emissions of 75 g/km costing £12,260. It is used solely for business purposes by Andrew.

What are the maximum capital allowances Andrew may claim for the eight month period ended 31 March 2017?

A   £15,500

B   £14,420

C   £10,333

D   £12,260

34   Ronald has always prepared his accounts to 31 March. On 31 March 2017 Ronald ceased trading. The tax written down value of the main pool at 1 April 2016 was £15,000.

On 1 January 2017 Ronald purchased a laptop solely for business use costing £4,500.

On 31 March 2017 all the items in the main pool were sold for £14,550 apart from the laptop which was retained by Ronald. The market value of the laptop at 31 March 2017 was £4,150. None of the items in the main pool was sold for more than its original cost.

What are the capital allowances/(balancing charge) for the year ended 31 March 2017?

A   £144

B   £450

C   (£800)

D   £800

35   Jacinta started trading on 1 August 2016 and prepares accounts to 31 December each year. Her trading profits for the first two periods are as follows:

5 months ended 31 December 2016   £10,500
Year ended 31 December 2017   £24,000

What is the trading income assessment for Jacinta for the tax year 2016/17?

£ [   ]

36   Lee decided to cease trading on 31 January 2017 after trading for many years. His tax adjusted profits for recent years have been:

Year ended 30 April 2015   £40,000

Year ended 30 April 2016   £10,000

Period ended 31 January 2017   £14,000

Lee has overlap profits of £3,000 brought forward from the commencement of trade.

What is Lee's trading income assessment for the tax year 2016/17?

A   £11,000

B   £14,000

C   £21,000

D   £24,000

PARTNERSHIPS

37 Elizabeth and Henry have been in partnership for many years, preparing accounts to 31 December each year.

Until 31 July 2016 profits were shared in the ratio 70:30 to Elizabeth and Henry respectively, with no salary allocated to either partner. From 1 August 2016 the profit sharing ratio was adjusted to 80:20 to Elizabeth and Henry respectively, after allocating a salary of £24,000 per annum to Henry.

The adjusted trading profits for the accounting year ended 31 December 2016 are £120,000.

How much of the profit for the year ended 31 December 2016 is allocated to Henry?

A   £41,000

B   £31,000

C   £43,200

D   £39,000

38 Albert and Jolene have been in partnership for many years, preparing accounts to 30 September each year. Albert and Jolene have balances on their capital accounts of £50,000 and £40,000 respectively.

The partnership agreement provides for Albert to receive an annual salary of £25,000 and both partners to receive interest on capital of 4% per year.

The agreed profit sharing ratio is 1:3 to Albert and Jolene respectively.

The adjusted trading profits for the accounting year ended 30 September 2016 are £80,000.

How much trading profit is assessable on Albert in the tax year 2016/17?

A   £39,850

B   £20,000

C   £12,850

D   £40,250

39 Tim, Abhiroop and Angela have been in partnership for many years, preparing accounts to 31 December each year.

The partnership agreement provides for Tim to receive an annual salary of £15,000.

The agreed profit sharing ratio is 1:3:2 to Tim, Abhiroop and Angela respectively.

Tim left the partnership on 31 May 2016.

The adjusted trading profits for the accounting year ended 31 December 2016 are £360,000.

How much of the profit for the year ended 31 December 2016 is allocated to Tim?

A   £25,000

B   £30,208

C   £72,500

D   £23,958

40 Nazim and Laura have been in partnership for many years, preparing accounts to 31 October each year and sharing profits equally.

On 1 June 2016 Fabiola joined the partnership. The agreed profit sharing ratio was 2: 2:1 to Nazim, Laura and Fabiola respectively.

The adjusted trading profits for the accounting years ended 31 October 2016 and 2017 were £240,000 and £300,000 respectively.

What is Fabiola's trading income assessment for the tax year 2016/17?

A   £20,000

B   £55,000

C   £48,000

D   £45,000

TRADING LOSSES

41   *June 2015 OT question*

Naomi is self-employed. For the year ended 5 April 2017 she made a trading loss of £110,000, having made a trading profit of £24,000 for the year ended 5 April 2016. Naomi also had employment income of £92,000 for the tax year 2015/16.

What is the maximum loss relief claim which Naomi can make against her total income for the tax year 2015/16?

A   £74,000

B   £50,000

C   £110,000

D   £29,000

42 Brooke has been trading profitably as a sole trader for many years. However, in the year ended 31 August 2015 she made a trading loss of £65,000.

Brooke has the following income in the tax year 2016/17:

	£
Trading profit for year ended 31 August 2016	12,000
Dividend income	9,000
Property income (furnished holiday accommodation)	4,000
NS&I savings certificate interest	1,000

What is Brookes' net income for the tax year 2016/17 assuming she carries the trading loss forward?

£ _____

43 Damyanti has been trading as a sole trader for many years. Her recent tax adjusted trading profits/(losses) have been:

Year ended 31 August 2015 £55,000

Year ended 31 August 2016 (£90,000)

Damyanti also receives bank interest of £14,000 each tax year.

What is the amount of trading loss carried forward to the tax year 2017/18 assuming that Damyanti makes a claim to use the loss in the current and prior tax years?

A   £35,000

B   £7,000

C   £29,000

D   £26,000

44 Sabine started to trade as a sole trader on 1 November 2014. Her tax adjusted trading profits/(losses) for the first two years are:

Year ended 31 October 2015   (£25,000)

Year ended 31 October 2016   £5,000

Sabine was employed until 31 March 2014 earning £45,000 per annum.

How much, if any, of the loss can be offset against Sabine's employment income in 2011/12?

A   £25,000

B   £10,417

C   £14,583

D   £0

45 Sally has been trading as a sole trader for many years. In the year ended 31 July 2016 she made a trading loss of £45,000.

Sally's only other source of income is property income of £8,000 each tax year.

In the tax year 2016/17 Sally realised a chargeable gain of £32,000 on the sale of a necklace and a capital loss of £4,000 on the sale of a painting. She has capital losses brought forward of £18,000.

What is the amount of trading loss that Sally can offset against her chargeable gains in the tax year 2016/17?

A   £37,000

B   £28,000

C   £10,000

D   £16,900

46 Carol ceased trading on 30 September 2016.

Her recent tax adjusted trading profits/(losses) have been:

Year ended 31 January 2016 £39,000

Period ended 30 September 2016 (£24,000)

Carol had unused overlap profits from the commencement of trade of £12,000.

What is the amount of terminal loss available to Carol?

A £30,000

B £23,000

C £18,000

D £11,000

PENSIONS AND NIC

47 *June 2015 OT question*

Which classes of national insurance contribution is an employer responsible for paying?

A Both class 2 and class 4

B Class 1 only

C Both class 1 and class 1A

D Class 2 only

48 *September 2015 OT question*

Lorna has the choice of being either employed or self-employed. If employed, Lorna's gross annual salary for the tax year 2016/17 will be £36,000. If self-employed, Lorna's trading profit for the year ended 5 April 2017 will be £36,000.

How much more national insurance contributions will Lorna suffer for the tax year 2016/17 if she chooses to be employed rather than self-employed?

A £838

B £934

C £692

D £1,080

49 Hamid runs a sole trader business, in which he employs an employee who earns £40,000 per annum and is provided with a company car for private and business use.

For each class of NIC select whether it is paid by Hamid and also whether it represents part of the total tax cost suffered by Hamid.

	Paid by Hamid	Suffered by Hamid
Employee class 1 primary		
Employer's class 1 secondary		
Class 1A		
Class 2		
Class 4		

50 *Specimen paper June 2015*

During the tax year 2016/17, William was paid a gross annual salary of £82,700. He also received taxable benefits valued at £5,400.

What amount of employee class 1 national insurance contributions (NICs) will have been suffered by William for the tax year 2016/17?

A £5,095

B £8,957

C £4,987

D £4,193

51 Efe is a director of Mulch Ltd, and is paid an annual salary of £60,000. During the tax year 2016/17 he also received an annual bonus of £3,000 and childcare vouchers of £20 per week for 52 weeks.

How much employee class 1 primary NICs does Efe suffer for the tax year 2016/17?

A £4,593

B £4,614

C £4,533

D £6,593

52 Bob is an employee of Dibbit Ltd, and is paid an annual salary of £50,000. He makes contributions of £3,000 into the company's occupational pension scheme each year.

In the tax year 2016/17 he drove 12,000 business miles in his own car for which he was paid 50p per mile by Dibbit Ltd.

How much employer's class 1 NICs is Dibbit Ltd required to pay in respect of Bob's earnings and reimbursed mileage for the tax year 2016/17?

A £5,781

B £5,863

C £5,919

D £5,505

53 Kolo is an employee of Lapsang Ltd. He is paid a salary of £20,000 and has use of a petrol-driven company car for private purposes throughout the tax year 2016/17. The car has a list price of £15,000 and CO_2 emissions of 109g. No petrol is provided for private mileage.

How much class 1A NICs is payable by Lapsang Ltd in respect of Kolo's company car?

A · £2,700

B £373

C £3,133

D £393

54 Broadman Ltd provides employment benefits to its employees.

On which TWO of the following benefits is class 1A NIC payable by Broadman Ltd?

A Occupational pension scheme contributions of 5% of the employees' salaries

B Payment for a parking space in a public car park near the office

C Annual summer event costing £200 per head

D Provision of a smart phone for business and private use including the cost of private calls

E Membership of local sports club at a cost of £400 per annum

F Mileage allowance of 5p per mile for cost of travel between employee's home and the company's office premises

55 Mohammed, age 35, runs a sole trader business. In the year ended 5 April 2017 his accounting profit and tax adjusted trading profit were £5,400 and £6,800 respectively.

Nicole is aged 75 and receives the state retirement pension. She also has a sole trader business. In the year ended 5 April 2017 her accounting profit and tax adjusted trading profit were £5,900 and £6,200 respectively.

Identify who is required to pay class 2 NIC for the tax year 2016/17:

	Class 2 NICs payable	Class 2 NICs not payable
Mohammed		
Nicole		

56 Marion runs a sole trader business. Her tax adjusted trading profit is £68,000 for the year ended 31 December 2016.

How much class 4 NICs is Marion required to pay for the tax year 2016/17?

A £3,645

B £5,395

C £4,693

D £4,370

57   Robin is a sole trader. His tax adjusted trading profit for the year ended 31 July 2016 is £70,000. In the year ended 31 July 2015 he had a trading loss of £20,000 which he decided to carry forward rather than offset against total income of the current or prior year.

Robin's other income in the tax year 2016/17 comprises £3,000 of savings income.

How much are his assessable profits for class 4 NIC purposes for the tax year 2016/17?

A   £70,000

B   £53,000

C   £50,000

D   £73,000

58   Isaac is self-employed and for the year ended 31 March 2017 he paid £40,000 (net) into his personal pension plan. Isaac's relevant earnings for the tax year 2016/17 were £110,000.

What amount of income tax will Isaac pay at the basic rate for the tax year 2016/17?

£ [   ]

59   Padma became a member of a personal pension scheme on 6 April 2013 and has made gross personal pension contributions as follows:

2013/14   £23,000
2014/15   £40,000
2015/16   £35,000

Padma's tax adjusted trading income in the tax year 2016/17 is £190,000. She has no other sources of income.

What is the maximum gross personal pension contribution that Padma can make in the tax year 2016/17 without incurring an annual allowance charge?

A   £72,000

B   £40,000

C   £52,000

D   £20,000

60 Griff is employed by Gargoyle plc on an annual salary of £50,000. In addition Griff lets out two properties:

- qualifying furnished holiday accommodation which generates taxable income of £5,000 per annum, and

- a warehouse, let to a local business, which generates taxable income of £8,000 per annum.

In the tax year 2016/17 he made a £4,000 (gross) donation to a national charity under the gift aid scheme.

What are Griff's net relevant earnings for the tax year 2016/17?

A   £51,000

B   £63,000

C   £59,000

D   £55,000

61 Austin, age 47, runs a sole trader business. In the tax year 2016/17 his trading income was £51,200. During the tax year 2016/17 he paid £22,400 (net) into a personal pension scheme.

Petra, age 45, has employment income of £120,000 in the tax year 2016/17. She has never been a member of a pension scheme until the tax year 2016/17 when she paid £50,000 (net) into a personal pension scheme.

Identify who has made fully tax-relievable pension contributions in the tax year 2016/17?

	Fully tax relievable pension contributions	Not fully tax relievable pension contributions
Austin		
Petra		

62 Roger is employed on an annual salary of £145,000. His employer has an occupational pension scheme into which Roger paid 2% of his salary and the company paid 5% of his salary in the tax year 2016/17. Roger also made a payment of £20,000 into a personal pension scheme in the tax year 2016/17.

What is Roger's net income (before deducting the personal allowance) for the tax year 2016/17?

£ [   ]

63 Natalia's only income in the tax year 2016/17 is trading income of £80,000. She also has an annual allowance charge of £10,000 as a result of making gross personal pension contributions of £50,000 in the tax year 2016/17.

What is Natalia's income tax liability for the tax year 2016/17?

A   £25,200

B   £19,600

C   £15,800

D   £23,800

ADMINISTRATION AND ETHICS

64   *September 2015 OT question*

Taxes can be either capital taxes or revenue taxes, although some taxes are neither type of tax.

Which is the correct classification for the following three taxes?

	Value added tax	Inheritance tax	National insurance contributions
A	Neither type	Revenue tax	Capital tax
B	Revenue tax	Capital tax	Neither type
C	Capital tax	Neither type	Revenue tax
D	Neither type	Capital tax	Revenue tax

65   *June 2015 OT question*

Which of the following statements correctly explains the difference between tax evasion and tax avoidance?

A   Both tax evasion and tax avoidance are illegal, but tax evasion involves providing HM Revenue and Customs with deliberately false information

B   Tax evasion is illegal, whereas tax avoidance involves the minimisation of tax liabilities by the use of any lawful means

C   Both tax evasion and tax avoidance are illegal, but tax avoidance involves providing HM Revenue and Customs with deliberately false information

D   Tax avoidance is illegal, whereas tax evasion involves the minimisation of tax liabilities by the use of any lawful means

66 **Which TWO of the following are true of tax evasion?**

A   Tax evasion means using the taxation regime to ones' own advantage by arranging your affairs to minimise your tax liability

B   Tax evasion includes not providing all relevant information to HMRC

C   Tax evasion is legal and does not involve misleading HMRC

D   Tax evasion utilises loopholes in tax legislation

E   Tax evasion encompasses any attempt to avoid or reduce tax by illegal means

F   Tax evasion includes utilising tax-free investments, such as ISAs

67 *Specimen paper June 2015*

You are a trainee Chartered Certified Accountant and your firm has a client who has refused to disclose a chargeable gain to HM Revenue and Customs (HMRC).

From an ethical viewpoint, which of the following actions could be expected of your firm?

(1)   Reporting under the money laundering regulations

(2)   Advising the client to make disclosure

(3)   Ceasing to act for the client

(4)   Informing HMRC of the non-disclosure

(5)   Warning the client that your firm will be reporting the non-disclosure

(6)   Notifying HMRC that your firm has ceased to act for the client

A   (2), (3) and (5)

B   (1), (2), (3) and (6)

C   (2), (3) and (4)

D   (1), (4), (5) and (6)

68 **Which of the following is true of a tax adviser?**

A   A tax adviser can only disclose information about the client to third parties with the clients' consent

B   A tax adviser must not assist a client to plan or commit any tax offences

C   If a tax adviser becomes aware that a client has committed a tax irregularity they must disclose it to HMRC

D   A tax adviser acting for a client has no duties and responsibilities towards HMRC

69   *September 2015 OT question*

For the tax year 2015/16, what are the latest dates by which a taxpayer, who does not wish to incur a penalty, should file a self-assessment tax return on paper or online?

	Paper tax return	Online tax return
A	31 October 2015	31 January 2018
B	31 October 2016	31 January 2017
C	31 October 2017	31 January 2017
D	31 October 2017	31 January 2018

70   *June 2015 OT question*

For the tax year 2015/16, Willard filed a paper self-assessment tax return on 10 August 2016.

What is the deadline for Willard to make an amendment to his tax return for the tax year 2015/16, and by what date will HM Revenue and Customs (HMRC) have to notify Willard if they intend to carry out a compliance check into this return?

	Amendment	Compliance check
A	10 August 2017	31 January 2018
B	10 August 2017	10 August 2017
C	31 January 2018	10 August 2017
D	31 January 2018	31 January 2018

71   Philip is a sole trader and is married to Harriet. Harriet is in employment. They jointly own a residential investment property which is rented out.

Select the dates until which Philip and Harriet must keep the records which support their tax returns for the tax year 2016/17.

	Phillip	Harriet
31 January 2019		
31 January 2022		
31 January 2023		

72 *June 2015 OT question*

Abdul's tax liabilities for the tax years 2015/16 and 2016/17 are as follows:

	2015/16	2016/17
	£	£
Income tax payable	300	2,400
Class 4 national insurance contributions	320	1,260
Capital gains tax liability	240	0
	860	3,660

What payment on account will Abdul have to make on 31 July 2017 in respect of his tax liability for the tax year 2016/17?

A   £310

B   £1,830

C   £430

D   £0

73 *June 2015 OT question*

Quinn will not make the balancing payment in respect of her tax liability for the tax year 2016/17 until 17 October 2018.

What is the total percentage of penalty which Quinn will be charged by HM Revenue and Customs (HMRC) in respect of the late balancing payment for the tax year 2016/17?

A   15%

B   10%

C   5%

D   30%

74   Jeanette's income tax and capital gains tax liabilities for the tax year 2016/17 were £25,000 and £5,000 respectively. Of the £25,000 income tax liability, tax of £5,400 was deducted at source under PAYE. She made payments on account totalling £18,000 for the tax year 2016/17.

What is the balancing payment Jeanette should pay on 31 January 2018?

A   £16,400

B   £6,600

C   £12,000

D   £1,600

75 Belinda paid the balancing payment of income tax of £7,400 for the tax year 2016/17 on 10 March 2018.

For each of the following statements select whether it is true or false:

	True	False
Belinda will have to pay interest on late paid tax from 31 January 2018 to 10 March 2018		
Belinda will have to pay a £100 fixed penalty because the payment is late		
Belinda will have to pay a 5% penalty because the payment is more than 30 days late		

76 Florence filed her return for the tax year 2016/17, showing income tax payable of £6,500, 8 months late.

In addition to the initial £100 late filing penalty, what is the maximum further penalty that she can be charged for filing the tax return late?

£ ☐

77 Welan Ltd pays its employees monthly on the 15th of every month.

For each of the following statements select whether it is true or false:

	True	False
Under the Real Time Information PAYE system, Welan Ltd must submit income tax and NIC information in respect of the monthly salary payments to HM Revenue & Customs electronically by the 15th day of each month		
Welan Ltd must pay the income tax and NIC due on the monthly salary payments to HM Revenue & Customs electronically by the 22nd of the month following the month the salaries are paid		
Welan Ltd must provide each employee with a year-end summary form (P60) for the tax year 2016/17 by 6 July 2017		

PRACTICE SECTION B OBJECTIVE TEST CASES

INCOME TAX BASICS AND EMPLOYMENT INCOME

78   PHILIP & CHARLES (ADAPTED) *Walk in the footsteps of a top tutor*

Philip and Charles are father and son. The following information is available for the tax year 2016/17:

Philip Wind

Philip retired early at the age of 55. During the tax year 2016/17 Philip received pension income of £13,500 and building society interest of £14,600.

Charles Wind

Charles is self-employed, and his tax adjusted trading profit for the year ended 31 December 2016 was £109,400.

During the tax year 2016/17 Charles made a gift aid donation of £800 (gross) to a national charity.

Charles has been a member of a registered personal pension scheme since May 2014. He made a gross contribution of £25,000 in the tax year 2014/15 but has not made any subsequent contributions.

1   What is Philip's income tax liability for the tax year 2016/17?

    A   £3,420

    B   £2,720

    C   £3,220

    D   £2,920

2   What amount of personal allowance is available to Charles for the tax year 2016/17?

    A   £2,400

    B   £11,000

    C   £6,700

    D   £6,800

3   What is the amount of class 4 national insurance liability in respect of Charles for the tax year 2016/17?

    A   £4,473

    B   £4,453

    C   £4,457

    D   £4,253

4   **What was the total available annual allowance available to Charles for pension contribution purposes in the tax year 2016/17?**

   A   £95,000

   B   £40,000

   C   £145,000

   D   £88,750

5   **If Charles had made payments of £6,880 into a personal pension scheme during the tax year 2016/17 which of the following statements are correct?**

   (1)   His basic rate band for the tax year 2016/17 would have been increased by £8,600 in relation to this contribution.

   (2)   His taxable income for the tax year 2016/17 would have been reduced by £8,600

   (3)   HM Revenue and Customs would have paid £1,376 into the pension fund on his behalf

   (4)   His tax liability at the 40% rate would have been £3,440 lower in the tax year 2016/17

   A   (2) and (3)

   B   (1) and (4)

   C   (1) and (3)

   D   (2) and (4)

79   KIM BAXTER (ADAPTED) *Walk in the footsteps of a top tutor*

This objective test case question contains question types which will only appear in a computer based examination, but this question provides valuable practice for all students whichever version of the examination they are taking.

Kim is employed as a sales person by Sharp-Suit plc. During the tax year 2016/17 her employment package included the following benefits:

(1)   On 1 June 2016 Sharp-Suit plc provided Kim with a loan of £14,600, at an annual interest rate of 1%, so that she could purchase a new motor car.

(2)   During the period from 1 June 2016 to 5 April 2017 Kim used her private motor car for business and private purposes. She received no reimbursement from Sharp-Suit plc for any of the expenditure incurred.

   Kim's mileage during this period included the following:

	Miles
Normal daily travel between home and permanent workplace	3,400
Travel between permanent workplace and Sharp-Suit plc's customers	9,200
Travel between home and a temporary workplace for one month	1,300

(3)   On 6 April 2016 Kim purchased a television from Sharp-Suit plc for £50 when its market value was £200. The company had purchased the television for £800 on 6 April 2015 and Kim had used it at home since that date.

Kim's total employment income, including the above benefits and deductions, for the tax year 2016/17 was £25,000.

Other information

During the tax year 2016/17 Kim paid interest of £140 on a personal loan, taken out on 1 January 2016 to purchase a laptop computer for use in her employment with Sharp-Suit plc. She also paid a charitable contribution of £800 under the gift aid scheme. She had no other sources of income.

Kim's husband Richard stays at home to look after their children while Kim is at work. Richard's only income in the tax year 2016/17 is savings income of £10,200.

1   **What is the taxable benefit in respect of the loan from Kim's employer for the tax year 2016/17?**

   A   £292

   B   £365

   C   £122

   D   £243

2   **What amount will be deducted from Kim's taxable employment income in the tax year 2016/17 in respect of the use of her car for business purposes?**

   A   £4,140

   B   £4,625

   C   £4,725

   D   £5,475

3   **What is the taxable benefit in respect of the purchase of the television from Sharp-Suit plc in the tax year 2016/17?**

   A   £590

   B   £750

   C   £150

   D   £640

4   **What is the amount of Kim's taxable income for the tax year 2016/17?**

   £ [   ]

5 **Assuming that Kim and Richard make a marriage allowance election in respect of the tax year 2016/17, match the appropriate tax impact to each individual.**

	Richard	Kim
Personal allowance reduced by £800		
Personal allowance reduced by £1,100		
Personal allowance increased by £800		
Personal allowance increased by £1,100		
Income tax liability reduced by £160		
Income tax liability reduced by £220		

INCOME TAX BASICS AND INCOME FROM SELF-EMPLOYMENT

80 FOO DEE (ADAPTED)

On 31 December 2016 Foo Dee resigned as an employee of Gastronomic Food plc and on 1 January 2017 Foo commenced self-employment running her own restaurant, preparing accounts to 30 September.

The following information is available for the tax year 2016/17:

Employment

During the period 6 April 2016 to 31 December 2016 Foo earned a salary of £38,000 and was provided with the following benefits:

(1) A diesel driven car with CO_2 emissions of 180 g/km and a list price of £21,000. Foo paid £2,000 to Gastronomic Food plc towards the purchase price of the car. Foo was not provided with fuel for private mileage.

(2) Gastronomic Food plc paid Foo a cash allowance of £55 per week for 39 weeks. She gave this to her mother who looks after her two children, on an informal basis, while Foo is at work.

(3) The company contributed 6% of Foo's gross salary of £38,000 into Gastronomic-Food plc's HM Revenue & Customs' registered occupational pension scheme.

Self-employment

(1) Foo's statement of profit or loss for her restaurant business for the nine-month period ended 30 September 2017 is as follows:

	£	£
Gross profit		202,054
Depreciation	3,500	
Legal fees (Note 2)	4,200	
Property expenses (Note 3)	12,800	
Other expenses (all allowable)	50,700	
	———	(71,200)
Net profit		130,854

(2)   Legal fees include conveyancing fees of £1,400 for the purchase of the restaurant.

(3)   Foo purchased her restaurant on 1 January 2017. She lives in a flat that is situated above the restaurant, and one quarter of the total property expenses of £12,800 relate to this flat.

(4)   On 30 September 2017 Foo purchased a motor car with CO_2 emissions of 115 grams per kilometre for £14,600. Private use of the car by Foo is 30%.

Foo never had to complete a tax return whilst she was employed by Gastronomic Food plc.

1   **What is the taxable benefit in respect of the company car for the tax year 2016/17?**

   A   £6,840

   B   £5,670

   C   £4,702

   D   £5,130

2   **How much is the total taxable benefit of the provision of childcare and the pension contribution by the company for the tax year 2016/17?**

   A   £0

   B   £2,145

   C   £1,053

   D   £4,425

3   **What is Foo's taxable trading profit before capital allowances for the nine-month period ended 30 September 2017?**

   A   £135,454

   B   £137,554

   C   £138,954

   D   £135,754

4   **What is the maximum capital allowances claim that Foo can make in respect of the nine-month period ended 30 September 2017?**

   A   £1,380

   B   £1,971

   C   £1,840

   D   £818

5   Foo has not previously been required to submit a tax return to HMRC.

By what date must Foo inform HMRC of her new source of self-employment income and what is the filing date for the first tax return that includes income from self-employment?

	New source	Tax return
A	5 October 2017	31 January 2019
B	5 October 2017	31 January 2018
C	30 September 2017	31 January 2018
D	30 September 2018	31 January 2019

PRACTICE SECTION C CONSTRUCTED RESPONSE QUESTIONS

INCOME TAX BASICS AND EMPLOYMENT INCOME

81   SALLY BURTON (ADAPTED)

The following information is available in respect of Sally Burton for the tax year 2016/17:

Sally Burton

(1)   Sally is employed by Burton plc as a senior manager. She is paid a gross annual salary of £90,000 from which PAYE of £30,000 was deducted by her employer.

(2)   On 6 June 2016 Sally was provided with a petrol powered motor car which has a list price of £17,118. Sally made a capital contribution of £2,000 towards the cost of the motor car when it was first provided. The official CO_2 emission rate for the motor car is 152 grams per kilometre. Burton plc paid for all of the motor car's maintenance costs of £2,400 during the tax year 2016/17 as well as a car parking space near to its premises costing £1,200. Her employer did not provide any fuel for private journeys.

(3)   Burton plc has provided Sally with living accommodation since 2015. The property was purchased in 2008 for £105,000, and was valued at £120,000 when first provided to Sally. It has an annual value of £1,632. Sally was not required by her job to live in the accommodation provided by her employer. Sally was required to reimburse her employer £75 each month for the use of the accommodation.

(4)   On 1 February 2017 Sally purchased £100,000 (nominal value) of gilts for £115,000 (including accrued interest). The gilts pay interest at 2% half yearly on 31 March and 30 September.

(5)   Sally also received building society interest of £1,917.

(6)   On 5 April 2017 Sally granted a 15 year lease on a property she owns in return for a premium of £10,680.

Required:

Calculate Sally's income tax payable for the tax year 2016/17.   **(15 marks)**

82 VIGOROUS PLC (ADAPTED)

Vigorous plc runs a health club. The company has three employees who received benefits during the tax year 2016/17. Each of the employees is paid an annual salary of £60,000. It has been decided not to payroll the employee benefits, therefore P11D forms will be prepared for each employee.

The following information is relevant:

Andrea Lean

(1) Andrea was employed by Vigorous plc throughout the tax year 2016/17.

(2) Throughout 2016/17 Vigorous plc provided Andrea with a petrol powered company motor car with a list price of £19,400. The official CO_2 emission rate for the motor car is 240 grams per kilometre. Vigorous plc paid for all of the motor car's running costs of £6,200 during 2016/17, including petrol used for private journeys. During the tax year 2016/17 Andrea paid £150 per month to Vigorous plc for the private use of the motor car.

(3) Vigorous plc has provided Andrea with living accommodation since 1 November 2014. The property was purchased on 1 January 2012 for £130,000. The company spent £14,000 improving the property during March 2013, and a further £8,000 was spent on improvements during May 2016.

The value of the property on 1 November 2014 was £170,000, and it has an annual value of £7,000. The furniture in the property cost £6,000 during November 2014. Andrea personally pays for the annual running costs of the property amounting to £4,000.

(4) On 1 March 2016 Vigorous plc gave Andrea a large bouquet of flowers, costing £40, on the occasion of her 50th birthday.

Ben Slim

(1) Ben commenced employment with Vigorous plc on 1 July 2016.

(2) On 1 July 2016 Vigorous plc provided Ben with an interest free loan of £120,000 so that he could purchase a new main residence. He repaid £20,000 of the loan on 1 December 2016.

(3) During the tax year 2016/17 Vigorous plc paid £9,300 towards the cost of Ben's relocation. His previous main residence was 125 miles from his place of employment with the company. The £9,300 covered the cost of disposing of Ben's old property and of acquiring his new property.

(4) On 1 July 2016 Ben joined the company's childcare scheme which provides employees with childcare vouchers of £60 per week to buy care from an approved child carer. Ben received vouchers to provide care for 36 weeks in the tax year 2016/17.

Chai Trim

(1) Chai was employed by Vigorous plc throughout the tax year 2016/17.

(2) During the tax year 2016/17 Vigorous plc provided Chai with a two-year old company van, which was available for private use. The van was unavailable during the period 1 August to 30 September 2016. Chai paid for fuel for all private journeys.

(3) Vigorous plc has provided Chai with a television for her personal use since 6 April 2014. The television cost Vigorous plc £800 in April 2014. On 6 April 2016 the company sold the television to Chai for £150, although its market value on that date was £250.

(4) Throughout the tax year 2016/17 Vigorous plc provided Chai with free membership of its health club. The normal annual cost of membership is £800. This figure is made up of direct costs of £150, fixed overhead costs of £400 and profit of £250. The budgeted membership for the year has been exceeded, but the health club has surplus capacity.

Required:

(a) Calculate the benefit figures that Vigorous plc will have to include on the forms P11D for Andrea, Ben, and Chai for the tax year 2016/17. **(12 marks)**

(b) Explain how the income tax liability in respect of benefits is collected by HM Revenue & Customs. **(3 marks)**

(Total: 15 marks)

83 ALI PATEL (ADAPTED) *Walk in the footsteps of a top tutor*

You should assume that today's date is 15 March 2016.

Ali Patel has been employed by Box plc since 1 January 2013, and is currently paid an annual salary of £29,000. On 6 April 2016 Ali is to be temporarily relocated for a period of 12 months from Box plc's head office to one of its branch offices. He has been offered two alternative remuneration packages:

First remuneration package

(1) Ali will continue to live near Box plc's head office, and will commute on a daily basis to the branch office using his private motor car.

(2) He will be paid additional salary of £500 per month.

(3) Box plc will pay Ali an allowance of 38 pence per mile for the 1,600 miles that Ali will drive each month commuting to the branch office.

Ali's additional cost of commuting for the tax year 2016/17 will be £1,800.

Second remuneration package

(1) Box plc will provide Ali with rent-free living accommodation near the branch office.

(2) The property will be rented by Box plc at a cost of £800 per month. The annual value of the property is £4,600.

(3) Ali will rent out his main residence near Box plc's head office, and this will result in property business income of £6,000 for the tax year 2016/17.

Required:

(a) Calculate Ali's income tax liability and employee class 1 national insurance contributions for the tax year 2016/17, if he:

(1) accepts the first remuneration package offered by Box plc, **(6 marks)**

(2) accepts the second remuneration package offered by Box plc. **(5 marks)**

(b) Advise Ali as to which remuneration package is the most beneficial from a financial perspective.

Your answer should be supported by a calculation of the amount of income, net of all costs including income tax and class 1 national insurance contributions, which he would receive for the tax year 2016/17 under each alternative.   **(4 marks)**

(Total: 15 marks)

84   PATIENCE (ADAPTED)   *Walk in the footsteps of a top tutor*

Patience retired on 31 December 2016, and on that date ceased employment and self-employment. The following information is available in respect of the tax year 2016/17:

Employment

(1)   Patience was employed by a private school as a teacher. From 6 April to 31 December 2016, she was paid a salary of £3,750 per month.

(2)   During the period 6 April to 31 December 2016, Patience contributed 6% of her monthly gross salary of £3,750 into her employer's HM Revenue and Customs' (HMRC's) registered occupational pension scheme. Patience's employer contributed a further 10% on her behalf.

(3)   During the period 6 April to 30 June 2016, Patience's granddaughter was provided with a free place at the private school run by Patience's employer. The normal fee payable would have been £4,600. The additional marginal expense of providing the place for the grandchild was £540.

(4)   On 25 June 2016, Patience was given a clock valued at £600 as an award for her 25 years of teaching at her employer's school. She has not previously received any similar awards.

(5)   Patience's employer provided her with an interest-free loan so that she could purchase a season ticket for the train to work. The balance of the loan outstanding at 6 April 2016 was £8,000, and Patience repaid the loan in full on 31 December 2016.

Self-employment

(1)   Patience was self-employed as a private tutor. Her trading profit for the year ended 31 July 2016 was £14,800. This figure is **after** taking account of capital allowances.

(2)   Patience's trading profit for the final five-month period of trading from 1 August to 31 December 2016 was £6,900. This figure is **before** taking account of capital allowances.

(3)   The tax written down value of the capital allowances main pool at 1 August 2016 was £2,200. On 10 August 2016, Patience purchased a laptop computer for £1,700.

On the cessation of trading, Patience personally retained the laptop computer. Its value on 31 December 2016 was £1,200. The remainder of the items included in the main pool were sold for £800 on 31 December 2016.

(4)   Patience has unused overlap profits brought forward of £3,700.

Personal pension contributions

During the period 6 April to 31 December 2016, Patience contributed a total of £3,600 (net) into a personal pension scheme.

Pension income

During the period 1 January to 5 April 2017, Patience received the state pension of £1,450, a pension of £6,000 from her employer's occupational pension scheme, and a private pension of £3,300. These were the total gross amounts received.

Property

Patience owned two residential properties which were let out unfurnished until both properties were sold on 31 December 2016. The following information is available in respect of the two properties:

	Property one	Property two
	£	£
Rent received during the tax year 2016/17	3,600	7,200
Sale proceeds on 31 December 2016	122,000	98,000
Allowable revenue expenditure during the tax year 2016/17	(4,700)	(2,600)
Purchase cost	(81,400)	(103,700)

Patience has never occupied either of the two properties as her main residence.

Required:

Calculate Patience's income tax and capital gains tax liabilities for the tax year 2016/17.

Notes:

1   You should indicate by the use of zero (0) any items which are not taxable or deductible.

2   The following mark allocation is provided as guidance for this question:

Income tax   (13 marks)

Capital gains tax   (2 marks)

(Total: 15 marks)

85   SAMMI SMITH (ADAPTED)   *Walk in the footsteps of a top tutor*

You should assume that today's date is 20 March 2016.

Sammi Smith is a director of Smark Ltd. The company has given her the choice of being provided with a leased company motor car or alternatively being paid additional director's remuneration and then privately leasing the same motor car herself.

Company motor car

The motor car will be provided throughout the tax year 2016/17, and will be leased by Smark Ltd at an annual cost of £26,540. The motor car will be petrol powered, will have a list price of £81,858, and will have an official CO_2 emission rate of 295 grams per kilometre.

The lease payments will cover all the costs of running the motor car except for fuel. Smark Ltd will not provide Sammi with any fuel for private journeys.

Additional director's remuneration

As an alternative to having a company motor car, Sammi will be paid additional gross director's remuneration of £24,870 during the tax year 2016/17. She will then privately lease the motor car at an annual cost of £26,540.

Other information

The amount of business journeys that will be driven by Sammi will be immaterial and can therefore be ignored.

Sammi's current annual director's remuneration is just in excess of £45,000. Smark Ltd prepares its accounts to 5 April. The lease of the motor car will commence on 6 April 2016.

Required:

(a) **Advise Sammi Smith of the income tax and national insurance contribution implications for the tax year 2016/17 if she**

    (1) **is provided with the company motor car, and**

    (2) **receives additional director's remuneration of £24,870.**   **(5 marks)**

(b) **Advise Smark Ltd of the corporation tax and national insurance contribution implications for the year ended 5 April 2017 if the company**

    (1) **provides Sammi Smith with the company motor car, and**

    (2) **pays Sammi Smith additional director's remuneration of £24,870.**

    You should ignore value added tax (VAT).   **(5 marks)**

(c) **Determine which of the two alternatives is the most beneficial from each of the respective points of view of Sammi Smith and Smark Ltd.**   **(5 marks)**

        (Total: 15 marks)

86   **LETICIA STONE** *Walk in the footsteps of a top tutor*

Leticia Stone owns three properties which are let out. The following information relates to the tax year 2016/17:

Property one

This is a freehold house that qualifies as a trade under the furnished holiday letting rules. Leticia purchased this property on 1 July 2016 for £282,000. The purchase price included £4,600 for furniture and kitchen equipment.

Leticia borrowed £220,000 to purchase this property. During the period 1 July 2016 to 5 April 2017 she made loan repayments totalling £14,300, of which £12,700 was in respect of loan interest.

The property was let for 22 weeks at £425 per week during the period 1 July 2016 to 5 April 2017.

Due to a fire, £12,200 was spent on replacing the roof of the house during March 2017. Only £10,900 of this was paid for by Leticia's property insurance.

During the tax year 2016/17 Leticia drove 1,170 miles in her motor car in respect of the furnished holiday letting business. She uses HM Revenue and Customs' authorised mileage rates to calculate her expense deduction. The mileage was for the following purposes:

	Miles
Purchase of property	160
Running the business on a weekly basis	880
Property repairs	130

The other expenditure on this property for the period 1 July 2016 to 5 April 2017 amounted to £3,770, and this is all allowable.

Property two

This is a leasehold shop that is let out unfurnished. The property was acquired on 1 May 2016 and was immediately let to a tenant, with Leticia receiving a premium of £45,000 for the grant of a five-year lease. During the period 1 May 2016 to 5 April 2017 Leticia received four quarterly rental payments of £2,160 per quarter, payable in advance.

Leticia pays a monthly rent of £1,360 for this property, but did not pay a premium when she acquired it.

Property three

This is a freehold house that is let out unfurnished. The property was let from 6 April 2016 to 31 January 2017 at a monthly rent of £580. On 31 January 2017 the tenant left, owing three months' rent. Leticia recovered two months of the outstanding rent by retaining the tenant's security deposit, but was unable to recover the balance.

On 1 March 2017 a new tenant paid Leticia a security deposit of £1,200, being two months' rent, although the new tenancy did not commence until 15 April 2017.

During the tax year 2016/17 Leticia paid loan interest of £9,100 in respect of a loan that was taken out to purchase this property.

Other expenditure

The other expenditure on properties two and three for the tax year 2016/17 amounted to £36,240, and this is all allowable.

Furnished room

During the tax year 2016/17 Leticia rented out one furnished room of her main residence. During the year she received rent of £3,170, and incurred allowable expenditure of £4,840 in respect of the room. Leticia always uses the most favourable basis as regards the tax treatment of the furnished room.

Required:

(a) Calculate Leticia Stone's property loss for the tax year 2016/17.

  Your answer should separately identify the furnished holiday letting loss. (13 marks)

(b) Advise Leticia Stone as to the possible ways in which her property loss for the tax year 2016/17 can be relieved. (2 marks)

(Total: 15 marks)

87   RICHARD TRYER (ADAPTED) *Walk in the footsteps of a top tutor*

Richard Tryer is employed by Prog plc as a computer programmer.

Richard has tried to prepare his own income tax computation for the tax year 2016/17, but he has found it more difficult than expected. Although the sections which Richard has completed are correct, there are a significant number of omissions. The omissions are marked as outstanding (O/S).

The partly completed income tax computation is as follows:

Richard Tryer

Income tax computation – 2016/17

	Notes	£	£
Employment income			
Salary		41,000	
Car benefit	1	O/S	
Fuel benefit	1	O/S	
Living accommodation	2	O/S	
		———	O/S
Property income	3		O/S
Building society interest			1,260
Dividends			8,800
			O/S
Personal allowance			(11,000)
			———
Taxable income			O/S
			———

£		
32,000 at 20%		6,400
O/S at 40%		O/S
O/S at 0%		O/S
O/S at 40%		O/S
O/S at 0%		O/S
O/S at 32·5%		O/S
———		
O/S		
———		

Income tax liability	O/S
Less: PAYE	(9,130)
	———
Income tax payable	O/S
	———

Note 1 – Car and fuel benefits

Throughout the tax year 2016/17, Prog plc provided Richard with a petrol-powered motor car which has a list price of £17,900. The motor car cost Prog plc £17,200, and it has a CO_2 emission rate of 119 grams per kilometre. During the tax year 2016/17, Richard made contributions of £1,200 to Prog plc for the use of the motor car.

During the period 1 July 2016 to 5 April 2017, Prog plc also provided Richard with fuel for private journeys. The total cost of fuel during the period 1 July 2016 to 5 April 2017 was £4,200, of which 45% was for private journeys. Richard did not make any contributions towards the cost of the fuel.

Note 2 – Living accommodation

Throughout the tax year 2016/17, Prog plc provided Richard with living accommodation. The property has been rented by Prog plc since 6 April 2016 at a cost of £1,100 per month. On 6 April 2016, the market value of the property was £122,000, and it has an annual value of £8,600.

On 6 April 2016, Prog plc purchased furniture for the property at a cost of £12,100. The company pays for the running costs relating to the property, and for the tax year 2016/17 these amounted to £3,700.

Note 3 – Property income

Richard owns a freehold shop which is let out unfurnished. The shop was purchased on 1 October 2016, and during October 2016 Richard spent £8,400 replacing the building's roof. The shop was not usable until this work was carried out, and this fact was represented by a reduced purchase price.

On 1 December 2016, the property was let to a tenant, with Richard receiving a premium of £12,000 for the grant of a 30-year lease. The monthly rent is £830 payable in advance, and during the period 1 December 2016 to 5 April 2017 Richard received five rental payments.

Due to a fire, £8,600 was spent on repairing the roof of the shop during February 2017. Only £8,200 of this was paid for by Richard's property insurance.

Richard paid insurance of £480 in respect of the property. This was paid on 1 October 2016 and is for the year ended 30 September 2017.

Required:

Calculate the income tax payable by Richard Tryer for the tax year 2016/17.   (15 marks)

88   SAMSON AND DELILAH *Walk in the footsteps of a top tutor*

Samson and Delilah are a married couple. They are both employed by Rope plc, and Delilah is also a partner in a partnership. The following information is available in respect of the tax year 2016/17:

Samson

During the tax year 2016/17, Samson was paid a gross annual salary of £112,000 in respect of his employment with Rope plc.

Delilah

(1)   During the tax year 2016/17, Delilah was paid a gross annual salary of £184,000 in respect of her employment with Rope plc.

(2)   Throughout the tax year 2016/17, Rope plc provided Delilah with a petrol powered motor car which has a list price of £67,200, and an official CO_2 emission rate of 195 grams per kilometre. Rope plc does not provide Delilah with any fuel for private journeys. Delilah was unable to drive her motor car for a period during the tax year 2016/17 because of a skiing accident, and during this period Rope plc provided her with a chauffeur at a total cost of £9,400.

(3)   Delilah pays an annual professional subscription of £450 which is relevant to her employment with Rope plc. Delilah also pays an annual membership fee of £1,420 to a golf club which she uses to entertain Rope plc's clients. Rope plc does not reimburse Delilah for either of these costs.

(4)   During the tax year 2016/17, Delilah donated £250 (gross) per month to charity under the payroll deduction scheme operated by Rope plc.

(5)   Delilah has been in partnership with Esther and Felix for a number of years. The partnership's tax adjusted trading profit for the year ended 31 December 2016 was £93,600. Esther is paid an annual salary of £8,000, with the balance of profits being shared 40% to Delilah, 30% to Esther and 30% to Felix.

(6)   During the tax year 2016/17, Delilah paid interest of £6,200 on a personal loan taken out to purchase her share in the partnership.

(7)   During the tax year 2016/17, Delilah made charitable gift aid donations totalling £6,000 (gross).

Joint income – Building society deposit account

Samson and Delilah have savings in a building society deposit account which is in their joint names. During the tax year 2016/17, they received building society interest totalling £9,600 from this joint account.

Required:

(a)   **Calculate Samson and Delilah's respective income tax liabilities for the tax year 2016/17.**

        Note: The following mark allocation is provided as guidance for this requirement:

        Samson   (3.5 marks)

        Delilah   (9.5 marks)   **(13 marks)**

(b)   **Calculate Samson's income tax saving for the tax year 2016/17 if the building society deposit account had been in Delilah's sole name instead of in joint names for the entire year.**   **(2 marks)**

                                                                                        (Total: 15 marks)

INCOME TAX BASICS AND INCOME FROM SELF-EMPLOYMENT

89   CAROL COURIER (ADAPTED)

For the purposes of this question you should assume that today's date is 15 March 2016.

Carol Courier is employed by Quick-Speed plc as a delivery driver, and is paid a salary of £37,500 per year. She contributes 5% of her gross salary into Quick-Speed plc's HM Revenue & Customs registered occupational pension scheme.

As an alternative to being employed, Quick-Speed plc have offered Carol the opportunity to provide delivery services to the company on a self-employed basis.

The details of the proposed arrangement for the year ended 5 April 2017 are as follows:

(1)   Carol will commence being self-employed on 6 April 2016.

(2)   Her income from Quick-Speed plc is expected to be £43,500.

(3)   Carol will also provide delivery services to other clients. Her income from these contracts is expected to be £8,000.

(4)   Carol will lease a delivery van and 100% of the mileage will be for business purposes. The cost of leasing and running the van will be £4,400.

(5)   When she is unavailable Carol will have to provide a replacement driver to deliver for Quick-Speed plc. This will cost her £2,800.

(6)   Carol will contribute £3,000 (gross) into a personal pension scheme during the tax year 2016/17. This will provide her with the same benefits as the occupational pension scheme provided by Quick-Speed plc.

Required:

(a)   **Assuming that Carol does not accept the offer from Quick-Speed plc and continues to be employed by the company, calculate her income tax and class 1 NIC liability for the tax year 2016/17.**   **(5 marks)**

(b)   **Assuming that Carol accepts the offer to provide delivery services to Quick-Speed plc on a self-employed basis from 6 April 2016 onwards, calculate her income tax, class 2 NIC and class 4 NIC liabilities for the tax year 2016/17.**   **(6 marks)**

(c)   **Advise Carol as to whether it will be beneficial to accept the offer to provide delivery services to Quick-Speed plc on a self-employed basis.**

Your answer should be supported by a calculation of the amount by which Carol's income for the tax year 2016/17 (net of outgoings, income tax and NIC) will increase or decrease if she accepts the offer.   **(4 marks)**

(Total: 15 marks)

90   IDRIS WILLIAMS *Walk in the footsteps of a top tutor*

(a)   Idris Williams has opened a small bed and breakfast and is considering whether to prepare his accounts to 5 April or 30 June.

Required:

Advise Idris of the advantages for tax purposes of choosing an accounting date of either 5 April or 30 June.   **(4 marks)**

(b)   Idris commenced trade on 6 April 2016 and has decided to prepare his first set of accounts to 5 April 2017.

The following information is available regarding his statement of profit or loss for the first year of trading:

	Notes	£	£
Revenue	(1)		49,910
Less: Food, utilities and other household goods	(2)		(17,660)
			————
Gross profit			32,250
Expenses:			
Depreciation	(3)	1,250	
Motor expenses	(4)	9,340	
Other expenses	(5)	1,485	
		———	(12,075)
			————
Net profit			20,175
			————

Notes:

(1)   Revenue includes £10,275 which is still receivable at 5 April 2017.

(2)   Idris paid for 95% of his purchases by 5 April 2017 and the remainder in May 2017. There is no closing inventory at 5 April 2017.

Idris is also living in part of the bed and breakfast and £4,500 of the purchases relate to Idris's personal use.

(3)   The depreciation charge relates to furniture bought in the period for £3,500 and a motor car purchased on 6 April 2016 for £9,000. The motor car has CO_2 emissions of 105 g/km.

(4)   The motor expenses of £9,340 relate to Idris' car and in the period he drove 13,000 business miles and 20,000 miles in total.

(5)   The other expenses are all allowable for tax purposes. £400 of these expenses were unpaid at 5 April 2017.

The cash basis private use adjustment for one occupant in a business premises for a 12 month period is £4,200.

Required:

(1)   Calculate Idris' tax adjusted trading profit for the year ended 5 April 2017, assuming he uses the normal accruals basis.   **(4 marks)**

(2)   State why Idris is entitled to use the cash basis and calculate Idris' tax adjusted trading profit for the year ended 5 April 2017, assuming he uses the cash basis.   **(6 marks)**

(3)   State which basis would be more beneficial for Idris for the tax year 2016/17.   **(1 mark)**

   (Total: 15 marks)

91   SAM WHITE (ADAPTED) *Walk in the footsteps of a top tutor*

(1)   Sam is self-employed running a retail clothing shop. His statement of profit or loss for the year ended 5 April 2017 is as follows:

	Notes	£	£
Gross profit			190,300
Depreciation		7,600	
Motor expenses	2	8,800	
Patent royalties	3	700	
Professional fees	4	1,860	
Other expenses	5	71,340	
		———	(90,300)
			———
Net profit			100,000
			———

(2)   During the year ended 5 April 2017 Sam drove a total of 25,000 miles, of which 5,000 miles were driven when he visited his suppliers in Europe. The balance of the mileage is 25% for private journeys and 75% for business journeys in the United Kingdom.

(3)   During the year ended 5 April 2017 Sam paid patent royalties of £700 in respect of specialised technology that he uses when altering clothes for customers.

(4)   The figure for professional fees consists of £1,050 for legal fees in connection with an action brought against a supplier for breach of contract and £810 for accountancy. Included in the figure for accountancy is £320 in respect of personal capital gains tax advice for the tax year 2016/17.

(5)   The figure for other expenses of £71,340 includes £560 for gifts to customers of food hampers costing £35 each and £420 for gifts to customers of pens carrying an advertisement for the clothing shop costing £60 each.

(6)   Sam uses one of the eight rooms in the couple's house as an office for when he works at home. The total running costs of the house for the year ended 5 April 2017 were £5,120. This cost is not included in the expenses in the statement of profit or loss of £90,300.

(7) Sam uses his private telephone to make business telephone calls. The total cost of the private telephone for the year ended 5 April 2017 was £1,600, and 25% of this related to business telephone calls. The cost of the private telephone is not included in the expenses in the statement of profit or loss of £90,300.

(8) During the year ended 5 April 2017 Sam took goods out of the clothing shop for his personal use without paying for them and no entry has been made in the accounts to record this. The goods cost £820, and had a selling price of £1,480.

(9) The tax written down values for capital allowance purposes at 6 April 2016 were:

Main pool	£14,800
Motor car bought January 2017	£20,200

The motor car is used by Sam (see note 2) and has an official CO_2 emission rate of 190 g/km.

Required:

Calculate Sam's tax adjusted trading profit for the year ended 5 April 2017.

Your computation should start with the net profit of £100,000 and should list all the items referred to in Notes (1) to (8), indicating with a zero (0) any items that do not require adjustment. **(10 marks)**

92 GEORGE (ADAPTED) *Walk in the footsteps of a top tutor*

You should assume that today's date is 1 March 2016.

George, a software developer has accepted a one-year contract to update software for Xpee plc.

(1) The contract will run from 6 April 2016 to 5 April 2017, with a fee of £40,000 payable for the entire year of the contract. A condition of the contract is that George will have to do the work personally and not be permitted to sub-contract the work to anyone else.

(2) George will work from home, but will have to attend weekly meetings at Xpee plc's offices to receive instructions regarding the work to be performed during the following week.

(3) George will not incur any significant expenses in respect of the contract apart from the purchase of a new laptop computer for £3,600 on 6 April 2016. This laptop will be used 100% for business purposes.

(4) During the term of the contract, George will not be permitted to work for any other clients. He will therefore not have any other income during the tax year 2016/17.

(5) George's tax liability for the tax year 2015/16 was collected through PAYE, so he will not be required to make any payments on account in respect of the tax year 2016/17.

George has several friends who are also software developers. He understands that his employment status is not clear cut but that his income tax liability for the tax year 2016/17 will be the same regardless of whether he is treated as employed or as self-employed. However, George appreciates that there are advantages to being classed as self-employed.

Required:

(a) List FOUR factors which are indicators of George being treated as an employee in relation to his contract with Xpee plc rather than as self-employed.

Note: You should confine your answer to the information given in the question.

(2 marks)

(b) Calculate George's income tax liability and national insurance contributions for the tax year 2016/17 if he is treated as self-employed in respect of his contract with Xpee plc. **(4 marks)**

(c) If George is treated as being an employee of Xpee plc instead of self-employed:

(1) Explain why his income tax liability will be payable earlier. **(2 marks)**

(2) Calculate the additional amount of national insurance contributions which he personally will suffer for the tax year 2016/17. **(2 marks)**

(Total: 10 marks)

---

93 **SOPHIA WONG (ADAPTED)** *Walk in the footsteps of a top tutor*

You should assume that today's date is 15 March 2016.

(a) Sophia Wong is self-employed as a lawyer. For the year ended 5 April 2017 Sophia has forecast that her tax adjusted trading profit will be £80,000.

This will be her only income for the tax year 2016/17, and Sophia's total income tax liability and national insurance contributions (NIC) for this year if she continues to trade on a self-employed basis will be as follows:

	£
Income tax	21,200
Class 2 NIC	146
Class 4 NIC	3,885
	–––––––
	25,231
	–––––––

Sophia understands that she could save tax and NIC if she instead traded as a limited company, and she is therefore considering incorporating her business on 6 April 2016. The forecast taxable total profits of the new limited company for the year ended 5 April 2017 are unchanged at £80,000 (before taking account of any director's remuneration).

Required:

Assuming that Sophia Wong incorporates her business on 6 April 2016, advise her whether or not there will be an overall saving of tax and national insurance contributions (NIC) for the tax year 2016/17 if she withdraws all of the profits from the new company as:

(1) director's remuneration (after allowing for employer's class 1 NIC, gross director's remuneration will be £71,282), or **(6 marks)**

(2) dividends (after allowing for corporation tax, dividends will be £64,000). **(5 marks)**

Notes:

(1) For both alternatives, you are expected to calculate the corporation tax liability (if any) of the new limited company for the year ended 5 April 2017, the income tax liability of Sophia Wong, and the class 1 NIC (if any) payable by Sophia and the new company.

(2) You should assume that the rates of corporation tax remain unchanged.

(b) Since receiving your advice in (a) above Sophia has unexpectedly received a very generous offer to buy her business. This coincided with discussions she has been having with a major law firm who are interested in employing her.

She has therefore now decided not to incorporate her business but instead to sell it to an unconnected third party for £200,000, to be received in cash on 1 May 2016. The only chargeable asset of Sophia Wong's business is goodwill, the value of this asset has increased over a number of years to £150,000. The goodwill has a nil cost.

On 15 April 2016 Sophia sold a necklace realising a chargeable gain of £11,153.

Sophia will not make any other disposals during the tax year 2016/17. She will take a long holiday before starting her new job and her taxable income (after deduction of the personal allowance) for the tax year 2016/17 will be £20,000.

Required:

Calculate Sophia Wong's capital gains tax liability for the tax year 2016/17 assuming she sells her business on 1 May 2016 for £200,000 cash and she makes any beneficial elections.

State the deadline(s) for making any elections you have identified as being beneficial.

(4 marks)

(Total: 15 marks)

94 FERGUS *Walk in the footsteps of a top tutor*

You should assume that today's date is 15 March 2016.

Fergus is currently self-employed, and if he continues to trade on a self-employed basis, his total income tax liability and national insurance contributions (NIC) for the tax year 2016/17 will be £33,631.

However, Fergus is considering incorporating his business on 6 April 2016. The forecast taxable total profits of the new limited company for the year ended 5 April 2017 are £100,000 (before taking account of any director's remuneration).

Fergus will pay himself gross director's remuneration of £19,000 and dividends of £40,000. The balance of the profits will remain undrawn within the new company.

Required:

Determine whether or not there will be an overall saving of tax and national insurance contributions (NIC) for the year ended 5 April 2017 if Fergus incorporates his business on 6 April 2016.

Notes:

1 You are expected to calculate the income tax payable by Fergus, the class 1 NIC payable by Fergus and the new limited company, and the corporation tax liability of the new limited company for the year ended 5 April 2017.

2 You should assume that the rates of corporation tax remain unchanged. (10 marks)

95   JOHN AND LIAN (ADAPTED)   *Walk in the footsteps of a top tutor*

(a)   John Higgins left employment on 30 April 2016 and started an unincorporated business on 1 June 2016. He will prepare his first set of accounts for the 12 months to 31 May 2017 and expects to make a taxable profit of £80,000.

Prior to starting the business his only income was from his employment and his income tax liability was paid at source through the Pay As You Earn (PAYE) system.

Required:

(1)   State the date by which John must notify HM Revenue & Customs that he is chargeable to income tax in respect of his trading income if he does not receive a notice to complete a tax return.

(2)   State the date that John must keep records which relate to his tax return for the tax year 2016/17.

(3)   State the first date by which John will first be required to pay an amount of income tax in relation to the taxable profits arising from his business.

(3 marks)

(b)   Lian Zhang commenced in self-employment on 1 May 2014. She prepared accounts to 30 April and her trading profits for the first two years of trading were as follows:

	Tax adjusted trading profit before capital allowances	Capital allowances
	£	£
Year ended 30 April 2015	62,300	11,900
Year ended 30 April 2016	75,400	38,200

In 2017 Lian was offered an employment contract with a large company which she decided to accept. She ceased trading and prepared her final set of accounts for the 14-month period to 30 June 2017.

Lian's tax adjusted trading profit (before capital allowances) for the 14-month period ended 30 June 2017 will be £61,500.

The tax written down value of her capital allowances main pool at 1 May 2016 was £14,400. She acquired a new machine on 1 June 2016 for £12,000 and sold all of the plant and machinery which was still owned by the business on 30 June 2017 for £22,000. No item was sold for more than its original cost.

Required:

Calculate the amount of trading profit that will be assessed on Lian Zhang for each of the tax years 2014/15, 2015/16, 2016/17 and 2017/18.

You should assume that the capital allowance rates for the tax year 2016/17 apply throughout.   **(7 marks)**

(Total: 10 marks)

96   FANG, HONG AND KANG *Walk in the footsteps of a top tutor*

 Timed question with Online tutor debrief

(a)   Fang commenced self-employment on 1 August 2014. She has a trading profit of £45,960 for the year ended 31 July 2015, and a trading profit of £39,360 for the year ended 31 July 2016.

Required:

(1)   Calculate the amount of trading profit which will have been assessed on Fang for each of the tax years 2014/15, 2015/16 and 2016/17, and state the amount of any overlap profit.   (3 marks)

(2)   Explain how Fang would have obtained relief for trading expenditure incurred prior to 1 August 2014 and for computer equipment which Fang already owned which was brought into business use on 1 August 2014.

(2 marks)

(b)   Hong has been in self-employment since 2005, preparing accounts to 5 April. For the year ended 5 April 2017 she made a trading loss of £45,800, and has claimed this against her total income and chargeable gain for the tax year 2015/16.

For the year ended 5 April 2016 Hong made a trading profit of £29,700. She also has property income of £3,900 for the tax year 2015/16. Hong has an unused trading loss of £2,600 brought forward from the tax year 2014/15.

During the tax year 2015/16 Hong disposed of an investment property and this resulted in a chargeable gain (before the annual exempt amount) of £17,800. Hong has unused capital losses of £6,200 brought forward from the tax year 2013/14.

Required:

After taking account of the loss relief claims made, calculate Hong's taxable income and taxable gain for the tax year 2015/16, and state the amount of any trading loss carried forward.

You should assume that the tax allowances for the tax year 2016/17 apply throughout.   (5 marks)

(c)   Kang, Ling and Ming have been in partnership since 2007, preparing accounts to 30 June. Ming left the partnership on 31 October 2015. Profits have always been shared equally.

The partnership had a trading profit of £148,800 for the year ended 30 June 2015, and a profit of £136,800 for the year ended 30 June 2016. Each partner has unused overlap profits brought forward of £29,400.

Required:

Calculate the trading income assessments of Kang, Ling and Ming for each of the tax years 2015/16 and 2016/17. **(5 marks)**

(Total: 15 marks)

 Calculate your allowed time, allocate the time to the separate parts................

97 NA STYLE (ADAPTED) *Walk in the footsteps of a top tutor*

Na Style commenced self-employment as a hairdresser on 1 January 2014. She had tax adjusted trading profit as follows:

	£
Six months ended 30 June 2014	25,200
Year ended 30 June 2015	21,600
Year ended 30 June 2016	30,665

Other information

(1) During the tax year 2016/17 Na received dividends of £8,200, building society interest of £700, interest of £310 from an individual savings account (ISA), interest of £1,100 on the maturity of a NS&I savings certificate, and interest of £370 from government stocks (gilts).

(2) Na's payments on account of income tax in respect of the tax year 2016/17 totalled £3,200.

Required:

(a) Calculate the amount of trading profit that will have been assessed on Na Style for the tax years 2013/14 to 2016/17 inclusively, clearly identifying the amount of any overlap profits. **(6 marks)**

(b) (1) Calculate the income tax payable by Na Style for the tax year 2016/17.

(6 marks)

(2) Calculate Na Style's balancing payment for the tax year 2016/17 and her payments on account for the tax year 2017/18, stating the relevant due dates.

You should ignore national insurance contributions. **(3 marks)**

(Total: 15 marks)

98   SIMON HOUSE (ADAPTED) *Walk in the footsteps of a top tutor*

On 1 May 2016 Simon House purchased a derelict freehold house for £127,000. Legal fees of £1,800 were paid in respect of the purchase.

Simon then renovated the house at a cost of £50,600, with the renovation being completed on 10 August 2016. He immediately put the house up for sale, and it was sold on 31 August 2016 for £260,000. Legal fees of £2,600 were paid in respect of the sale.

Simon financed the transaction by a bank loan of £150,000 that was taken out on 1 May 2016 at an annual interest rate of 6%. The bank loan was repaid on 31 August 2016.

Simon had no income or capital gains for the tax year 2016/17 except as indicated above.

Simon has been advised that whether or not he is treated as carrying on a trade will be determined according to the 'badges of trade', which include:

(1)   Subject matter of the transaction.

(2)   Length of ownership.

(3)   Frequency of similar transactions.

(4)   Work done on the property.

(5)   Circumstances responsible for the realisation.

(6)   Motive.

Required:

(a)   **Briefly explain the meaning of each of the six 'badges of trade' listed in the question.**

       You are not expected to quote from decided cases.   **(3 marks)**

(b)   **Calculate Simon House's income tax liability and his class 2 and class 4 national insurance contributions for the tax year 2016/17, if he is treated as carrying on a trade in respect of the disposal of the freehold house.**   **(8 marks)**

(c)   **Calculate Simon House's capital gains tax liability for the tax year 2016/17, if he is not treated as carrying on a trade in respect of the disposal of the freehold house.**
                                                                                                (4 marks)

                                                                                        (Total: 15 marks)

99   TIM BURR (ADAPTED) *Walk in the footsteps of a top tutor*

Tim Burr is a self-employed tree surgeon. His business has grown rapidly over the last few years and Tim is struggling to keep up with his workload.

On 1 December 2016, he is planning to bring a newly qualified tree surgeon, Hazel Grove into his business. Hazel will either be taken on as an employee, being paid a gross monthly salary of £3,300, or join Tim as a partner, receiving a 20% share of the new partnership's profits.

Tim has forecast that his tax adjusted trading profit will be £216,000 for the year ended 30 September 2017, and £240,000 for the year ended 30 September 2018.

Hazel does not have any other income for the tax year 2016/17.

Required:

(a)   Assuming that Hazel Grove is employed from 1 December 2016, calculate the total amount of national insurance contributions that will be paid by Tim Burr and Hazel Grove, if any, in respect of her earnings for the tax year 2016/17.

You are not expected to calculate the national insurance contributions that will be paid in respect of Tim Burr's earnings.   **(4 marks)**

(b)   Assuming that Hazel Grove becomes a partner from 1 December 2016:

(2)   Calculate her trading income assessments for the tax years 2016/17 and 2017/18.

You are not expected to calculate any overlap profits.   **(4 marks)**

(2)   Calculate the total amount of national insurance contributions that will be paid by Tim Burr and Hazel Grove, if any, in respect of her trading income assessment for the tax year 2016/17.

You are not expected to calculate the national insurance contributions that will be paid in respect of Tim Burr's trading income assessment.   **(2 marks)**

(Total: 10 marks)

100   RICHARD FEAST (ADAPTED)   *Walk in the footsteps of a top tutor*

(a)   On 6 April 2016, Richard Feast commenced in self-employment, running a restaurant. Richard's statement of profit or loss for the year ended 5 April 2017 is as follows:

	Notes	£	£
Gross profit			73,440
Expenses			
Motor expenses	1	7,660	
Property expenses	2	16,200	
Repairs and renewals	3	6,420	
Other expenses	4	10,960	
			(41,240)
Net profit			32,200

Note 1 – Motor expenses

	£
Cost of running Richard's motor car	4,710
Cost of running a motor car used by the restaurant's chef	2,670
Parking fines incurred by Richard	280
	7,660

Richard's motor car is used 70% for private journeys, and the chef's motor car is used 20% for private journeys.

Note 2 – Property expenses

Richard lives in an apartment which is situated above the restaurant, and one-fifth of the total property expenses of £16,200 relate to this apartment.

Note 3 – Repairs and renewals

	£
Decorating the restaurant	5,100
Decorating the apartment	1,320
	─────
	6,420
	─────

The property was in a usable state when it was purchased.

Note 4 – Other expenses

The figure of £10,960 for other expenses includes legal fees of £2,590 in connection with the purchase of the restaurant property. The remaining expenses are all allowable.

Additional information: Plant and machinery

The following motor cars were purchased during the year ended 5 April 2017:

	Date of purchase	Cost	CO_2 emission rate
		£	
Motor car (1)	6 April 2016	14,000	124 grams per kilometre
Motor car (2)	6 April 2016	16,800	103 grams per kilometre

Motor car (1) is used by Richard, and motor car (2) is used by the restaurant's chef.

Required:

Calculate Richard Feast's tax adjusted trading profit for the year ended 5 April 2017.

Notes:

1   Your computation should commence with the net profit figure of **£32,200**, and should list all of the items referred to in Notes (1) to (4), indicating by the use of zero (0) any items which do not require adjustment.

2   In answering this part of the question you are not expected to take account of any of the information provided in parts (b) or (c) below.   **(7 marks)**

(b)   Richard's only employee is a chef who is employed throughout the 2016/17 tax year on a gross annual salary of £46,000. The chef was provided with a petrol powered motor car (see the plant and machinery information in part (a) above) throughout the tax year. The list price of the motor car is the same as its cost. Richard did not provide any fuel for private journeys.

Required:

Calculate the employers' class 1 and class 1A national insurance contributions which Richard Feast would have incurred in respect of the chef's earnings and benefit for the tax year 2016/17.

You are not expected to calculate the national insurance contributions suffered by the employees or by Richard in respect of his self-employment.   **(3 marks)**

(c)   Richard has not previously filed a self-assessment tax return, and therefore wants to know when he will have to file his return for the tax year 2016/17. He is not sure whether to file a paper tax return or to file the return online.

As this will be his first self-assessment tax return, Richard is concerned that HM Revenue and Customs might carry out a compliance check.

Required:

(1)   Advise Richard Feast of the latest dates by which his self-assessment tax return for the tax year 2016/17 should be filed in order to avoid a penalty.

(2 marks)

(2)   State the period during which HM Revenue and Customs will have to notify Richard Feast if they intend to carry out a compliance check in respect of his self-assessment tax return for the tax year 2016/17, and the possible reasons why such a check would be made.

You should assume that Richard will file his tax return by the filing date.

(3 marks)

(Total: 15 marks)

101   ALFRED KING (ADAPTED)   *Walk in the footsteps of a top tutor*

(a)   Alfred King is trying to calculate his balancing payment for the tax year 2016/17, and the following information is available:

(1)   He has been in partnership with Anne Royal and Mary Regal running a retail shop since 6 April 2007, but Mary resigned as a partner on 1 January 2017.

(2)   The partnership's tax adjusted trading profit for the year ended 5 April 2017 is £228,000. This figure is **before** taking account of capital allowances.

(3)   The tax written down value of the partnership's capital allowances main pool at 6 April 2016 was £10,000. The only capital expenditure during the year ended 5 April 2017 was the cost of £82,000 for refurbishing the second floor of the partnership's shop during December 2016. The cost was made up as follows:

	£
False ceiling	17,600
Display units	15,100
Tiled flooring	32,200
Movable partition walls	17,100
	——
	82,000
	——

(4)   The partners have always shared profits equally, and continued to do so after Mary resigned.

(5)   During the tax year 2016/17, Alfred received dividends totalling £3,320, of which £720 were from an individual savings account (ISA).

(6)   During the tax year 2016/17, Alfred made gift aid donations totalling £1,920 (net) to national charities.

(7)   Alfred's payments on account of income tax and class 4 national insurance contributions in respect of the tax year 2016/17 totalled £20,200.

Required:

Calculate Alfred King's balancing payment for the tax year 2016/17. You should take account of class 4 national insurance contributions.   **(12 marks)**

(b)   The partnership of Alfred King and Anne Royal is planning to replace Mary Regal by employing either one full-time employee or two part-time employees. A full-time employee would be paid a gross annual salary of £22,000, whilst the part-time employees would each be paid gross annual salaries of £11,450. Alfred would prefer to employ two part-time employees, but is concerned that this will be more expensive.

Required:

Explain to Alfred King why employing two part-time employees will not be any more expensive than employing one full-time employee. Ignore the NIC employment allowance.

Note: You should include calculations to support your explanation, and should confine your answer to the information given in this part of the question. (3 marks)

(Total: 15 marks)

102   CHI NEEDLE (ADAPTED)   *Walk in the footsteps of a top tutor*

Chi Needle commenced self-employment as an acupuncturist on 6 April 2016, and for the year ended 5 April 2017 her trading profit using the normal accruals basis was £52,400, calculated as follows:

	Notes	£	£
Revenue	1		71,900
Expenses			
Motor expenses	2	4,400	
Other expenses	3	8,200	
Capital allowances	4	6,900	
		─────	(19,500)
Trading profit			52,400

Note 1 – Revenue

The revenue figure of £71,900 includes receivables of £1,600 which were owed as at 5 April 2017.

Note 2 – Motor expenses

The total motor expenses for the year ended 5 April 2017 were £5,500, of which 20% was for private journeys. This proportion has been disallowed in calculating the trading profit. During the year ended 5 April 2017, Chi drove 13,200 business miles.

Note 3 – Other expenses

The other expenses figure of £8,200 includes payables of £900 which were owed as at 5 April 2017.

Note 4 – Capital allowances

Capital allowances consist of an annual investment allowance claim of £4,020 in respect of office equipment purchased on 6 April 2016, and a writing down allowance of £2,880 claimed in respect of Chi's motor car. The motor car had cost £20,000 on 6 April 2016.

Additional information

Chi has no other income for the tax year 2016/17.

She did not make any payments on account in respect of the tax year 2016/17.

Required:

(a)   Based on the trading profit of £52,400 for the year ended 5 April 2017:

    (1)   Calculate Chi Needle's income tax liability for the tax year 2016/17.   **(2 marks)**

    (2)   Calculate the class 2 and class 4 national insurance contributions payable by Chi Needle for the tax year 2016/17.   **(3 marks)**

(b)   Calculate Chi Needle's trading profit for the year ended 5 April 2017 if she had used the cash basis instead of the accruals basis.

    Notes:

    (1)   Where relevant, expenses should be claimed on a flat rate basis.

    (2)   You are not expected to recalculate the income tax liability or the national insurance contributions payable.   **(5 marks)**

(Total: 10 marks)

TRADING LOSSES

103   NORMA (ADAPTED)

Norma, who had been in business as a confectioner since 1 May 2012, disposed of the business and retired on 31 May 2016. She does not intend to start any other business, but will be employed part time from 1 June 2016 on an annual salary of £11,400.

Her trading profits/(losses), as adjusted for taxation were:

	£	
Period ended 31.12.12	21,000	Profit
Year ended 31.12.13	17,000	Profit
Year ended 31.12.14	16,900	Profit
Year ended 31.12.15	8,835	Profit
Period ended 31.5.16	(11,000)	Loss

Norma has received bank interest of £2,400 each year since April 2012. In addition she realised a taxable gain (i.e. after the annual exempt amount), of £35,000 in June 2015.

The taxable gain does not qualify for entrepreneurs' relief and it is not in relation to residential property.

Required:

(a) Calculate Norma's taxable income and gains for each tax year that she was in business before any relief for the loss arising in the period ended 31 May 2016.

(b) Explain the options available to Norma to utilise the loss and explain the effect on her tax liability of the loss relief claims identified.

Assume that the tax rules, rates and allowances for the tax year 2016/17 apply throughout. **(15 marks)**

104 LEONARDO *Walk in the footsteps of a top tutor*

Leonardo commenced to trade as an art dealer on 1 September 2013. His trading results, adjusted for income tax, are:

	£	
Period ended 31.5.14	40,500	Profit
Year ended 31.5.15	(54,000)	Loss
Year ended 31.5.16	(27,000)	Loss
Year ended 31.5.17	11,000	Profit

Leonardo does not foresee making any significant profits in the next 2 or 3 years.

Leonardo has not had any other income in any of the years in question, or earlier.

Required:

(a) Show how his trading loss can be utilised most effectively, giving your reasons.

(8 marks)

(b) State by what date(s) the claims you are proposing in part (a) should be submitted to HM Revenue & Customs. **(2 marks)**

(Total: 10 marks)

105 DEE ZYNE (ADAPTED) *Walk in the footsteps of a top tutor*

On 5 July 2016 Dee Zyne resigned as an employee of Trendy-Wear plc. The company had employed her as a fashion designer since 2006. On 6 July 2016 Dee commenced self-employment running her own clothing business, preparing accounts to 5 April.

The following information is available for the tax year 2016/17:

Self-employment

(1) Dee's tax adjusted trading loss for the period 6 July 2016 to 5 April 2017 was £11,440. This figure is before taking account of the information in Note (2) and capital allowances.

(2)   During the period 6 July 2016 to 5 April 2017 Dee paid patent royalties of £500 in respect of specialised technology that she uses in her clothing business.

(3)   Dee purchased the following assets during the period ended 5 April 2017:

		£
10 July 2016	Computer	1,257
16 August 2016	Office furniture	2,175
13 November 2016	Motor car (1)	10,400
21 January 2017	Motor car (2)	17,800

Motor car (1) purchased on 13 November 2016 has CO_2 emissions of 105 grams per kilometre, is used by an employee, and 15% of the mileage is for private purposes.

Motor car (2) purchased on 21 January 2017 has CO_2 emissions of 135 grams per kilometre, is used by Dee, and 20% of the mileage is for private purposes.

Other information

(1)   Dee's employment income for the period 6 April 2016 – 5 July 2016 was £28,875.

(2)   Dee's total income for each of the tax years 2010/11 to 2015/16 was £80,000.

Required:

(a)   Calculate Dee's tax adjusted trading loss for the tax year 2016/17.   **(6 marks)**

(b)   Describe the ways in which Dee could have relieved her trading loss for the tax year 2016/17 against total income, and explain which of these claims would have been most beneficial.

You should assume that the tax rates for the tax year 2016/17 apply throughout.

(4 marks)

(Total: 10 marks)

106 SAMANTHA FABRIQUE (ADAPTED)   *Walk in the footsteps of a top tutor*

Samantha Fabrique has been a self-employed manufacturer of clothing since 2005. She has the following income and chargeable gains for the tax years 2015/16 to 2017/18:

	2015/16	2016/17	2017/18
	£	£	£
Trading profit/(loss)	21,600	(81,900)	10,500
Building society interest	52,100	3,800	1,500
Chargeable gains/(loss)	53,300	(3,400)	11,300

The chargeable gains do not qualify for entrepreneurs' relief and are not in relation to residential property.

Required:

(a)   State the factors that will influence an individual's choice of loss relief claims.

(3 marks)

(b) Calculate Samantha's taxable income and taxable gains for each of the tax years 2015/16, 2016/17 and 2017/18 on the assumption that she relieves the trading loss of £81,900 for the tax year 2016/17 on the most favourable basis.

Explain your reasoning behind relieving the loss on the most favourable basis.

You should assume that the tax allowances for the tax year 2016/17 apply throughout. **(12 marks)**

(Total: 15 marks)

107 MICHAEL AND SEAN *Walk in the footsteps of a top tutor*

(a) The UK Government uses tax policies to encourage certain types of activity.

Required:

Briefly explain how the UK Government's tax policies encourage:

(1) Individuals to save, **(1 mark)**

(2) Individuals to support charities, **(1 mark)**

(3) Entrepreneurs to build their own businesses and to invest in plant and machinery. **(2 marks)**

(b) You are a trainee chartered certified accountant and your manager has asked for your help regarding two taxpayers who have both made trading losses.

Michael

Michael commenced in self-employment on 1 July 2015, preparing accounts to 5 April. His results for the first two periods of trading were as follows:

		£
Nine-month period ended 5 April 2016	– Trading loss	(24,600)
Year ended 5 April 2017	– Trading profit	7,100

For tax years 2011/12 to 2013/14, Michael had the following employment income:

	£
2011/12	44,500
2012/13	17,200
2013/14	51,000

Michael did not have any income during the period 6 April 2014 to 30 June 2015.

Sean

Sean has been in self-employment since 2006, but ceased trading on 31 December 2016. He has always prepared accounts to 31 December. His results for the final five years of trading were as follows:

	£
Year ended 31 December 2012 – Trading profit	21,300
Year ended 31 December 2013 – Trading profit	14,400
Year ended 31 December 2014 – Trading profit	18,900
Year ended 31 December 2015 – Trading profit	3,700
Year ended 31 December 2016 – Trading loss	(23,100)

For each of the tax years 2012/13 to 2016/17 Sean has property business profits of £11,000. Sean has unused overlap profits brought forward of £3,600.

Required:

For each of the two taxpayers Michael and Sean, identify the loss relief claims that are available to them, and explain which of the available claims would be the most beneficial.

Notes:

(1) You should clearly state the amount of any reliefs claimed and the rates of income tax saved. However, you are not expected to calculate any income tax liabilities.

(2) You should assume that the tax rates and allowances for the tax year 2016/17 apply throughout.

The following mark allocation is provided as guidance for this requirement:

Michael	**(5 marks)**
Sean	**(6 marks)**
	(Total: 15 marks)

PARTNERSHIPS

108 PETER, QUINTON AND ROGER (ADAPTED) *Walk in the footsteps of a top tutor*

Peter and Quinton commenced in partnership on 1 January 2014. Roger joined as a partner on 1 January 2015, and Peter resigned as a partner on 31 December 2016. Profits and losses have always been shared equally.

The partnership's tax adjusted profits and losses are as follows:

	£	
Year ended 31 December 2014	40,000	Profit
Year ended 31 December 2015	90,000	Profit
Year ended 31 December 2016	(30,000)	Loss

All of the partners were in employment prior to becoming partners, and each of them has investment income. None of the partners has any capital gains.

Required:

(a) Briefly explain the basis by which trading profits are assessed on partners when they join a partnership. **(2 marks)**

(b) Calculate the trading income assessments of Peter, Quinton and Roger for the tax years 2013/14, 2014/15 and 2015/16. **(6 marks)**

(c) State the possible ways in which Peter, Quinton and Roger can relieve their share of the trading loss for the tax year 2016/17.

Your answer should include a calculation of the amount of loss available for relief to each partner. **(7 marks)**

(Total: 15 marks)

109 AE, BEE, CAE, AND DEE (ADAPTED) *Walk in the footsteps of a top tutor*

(a) Ae and Bee commenced in partnership on 1 July 2014 preparing accounts to 30 June. Cae joined as a partner on 1 July 2016. Profits have always been shared equally.

The partnership's tax adjusted trading profit since the commencement of trading have been:

	£
Year ended 30 June 2015	54,000
Year ended 30 June 2016	66,000
Year ended 30 June 2017	87,000

Required:

Calculate the trading income assessments of Ae, Bee and Cae for each of the tax years 2014/15, 2015/16 and 2016/17.   **(5 marks)**

(b) Dee has been self-employed for many years. The business has been loss making for the last two years. In the year ended 5 April 2018 she is planning to bring her sister, Eae, into the business as a partner, in an attempt to turn the business around. She anticipates that the business will make a small loss in the year ended 5 April 2018, but will make growing profits going forward.

Dee's losses have been as follows:

	£
Year ended 5 April 2016	5,000
Year ended 5 April 2017	165,000

Dee has savings income of £85,000 each year.

Required:

(1) **Explain how the loss in the year ended 5 April 2017 can be relieved, assuming Dee always claims relief for her losses as soon as possible.**   **(3 marks)**

(2) **Explain the claims available to Eae to obtain relief for her share of any trading losses in the year ended 5 April 2018.**   **(2 marks)**

(Total: 10 marks)

110 AUY MAN AND BIM MEN (ADAPTED) *Walk in the footsteps of a top tutor*

Auy Man and Bim Men have been in partnership since 6 April 2006 as management consultants. The following information is available for the tax year 2016/17:

Personal information

Auy spent 190 days in the United Kingdom (UK) during the tax year 2016/17. Auy was resident in the UK during the tax year 2015/16.

Bim spent 100 days in the UK during the tax year 2016/17. Bim also spent 100 days in the UK in each of the previous five tax years, and was treated as resident in the UK during each of the previous three years. Bim's time in the UK is spent living in her holiday home in the Lake District.

Statement of profit or loss for the year ended 5 April 2017

The partnership's summarised statement of profit or loss for the year ended 5 April 2017 is:

	Notes	£	£
Sales			143,880
Expenses:			
Depreciation		3,400	
Other expenses	1	1,800	
Wages and salaries	2	50,900	
		———	(56,100)
Net profit			87,780

Notes:

(1)   The figure of £1,800 for other expenses includes £720 for entertaining employees. The remaining expenses are all allowable.

(2)   The figure of £50,900 for wages and salaries includes the annual salary of £4,000 paid to Bim (see the profit sharing note below).

Plant and machinery

On 6 April 2016 the tax written down values of the partnership's plant and machinery were:

	£
Main pool	3,100
Motor car (1)	18,000

The following transactions took place during the year ended 5 April 2017:

		Cost
		£
8 May 2016	Purchased motor car (2)	11,600
21 November 2016	Purchased motor car (3)	14,200
14 January 2017	Purchased motor car (4)	8,700

Motor car (1) was purchased in March 2014 and has a CO_2 emission rate of 175 grams per kilometre. It is used by Auy, and 70% of the mileage is for business journeys.

Motor car (2) is a new car purchased on 8 May 2016 has a CO_2 emission rate of 70 grams per kilometre. It is used by Bim, and 70% of the mileage is for business journeys.

Motor car (3) purchased on 21 November 2016 has a CO_2 emission rate of 105 grams per kilometre. Motor car (4) purchased on 14 January 2017 has a CO_2 emission rate of 140 grams per kilometre. These two motor cars are used by employees of the business.

Profit sharing

Profits are shared 80% to Auy and 20% to Bim. This is after paying an annual salary of £4,000 to Bim, and interest at the rate of 5% on the partners' capital account balances.

The capital account balances are:

	£
Auy Man	56,000
Bim Men	34,000

Required:

(a)   Explain why both Auy Man and Bim Men will each be treated for tax purposes as resident in the United Kingdom for the tax year 2016/17.   **(2 marks)**

(b)   Calculate the partnership's tax adjusted trading profit for the year ended 5 April 2017, and the trading income assessments of Auy Man and Bim Men for the tax year 2016/17.

Your computation should commence with the net profit figure of £87,780, and should also list all of the items referred to in Notes (1) and (2) indicating by the use of zero (0) any items that do not require adjustment.   **(10 marks)**

(c)   Calculate the class 4 national insurance contributions payable by Auy Man and Bim Men for the tax year 2016/17.   **(3 marks)**

(Total: 15 marks)

111   DANIEL, FRANCINE AND GREGOR   *Walk in the footsteps of a top tutor*

(a)   Amanda, Beatrice and Claude have been in partnership since 1 November 2010, preparing accounts to 31 October annually. Daniel joined as a partner on 1 May 2016. Profits have always been shared equally. The partnership's recent tax adjusted trading profits are as follows:

	£
Year ended 31 October 2015	147,000
Year ended 31 October 2016	96,000
Year ended 31 October 2017 (forecast)	180,000

Required:

Calculate Daniel's trading income assessment for the tax year 2016/17.   **(3 marks)**

(b)   Francine is employed by Fringe plc. On 1 August 2016, Fringe plc provided Francine with a loan of £96,000 to help her purchase a holiday cottage. On 1 October 2016, the loan was increased by a further £14,000 so that Francine could renovate the cottage. Francine pays interest at an annual rate of 1.5% on this loan.

The taxable benefit in respect of this loan is calculated using the average method.

Required:

Calculate Francine's taxable benefit for the tax year 2016/17 in respect of the loan from Fringe plc.   **(3 marks)**

(c)   Gregor has been self-employed since 6 April 2003. He has the following income and chargeable gains for the tax years 2015/16 and 2016/17:

	2015/16	2016/17
	£	£
Trading profit/(loss)	14,700	(68,800)
Property income/(loss)	4,600	(2,300)
Building society interest	1,300	900
Chargeable gain/(loss)	(2,900)	17,400

Required:

On the assumption that Gregor relieves his trading loss of £68,800 as early as possible, calculate the amount of trading loss carried forward to the tax year 2017/18.

Note: You should assume that the tax allowances for the tax year 2016/17 apply throughout.
(4 marks)

(Total: 10 marks)

PENSIONS AND NIC

112 JOHN BEACH (ADAPTED)   *Walk in the footsteps of a top tutor*

The following information is available in respect of John Beach for the tax year 2016/17:

(1) John has been employed by Surf plc as a sales director since 1 December 1995. During the tax year 2016/17, he was paid gross director's remuneration of £141,000.

(2) During the tax year 2016/17, John contributed £28,000 into Surf plc's HM Revenue and Customs' registered occupational pension scheme. The company contributed a further £11,000 on his behalf. Both John and Surf plc made exactly the same contributions in the tax years 2015/16 and 2014/15. In the tax year 2013/14 John's contributions were £30,000 and the company's were £18,000.

(3) During the period 6 April to 31 October 2016, John used his private motor car for both private and business journeys. He was reimbursed by Surf plc at the rate of 60p per mile for the following mileage:

	Miles
Normal daily travel between home and Surf plc's offices	1,180
Travel between Surf plc's offices and the premises of Surf plc's clients	4,270
Travel between home and the premises of Surf plc's clients (none of the clients' premises were located near the offices of Surf plc)	510
Total mileage reimbursed by Surf plc	5,960

(4) During 2013 Surf plc provided John with a loan which was used to purchase a yacht. The amount of loan outstanding at 6 April 2016 was £84,000. John repaid £12,000 of the loan on 31 July 2016, and then repaid a further £12,000 on 31 December 2016. He paid loan interest of £1,270 to Surf plc during the tax year 2016/17. The taxable benefit in respect of this loan is calculated using the average method.

(5) Surf plc gave John an engraved gold watch costing £465 on 1 December 2016 in recognition of his long service with the company.

(6) During the tax year 2016/17, John made personal pension contributions up to the maximum amount of available annual allowances, including any unused amounts brought forward from previous years. These contributions were in addition to the contributions he made to Surf plc's occupational pension scheme (see Note (2)). John has not made any personal pension contributions in previous tax years.

Required:

(a) Calculate John Beach's income tax liability for the tax year 2016/17. **(12 marks)**

(b) Calculate the class 1 national insurance contributions that will have been suffered by John Beach and Surf plc in respect of John's earnings and benefits for the tax year 2016/17. **(3 marks)**

(Total: 15 marks)

113 DUKE AND EARL UPPER-CRUST (ADAPTED)

Duke and Earl Upper-Crust are twin brothers.

Duke is employed by the High-Brow Bank plc as a financial adviser. During the tax year 2016/17 Duke was paid a gross salary of £114,000. He also received a bonus of £20,000 on 15 March 2017. On 31 March 2017 Duke made a contribution of £35,000 (gross) into a personal pension scheme. He is not a member of High-Brow Bank plc's occupational pension scheme.

Earl is self-employed as a financial consultant. His trading profit for the year ended 5 April 2017 was £34,000. During the tax year 2016/17 Earl has made contributions of £40,000 (gross) into a personal pension scheme.

Neither Duke nor Earl has any other income.

In previous tax years Duke and Earl Upper-Crust had the same level of income as in the tax year 2016/17. Duke paid £40,000 (gross) into his pension scheme and Earl paid £10,000 (gross).

Required:

(a) Calculate Duke and Earl's income tax liabilities for the tax year 2016/17, together with the net amounts that Duke and Earl will have paid to their personal pension companies. **(9 marks)**

(b) Explain the effect of the pension scheme annual allowance limit, and the tax implications if contributions are made in excess of this limit. **(2 marks)**

(c) Advise Duke and Earl of the maximum additional amounts that they could have contributed into personal pension schemes for the tax year 2016/17 for which they would get tax relief and which would not incur an annual allowance charge, and the date by which any qualifying contributions would have had to have been paid. **(4 marks)**

(Total: 15 marks)

114 VANESSA AND SERENE (ADAPTED) *Walk in the footsteps of a top tutor*

Vanessa Serve and Serene Volley are sisters. The following information is available for the tax year 2016/17:

Vanessa Serve

(1)   Vanessa is self-employed as a tennis coach. Her tax adjusted trading profit for the year ended 31 March 2017 is £52,400. However, this figure is before taking account of capital allowances.

(2)   The only item of plant and machinery owned by Vanessa is her motor car. This was bought in May 2015 and has an official CO_2 emission rate of 100 grams per kilometre. At 1 April 2016 it had a tax written down value of £10,400.

         During the year ended 31 March 2017 Vanessa drove a total of 20,000 miles, of which 6,000 were for private journeys.

(3)   Vanessa contributed £6,400 (gross) into a personal pension scheme during the tax year 2016/17.

(4)   In addition to her self-employed income, Vanessa received bank interest of £1,100 during the tax year 2016/17.

Serene Volley

(1)   Serene is employed as a sports journalist by Backhand plc, a newspaper publishing company.

         During the tax year 2016/17 she was paid a gross annual salary of £26,400. Income tax of £3,016 was deducted from this figure under PAYE.

(2)   Throughout the tax year 2016/17 Backhand plc provided Serene with a diesel powered motor car which has a list price of £24,700. The official CO_2 emission rate for the motor car is 74 grams per kilometre.

         The company did not provide Serene with any fuel for private journeys.

(3)   Serene contributed 5% of her gross salary of £26,400 into Backhand plc's HM Revenue and Customs' registered occupational pension scheme.

(4)   In addition to her employment income, Serene received interest of £1,200 on the maturity of a NS&I Savings Certificate during the tax year 2016/17.

Required:

(a)   Calculate the income tax payable by both Vanessa and Serene for the tax year 2016/17.   **(11 marks)**

(b)   Calculate the national insurance contributions payable by both Vanessa and Serene for the tax year 2016/17.   **(4 marks)**

(Total: 15 marks)

115 ANN, BASIL AND CHLOE (ADAPTED) *Walk in the footsteps of a top tutor*

You are a trainee accountant and your manager has asked for your help regarding three taxpayers who have all made personal pension contributions during the tax year 2016/17.

Ann Peach

Ann is self-employed as an estate agent. Her trading profit for the year ended 5 April 2017 was £38,000. Ann made contributions of £42,000 (gross) into a personal pension scheme during the tax year 2016/17.

Basil Plum

Basil is employed by the Banana Bank plc as a fund manager. During the tax year 2016/17 Basil was paid a gross salary of £152,000.

Basil has made contributions into a personal pension plan totalling £40,000 (gross) each year for the last four years. During the tax year 2016/17 he also makes total gross contributions of £40,000.

He is not a member of Banana Bank plc's occupational pension scheme but the bank contributed £5,000 to Basil's personal pension in the tax year 2016/17.

Chloe Pear

Chloe Pear lets out unfurnished property. For the tax year 2016/17 her property business profit was £23,900. Chloe made contributions of £8,200 (gross) into a personal pension scheme during the tax year 2016/17.

Neither Ann nor Basil nor Chloe has any other income.

Required:

(a) **For each of the three taxpayers Ann Peach, Basil Plum and Chloe Pear, state, giving reasons, the amount of personal pension contributions that will have qualified for tax relief for the tax year 2016/17, and calculate their income tax liabilities for that year.**

Marks are allocated as follows:

Ann Peach 3 marks; Basil Plum 5 marks; and Chloe Pear 2 marks. **(10 marks)**

(b) **Explain the tax consequences of Banana Bank plc contributing £100,000 instead of £5,000 into Basil's personal pension in the tax year 2016/17 and the purpose of the annual allowance.** **(5 marks)**

(Total: 15 marks)

SELF-ASSESSMENT

116 PI CASSO (ADAPTED)

(a) Pi Casso has been a self-employed artist since 2005, preparing her accounts to 30 June.

Pi's tax liabilities for the tax years 2014/15, 2015/16 and 2016/17 are as follows:

	2014/15	2015/16	2016/17
	£	£	£
Income tax liability	3,240	4,100	2,730
Class 2 national insurance contributions	143	146	146
Class 4 national insurance contributions	1,240	1,480	990
Capital gains tax liability	0	4,880	0

Required:

(1) **Prepare a schedule showing the payments on account and balancing payments that Pi will have made or will have to make during the period from 1 July 2016 to 31 March 2018, assuming that Pi makes any appropriate claims to reduce her payments on account.**

Your answer should clearly identify the relevant due date of each payment.

(7 marks)

(2) **State the implications if Pi had made a claim to reduce her payments on account for the tax year 2016/17 to £Nil.** **(2 marks)**

(3) **State the latest date by which Pi must make a claim to reduce her payments on account for the tax year 2016/17.** **(1 mark)**

Assume that the tax rules for the tax year 2016/17 apply to all tax years.

(b) Turner is married to Andrea. In the tax year 2016/17 Turner had trading income of £250,000 and interest income of £5,000.

Andrea had employment income of £20,000 and dividend income of £23.000.

Required:

Explain, with supporting calculations, the maximum joint tax saving that Turner and Andrea could have made in the tax year 2016/17by transferring investments between them. **(5 marks)**

(Total: 15 marks)

117   ERNEST VADER (ADAPTED)   *Walk in the footsteps of a top tutor*

You should assume that today's date is 30 June 2018.

You are a trainee Chartered Certified Accountant and are dealing with the tax affairs of Ernest Vader.

Ernest's self-assessment tax return for the tax year 2016/17 was submitted to HM Revenue & Customs (HMRC) on 15 May 2017, and Ernest paid the resulting income tax liability by the due date of 31 January 2018. However, you have just discovered that during the tax year 2016/17 Ernest disposed of a freehold property, the details of which were omitted from his self-assessment tax return. The capital gains tax liability in respect of this disposal is £18,000, and this amount has not been paid.

Ernest has suggested that since HMRC's right to initiate a compliance check into his self-assessment tax return for the tax year 2016/17 expired on 15 May 2018, no disclosure should be made to HMRC of the capital gain.

Required:

(a)   Briefly explain the difference between tax evasion and tax avoidance, as well as the general anti-abuse rule and how HMRC would view the situation if Ernest Vader does not disclose his capital gain.   **(4 marks)**

(b)   Briefly explain from an ethical viewpoint how you, as a trainee Chartered Certified Accountant, should deal with the suggestion from Ernest Vader that no disclosure is made to HMRC of his capital gain.   **(3 marks)**

(c)   Explain the penalties which your firm, as tax agents, could be liable to, if a compliance check is commenced by HMRC and the firm fails to supply the information requested by HMRC.   **(2 marks)**

(d)   State the period for which late payment interest will run assuming that HMRC discover the capital gain and raise an assessment on 15 July 2018 in respect of Ernest Vader's capital gains tax liability of £18,000 for the tax year 2016/17, and that this amount is then paid on 31 July 2018.   **(1 mark)**

(Total: 10 marks)

118   SOPHIE SHAPE (ADAPTED)

 Timed question with Online tutor debrief

Sophie Shape has been a self-employed sculptor since 1998, preparing her accounts to 5 April. Sophie's tax liabilities for the tax years 2015/16 and 2016/17 are as follows:

	2015/16	2016/17
	£	£
Income tax liability	5,240	6,100
Class 2 national insurance contributions	146	146
Class 4 national insurance contributions	1,820	1,910
Capital gains tax liability	0	5,280

Required:

(a)   Prepare a schedule showing the payments on account and balancing payment which Sophie Shape will have made, or will have to make, during the period from 1 April 2017 to 31 March 2018.

Your answer should clearly identify the relevant due date of each payment.

(4 marks)

(b)   State the implications if Sophie Shape had made a claim to reduce her payments on account for the tax year 2016/17 to nil without any justification for doing so.

(2 marks)

(c)   Advise Sophie Shape of the latest date by which she can file a paper self-assessment tax return for the tax year 2016/17.   (1 mark)

(d)   State the period during which HM Revenue and Customs (HMRC) will have to notify Sophie Shape if they intend to carry out a compliance check in respect of her self-assessment tax return for the tax year 2016/17, and the possible reasons why such a check would be made.

You should assume that Sophie will file her tax return by the filing date.   (3 marks)

(Total: 10 marks)

 Calculate your allowed time, allocate the time to the separate parts.................

Section 2

PRACTICE CHARGEABLE GAINS QUESTIONS

PRACTICE SECTION A OBJECTIVE TEST QUESTIONS

INDIVIDUALS – CAPITAL GAINS TAX

119 Massita is planning to dispose of several assets in the tax year 2016/17 and wants to avoid any capital gains tax liability. He is unsure which of his assets to sell and which to retain.

Which TWO of the following assets would potentially realise a chargeable gain?

A   Qualifying corporate bonds

B   Painting by a famous artist

C   Gilt-edged securities

D   Main residence that he has always lived in

E   A car used in his trade, on which he has claimed capital allowances and which would be sold for £15,000 and realise a profit

F   A machine used in his trade, on which he has claimed capital allowances and which would be sold for £22,000 and realise a profit

120 Lexie sold a residential property, which she had never lived in, for £340,000 in the tax year 2016/17 incurring legal expenses of £2,500. She had acquired the building for £150,000 in 2007.

Lexie has taxable income of £54,000 for the tax year 2016/17. She sold no other assets in the tax year 2016/17.

What is Lexie's capital gains tax liability?

A   £35,280

B   £49,392

C   £52,500

D   £31,752

121 Jackson acquired a holiday villa for £115,000 on 1 May 2006. He gave it to his wife Sophia on 30 September 2011 when it was worth £100,000. Sophia sold the villa for £165,000 on 1 July 2016.

Sophia had no other capital disposals in the tax year 2016/17 and has capital losses brought forward of £5,000. Her taxable income for the tax year 2016/17 is £60,000.

What is Sophia's capital gains tax payable in the tax year 2016/17?

A   £9,492

B   £6,780

C   £10,892

D   £13,692

122 Aiden bought 30 acres of land on 1 March 2010 for £300,000.

On 1 January 2012 he sold 10 acres of the land for £150,000. At this time the remaining land was worth £250,000.

On 1 March 2017 Aiden sold the remaining acres for £425,000.

Aiden has no other capital disposals during the tax year 2016/17.

What is Aiden's taxable gain for the tax year 2016/17?

A   £113,900

B   £226,400

C   £237,500

D   £263,900

123 Noah sold two paintings at an auction on 14 May 2016 for £4,000 and £7,200 respectively. He had purchased the two paintings for £1,000 each on 22 May 2005.

What is Noah's total chargeable gain arising on the sale of the two paintings?

£ ☐

124 Liam purchased an antique glass vase for £22,000 on 30 March 2002, incurring legal fees of £800.

The market for antique glassware has since slumped and Liam sold the vase for £5,500 on 1 January 2017 incurring auctioneer fees of £300.

What is Liam's allowable loss on this disposal?

A   £16,000

B   £16,800

C   £17,100

D   £17,600

125 *June 2015 OT question*

For the tax year 2016/17, Nog has a chargeable gain of £23,700 and a capital loss of £10,400. She has unused capital losses of £6,000 brought forward from the tax year 2015/16.

What amount of capital losses can Nog carry forward to the tax year 2017/18?

A   £3,800

B   £0

C   £6,000

D   £2,200

126 *September 2015 OT question*

On 31 March 2017, Jessica sold a copyright for £28,800. The copyright had been purchased on 1 April 2011 for £21,000 when it had an unexpired life of 15 years.

What is Jessica's chargeable gain in respect of the disposal of the copyright?

A   £0

B   £20,400

C   £16,200

D   £7,800

127   On 1 June 2004 Aaliyah purchased a copyright at a cost of £35,000. The copyright had an estimated useful life of 20 years.

Aaliyah sold the copyright on 1 June 2016 for £44,000.

What is the chargeable gain arising on this sale?

A   £9,000

B   £18,900

C   £23,000

D   £30,000

128   Cooper purchased a holiday home for £142,000 on 1 October 2010. The property was damaged in a fire on 1 January 2012.

Cooper received compensation of £60,000 from his insurance company on 31 January 2012. He spent £70,000 on restoring the home in March 2012 and it was worth £180,000 after restoration. Cooper made an election such that a part disposal did not arise in the tax year 2011/12.

Cooper sold the holiday home for £230,000 on 1 March 2017.

What is Cooper's chargeable gain on the sale?

A   £18,000

B   £88,000

C   £148,000

D   £78,000

129 *September 2015 OT question*

On 10 January 2017, a freehold property owned by Winifred was damaged by a fire. The property had been purchased on 29 May 2004 for £73,000. Winifred received insurance proceeds of £37,200 on 23 February 2017, and she spent a total of £41,700 during March 2017 restoring the property. Winifred has elected to disregard the part disposal.

What is the base cost of the restored freehold property for capital gains tax purposes?

A   £68,500

B   £77,500

C   £114,700

D   £35,800

130 Madison gave 10,000 shares in Miles plc to her daughter during the tax year 2016/17.

The shares were quoted in the Stock Exchange Official List at 120p – 136p per share on the day of the sale.

Madison acquired 15,000 shares in Miles plc on 1 January 2011 for £4,000.

What is the chargeable gain on the gift of the 10,000 shares?

£ [   ]

131 Clarissa has disposed of the following shares and securities during the tax year 2016/17:

(1)   Gilts for £8,000 which were purchased in 2014 for £2,500.

(2)   20,000 shares in Martin plc sold to her sister for £7,000.

The market value of the shares on the day of the sale was £12,300.

The shares were purchased for £8,000 in February 2014.

What is Clarissa's total chargeable gain on these disposals in the tax year 2016/17?

A   £4,500

B   £4,300

C   £5,500

D   £9,800

132 Emily had the following transactions in the shares of Elijah Plc:

		Number of shares	Cost	Proceeds
			£	£
1 June 2016	Purchase	22,000	88,000	
1 October 2016	Purchase	2,000	7,440	
1 October 2016	Sale	20,000		59,000
23 October 2016	Purchase	3,000	10,800	

Select the share purchases which will be matched to the 20,000 shares sold on 1 October 2016?

Share purchases

20,000 shares from the purchase on 1 June 2016

2,000 shares from the purchase on 1 October 2016

3,000 shares from the purchase on 23 October 2016

15,000 shares from the share pool as at 1 October 2016

17,000 shares from the share pool as at 1 October 2016

18,000 shares from the share pool as at 1 October 2016

20,000 shares from the share pool as at 1 October 2016

No further matches needed

No further matches needed

Matching order

Matched first

Matched second

Matched third

133 Carter sold 4,500 shares in Brody Ltd on 28 February 2017 for £42,500.

He had purchased shares in Brody Ltd as follows:

21 April 1998   9,000 shares for £27,050

30 April 2012   2,600 shares for £9,750

What is Carter's chargeable gain on the disposal of the Brody Ltd shares?

A   £28,224

B   £28,975

C   £5,700

D   £27,039

134 Caleb had the following transactions in Harper plc shares:

26 April 2005   Purchased 40,000 shares in Harper plc for £200,000

19 May 2008   Harper plc announced a 1:4 rights issue at £4 per share. Elijah took up his rights in full

3 May 2012   Harper plc announced a 1:5 bonus issue

25 March 2017   Elijah sold 12,500 shares for £175,000

What is the allowable cost for capital gains tax purposes of the shares disposed of on 25 March 2017?

A   £62,500

B   £60,000

C   £50,000

D   £41,667

135 Hunter purchased 50,000 shares in Grayson Ltd for £90,000 on 30 May 2006.

On 1 November 2016 Grayson Ltd was taken over by Riley plc. Grayson Ltd shareholders received £3 cash and 2 Riley plc ordinary £1 shares for every Grayson Ltd share.

Immediately after takeover Riley plc shares were worth £1.20 each.

What is Hunter's chargeable gain as a result of the takeover?

A   £0

B   £150,000

C   £100,000

D   £180,000

136 Zofia sold her only home after 17 years of ownership. She lived in it for the first year and last eight years of ownership. She did not live in it for the middle eight years.

Under which of the following circumstances would the entire eight year period when she did not live in the property qualify as deemed occupation?

A   She was employed abroad

B   She rented it out to someone else who lived in it as their main residence

C   She was working in a different part of the UK

D   She was travelling

137 Masuma sold her only home and realised a gain before reliefs of £120,000. She had used six of the ten rooms herself and let out the other four for the duration of her ownership.

What is her chargeable gain, assuming she claims all available reliefs?

A   £0

B   £8,000

C   £48,000

D   £72,000

138 The four shareholders of Elephant Ltd are selling their shares. They own the share capital as follows:

Amin: 32%

Ben: 32%

Camilla: 32%

Dimitri: 4%

All shares have equal voting rights. Amin has never worked for the company. Ben works part time, and Camilla and Dimitri work full time, for the company. Camilla only joined Elephant Ltd six months ago and has owned her shares for three months, whereas Ben and Dimitri have worked for the company and owned their shares for five years.

Only _____ will qualify for entrepreneurs' relief on the sale of their shares.

Select the individual that appropriately fills the gap above:

A   Amin

B   Ben

C   Camilla

D   Dimitri

139 In October 2016 Bhavin sold his business which he had run for nine years as a sole trader, realising chargeable gains on disposal of the business assets of £13,250,000.

Bhavin is a higher rate taxpayer and has not made any previous disposals.

What is Bhavin's capital gains tax liability for the tax year 2016/17 assuming he has made no other gains during the tax year or any previous tax years, and claims all available reliefs?

A   £1,906,892

B   £1,647,780

C   £1,648,890

D   £1,650,000

140 **The disposal of which TWO of the following assets qualifies for rollover relief?**

A   A portable sewing machine used by a sole trader in his business

B   Shares in an individual's personal trading company

C   Land used by a sole trader in his business

D   Shares in the company of which the individual is an employee

E   A building owned by a company and let out to other businesses

F   The goodwill in a sole trader's business

141 *June 2015 OT question*

Alice is in business as a sole trader. On 13 May 2016, she sold a freehold warehouse for £184,000, and this resulted in a chargeable gain of £38,600. Alice purchased a replacement freehold warehouse on 20 May 2016 for £143,000. Where possible, Alice always makes a claim to roll over gains against the cost of replacement assets. Both buildings have been, or will be, used for business purposes by Alice.

What is the base cost of the replacement warehouse for capital gains tax purposes?

A   £181,600

B   £104,400

C   £143,000

D   £102,000

142   In October 2005 Hitesh sold a factory for £230,574 and realised a gain of £31,083.

In May 2006 he bought a warehouse for £231,211. He then sold the warehouse in December 2016 for £270,213.

Both of the buildings were used for the purposes of his sole trader business.

What is the chargeable gain arising on the disposal of the warehouse in December 2016 assuming all available reliefs are claimed?

A   £31,083

B   £39,002

C   £58,985

D   £70,085

143   Lionel owns 50% of the ordinary share capital in Giraffe Ltd and 2% of the ordinary share capital in Zebra plc. Both are trading companies and Lionel has 50% and 2% of the voting rights respectively.

Which TWO of the following would be a qualifying asset for the purposes of gift relief?

A   Part of Lionel's shareholding in Giraffe Ltd, representing 2% of the total ordinary share capital in Giraffe Ltd

B   A building owned by Lionel and used in the trade of Zebra plc

C   Lionel's entire holding of Zebra plc shares

D   A warehouse owned by Lionel and used by Giraffe Ltd for storing raw materials

COMPANIES – CHARGEABLE GAINS

144 Forrest Ltd bought a warehouse for £250,000 in December 2007, incurring £20,000 legal fees in connection with the acquisition. The warehouse was sold for £800,000 in May 2016.

Assume the relevant RPIs are as follows:

December 2007   210.9

May 2016   261.9

What is the chargeable gain arising on the sale of the warehouse?

A   £464,660

B   £464,708

C   £469,500

D   £477,350

145 Harrop Ltd sold two assets in the year ended 31 December 2016.

(1)   Two acres of land which it had acquired for £20,000 in May 1987 were sold for £45,000 in October 2016.

(2)   A warehouse which it had acquired for £80,000 in June 1996 was sold for £75,000 in October 2016.

Assume the relevant RPIs are as follows:

May 1987   101.9

June 1996   153.0

October 2016   263.9

What is the company's allowable loss for the year ended 31 December 2016, assuming it sold no other assets?

A   £69,800

B   £11,800

C   £5,000

D   £69,787

146 In the year ended 30 June 2016 Lompy Ltd had a tax adjusted trading profit of £800,200 and property income of £45,000. It also realised a chargeable gain of £25,000 and a capital loss of £80,000 on assets that were used for the purposes of the property business.

In the year ended 30 June 2015 it had a tax adjusted trading profit of £520,000 and chargeable gains of £9,000.

How much, if any, of the capital loss arising in the year ended 30 June 2016 is carried forward to the year ended 30 June 2017?

£ [   ]

147 Rimbo Ltd had the following transactions in the shares of Profitable Ltd, an investment company:

		Number	£
April 1993	Purchase	25,000	33,000
June 2016	Sale	8,000	26,000

Assume the relevant RPIs are as follows:

April 1993	140.6
June 2016	262.3

What is the amount of the indexed cost available on the sale of the shares in June 2016?

A   £19,700

B   £10,560

C   £61,564

D   £28,564

148 On 1 October 2016 Smooth Ltd sold a factory for £850,000, realising a gain of £250,000.

On 1 November 2015 the company had purchased an immovable machine for £900,000. The machine is expected to be used by the company for at least 25 years.

The company prepares accounts to 31 December.

The company wishes to defer the gain arising on the sale of the factory by making a rollover relief election in respect of the acquisition of the machine.

For each of the following statements select whether it is true or false:

	True	False
The £250,000 gain which could be deferred as a result of the acquisition of the machine will become chargeable on 1 October 2026		
The company must make a rollover relief election by 31 December 2020		

PRACTICE SECTION B OBJECTIVE TEST CASES

INDIVIDUALS – CAPITAL GAINS TAX

149 MICHAEL CHIN (ADAPTED)

Michael Chin made the following disposals of assets during the tax year 2016/17:

(1) On 30 June 2016 Michael sold a business that he had run as a sole trader since 1 January 2012. He realised the following gains and losses on the chargeable assets of the business:

	£
Goodwill	60,000
Freehold property	64,000
Storage unit	(13,000)

The goodwill has been built up since 1 January 2012. The freehold property had been acquired 6 months prior to the date of disposal and the storage unit had been acquired on 1 June 2013.

(2) On 8 December 2016 Michael gave Mika, his daughter, his entire holding of 50,000 50p ordinary shares (a 60% holding) in Minnow Ltd, an unquoted trading company. The market value of the shares on that date was £180,000.

Michael had originally purchased the shares on 5 January 2016 for £87,500. On 8 December 2016 the market value of Minnow Ltd's chargeable assets was £250,000, of which £200,000 was in respect of chargeable business assets. Michael has never been employed by Minnow Ltd.

(3) On 28 February 2017 Michael sold a painting for £5,900 after auctioneer's fees of £656. He had originally acquired the painting on 1 June 2015 for £4,000.

(4) On 15 March 2017 Michael gave Mika, his daughter, the following assets:

 – Necklace valued at £4,000. Acquired by Michael for £5,000.

 – Boat valued at £80,000. Acquired by Michael for £70,000.

 – Machine used for trading activities valued at £7,000. Acquired by Michael for £8,000.

Michael incurred a capital loss of £16,800 during the tax year 2014/15, and made a chargeable gain of £17,100 and a capital loss of £7,000 during the tax year 2015/16.

Assume that the tax rates and allowances for the tax year 2016/17 apply throughout.

1 **What is the net chargeable gain on the disposal of the sole trader business on 30 June 2016 that qualifies for entrepreneurs' relief?**

 A £124,000

 B £111,000

 C £60,000

 D £51,000

2   What amount of gift relief, if any, is available on the gift of shares in Minnow Ltd on 8 December 2016?

   A   £74,000

   B   £0

   C   £18,500

   D   £92,500

3   What is the chargeable gain, if any, arising on the sale of the painting on 28 February 2017?

   A   £1,244

   B   £0

   C   £1,900

   D   £927

4   Which of the following gifts made by Michael on 15 March 2017 will result in a chargeable gain or allowable loss?

   (1)   Necklace

   (2)   Boat

   (3)   Machine

   A   None of them

   B   (2) only

   C   (3) only

   D   (1) and (2)

5   What amount of capital losses are brought forward from the tax year 2015/16?

   A   £17,800

   B   £6,700

   C   £16,800

   D   £23,800

150   WILSON BIAZMA (ADAPTED)

This objective test case question contains question types which will only appear in a computer based examination, but this question provides valuable practice for all students whichever version of the examination they are taking.

Wilson Biazma was treated as automatically resident in the United Kingdom for tax purposes in the tax year 2016/17.

He disposed of a number of assets during the tax year 2016/17. His disposals included the following:

(1)   On 21 July 2016 Wilson sold a freehold office building for £246,000. The office building had been purchased on 3 January 1996 for £104,000. The office building has always been used entirely for business purposes in a wholesale business run by Wilson as a sole trader.

Wilson purchased a replacement office building on 14 January 2017 for £136,000.

(2)   On 26 July 2016 Wilson sold a retail business that he had run as a sole trader since 1 June 2010. The disposal proceeds for the business were £200,000.

The only chargeable asset of the business was goodwill and this was valued at £120,000 on 26 July 2016. The goodwill has a cost of £0.

(3)   On 24 August 2016 Wilson sold 500 shares in STU plc (a trading company which has an issued share capital of 1 million shares). Wilson has worked part time for the company for many years. His shares in STU plc were acquired as follows:

	Number of shares
1 May 1999	500
10 June 2014	200
20 August 2016	400
24 August 2016	200

Wilson made a number of other chargeable disposals during the tax year such that his total chargeable gains including the above disposals, were £800,000 of which £500,000 qualified for entrepreneurs' relief. None of the gains related to residential property. Wilson's taxable income in the tax year 2016/17 was £25,000.

1   Which of the following criteria would mean that Wilson is treated as automatically UK resident in the tax year 2016/17?

	Automatically UK resident	Not automatically UK resident
Wilson had close family in the UK in the tax year		
Wilson was in the UK for 180 days in the tax year		
Wilson worked in the UK in the tax year		
Wilson's only home during the tax year was in the UK		
Wilson spent more time in the UK than any other country in the tax year		

2   Which of the following disposals made by Wilson will qualify for entrepreneurs' relief?

(1)   Freehold office building

(2)   Goodwill

(3)   Shares in STU plc

A   (2) and (3)

B   (1) only

C   (2) only

D   (1) and (3)

3   What is the amount of the chargeable gain (after all reliefs) arising on the sale of the freehold office building assuming that Wilson has made a claim to rollover the gain on the office building against the replacement office building?

£ [   ]

4   How will the disposal of shares in STU plc be matched against the share acquisitions?

A   200 acquired on 24 August 2016 and 300 acquired on 20 August 2016

B   400 acquired on 20 August 2016 and 100 out of the pool of 700 shares acquired before 20 August 2016

C   400 acquired on 20 August 2016 and 100 out of 500 acquired on 1 May 1999

D   200 acquired on 24 August 2016 and 300 out of the pool of 1,100 shares acquired before 24 August 2016

5   What is the amount of Wilson's capital gains tax liability for the tax year 2016/17?

A   £107,780

B   £110,000

C   £130,892

D   £108,890

151 BO (ADAPTED)

You are a trainee accountant and your manager has asked for your help regarding a client whodisposed of assets during the tax year 2016/17.

Bo Neptune

On 31 July 2016 Bo made a gift to his son, Chi, of his entire holding of 50,000 £1 ordinary shares (a 100% holding) in Botune Ltd, an unquoted trading company. The market value of the shares on that date was £210,000. The shares had been purchased by Bo on 22 January 2009 for £94,000. Bo and Chi have elected to hold over the gain as a gift of a business asset.

Bo has taxable income in the tax year 2016/17 of £25,000 and had made a chargeable gain on the sale of a painting of £20,000. Bo has never made any other chargeable disposals.

On 30 September 2016 Bo sold a house for £282,000, resulting in a chargeable gain of £172,000. The house had been purchased on 1 October 2004.

He occupied the house as his main residence from the date of purchase until 30 September 2006. Bo then moved in with his girlfriend and the house was unoccupied between 1 October 2006 and 30 September 2016.

Throughout the period 1 October 2004 to 30 September 2016 Bo did not have any other main residence.

1   **What is the Chi's base cost in the 50,000 £1 ordinary shares in Botune Ltd?**

   A   £116,000

   B   £210,000

   C   £94,000

   D   £105,100

2   **Assuming that no other chargeable gains arise in the tax year, how much capital gains tax would Bo pay on the disposal of the painting in the tax year 2016/17?**

   A   £1,780

   B   £890

   C   £1,080

   D   £3,300

3   **When is the capital gains tax due date(s) for the tax year 2016/17 and by what date must Bo and Chi make the election to hold over the gain on the Botune Ltd shares?**

	CGT due date	Election date
A	31 January 2018	5 April 2021
B	31 July 2017 and 31 January 2018	5 April 2021
C	31 January 2018	31 July 2020
D	31 July 2017 and 31 January 2018	31 January 2020

4   **If Bo had instead sold the shares in Botune Ltd to Chi for £160,000 how much would Bo's chargeable gain in the tax year 2016/17 have been?**

A   £66,000

B   £116,000

C   £50,000

D   £160,000

5   **How much principle private residence relief is Bo entitled to on the sale of his main residence?**

A   £121,833

B   £93,167

C   £46,929

D   £50,167

152 ALPHABET LTD (ADAPTED) *Walk in the footsteps of a top tutor*

On 15 October 2016 Alphabet Ltd, an unquoted trading company, was taken over by XYZ plc. Prior to the takeover Alphabet Ltd's share capital consisted of 100,000 £1 ordinary shares and under the terms of the takeover the shareholders received either cash of £6 per share or one £1 ordinary share in XYZ plc for each £1 ordinary share in Alphabet Ltd.

The following information is available regarding three shareholders of Alphabet Ltd:

Aloi

Aloi has been the managing director of Alphabet Ltd since the company's incorporation on 1 January 2006, and she accepted XYZ plc's cash alternative of £6 per share in respect of her shareholding of 60,000 £1 ordinary shares in Alphabet Ltd. Aloi had originally subscribed for 50,000 shares in Alphabet Ltd on 1 January 2006 at their par value, and purchased a further 10,000 shares on 20 May 2008 for £18,600.

Bon

Bon has been the sales director of Alphabet Ltd since 1 February 2016, having not previously been an employee of the company. She accepted XYZ plc's share alternative of one £1 ordinary share for each of her 25,000 £1 ordinary shares in Alphabet Ltd. Bon had purchased her shareholding on 1 February 2016 for £92,200.

On 4 March 2017 Bon gave 10,000 of her £1 ordinary shares in XYZ plc to her brother for £50,000. On that date the shares were quoted on the Stock Exchange Daily Official List at £7.10 – £7.18. Gift relief is not available in respect of this disposal.

Cherry

Cherry has been an employee of Alphabet Ltd since 1 May 2007. She accepted XYZ plc's share alternative of one £1 ordinary share for each of her 3,000 £1 ordinary shares in Alphabet Ltd. Cherry had purchased her shareholding on 20 June 2008 for £4,800.

On 13 November 2016 Cherry sold 1,000 of her £1 ordinary shares in XYZ plc for £6,600.

Cherry died on 5 April 2017, and her remaining 2,000 £1 ordinary shares in XYZ plc were inherited by her daughter. On that date these shares were valued at £15,600.

1   **Which of the following individuals met the qualifying conditions for entrepreneurs' relief as regards their shareholdings in Alphabet Ltd?**

     A   Neither Bon nor Cherry

     B   Bon only

     C   Cherry only

     D   Both of them

2   **What is the chargeable gain, if any, arising on Aloi on the takeover of Alphabet Ltd?**

     A   £0

     B   £291,400

     C   £341,400

     D   £280,300

3   **What is the chargeable gain or allowable loss on the disposal of shares in XYZ plc by Bon to her brother on 4 March 2017?**

     A   £13,120

     B   £34,120

     C   £34,520

     D   (£20,800)

4   **By what date(s) must Bon pay any capital gains tax due as a result of the disposal of shares in XYZ plc?**

     A   31 January 2018

     B   30 September 2017

     C   4 March 2018

     D   5 December 2017

5   **What is the allowable cost that will be used by Cherry's daughter in the capital gains computation on a subsequent disposal by her of the shares in XYZ plc which she inherited on 4 March 2017?**

     A   £15,600

     B   £4,800

     C   £2,000

     D   £3,200

153 JORGE JUNG (ADAPTED)

This objective test case question contains question types which will only appear in a computer-based examination, but this question provides valuable practice for all students whichever version of the examination they are taking.

Jorge Jung disposed of the following assets during the tax year 2016/17:

(1) On 30 September 2016 Jorge sold a copyright for £8,200. The copyright had been purchased on 1 October 2014 for £7,000 when it had an unexpired life of 10 years.

(2) On 6 October 2016 Jorge sold a painting for £6,400. The painting had been purchased on 18 May 2021 for £2,200. Jorge incurred selling fees of £350 on the disposal.

(3) On 3 December 2016 Jorge sold two acres of land for £92,000. Jorge's father had originally purchased three acres of land on 4 August 2004 for £19,500.

His father died on 17 June 2011, and the land was inherited by Jorge. On that date the three acres of land were valued at £28,600. On 1 December 2011 Jorge incurred legal fees of £500 defending his title to the three acres of land.

The market value of the unsold acre of land as at 3 December 2016 was £38,000.

(4) On 14 January 2017 Jorge disposed of 5,000 £1 ordinary shares in a UK company to another individual. The market value of the shares on that date was £64,800. Jorge had purchased the shares for £26,300.

---

1   What is the amount of the chargeable gain arising on the disposal of the copyright?

    A   £6,800

    B   £2,600

    C   £1,200

    D   £960

2   What is the amount of the chargeable gain arising on the disposal of the painting?

£ [   ]

3   What is the allowable cost used in the capital gains tax disposal computation for the sale of the two acres of land on 3 December 2016?

    A   £20,740

    B   £14,154

    C   £20,594

    D   £19,400

4   Jorge wishes to make a holdover (gift relief) claim in respect of the gain on the disposal of the shares on 14 January 2017. Which of the following conditions must be met?

(1)   The company must be an unquoted company

(2)   The company must not own any non-business assets

(3)   The company must be a trading company

(4)   Jorge must have owned the shares for at least two years

A   (2), (3) and (4)

B   (1) and (2)

C   (3) only

D   (1) and (3)

5   Assuming Jorge sold the shares on 14 January 2017 realising a chargeable gain, which TWO of the following conditions must be met for entrepreneurs' relief to be available?

A   Jorge must make a claim for the relief by 31 January 2019

B   Jorge must have worked full time for the company for at least one year prior to the disposal

C   Jorge must have owned the shares for at least one year prior to the disposal

D   Jorge must be disposing of at least 5% of the company's shares

154   ALBERT AND CHARLES (ADAPTED) *Walk in the footsteps of a top tutor*

 Timed question with Online tutor debrief

Albert and Victoria

On 12 February 2017, Albert sold a house for £840,000, which he had owned individually. The house had been purchased on 12 February 2001 for £222,900.

Throughout the period of ownership the house was occupied by Albert and his wife, Victoria, as their main residence. One-quarter of the house was always used exclusively for business purposes by the couple.

For the tax year 2016/17 Albert is a higher rate taxpayer and did not make any other disposals of assets.

For the tax year 2016/17 Victoria had taxable income of £15,740 and made chargeable gains on other disposals of £11,100.

Charles and Daphne

On 23 October 2016 Charles sold 4,000 £1 ordinary shares in Restoration plc, a quoted trading company, to his daughter, Daphne, for £20,000 when they were valued at £31,600. Gift relief is not available in respect of this gift.

The company has 4 million £1 ordinary shares in issue. Charles has never worked for the company but Daphne has worked for the company for the previous 5 years.

Charles acquired his shares in the company as follows:

1 March 2008	Purchased 20,000 shares for £19,800
20 July 2012	Purchased 8,000 shares for £27,800

Charles is retired and has taxable income of £15,000 in the tax year 2016/17. He has not made any other disposals in the tax year 2016/17.

On 4 April 2017 Daphne sold a painting for gross proceeds of £5,300. The painting had been purchased for £13,000 in September 2000. Daphne incurred auctioneer's fees of £300 in relation to the disposal.

For the tax year 2016/17 Daphne is a higher rate taxpayer, and regularly makes disposals of other investments, so no annual exempt amount is available the tax year 2016/17.

Charles and Daphne always make any available claims and elections in connection with their tax affairs.

1   **What is the amount of principal private residence relief available on the disposal of the house by Albert?**

   A   £154,275

   B   £462,825

   C   £477,288

   D   £454,400

2   **What is the amount of capital gains tax that would have been saved if Albert had transferred 50% ownership of the house to Victoria prior to its disposal?**

   A   £1,626

   B   £4,553

   C   £3,252

   D   £3,200

3   **What is the allowable base cost used in the capital gains tax computation on the sale of shares to Charles' daughter?**

   A   £13,900

   B   £31,600

   C   £3,960

   D   £6,800

4   **What is Daphne's chargeable gain or allowable loss in respect of the sale of the painting on 4 April 2017?**

   A   (£7,300)

   B   £7,400

   C   £0

   D   (£8,000)

5   **Which of the following are valid reasons why gift relief WAS NOT available on the sale of shares to Daphne?**

(1)   Charles has never worked for the company

(2)   Daphne paid Charles for the shares

(3)   Charles did not own at least 5% of the ordinary shares and voting rights in Restoration plc

A   (1) only

B   (2) and (3)

C   (3) only

D   (1) and (2)

 Calculate your allowed time, allocate the time to the separate parts.................

COMPANIES – CHARGEABLE GAINS

155 HAWK LTD (ADAPTED) *Walk in the footsteps of a top tutor*

Hawk Ltd sold the following assets during the year ended 31 March 2017:

(1)   On 15 April 2016 a freehold office building was sold for £260,000. The office building had been purchased on 2 July 1996 for £81,000, and had been extended at a cost of £43,000 during May 2008. Hawk Ltd incurred legal fees of £3,200 in connection with the purchase of the office building.

(2)   On 30 April 2016 a freehold factory was sold for £500,000 (before deducting legal fees of £3,840) realising an unindexed gain of £300,000 and an indexed gain of £240,000. The factory has always been used by Hawk Ltd for business purposes.

Hawk Ltd plans to reinvest some or all of the proceeds in the purchase of a new freehold factory.

(3)   In July 2016 White plc was taken over by Black plc. Hawk Ltd had purchased 3,000 ordinary shares in White plc for £8,000 in June 2000. On takeover, Hawk Ltd received 2 ordinary shares and 2 preference shares in Black plc for each ordinary share in White plc.

Immediately after the takeover the ordinary shares in Black plc were quoted at £3 and the preference shares at £2.

Indexation factors are as follows:

July 1996 to May 2008	0.411
July 1996 to April 2016	0.716
June 2000 to July 2016	0.535
May 2008 to April 2016	0.216

1   What is the amount of indexation allowance available on the disposal of the freehold office building on 15 April 2016?

A   £67,284

B   £60,287

C   £69,575

D   £67,975

2   Which of the following assets is/are qualifying assets for companies for rollover relief?

(1)   Goodwill acquired on the purchase of the trade and assets of another business

(2)   Land acquired for business use

(3)   Vehicle costing £150,000 with an estimated useful life of 50 years

(4)   75% shareholding of an unquoted trading company

A   (1), (2) and (3)

B   (1) and (3) only

C   (2) only

D   (2) and (4)

3   What is the maximum amount of rollover relief that Hawk Ltd can claim in respect of the gain on the factory and what is the latest date by which the reinvestment must take place?

	Maximum rollover relief	Latest date
A	£300,000	30 April 2019
B	£240,000	30 April 2019
C	£300,000	31 March 2020
D	£240,000	31 March 2020

4   What is the minimum amount that will have to be reinvested in qualifying replacement business assets in order for the company to claim the maximum possible amount of rollover relief in respect of the gain on the factory?

A   £240,000

B   £496,160

C   £236,160

D   £500,000

5   What is the indexed cost of the ordinary shares in Black plc on 30 June 2016?

A   £7,368

B   £4,280

C   £18,000

D   £30,000

156 ACEBOOK LTD (ADAPTED) *Walk in the footsteps of a top tutor*

Acebook Ltd had a number of capital transactions during the year ended 31 December 2016 including the following:

(1)   On 10 March 2016 Acebook Ltd took up its allocation under a 1 for 5 rights issue by Oogle plc, paying £4.30 for each new share issued. The company had originally purchased 24,000 shares in Oogle plc on 28 June 2007 for £25,200.

Indexation factors are as follows:

June 2007 to March 2016   0.260

(2)   On 30 June 2016 Acebook sold three acres of land for £192,000. Acebook Ltd had originally purchased four acres of land, and the indexed cost of the four acres on 30 June 2016 was £196,000. The market value of the unsold acre of land as at 30 June 2016 was £53,000. During June 2016 Acebook Ltd spent £29,400 clearing and levelling all four acres of land.

(3)   On 1 October 2016 two adjacent investment properties accidentally caught fire. The following information is available:

(1)   The first investment property was destroyed. The indexed cost of the property on that date was £138,400. Acebook Ltd received insurance proceeds of £189,000 on 20 October 2016, and on 31 October 2016 the company paid £172,400 for a replacement investment property.

(2)   The second investment property was damaged. The indexed cost of the property on that date was £216,500. Acebook Ltd received insurance proceeds of £100,000 on 20 October 2016, all of which were used to repair the property.

Acebook Ltd has made a claim to defer the gains arising from the receipt of the insurance proceeds in respect of both properties.

1   **Which of the following statements concerning indexation allowance is/are INCORRECT?**

(1)   The indexation allowance is not available where shares acquired on 29 August 2016 are sold at a gain on 5 September 2016

(2)   The indexation factor must always be rounded to 3 decimal places

(3)   The indexation allowance can increase an allowable loss but cannot turn a chargeable gain into an allowable loss

(4)   The indexation allowance is not available where a chargeable gain is deferred by rollover relief

A   (2) and (3) only

B   (1) and (4) only

C   All of them

D   (2), (3) and (4) only

2   What is the indexed cost of the share pool of Oogle plc shares on 10 March 2016 after the rights issue has been taken up by Acebook Ltd?

A   £45,840

B   £52,392

C   £547,752

D   £541,200

3   What is the allowable cost that will be deducted in the capital gains computation on the disposal of the three acres of land on 30 June 2016?

A   £153,600

B   £169,050

C   £183,000

D   £176,640

4   What is the chargeable gain arising in the year ended 31 December 2016 as a result of the destruction of the first investment property and subsequent reinvestment in a replacement property?

A   £16,600

B   £50,600

C   £189,000

D   £34,000

5   In relation to the second investment property, that was damaged in the fire, which of the following statements is CORRECT?

A   There is a chargeable disposal, in the year ended 31 December 2016, for chargeable gains purposes and the deemed proceeds are the market value of the property before restoration

B   The indexed cost of the property in October 2016 after the restoration will be £100,000

C   The indexed cost of the property in October 2016 after the restoration will be £216,500

D   There is a chargeable disposal, in the year ended 31 December 2016, for chargeable gains purposes and the deemed proceeds are £100,000

PRACTICE SECTION C CONSTRUCTED RESPONSE QUESTIONS

INDIVIDUALS – CAPITAL GAINS TAX

157   DAVID AND ANGELA BROOK (ADAPTED) *Walk in the footsteps of a top tutor*

David and Angela Brook are a married couple. They disposed of the following assets during the tax year 2016/17:

Jointly owned property

(1)   On 29 July 2016 David and Angela sold a classic Ferrari motor car for £34,400. The motor car had been purchased on 17 January 2004 for £27,200.

(2)   On 30 September 2016 David and Angela sold a house for £381,900. The house had been purchased on 1 October 1996 for £86,000.

David and Angela occupied the house as their main residence from the date of purchase until 31 March 2000. The house was then unoccupied between 1 April 2000 and 31 December 2003 due to Angela being required by her employer to work elsewhere in the United Kingdom.

From 1 January 2004 until 31 December 2010 David and Angela again occupied the house as their main residence. The house was then unoccupied until it was sold on 30 September 2016.

Throughout the period 1 October 1996 to 30 September 2016 David and Angela did not have any other main residence.

David Brook

On 5 May 2016 David transferred his entire shareholding of 20,000 £1 ordinary shares in Bend Ltd, an unquoted trading company, to Angela. On that date the shares were valued at £64,000. David's shareholding had been purchased on 21 June 2014 for £48,000.

Angela Brook

On 7 July 2016 Angela sold 15,000 of the 20,000 £1 ordinary shares in Bend Ltd that had been transferred to her from David. The sale proceeds were £62,400.

Neither David nor Angela has ever worked for Bent Ltd. Angela has taxable income of £31,445 for the tax year 2016/17. David does not have any taxable income.

Required:

Compute David and Angela's respective capital gains tax liabilities for the tax year 2016/17. **(10 marks)**

158 BILL DING *Walk in the footsteps of a top tutor*

Bill Ding has run a construction company, High Rise Ltd since he purchased the entire shareholding for £112,000 in 1999. He has worked for the company since purchase.

Bill has decided to retire and on 17 August 2016 Bill made a gift of his entire holding of High Rise Ltd shares to his daughter, Belle, who also works for the company. The market value of the shares on that date was £260,000.

On 17 August 2016 the market value of High Rise Ltd's chargeable assets was £180,000, of which £150,000 was in respect of chargeable business assets. Bill and his daughter have elected to hold over the gain on this gift of a business asset.

Belle plans to sell the shares in High Rise Ltd on 31 March 2017, when they are expected to be worth £265,000 in order to fund a new business venture.

Neither Bill nor Belle has made any previous disposals chargeable to capital gains tax, and both are higher rate taxpayers.

Required:

(a) Calculate the gains arising and capital gains tax liabilities for Bill and Belle on the gift of High Rise Ltd shares to Belle and the subsequent sale by Belle.

Assume that Bill and Belle make a joint claim for gift relief, and state the due date for this claim. **(5 marks)**

(b) Recalculate the gains arising and capital gains tax liabilities for Bill and Belle, assuming a joint claim for gift relief is not made. **(3 marks)**

(c) Briefly conclude, including a calculation of the tax saving, on which route would be preferable for Bill and Belle. **(2 marks)**

(Total: 10 marks)

159 JEROME *Walk in the footsteps of a top tutor*

Jerome made the following gifts to family members during the tax year 2016/17:

(1) On 28 May 2016, Jerome made a gift of a house valued at £187,000 to his wife. Jerome's uncle had originally purchased the house on 14 July 1995 for £45,900. The uncle died on 12 June 2004, and the house was inherited by Jerome. On that date, the house was valued at £112,800. Jerome has never occupied the house as his main residence.

(2) On 24 June 2016, Jerome made a gift of his entire 12% holding of 12,000 £1 ordinary shares in Reward Ltd, an unquoted trading company, to his son. The market value of the shares on that date was £98,400. The shares had been purchased on 15 March 2006 for £39,000. On 24 June 2016, the market value of Reward Ltd's chargeable assets was £540,000, of which £460,000 was in respect of chargeable business assets. Jerome and his son have elected to hold over the gain on this gift of a business asset.

(3) On 7 November 2016, Jerome made a gift of an antique bracelet valued at £12,200 to his granddaughter. The antique bracelet had been purchased on 1 September 2001 for £2,100.

(4) On 29 January 2017, Jerome made a gift of nine acres of land valued at £78,400 to his brother. He had originally purchased ten acres of land on 3 November 2005 for £37,800. The market value of the unsold acre of land as at 29 January 2017 was £33,600. The land has never been used for business purposes.

Required:

(a) **Calculate Jerome's chargeable gains for the tax year 2016/17.**

   Note: You should ignore inheritance tax. **(7 marks)**

(b) **For each of the four recipients of assets (1) to (4) gifted from Jerome, state their respective base cost for capital gains tax purposes.** **(3 marks)**

   (Total: 10 marks)

160 GINGER AND NIGEL (ADAPTED) *Walk in the footsteps of a top tutor*

You should assume that today's date is 1 March 2017.

(a) Ginger has a holding of 10,000 £1 ordinary shares in Nutmeg Ltd, an unquoted trading company, which she had purchased on 13 February 2007 for £2.39 per share. The current market value of the shares is £6.40 per share, but Ginger intends to sell some of the holding to her daughter at £4.00 per share during March 2017. Ginger and her daughter will elect to hold over any gain as a gift of a business asset.

For the tax year 2016/17, Ginger will not make any other disposals, and has therefore not utilised her annual exempt amount.

Required:

Explain how many £1 ordinary shares in Nutmeg Ltd Ginger can sell to her daughter for £4.00 per share during March 2017 without incurring any capital gains tax liability for the tax year 2016/17.

Your answer should be supported by appropriate calculations. **(4 marks)**

(b) Innocent and Nigel, a married couple, both have shareholdings in Cinnamon Ltd, an unquoted trading company with a share capital of 100,000 £1 ordinary shares.

Innocent has been the managing director of Cinnamon Ltd since the company's incorporation on 1 July 2007, and she currently holds 20,000 shares (with matching voting rights) in the company. These shares were subscribed for on 1 July 2007 at their par value.

Nigel has never been an employee or a director of Cinnamon Ltd, and he currently holds 3,000 shares (with matching voting rights) in the company. These shares were purchased on 23 April 2011 for £46,200.

Either Innocent or Nigel will sell 2,000 of their shares in Cinnamon Ltd during March 2017 for £65,000, but they are not sure which of them should make the disposal. For the tax year 2016/17, both Innocent and Nigel have already made disposals which will fully utilise their annual exempt amounts, and they will each have taxable income of £80,000.

Required:

Calculate the capital gains tax saving if the disposal of 2,000 shares in Cinnamon Ltd during March 2017 is made by Innocent rather than Nigel. **(6 marks)**

(Total: 10 marks)

161 MICK STONE (ADAPTED) *Walk in the footsteps of a top tutor*

Mick Stone disposed of the following assets during the tax year 2016/17:

(1) On 19 May 2016, Mick sold a freehold warehouse for £522,000. The warehouse was purchased on 6 August 2003 for £258,000. In January 2009, the floor of the warehouse was damaged by flooding and had to be replaced at a cost of £63,000. The warehouse was sold because it was surplus to the business's requirements as a result of Mick purchasing a newly built warehouse during 2015. Both warehouses have always been used for business purposes in a wholesale business run by Mick as a sole trader.

(2) On 24 September 2016, Mick sold 700,000 £1 ordinary shares in Rolling Ltd, an unquoted trading company, for £3,675,000. He had originally purchased 500,000 shares in Rolling Ltd on 2 June 2007 for £960,000. On 1 December 2012, Rolling Ltd made a 3 for 2 bonus issue. Mick has been a director of Rolling Ltd since 1 January 2007.

Required:

(a) **Assuming that no reliefs are available, calculate the chargeable gain arising from each of Mick Stone's asset disposals during the tax year 2016/17.**

You are not required to calculate the taxable gains or the amount of tax payable.

(4 marks)

(b) **State which capital gains tax reliefs might be available to Mick Stone in respect of each of his disposals during the tax year 2016/17, and what further information you would require in order to establish if the reliefs are actually available and to establish any restrictions as regards the amount of relief.**

For this part of the question you are not expected to perform any calculations.

(6 marks)

(Total: 10 marks)

162 RUBY (ADAPTED) *Walk in the footsteps of a top tutor*

You should assume that today's date is 1 March 2017.

(a) On 27 August 2016, Ruby disposed of a residential investment property, and this resulted in a chargeable gain of £45,800.

For the tax year 2016/17, Ruby has taxable income of £17,815.

Required:

Calculate Ruby's capital gains tax liability for the tax year 2016/17 if this is her only disposal in that tax year. **(2 marks)**

(b) In addition to the disposal already made on 27 August 2016, Ruby is going to make one further disposal during the tax year 2016/17. This disposal will be of either Ruby's holding of £1 ordinary shares in Pola Ltd, or her holding of 50p ordinary shares in Aplo plc.

Shareholding in Pola Ltd

Pola Ltd is an unquoted trading company, in which Ruby has a 10% shareholding. The shareholding was purchased on 14 July 2007 for £23,700 and could be sold for £61,000. Ruby has been an employee of Pola Ltd since 2005.

Shareholding in Aplo plc

Aplo plc is a quoted trading company, in which Ruby has a shareholding of 40,000 50p ordinary shares. Ruby received the shareholding as a gift from her father on 27 May 2010. On that date, the shares were quoted on the stock exchange at £2.12–£2.24. The shareholding could be sold for £59,000.

Neither entrepreneurs' relief nor holdover relief is available in respect of this disposal.

Required:

Calculate Ruby's revised capital gains tax liability for the tax year 2016/17 if, during March 2017, she also disposes of either (1) her shareholding in Pola Ltd, or alternatively (2) her shareholding in Aplo plc.

Note - the following mark allocation is provided as guidance for this requirement:

Pola Ltd	**(4.5 marks)**	
Aplo plc	**(3.5 marks)**	**(8 marks)**

(Total: 10 marks)

163 DALJEET *Walk in the footsteps of a top tutor*

Please assume today's date is 5 April 2016.

Daljeet wishes to sell personal assets to generate funds to pay his daughter's university fees and he has selected two assets that he is willing to sell. He will sell one of the assets to a third party on 31 December 2016 and will make his decision based on the asset that will generate the highest amount of net proceeds.

The assets Daljeet has identified as potential disposals are as follows:

1000 shares in ABC Ltd

Daljeet acquired 1,000 shares in ABC Ltd, a trading company, on 7 June 2011 for £60,000 when he became an employee of the company. On 7 June 2012 ABC Ltd underwent a rights issue, offering shareholders the opportunity to purchase 2 shares for every 5 shares already held for £50 per share. Daljeet purchased the maximum amount of shares.

ABC Ltd has 20,000 shares in issue.

If Daljeet sells the ABC Ltd shares, he will sell 1,000 shares worth £100,000 on 31 December 2016.

Holiday cottage

The cottage is currently worth £110,000 and legal fees in respect of the disposal are expected to be £1,300. Repairs costing £3,500 were made to the cottage roof in December 2015 following damage caused by a storm.

Daljeet originally bought the cottage in May 2007 at a cost of £65,000. It has always been let out and Daljeet has never occupied the property as his principal private residence.

Other information

Daljeet will be a higher rate taxpayer and will make no other disposals in the tax year 2016/17.

Required:

(a) Calculate which of the above asset disposals will result in the highest amount of proceeds, after deducting tax and any costs of sale.

You should assume that Daljeet will claim any relevant reliefs where possible and has not previously claimed any capital gains tax reliefs. **(8 marks)**

(b) Briefly explain why the disposal of either the ABC Ltd shares or the holiday cottage will not be subject to inheritance tax. **(2 marks)**

(Total: 10 marks)

COMPANIES – CHARGEABLE GAINS

164 FORWARD LTD (ADAPTED)

Forward Ltd sold the following assets during the year ended 31 March 2017:

(1) On 31 May 2016 Forward Ltd sold a freehold office building for £290,000. The office building had been purchased on 15 July 1996 for £148,000. The retail price index (RPI) for July 1996 was 152.4, and for May 2016 it was 261.9.

Forward Ltd purchased a replacement freehold office building on 1 June 2016 for £260,000.

(2) On 30 November 2016 Forward Ltd sold 5,000 £1 ordinary shares in Backward plc for £62,500. Forward Ltd had originally purchased 9,000 shares in Backward plc on 20 April 1990 for £18,000, and purchased a further 500 shares on 1 November 2016 for £6,500. Assume the retail price index for April 1990 was 125.1, and for November 2016 was 264.3. Forward Ltd has never owned more than 1% of the shares in Backward plc.

Forward Ltd purchased 10,000 £1 ordinary shares in Sideways plc on 1 December 2016 for £65,000.

Where possible, Forward Ltd has claimed to roll over any gains arising.

Forward Ltd's only other income for the year ended 31 March 2017 is its tax adjusted trading profit of £78,000. There are no related 51% group companies.

Required:

(a) Calculate Forward Ltd's corporation tax liability for the year ended 31 March 2017, and state by when this should be paid.

Your answer should clearly identify the amount of any gains that have been rolled over. Capital allowances should be ignored. **(7 marks)**

(b) Explain how Forward Ltd's rollover relief claim would have altered if on 1 June 2016 it had acquired a leasehold office building on a 15-year lease for £300,000, rather than purchasing the freehold office building for £260,000. **(3 marks)**

(Total: 10 marks)

165 LUNA LTD *Walk in the footsteps of a top tutor*

Luna Ltd had the following transactions in shares during the year ended 31 March 2017:

(1) On 29 November 2016, Luna Ltd sold its entire shareholding of £1 ordinary shares in Pluto plc for £53,400. Luna Ltd had originally purchased 16,000 shares in Pluto plc on 14 June 2009 for £36,800. On 22 May 2011, Luna Ltd sold 10,000 of the shares for £46,200.

Retail price indices (RPIs) are as follows:

June 2009	213.4
May 2011	235.2
November 2016	264.3

(2) On 12 February 2017, Luna Ltd's shareholding in Asteroid plc was taken over by Comet plc. Luna Ltd had originally purchased 10,000 £1 ordinary shares in Asteroid plc, and their indexed cost on 12 February 2017 was £33,000.

Under the terms of the takeover, for each of its £1 ordinary shares in Asteroid plc, Luna Ltd received £6.50 in cash plus one £1 ordinary share in Comet plc. Immediately after the takeover, Comet plc's £1 ordinary shares were quoted at £4.50.

Required:

(a) Explain how the indexation allowance can be used when a company makes a capital loss, or where the indexation allowance is greater than a company's unindexed gain. **(2 marks)**

(b) Calculate the chargeable gain arising from each of Luna Ltd's transactions in shares during the year ended 31 March 2017.

When calculating the chargeable gain arising from the disposal of the shareholding in Pluto plc, you should show full workings for the share pool. **(8 marks)**

(Total: 10 marks)

Section 3

PRACTICE INHERITANCE TAX QUESTIONS

PRACTICE SECTION A OBJECTIVE TEST QUESTIONS

166   Mario made a number of gifts during the tax year 2016/17:

Which of the following gifts are exempt transfers for inheritance tax purposes?

	Exempt	Not exempt
On 7 May 2016 he gave 100,000 shares in Lahm Ltd to his wife. The shares have been valued at that date at £500,000		
On 10 August 2016 he gave 50,000 shares in Hummells Ltd to a discretionary trust. The shares have been valued at that date at £75,000		
On 6 October 2016 he gave £2,000 to his son on the occasion of his marriage		
On 9 February 2017 he gave £300 to his daughter		

167   Shola made the following lifetime gifts during the 2016/17 tax year. He has previously made no other lifetime gifts.

(1)   27 September 2016   £30,000 to his daughter

(2)   29 December 2016   £475,000 into a trust – Shola paid any inheritance tax

What is the lifetime inheritance tax liability in relation to the lifetime gift on 29 December 2016?

A   £30,000

B   £36,000

C   £28,800

D   £37,500

168 Christiano made the following lifetime gifts, and agreed to pay any inheritance tax that arose as a result of the second gift.

(1) A gift into a discretionary trust on 18 February 2015 – the gross chargeable transfer was £274,000

(2) A cash gift of £150,000 into a discretionary trust on 20 May 2016

The nil rate band for the tax year 2014/15 was £325,000.

How much lifetime tax is paid by Christiano in respect of the gift on 20 May 2016?

A   £24,000

B   £0

C   £23,250

D   £24,750

169 Sully gave £210,000 to a discretionary trust on 1 May 2016.

The only other lifetime gifts that Sully has made are:

(1) On 1 June 2015 £2,000 to his nephew on the occasion of his marriage

(2) On 1 August 2015 £200,000 into a discretionary trust.

The nil rate band for the tax year 2015/16 was £325,000.

For inheritance tax purposes, how much nil rate band is available to set against the gift on 1 May 2016?

A   £130,000

B   £125,000

C   £131,000

D   £129,000

170 *September 2015 OT question*

Heng is a wealthy 45 year old who would like to reduce the potential inheritance tax liability on her estate when she dies.

Which of the following actions will NOT achieve Heng's aim of reducing the potential inheritance tax liability on her estate when she dies?

A   Changing the terms of her will so that the residue of her estate goes to her grandchildren rather than her children

B   Making lifetime gifts to trusts up to the value of the nil rate band every seven years

C   Changing the terms of her will so that the residue of her estate goes to her husband rather than her children

D   Making lifetime gifts to her grandchildren early in life

171   Amir died on 1 February 2017. During his lifetime, he made two gifts:

(1)   On 30 November 2009 he gave £200,000 to his son

(2)   On 15 June 2010 he gave £350,000 to his daughter

Select the correct chargeable amount of the above gifts (i.e. value before the deduction of the nil rate band) which becomes chargeable as a result of Amir's death?

	Chargeable amount £
30 November 2009	
15 June 2010	

A   £0

B   £194,000

C   £347,000

D   £344,000

172   *June 2015 OT question*

Chan died on 8 December 2016, having made a lifetime cash gift of £500,000 to a trust on 16 October 2015. Chan paid the inheritance tax arising from this gift.

Who will be responsible for paying the additional inheritance tax arising from the gift made to the trust as a result of Chan's death, and when will this be due?

A   The trustees on 30 June 2017

B   The personal representatives of Chan's estate on 8 June 2017

C   The personal representatives of Chan's estate on 30 June 2017

D   The trustees on 8 June 2017

173   Edin died on 16 July 2016. He made one lifetime gift on 10 November 2011 into a discretionary trust. He paid the lifetime tax of £52,250 and the gross chargeable transfer value of the gift was £586,250.

How much inheritance tax is due on the lifetime gift as a result of Edin's death?

A   £10,450

B   £62,700

C   £52,250

D   £104,500

174 Fabrice died on 20 January 2017. During his lifetime he made the following gifts:

(1)   20 February 2006   £300,000 to his son

(2)   22 March 2009   £400,000 to a discretionary trust

(3)   30 September 2015   half share in the family home, worth £250,000 to his daughter

(4)   24 December 2016   £800,000 to his wife

Select the gift(s) on which inheritance tax will be payable as a result of Fabrice's death?

	Inheritance tax payable
20 February 2006	
22 March 2009	
30 September 2015	
24 December 2016	

175 *June 2015 OT question*

Which of the following are NOT deducted when calculating the value of a person's chargeable estate for inheritance tax purposes?

(1)   An outstanding repayment mortgage

(2)   Funeral expenses

(3)   An outstanding interest-only mortgage

(4)   An outstanding endowment mortgage

(5)   A verbal promise to pay a friend's debt

(6)   Credit card debts

A   (1), (2) and (6)

B   (4) and (5)

C   (3) and (5)

D   (1), (3) and (4)

176 *September 2015 OT question*

Benjamin died on 30 November 2016 leaving an estate valued at £890,000. Inheritance tax of £276,000 was paid in respect of the estate. Under the terms of his will, Benjamin left £260,000 to his wife, a specific legacy of £120,000 (free of tax) to his brother, and the residue of the estate to his grandchildren.

What is the amount of inheritance received by Benjamin's grandchildren?

A   £614,000

B   £510,000

C   £354,000

D   £234,000

177 Fred died on 8 July 2016.

His estate consisted of the following assets:

(1)   A house worth £545,000 on which there is an outstanding endowment mortgage of £145,000, and

(2)   A life insurance policy with a market value of £300,000, but the proceeds paid to the executors from the policy were £350,000.

Under the terms of Fred's will £400,000 was left to his wife with the remainder of his estate to his son.

What is the gross chargeable value of Fred's death estate for inheritance tax purposes?

£ [ ]

178 Olivier died on 22 November 2016.

His estate comprised the following assets and liabilities:

(1)   A house worth £400,000 (with an outstanding repayment mortgage of £85,000)

(2)   Chattels worth £70,000

(3)   Cash in an ISA of £20,000

(4)   An outstanding gambling debt of £500 owed to a friend.

He left his whole estate to his children.

What is the chargeable value of Olivier's death estate for inheritance tax purposes?

A   £404,500

B   £385,000

C   £405,000

D   £384,500

179 Joel died on 20 December 2016, and left an estate worth £1,101,000 to his daughter.

Joel's only lifetime gift was a cash gift of £124,000 (after deducting all available exemptions) to his son on 8 August 2015.

How much inheritance tax is payable on Joel's death estate?

A   £310,400

B   £180,000

C   £440,400

D   £360,000

180   Dominic owned 7,500 shares in Halder Ltd. On 1 July 2016 he gave 3,000 shares to his son.

The company has an issued share capital of 10,000 shares.

The values of different shareholdings in the shares on 1 July 2016 are as follows:

Holding	Value per share
Up to 25%	£5
26% to 50%	£8
51% to 74%	£13
75% or more	£20

What is the transfer of value for inheritance tax purposes on the gift of the shares to his son?

£ ☐

181   On 15 September 2012 Elvis transferred £500,000 into a discretionary trust. On 15 September 2016 Elvis died.

When is the lifetime inheritance tax and any additional inheritance tax payable on death due in respect of the chargeable lifetime transfer?

		Additional tax on death		
		15 March 2017	**31 March 2017**	**30 April 2017**
Lifetime tax	**15 March 2013**	A	B	C
	31 March 2013	D	E	F
	30 April 2013	G	H	I

182   Melvin died on 6 March 2017 leaving an estate worth £2,000,000. His estate included a holiday home in the UK worth £400,000 which he left to his sister. He left the rest of his estate to his daughter and appointed a friend to act as executor.

For each of the following individuals, select whether they will pay the inheritance tax due on the estate, suffer the inheritance tax payable on the estate, or neither. It is possible to select more than one individual for the same answer.

	Pays tax	Suffers tax	Neither pays nor suffers tax
Sister			
Daughter			
Executor			

183 For each of the following statements select whether it is true or false:

	True	False
An advantage of giving an appreciating asset away during lifetime is that the increase in value up to the date of death will not be subject to inheritance tax		
For capital gains tax purposes lifetime gifts are taxable but gifts on death are not		
On a lifetime gift made more than three years before death, taper relief will reduce the amount of the gift chargeable to inheritance tax on death		

184 Willow died on 1 February 2009 with an estate valued at £280,000. She left £124,800 to her son and the remainder to her husband Stanley.

Stanley died on 1 March 2017 with an estate valued at £800,000, including the inheritance from Willow, which he left to his son.

Neither Willow nor Stanley had made any lifetime gifts.

What is the nil rate band available to Stanley's estate assuming all beneficial elections are made?

The nil rate band in 2008/09 was £312,000.

A £325,000

B £512,200

C £358,333

D £520,000

PRACTICE SECTION B OBJECTIVE TEST CASES

Tutorial note

You should expect inheritance tax to be tested in both sections A and B. The 10 mark question in Section C could also test inheritance tax topics.

There is however no set minimum or maximum number of marks for inheritance tax.

185 JIMMY (ADAPTED) *Walk in the footsteps of a top tutor*

Jimmy died on 14 February 2017. He had made a number of gifts during his lifetime:

(1) On 1 June 2009, Jimmy made a cash gift of £100,000 into a trust. There was no inheritance tax due at the time of this gift.

(2) On 2 August 2012 Jimmy made a cash gift of £5,000 to his grandson as a wedding gift when he got married.

(3) On 14 November 2012 Jimmy made a cash gift of £800,000 to a trust. Jimmy paid the inheritance tax arising from this gift.

At the date of his death Jimmy owned the following assets:

(1)   His main residence valued at £260,000.

(2)   A life assurance policy on his own life. On 14 February 2017 the policy had an open market value of £182,000, and proceeds of £210,000 were received following Jimmy's death.

Jimmy had promised to pay his godson £10,000 for being awarded a first class honours degree, but had not paid this at the date of death.

Under the terms of his will Jimmy left all of his estate to his daughter, Celine. As a result of her recent increased wealth, Celine is considering making a number of gifts to her friends and family but is unsure whether to do so during life or on death.

1   **What is the chargeable amount, after all available exemptions, of the cash gift of £800,000 to the trust on 14 November 2012?**

        A   £794,000

        B   £799,500

        C   £796,500

        D   £799,000

2   **What is the lifetime tax rate payable on the gift to the trust on 14 November 2012 and when was the lifetime tax payable?**

	Tax rate	Due date
A	20%	31 May 2013
B	20%	30 April 2013
C	25%	31 May 2013
D	25%	30 April 2013

3   **Which of the following statements concerning the calculation of the IHT payable on the gift into the trust on 14 November 2012 as a result of Jimmy's death is correct?**

        A   The taxable amount (after the nil rate band) of the gift will be reduced by 20% as the gift was made more than 3 years before death

        B   The nil rate band deductible from the chargeable amount will be reduced by the gross chargeable transfers in the seven years prior to the date of death

        C   The tax payable, after the deduction of the lifetime IHT payable will be reduced by 20% as the gift was made more than 3 years before death

        D   The nil rate band deductible from the chargeable amount will be reduced by the gross chargeable transfers in the seven years prior to the date of the gift

4   **What is the value of Jimmy's gross chargeable death estate?**

        A   £470,000

        B   £210,000

        C   £442,000

        D   £460,000

5   **Which of the following statements concerning the IHT implications of making gifts are correct?**

(1)   The payment of school fees for her children out of Celine's income throughout their school years would be an exempt gift if Celine's standard of living is not affected

(2)   Celine could give away £325,000 every seven years without incurring an IHT liability

(3)   A number of bequests, in Celine's will, of £200 per person would always be exempt from IHT

(4)   Giving away assets during lifetime that are appreciating in value will reduce any IHT payable on the gift on death

A   (1) and (3)

B   (1) and (2) only

C   (2) and (4) only

D   (1), (2) and (4)

186   NING GAO (ADAPTED) *Walk in the footsteps of a top tutor*

Ning Gao died on 15 April 2016.

Ning had made the following lifetime gifts:

(1)   On 1 March 2009 Ning made a cash gift of £50,000 to her daughter, Bao.

(2)   On 1 February 2010 Ning made a cash gift of £350,000 to her son, Shinya on the occasion of his marriage.

Ning's estate, after the deduction of various debts and liabilities, was valued at £750,000. Under the terms of her will Ning left £500,000 to her husband and £250,000 to her daughter, Bao.

After inheriting part of her mother's estate Bao decided to set up a discretionary trust. She owned 5,500 shares, which represented a 55% holding, in Prosper Ltd and on 1 March 2017 she transferred 1,375 shares into the discretionary trust.

The values of shareholdings in Prosper Ltd on 1 March 2017 were as follows:

Holding	Value per share
Up to 25%	£5
26% to 50%	£12
51% to 74%	£25
75% or more	£52

Bao's husband had died on 12 March 2007, and 70% of his inheritance tax nil rate band was not used.

The nil rate band for the tax year 2006/07 is £285,000 and for the tax year 2009/10 it is £325,000.

1   **What is the gross chargeable amount in relation to the gift to Shinya on 1 February 2010?**

    A   £346,000

    B   £342,000

    C   £350,000

    D   £339,000

2   **Which of the following conditions must be met for a debt outstanding at the date of death to be deducted from Ning's estate for inheritance tax purposes?**

    (1)   It must have been incurred in the seven years prior to death

    (2)   It must be legally enforceable

    (3)   It must be less than 10% of the gross estate

    (4)   If it is secured on an asset it must be less than the market value of the asset

    A   (2) only

    B   (1) and (3)

    C   (2) and (4)

    D   (1) and (4)

3   **By how much would the IHT payable on Ning's death estate of £750,000 have been reduced if she had instead died one year later, on 15 April 2017?**

    A   £140,000

    B   £130,000

    C   £97,600

    D   £100,000

4   **What is the amount of the transfer of value relating to the gift into the discretionary trust by Bao on 1 March 2017?**

    A   £6,875

    B   £34,375

    C   £88,000

    D   £49,500

5   **In the event of Bao's death, which of the following statements concerning the transfer of Bao's husband's nil rate band to Bao are correct?**

(1)   The executors of the husband's estate must elect to transfer the unused nil rate band within two years of the husband's death

(2)   The amount of the husband's nil rate band which can be transferred to Bao is 70% of the nil rate band when Bao dies

(3)   The nil rate band transferred from the husband can be used against the tax due as result of Bao's death on both lifetime transfers and her death estate

(4)   The husband's unused nil rate band can only be transferred to Bao if she dies within seven years of her husband

A   (3) and (4)

B   (1) and (4)

C   (2) and (3)

D   (1) and (2)

187   TOM (ADAPTED) *Walk in the footsteps of a top tutor*

Tom died on 1 May 2016.

He had made a gift with a chargeable amount of £450,000 (after all available exemptions) to a trust on 20 February 2010. Tom paid the inheritance tax arising on the gift.

Tom's estate at the date of death included the following assets as well as some cash in the bank:

(1)   A 50% share, valued at £150,000, in a successful racehorse

(2)   Cash winnings from betting on horse racing of £40,000

(3)   His main residence valued at £850,000 which has an outstanding repayment mortgage of £500,000.

The executors have determined that Tom's chargeable estate for IHT purposes was £2,250,000 and they filed their account of the estate assets with HM Revenue and Customs on 3 January 2017.

Tom left all of his estate to his children. His wife is still alive.

The nil rate band for the tax year 2009/10 was £325,000.

1   **What was the gross chargeable amount in respect of Tom's gift of £450,000 to the trust on 20 February 2010?**

A   £475,000

B   £450,000

C   £481,250

D   £473,750

2   If Tom had also made cash gifts of £5,500 to his daughter and £400 to his granddaughter on 20 December 2008 what would have been the amount of annual exemption available on the gift into the trust on 20 February 2010?

   A   £3,000

   B   £3,100

   C   £6,000

   D   £3,350

3   In respect of the gift to the trust on 20 February 2010, what rate of taper relief is applied to the IHT payable on Tom's death and who is liable to pay this additional IHT arising on death?

	Taper relief	Liability for tax
A	80%	Trustees
B	20%	Executors
C	80%	Executors
D	20%	Trustees

4   What is the net value of the estate assets (1)–(3) that will be included in Tom's chargeable death estate for IHT purposes?

   A   £540,000

   B   £350,000

   C   £390,000

   D   £1,000,000

5   How much IHT is payable on Tom's death estate and what is the due date for payment?

	Tax payable	Due date
A	£770,000	3 January 2017
B	£900,000	30 November 2016
C	£770,000	30 November 2016
D	£900,000	3 January 2017

188 AFIYA (ADAPTED) *Walk in the footsteps of a top tutor*

 Timed question with Online tutor debrief

This objective test case question contains question types which will only appear in a computer-based examination, but this question provides valuable practice for all students whichever version of the examination they are taking.

Afiya died on 29 November 2016. She had made a number of gifts during her lifetime as follows:

(1) Afiya's first gift was made on 14 September 2011, when she gave 6,500 £1 ordinary shares in Cassava Ltd, an unquoted investment company, to her daughter.

Before the transfer Afiya owned 8,000 shares out of Cassava Ltd's issued share capital of 10,000 £1 ordinary shares. On 14 September 2011, Cassava Ltd's shares were worth £3 each for a holding of 15%, £7 each for a holding of 65%, and £8 each for a holding of 80%.

(2) Afiya then made various other gifts such that as at 26 January 2016 the total gross chargeable value of all transfers made in the previous seven years was £220,000 comprising potentially exempt transfers of £100,000 and chargeable lifetime transfers of £120,000.

(3) On 27 January 2016, Afiya made a transfer of value (after all exemptions) of £400,000 to a trust. Afiya paid the inheritance tax arising from this gift.

Afiya's husband had died on 1 June 2008 leaving an estate valued at £200,000. He left £200 to his young nephew, £46,600 to his daughter and the balance to Afiya. He had never made any gifts during lifetime.

The nil rate band for the tax year 2008/09 is £312,000 and it is £325,000 thereafter.

1 **What is the gross chargeable transfer value (after all exemptions) of Afiya's gift to her daughter on 14 September 2011?**

 A £59,500

 B £39,500

 C £53,500

 D £45,500

2 **How much lifetime IHT is payable on the gift to the trust on 27 January 2016?**

 A £48,750

 B £39,000

 C £73,750

 D £43,750

3 Which **FOUR** of the following items will be included in, or deducted from, Afiya's chargeable death estate for inheritance tax purposes?

A Her principal private residence

B Funeral expenses

C Unpaid gambling debts

D Shares held in an Individual Savings Account

E £10,000 held in Gilts

F Endowment mortgage on her buy to let property

4 How much additional nil rate band is available on Afiya's death as a result of her husband's death?

A £276,250

B £276,458

C £265,200

D £265,400

5 What are the due dates of payment for the lifetime inheritance tax on the gift to the trust and the tax arising on Afiya's estate?

Dates	Lifetime tax on gift to trust	Tax on estate
30 April 2016		
27 July 2016		
31 July 2016		
30 April 2017		
29 May 2017		
31 May 2017		

🕐 Calculate your allowed time, allocate the time to the separate parts.................

PRACTICE SECTION C CONSTRUCTED RESPONSE QUESTIONS

189 ETHEL AND BLU (ADAPTED) *Walk in the footsteps of a top tutor*

(a) Ethel Brown started to run a small bed and breakfast business as a sole trader on 6 April 2016. She prepared her first accounts for the year to 5 April 2017.

She has read about the cash basis of accounting and HMRC flat rate expense adjustments which are intended to simplify tax accounting for small businesses.

In the year to 5 April 2017 she has the following transactions:

(1) Payments of £25,000 in respect of food, utilities and other household costs. She lives in part of the bed and breakfast premises with her husband and two children and 35% of the food, utilities and other household costs relate to their private use. The HMRC flat rate private use adjustment for four occupants of business premises is £7,800.

(2) On 1 June 2016 Ethel paid a car dealer £14,000 by cheque for a car with CO_2 emissions of 125g/km. She also made payments totalling £3,000 related to the running costs of the car for the year. She has used the car 40% of the time for private purposes and she drove 11,000 business miles during the year.

(3) On 1 March 2017 she acquired an item of kitchen equipment for £350 on credit terms. She paid the supplier's invoice on 15 April 2017.

Required:

Prepare brief notes which you can use to advise Ethel on how the transactions in Notes (1) to (3) should be treated for tax purposes in the accounts for the year to 5 April 2017 assuming that she opts to prepare her accounts using the cash basis and the HMRC flat rate expense adjustments.

You should ignore VAT **(4 marks)**

(b) On 15 January 2017 Blu Reddy made a gift of 200,000 £1 ordinary shares in Purple Ltd, an unquoted investment company, to a trust. Blu paid the inheritance tax arising from this gift.

Before the transfer Blu owned 300,000 shares out of Purple Ltd's issued share capital of 500,000 £1 ordinary shares.

On 15 January 2017 Purple Ltd's shares were worth £2 each for a holding of 20%, £3 each for a holding of 40%, and £4 each for a holding of 60%.

Blu has not made any previous gifts.

Required:

Calculate the inheritance tax that will be payable as a result of Blu Reddy's gift to the trust, and the additional inheritance tax that would be payable if Blu were to die on 31 May 2021.

You should ignore annual exemptions, and should assume that the nil rate band for the tax year 2016/17 remains unchanged. **(6 marks)**

(Total: 10 marks)

190 ROSIE AND TOM (ADAPTED) *Walk in the footsteps of a top tutor*

You should assume that today's date is 15 February 2017.

(a)   Rosie Rohan is the managing director of Hornburg plc. During the tax year 2016/17 Rosie was paid gross director's remuneration of £220,000.

She has made the following gross personal pension contributions:

Tax year	Pension contribution
	£
2013/14	41,000
2014/15	16,000
2015/16	Nil
2016/17	90,000

Rosie was a member of a pension scheme for the tax year 2015/16.

Required:

(1)   Advise Rosie Rohan of the total amount of pension scheme annual allowances that she has available for the tax year 2016/17

(2)   State whether Rosie has made contributions in the tax year 2016/17 in excess of the available annual allowances and explain the tax implications of doing so.

Notes:

1   You are not expected to calculate Rosie Rohan's income tax liability.

2   You are not expected to consider the situation where pension contributions do not attract tax relief.   (5 marks)

(b)   Tom Tirith made a cash gift of £200,000 to his daughter on 20 December 2015. He is now going to make a cash gift of £450,000 to a trust on 20 February 2017. The nil rate band for the tax year 2015/16 is £325,000.

Required:

(1)   Calculate the lifetime inheritance tax that will be payable in respect of Tom Tirith's gift of £450,000 to a trust if:

(1)   the trust pays the tax arising from the gift, or

(2)   Tom pays the tax arising from the gift,

and in the case of (2) only state the value of the gross chargeable transfer.

The total marks will be split equally between each part.   (3 marks)

(2)   Explain how your answer would be different if, instead of making a cash gift to his daughter on 20 December 2015, Tom made the same gift to a trust.

You are not required to do calculations for requirement (b)(2).   (2 marks)

(Total: 10 marks)

191 PERE JONES (ADAPTED)   *Walk in the footsteps of a top tutor*

On 23 August 2011, Pere Jones made a gift of a house valued at £420,000 to his son, Phil Jones. This was a wedding gift when Phil got married.

Pere Jones

Pere died on 20 March 2017 aged 76, at which time his estate was valued at £880,000. Under the terms of his will, Pere divided his estate equally between his wife and his son, Phil. Pere had not made any gifts during his lifetime except for the gift of the house to Phil.

The nil rate band for the tax year 2011/12 is £325,000.

Phil Jones

The house which Phil received as a wedding gift from Pere, his father, was always let out unfurnished until it was sold on 5 April 2017.

The following income and outgoings relate to the property for the tax year 2016/17:

	£
Sale proceeds	504,000
Cost of new boundary wall around the property (there was previously no boundary wall)	(5,300)
Cost of replacing the property's chimney	(2,800)
Legal fees paid in connection with the disposal	(8,600)
Property insurance	(2,300)

Phil has earnings from employment of £80,000 in the tax year 2016/17.

Required:

(a) Calculate the inheritance tax that will be payable as a result of Pere Jones' death,

(6 marks)

(b) Calculate Phil Jones' capital gains tax liability for the tax year 2016/17.   **(4 marks)**

(Total: 10 marks)

192 KENDRA OLDER (ADAPTED)   *Walk in the footsteps of a top tutor*

You should assume that today's date is 1 January 2017.

Kendra Older, aged 93, is unfortunately in poor health with just a few months left to live. She has made the following gifts during her lifetime:

(1) On 20 June 2009, Kendra made a gift to a trust with a gross chargeable transfer value of £140,000. No inheritance tax arose in respect of this gift.

(2) On 5 October 2015, Kendra made a cash gift of £253,000 to her children.

Kendra owns the following assets:

(1) A residential property valued at £970,000. The property is no longer occupied by Kendra, and if it were disposed of during the tax year 2016/17 the disposal would result in a chargeable gain of £174,000.

(2) A life assurance policy on her own life. The policy has an open market value of £210,000, and proceeds of £225,000 will be received following Kendra's death.

None of the above valuations are expected to change in the near future.

Under the terms of her will, Kendra has left her entire estate to her children.

The nil rate band of Kendra's husband was fully utilised when he died ten years ago.

The nil rate band for the tax years 2009/10 and 2015/16 is £325,000.

For the tax year 2016/17, Kendra will pay income tax at the higher rate.

Required:

(a) Calculate the inheritance tax which would be payable if Kendra Older were to die on 31 March 2017. **(7 marks)**

(b) Advise Kendra Older why it would not be beneficial to make an immediate lifetime gift of the property valued at £970,000 to her children.

Notes:

(1) Your answer should take account of both the capital gains tax and the inheritance tax implications of making the gift.

(2) For this part of the question you should ignore the capital gains tax annual exempt amount and inheritance tax annual exemptions. **(3 marks)**

(Total: 10 marks)

193 JAMES *Walk in the footsteps of a top tutor*

James died on 22 January 2017. He had made the following gifts during his lifetime:

(1) On 9 October 2009, a cash gift of £35,000 to a trust. No lifetime inheritance tax was payable in respect of this gift.

(2) On 14 May 2015, a cash gift of £420,000 to his daughter.

(3) On 2 August 2015, a gift of a property valued at £260,000 to a trust. No lifetime inheritance tax was payable in respect of this gift because it was covered by the nil rate band. By the time of James' death on 22 January 2017, the property had increased in value to £310,000.

On 22 January 2017, James' estate was valued at £870,000. Under the terms of his will, James left his entire estate to his children.

The nil rate band of James' wife was fully utilised when she died ten years ago.

The nil rate band for the tax years 2009/10 and 2015/16 is £325,000.

Required:

(a) Calculate the inheritance tax which will be payable as a result of James' death, and state who will be responsible for paying the tax. **(6 marks)**

(b) Explain why it might have been beneficial for inheritance tax purposes if James had left a portion of his estate to his grandchildren rather than to his children. **(2 marks)**

(c) Explain why it might be advantageous for inheritance tax purposes for a person to make lifetime gifts even when such gifts are made within seven years of death.

Notes:

1   Your answer should include a calculation of James' inheritance tax saving from making the gift of property to the trust on 2 August 2015 rather than retaining the property until his death.

2   You are not expected to consider lifetime exemptions in this part of the question.   **(2 marks)**

(Total: 10 marks)

194   OPAL ELDER (ADAPTED)

You should assume that today's date is 15 March 2017.

Opal Elder, aged 71, owns the following assets:

(1)   Two properties respectively valued at £374,000 and £442,000. The first property has an outstanding repayment mortgage of £160,000, and the second property has an outstanding endowment mortgage of £92,000.

(2)   Vintage motor cars valued at £172,000.

(3)   Investments in individual savings accounts (ISAs) valued at £47,000, savings certificates from NS&I (National Savings and Investments) valued at £36,000, and government stocks (gilts) valued at £69,000.

Opal owes £22,400 in respect of a personal loan from a bank, and she has also verbally promised to pay legal fees of £4,600 incurred by her nephew.

Under the terms of her will, Opal has left all of her estate to her children. Opal's husband is still alive.

On 14 August 2007, Opal had made a gift of £100,000 to her daughter, and on 7 November 2016, she made a gift of £220,000 to her son. Both these figures are after deducting all available exemptions.

The nil rate band for the tax year 2007/08 is £300,000.

Required:

(a)   (1)   Calculate Opal Elder's chargeable estate for inheritance tax purposes were she to die on 20 March 2017.   **(5 marks)**

(2)   Calculate the amount of inheritance tax which would be payable in respect of Opal Elder's chargeable estate, and state who will be responsible for paying the tax.   **(3 marks)**

(b)   Advise Opal Elder as to why the inheritance tax payable in respect of her estate would alter if she were to live for another seven years until 20 March 2024, and by how much.

You should assume that both the value of Opal Elder's estate and the nil rate band will remain unchanged.   **(2 marks)**

(Total: 10 marks)

195 MARCUS *Walk in the footsteps of a top tutor*

(a) Inheritance tax legislation does not actually contain a definition of who is, and who is not, a chargeable person.

Required:

(1) **Explain whether or not a married couple is treated as a chargeable person for inheritance tax purposes.** **(1 mark)**

(2) **State the special inheritance tax measures which are applicable to married couples.** **(2 marks)**

(b) Marcus died on 10 March 2017. He had made the following gifts during his lifetime:

(1) On 14 January 2008, Marcus made a chargeable lifetime transfer of £315,000 to a trust. The trustees paid the lifetime inheritance tax of £3,000 which arose in respect of this gift.

(2) On 3 February 2014, Marcus made a chargeable lifetime transfer of £395,000 to another trust. In addition to the gift, Marcus paid the related lifetime inheritance tax of £96,250 on this gift.

(3) On 17 March 2014, Marcus made a gift (a potentially exempt transfer) of 30,000 £1 ordinary shares in Scarum Ltd, an unquoted investment company, to his daughter.

Before the transfer, Marcus owned all of Scarum Ltd's issued share capital of 100,000 £1 ordinary shares. On 17 March 2014, Scarum Ltd's shares were worth £5 each for a holding of 30%, £9 each for a holding of 70%, and £12 each for a holding of 100%.

The nil rate band for the tax year 2007/08 is £300,000, and for the tax year 2013/14 it is £325,000.

Under the terms of his will, Marcus left his entire estate to his wife.

Required:

Calculate the inheritance tax which will be payable as a result of Marcus's death.

Note: You should ignore the inheritance tax annual exemption. **(7 marks)**

(Total: 10 marks)

Section 4

PRACTICE CORPORATION TAX QUESTIONS

PRACTICE SECTION A OBJECTIVE TEST QUESTIONS

CORPORATION TAX BASICS AND ADMINISTRATION

196 **Which of these options identify when a chargeable accounting period will come to an end? You can tick more than one box.**

	Chargeable accounting period end
At the end of a company's period of account	
The end of the tax financial year	
Twelve months after the beginning of the accounting period	
The date the company begins or ceases to trade	

197 *September 2015 OT question*

Which of the following companies will be treated as resident in the UK for corporation tax purposes?

(1) A Ltd, a company incorporated in the UK, with its central management and control exercised in the UK

(2) B Ltd, a company incorporated overseas, with its central management and control exercised in the UK

(3) C Ltd, a company incorporated in the UK, with its central management and control exercised overseas

(4) D Ltd, a company incorporated overseas, with its central management and control exercised overseas

A (1) only

B (1), (2), (3) and (4)

C (2) and (3) only

D (1), (2) and (3) only

198 In the year ended 31 March 2017, Easter Ltd had £100,000 of tax adjusted trading profits before capital allowances, and received bank interest received of £6,000 and dividends of £4,500. It also made qualifying charitable donations of £3,200. Capital allowances for the year were £2,000.

Bank interest receivable of £2,000 and £1,000 was accrued at 31 March 2016 and 31 March 2017 respectively.

What are Easter Ltd's taxable total profits for the year ended 31 March 2017?

A   £101,800

B   £99,800

C   £104,300

D   £103,000

199 You have been given some work to complete, which includes a draft calculation of taxable total profits for a client, Trains Ltd.

Your manager has asked you to check the following calculation and make any corrections necessary.

Year ended 31 December 2016	£
Tax adjusted trading profit	50,000
Property income	6,000
Dividends received from Track Ltd	5,400
Interest received	1,800
	———
Taxable total profits	63,200
	———

The amount of interest receivable for the year was £2,000. In addition the company realised a chargeable gain of £12,000.

What is the correct amount of taxable total profits for Trains Ltd for the year ended 31 December 2016?

A   £58,000

B   £70,000

C   £75,400

D   £69,800

200 In the year ended 31 March 2017 Biscuit Ltd had tax adjusted trading profits of £1,200,000. In addition, Biscuit Ltd had property income of £250,000, received dividends of £52,200 and paid a qualifying donation to a national charity of £7,000.

What is the corporation tax liability of Biscuit Ltd for the year ended 31 March 2017?

A   £299,040

B   £288,250

C   £290,000

D   £288,600

201 Shed Ltd had a tax adjusted trading profit for the year ended 31 March 2017 of £250,000. The company also received dividends of £5,000.

During the year the company sold a painting they had held as an investment for £110,000 realising a chargeable gain of £60,000. The directors had not been expecting the painting to sell for more than £50,000 so they decided to make a qualifying charitable donation with the excess proceeds of £60,000.

What is the corporation tax payable by Shed Ltd for the year ended 31 March 2017?

A £50,000

B £38,000

C £51,000

D £62,000

202 In the year ended 30 June 2016, Chelsea Ltd made a trading profit per the accounts of £25,580.

Included in the accounts was £1,000 spent on a Christmas party for the company's 5 employees and £2,000 for car lease payments.

The leased car has CO_2 emissions of 145g/km and has been leased by the company since 1 July 2015. During the year the car was used by one of the company's directors who drove 4,000 personal miles and 16,000 business miles in the car.

What is the tax adjusted trading profit for Chelsea Ltd for the year ended 30 June 2016?

A £25,980

B £26,880

C £25,580

D £25,880

203 During the year ended 31 March 2017, Swiss Ltd purchased a new car for £8,000, which has CO_2 emissions of 70g/km. It is used by an employee 30% of the time for private purposes and 70% of the time for business purposes.

On 1 April 2016, Swiss Ltd had a tax written down value brought forward on the main pool of £35,000.

What are the maximum capital allowances that Swiss Ltd could claim in the year ended 31 March 2017?

A £7,740

B £14,300

C £11,900

D £7,308

204 During the year ended 31 December 2016 Scotch Ltd rented out an unfurnished office building.

It was let from 1 August 2015 for an annual rent of £15,000, payable annually in advance, until 31 July 2016, when the tenant moved out. The office building was then unoccupied until 1 November 2016.

In August 2016 the company spent £500 replacing damaged fitted units in the kitchen area.

On 1 November 2016 a new tenant moved into the property. Under the new rental agreement annual rent of £8,000 is payable in advance on 1 November.

What is the property income to be included in Scotch Ltd's taxable total profits for the year ended 31 December 2016?

A   £9,583

B   £11,583

C   £10,083

D   £8,333

RELIEF FOR TRADING LOSSES

205 Toulon Ltd started trading on 1 April 2015. Its results for the first two accounting periods are as follows:

Year ended 31 March	2016	2017
	£	£
Tax adjusted trading (loss)/profit	(100,000)	20,000
Interest income	12,000	13,000
Chargeable gain	15,000	–
Qualifying charitable donations paid	(8,000)	(9,000)

What is the amount of loss carried forward at 31 March 2017 assuming the company makes a current year loss relief claim?

A   £73,000

B   £61,000

C   £53,000

D   £40,000

206 Hobart Ltd has had the following recent results:

Year ended 31 March	2016	2017
	£	£
Tax adjusted trading profit/(loss)	40,000	(50,000)
Property income	15,000	21,000
Qualifying charitable donations paid	(6,000)	(14,000)

What are Hobart Ltd's taxable total profits, if any, in the year ended 31 March 2016 assuming the company makes a claim to carry back the trading loss to the year ended 31 March 2016?

A   £20,000

B   £0

C   £6,000

D   £9,000

207 Tasman Ltd has had the following recent results:

	Year ended 30 June 2015	9 months ended 31 March 2016	Year ended 31 March 2017
	£	£	£
Tax adjusted trading profit/(loss)	40,000	22,000	(60,000)
Interest income	4,000	3,000	5,000

What is the amount of loss, if any, which is available to carry forward as at 31 March 2017 assuming Tasman Ltd claims to use the trading loss as soon as possible?

A   £0

B   £30,000

C   £19,000

D   £28,000

208 Darwin Ltd ceased to trade on 31 March 2017. Its recent results have been as follows:

Year ended	31.3.2014	31.3.2015	31.3.2016	31.3.2017
	£	£	£	£
Tax adjusted trading profit/(loss)	45,000	32,000	10,000	(100,000)
Chargeable gain	5,000	–	9,000	14,000

What are the company's taxable total profits for the year ended 31 March 2014 assuming the company makes a terminal loss relief claim?

A   £0

B   £6,000

C   £1,000

D   £15,000

209 Adelaide Ltd has had the following recent results:

Year ended 31 March	2015	2016	2017
	£	£	£
Tax adjusted trading profit	16,000	20,000	25,000
Property income/(loss)	5,000	(65,000)	10,000
Qualifying charitable donations paid	(800)	(900)	(1,100)

What is the amount of the unused property loss as at 31 March 2017?

A   £50,000

B   £10,000

C   £12,000

D   £55,000

WITH GROUP ASPECTS

210 *June 2015 OT question*

Ten Ltd is the parent company for a group of companies. The group structure is as follows:

Ten Ltd

90%

Twenty Ltd

75%

Thirty Ltd

70%

Forty Ltd

Each percentage holding represents a holding of ordinary share capital.

What is the group relationship between Forty Ltd and Ten Ltd?

A   They form a group for both group relief and chargeable gains purposes

B   They form a group for group relief purposes but not for chargeable gains purposes

C   They form a group for chargeable gains purposes but not for group relief purposes

D   They do not form a group for either group relief or chargeable gains purposes

211 Computer Ltd owns 75% of Chair Ltd, 60% of Bin Ltd and 100% of Paper Inc. Paper Inc owns 75% of Cardboard Ltd. All companies are resident in the UK except Paper Inc which is resident in the US.

Computer Ltd suffered a trading loss in the year ending 31 March 2017.

Which companies could Computer Ltd's trading loss be surrendered to?

	Loss can be surrendered to
Chair Ltd	
Bin Ltd	
Paper Inc	
Cardboard Ltd	

212 Battery Ltd owns 100% of Watch Ltd. During the year ended 31 March 2017 Battery Ltd had a trading loss of £100,000. During the 6 month period ended 30 June 2017 Watch Ltd had trading income of £50,000 and property income of £30,000.

What is the maximum loss that Watch Ltd can claim from Battery Ltd for the period ended 30 June 2017?

A   £50,000

B   £25,000

C   £40,000

D   £80,000

213 Brazil Ltd owns 100% of Germany Ltd and 75% of Holland Ltd. Germany Ltd owns 65% of Belgium Ltd and Holland owns 75% of Russia Ltd.

Which companies form a capital gains group for corporation tax purposes?

	Capital gains group
Brazil Ltd	
Germany Ltd	
Holland Ltd	
Belgium Ltd	
Russia Ltd	

214 Apple Ltd owns 75% of Grape Ltd. In the year ended 31 March 2017 Apple Ltd transferred a property with a market value of £300,000 to Grape Ltd. The original cost of the asset was £100,000 and the indexation allowance to the date of transfer was £50,000.

What is the deemed acquisition cost for chargeable gains purposes for Grape Ltd?

A   £150,000

B   £100,000

C   £0

D   £300,000

215 Telephone Ltd prepares accounts to 31 March each year. Throughout the year ended 31 March 2017 Telephone Ltd owned 62% of Desk Ltd, 75% of Chair Ltd, 55% of Table Ltd (a dormant company) and 100% of Window Inc (resident overseas). Telephone Ltd acquired 60% of the share capital of Curtain Ltd on 1 January 2017.

What is the total number of companies for the purposes of adjusting the £1,500,000 augmented profits threshold of Telephone Ltd for the year ended 31 March 2017?

A   2

B   3

C   4

D   5

216 Novak Ltd owns 80% of Roger Ltd. Roger Ltd owns 70% of Rafael Ltd and Rafael Ltd owns 55% of Andy Ltd. The group structure has been the same for a number of years.

What is the profits threshold for determining if Novak Ltd should pay corporation tax by instalments for the year ended 31 March 2017?

A   £375,000

B   £750,000

C   £1,500,000

D   £500,000

217 Custard Ltd started trading on 1 August 2016 and prepared its first set of accounts to 31 March 2017. The company's taxable total profits for the period to 31 March 2017 are £190,000.

Custard Ltd has three related 51% group companies from which it received dividends of £70,000. The company also received dividends from one non-related company of £27,000.

What is the amount of the augmented profits threshold that will be used to determine whether Custard Ltd is a large company for the period ended 31 March 2017?

A   £250,000

B   £375,000

C   £200,000

D   £333,333

218 Bourbon Ltd prepares annual accounts to 31 January. In the year ended 31 January 2017, the company had the following income:

	£
Trading income	1,450,000
Chargeable gain	100,000

Bourbon Ltd received dividends of £50,000 from related 51% group companies and dividends of £20,000 from non-related companies.

What are the augmented profits of Bourbon Ltd for the year ended 31 January 2017?

A   £1,470,000

B   £1,570,000

C   £1,620,000

D   £1,550,000

219 *September 2015 OT question (ADAPTED)*

During the year ended 31 March 2017, Luck Ltd received the following dividends:

	£
From unconnected companies	4,680
From a company in which Luck Ltd has a 80% shareholding	3,870
From a company in which Luck Ltd has a 45% shareholding	1,260

What is the amount that is included in Luck Ltd's augmented profits for the year ended 31 March 2017?

A   £5,940

B   £9,810

C   £3,870

D   £4,680

220 *Specimen paper June 2015*

For the year ended 31 March 2016, Sizeable Ltd had a corporation tax liability of £384,000, and for the year ended 31 March 2017 it had a liability of £456,000.

Sizeable Ltd is a large company, and is therefore required to make instalment payments in respect of its corporation tax liability.

The company's profits have accrued evenly throughout each year.

What is the amount of each instalment payable by Sizeable Ltd in respect of its corporation tax liability for the year ended 31 March 2017?

A   £228,000

B   £114,000

C   £96,000

D   £192,000

221 Hound Ltd started to trade on 1 June 2016 and prepared its first set of accounts for the 15 month period to 31 August 2017.

On which date(s) must Hound Ltd submit a corporation tax return in respect of the 15 month period of account?

A   1 March 2018 and 1 June 2018

B   31 August 2018 only

C   31 May 2018 and 31 August 2018

D   31 May 2018 only

222 All of the following companies are NOT large companies for the purposes of paying corporation tax.

(1)   W Ltd – prepared accounts for the year ended 30 June 2016

(2)   X Ltd – prepared accounts for the 15 months ended 30 September 2016

(3)   Y Ltd – prepared accounts for the year ended 31 March 2016

(4)   Z Ltd – prepared accounts for the 8 months to 30 June 2016

Which of the above companies have a due date in respect of corporation tax of 1 April 2017?

A   W Ltd, X Ltd and Z Ltd only

B   W Ltd and Z Ltd only

C   All of them

D   X Ltd and Y Ltd only

223 *September 2015 OT question*

Mammoth Ltd commenced trading on 1 January 2014. The company's augmented profits have been as follows:

Period	£
Year ended 31 December 2014	524,000
Year ended 31 December 2015	867,000
Year ended 31 December 2016	912,000

Throughout all of these periods, Mammoth Ltd had one related 51% group company.

What is the first year for which Mammoth Ltd will be required to pay its corporation tax liability by quarterly instalments?

A   Year ended 31 December 2015

B   None of the years ended 31 December 2014, 2015 or 2016

C   Year ended 31 December 2016

D   Year ended 31 December 2014

224 Gerber Ltd has been a large company for the purposes of paying its corporation tax liability for a number of years.

In 2016 it changed its accounting date and prepared an 8 month set of accounts to 31 December 2016.

When is the final corporation tax instalment in respect of the 8 month accounting period ended 31 December 2016 due?

A   14 February 2017

B   14 April 2017

C   14 May 2017

D   14 August 2017

225 *September 2015 OT question*

For the year ended 30 June 2016, Forgetful Ltd had a corporation tax liability of £166,250, which it did not pay until 31 July 2017. Forgetful Ltd is not a large company.

How much interest will Forgetful Ltd be charged by HM Revenue and Customs (HMRC) in respect of the late payment of its corporation tax liability for the year ended 30 June 2016?

A   £416

B   £2,909

C   £5,403

D   £1,662

PRACTICE SECTION B OBJECTIVE TEST CASES

CORPORATION TAX BASICS AND ADMINISTRATION

226 GREENZONE LTD (ADAPTED) *Walk in the footsteps of a top tutor*

Greenzone Ltd is a trading company.

Year ended 31 March 2017

Included in the company's statement of profit or loss for the year ended 31 March 2017 were the following expenses:

	£
Repairs and renewals	
Repainting the exterior of the company's office building	8,390
Extending the office building in order to create a new reception area	19,800
Entertaining expenses	
Entertaining UK customers	3,600
Entertaining overseas customers	1,840
Gifts and donations	
Political donations	740
Donation to a small, local charity where Greenzone Ltd received free advertising in the charity's newsletter.	430
Gifts to customers:	
– pens costing £30 each, not displaying Greenzone Ltd's name	660
– clocks costing £65 each and displaying Greenzone Ltd's name	910

Plant and machinery

On 1 April 2016 the tax written down value of Greenzone Ltd's main pool was £48,150.

The following motor cars were purchased during the year ended 31 March 2017:

	Date of purchase	Cost	CO$_2$ emission rate
		£	
New motor car (1)	10 April 2016	10,800	72 grams per kilometre
New motor car (2)	10 June 2016	20,400	120 grams per kilometre

The following motor car was sold during the year ended 31 March 2017:

	Date of sale	Proceeds	Original cost
		£	£
Motor car (3)	8 March 2017	9,100	8,500

The original cost of motor car (3) has previously been added to the main pool.

Period ended 30 September 2017

Greenzone Ltd changed its year end and prepared accounts for the six month period to 30 September 2017.

On 1 April 2017 the tax written down value of Greenzone Ltd's special rate pool was £9,200. During the six month period to 30 September 2017 the company installed a new air conditioning system throughout its offices at a cost of £150,000, which is expected to last 30 years.

1   What amount must be added back in the adjustment of trading profits computation in respect of repairs and renewals and entertaining expenses?

   A   £23,400

   B   £13,830

   C   £25,240

   D   £21,640

2   What amount must be added back in the adjustment of trading profits computation in respect of gifts and donations?

   A   £2,310

   B   £2,740

   C   £1,650

   D   £660

3   Assuming that Greenzone Ltd always claims the maximum capital allowances, what is the tax written down balance of the main pool at 31 March 2017?

   A   £58,097

   B   £48,749

   C   £56,211

   D   £49,241

4   Assuming that Greenzone Ltd always claims the maximum capital allowances, what capital allowances would be claimed in respect of the special rate pool for the six months ended 30 September 2017?

   A   £102,368

   B   £150,736

   C   £100,000

   D   £104,736

5   Assuming that Greenzone Ltd is a large company for the purposes of paying its corporation tax, on what dates are instalments of its corporation tax liability for the 6 months ended 30 September 2017 payable?

   A   14 July 2017, 14 October 2017, 14 January 2018 and 14 April 2018

   B   14 October 2017 and 14 January 2018 only

   C   14 October 2017, 14 January 2018, 14 April 2018 and 14 July 2018

   D   14 July 2017, 14 October 2017 and 14 January 2018 only

RELIEF FOR TRADING LOSSES

227   LOSER LTD (ADAPTED)

Loser Ltd 's recent results, together with a forecast for the year ended 31 March 2018 are:

	y/e 30.6.13	y/e 30.6.14	y/e 30.6.15	9 months ended 31.3.16	y/e 31.3.17	y/e 31.3.18
	£	£	£	£	£	£
Trading profit/(loss)	15,800	10,600	15,700	24,300	(78,300)	60,000
Property income	5,200	1,200	6,600	8,100	5,600	3,000
Qualifying charitable donations	(1,300)	(1,400)	(800)	(1,200)	(1,100)	(1,300)

The future prospects of Loser Ltd are currently uncertain.

Loser Ltd does not own shares in any other company.

1   **Which of the following factors are relevant to Loser Ltd's decision when choosing which loss relief claims to make?**

   (1)   Rate of tax

   (2)   Timing of relief

   (3)   Extent to which losses will be wasted

   (4)   Extent to which QCD relief will be wasted

   A   (2), (3) and (4)

   B   (2) and (4) only

   C   (1) and (3)

   D   (1) only

2   **Assuming that Loser Ltd decided not to make a specific loss relief claim, such that the trading loss was carried forward, what would be the amount of unrelieved loss at 31 March 2018?**

   A   £16,600

   B   £18,300

   C   £13,800

   D   £12,700

3   **Assuming that Loser Ltd elects to offset the loss as soon as possible what would be the amount of unrelieved loss at 31 March 2017?**

   A   £40,325

   B   £37,225

   C   £40,300

   D   £34,725

4 Assuming that Loser Ltd wishes to make a current year loss relief claim in respect of the trading loss, by which date must the claim be made?

A   1 January 2018

B   31 March 2023

C   31 March 2019

D   31 March 2018

5 Assuming that Loser Ltd had ceased trading on 31 March 2017 and claimed terminal loss relief in respect of its trading loss, what would be the amount of unrelieved loss at 31 March 2017?

A   £950

B   £5,775

C   £6,200

D   £23,750

WITH GROUP ASPECTS

228 DEUTSCH LTD (ADAPTED)   *Walk in the footsteps of a top tutor*

Deutsch Ltd has held shares in four trading companies for a number of years. All four companies prepare accounts to 31 March.

Year ended 31 March 2017

The following information is available for the year ended 31 March 2017:

	Eins Ltd	Zwei Ltd	Drei Ltd	Vier Co
Residence	UK	UK	UK	Overseas
Percentage shareholding	60%	20%	90%	70%
Trading profit/(loss)	£(74,800)	£68,900	£(52,700)	£22,600
Property income	£10,000	–	–	–
Chargeable gains		£204,400		
Qualifying charitable donations paid	–	–	£12,000	–

In the year ended 31 March 2017 Deutsch Ltd had a tax adjusted trading profit of £277,700 and no other income or gains.

Zwei Ltd

The remaining 80% of the Zwei Ltd shares are held by Berlin Ltd.

On 15 March 2017 Zwei Ltd sold a building for its market value of £500,000 to an independent third party. It had acquired the building for £200,000 on 1 May 2004. The indexed cost of the building at 15 March 2017 was £285,200. On 1 August 2016 Zwei Ltd acquired a factory at a cost of £460,000.

1   Which of the four trading companies will be treated as related 51% group companies of Deutsch Ltd?

    A   All four companies

    B   Eins Ltd, Drei Ltd and Vier Co only

    C   Eins Ltd, Zwei Ltd and Drei Ltd only

    D   Eins Ltd and Drei Ltd only

2   What is the maximum amount of group relief that Deutsch Ltd can claim for the year ended 31 March 2017?

    A   £64,700

    B   £52,700

    C   £139,500

    D   £47,430

3   What is the amount of gain arising on the sale of the building by Zwei Ltd that can be rolled over into the acquisition of the factory?

    A   £214,800

    B   £40,000

    C   £260,000

    D   £174,800

4   If instead of selling the building to an independent third party Zwei Ltd had sold it to Berlin Ltd for £450,000 on 15 March 2017, what would have been the capital gains base cost of the building for Berlin Ltd?

    A   £285,200

    B   £500,000

    C   £200,000

    D   £450,000

5   What are the dates by which Deutsch Ltd must make a group relief claim in respect of the year ended 31 March 2017 and Zwei Ltd must make a rollover relief claim in respect of the disposal of the building in the year ended 31 March 2017?

	Group relief	Rollover relief
A	31 March 2021	31 March 2021
B	31 March 2019	31 March 2021
C	31 March 2019	31 March 2019
D	31 March 2021	31 March 2019

PRACTICE SECTION C CONSTRUCTED RESPONSE QUESTIONS

CORPORATION TAX BASICS AND ADMINISTRATION

229 ARABLE LTD (ADAPTED)

Arable Ltd commenced trading on 1 April 2016 as a manufacturer of farm equipment, preparing its first accounts for the nine-month period ended 31 December 2016. The following information is available:

Trading profit

The tax adjusted trading profit is £376,611. This figure is before taking account of capital allowances and any deduction arising from the premium paid in respect of leasehold property.

Plant and machinery

Arable Ltd purchased the following assets in respect of the nine-month period ended 31 December 2016.

		£
20 April 2016	Delivery lorries	193,350
12 May 2016	Motor car (1)	11,200
14 May 2016	Motor car (2)	14,600
17 May 2016	Motor car (3)	13,000

Motor car (1) purchased on 12 May 2016 for £11,200 has a CO_2 emission rate of 106 grams per kilometre. Motor car (2) purchased on 14 May 2016 for £14,600 has a CO_2 emission rate of 138 grams per kilometre. Motor car (3), purchased on 17 May 2016 for £13,000, is a new car and has CO_2 emissions of 69 grams per kilometre.

The company will not make any short life asset elections.

Leasehold property

On 1 April 2016 Arable Ltd acquired a leasehold office building. A premium of £75,000 was paid for the grant of a 15-year lease. The office building was used for business purposes by Arable Ltd throughout the period ended 31 December 2016.

Freehold property

On 1 August 2016 Arable Ltd acquired the freehold of a second office building. This office building was empty until 30 September 2016, and was then let to a tenant. On that date Arable Ltd received a premium of £50,000 for the grant of a five-year lease, and annual rent of £14,800 which was payable in advance.

Loan interest received

Loan interest of £6,000 was received on 30 September 2016, and £3,000 was accrued at 31 December 2016. The loan was made for non-trading purposes.

Dividends received

During the period ended 31 December 2016 Arable Ltd received dividends of £20,000 from Ranch plc, an unrelated UK company.

Other information

Arable Ltd has two related 51% group companies.

Required:

(a) Calculate Arable Ltd's corporation tax liability for the nine-month period ended 31 December 2016. **(12 marks)**

(b) Explain, with supporting calculations, whether Arable Ltd is defined as a large company, for the purposes of determining the due date for payment of tax, for the nine-month period ended 31 December 2016. **(3 marks)**

(Total: 15 marks)

230 DO-NOT-PANIC LTD (ADAPTED)

Do-Not-Panic Ltd is a United Kingdom resident company that installs burglar alarms.

The company commenced trading on 1 January 2016 and its results for the fifteen-month period ended 31 March 2017 are summarised as follows:

(1) The trading profit as adjusted for tax purposes is £250,500. This figure is before taking account of capital allowances.

(2) Do-Not-Panic Ltd purchased a new car (CO_2 emission of 70g/km) for £18,000 on 1 December 2016 and equipment for £24,000 on 20 February 2017.

(3) On 21 December 2016 Do-Not-Panic Ltd disposed of some investments and this resulted in a capital loss of £4,250. On 28 March 2017 the company made a further disposal and this resulted in a chargeable gain of £42,000.

(4) The company opened a bank deposit account on 1 April 2016. Interest income of £25,000 was credited to the account on 31 March 2017. Interest accrued as at 31 December 2016 was £18,000.

(5) On 1 March 2017 the company took out a non-trade related bank loan to acquire a minority shareholding in a supplier company. Interest payable as at 31 March 2017 was £6,000.

Do-Not-Panic Ltd has no related 51% group companies.

Required:

Calculate Do-Not-Panic Ltd's corporation tax liabilities in respect of the fifteen-month period ended 31 March 2017 and advise the company by when these should be paid and the date that the tax return(s) should be filed.

Ignore VAT. **(10 marks)**

231 CRASH BASH LTD (ADAPTED) *Walk in the footsteps of a top tutor*

Crash-Bash Ltd commenced trading on 1 April 2016 as a manufacturer of motor cycle crash helmets in the United Kingdom. The company is incorporated overseas, although its directors are based in the United Kingdom and hold their board meetings in the United Kingdom.

Crash-Bash Ltd prepared its first accounts for the nine-month period ended 31 December 2016. The following information is available:

Trading profit

The tax adjusted trading profit based on the draft accounts for the nine-month period ended 31 December 2016 is £1,002,924.

This figure is before making any adjustments required for:

(1)   Capital allowances.

(2)   Advertising expenditure of £12,840 incurred during March 2016. This expenditure has not been deducted in arriving at the tax adjusted trading profit for the period ended 31 December 2016 of £1,002,924.

Plant and machinery

The accounts for the nine-month period ended 31 December 2016 showed the following additions and disposals of plant and machinery:

		Cost
		£
2 May 2016	Purchased machinery	271,250
28 June 2016	Purchased a motor car	13,200
3 July 2016	Purchased machinery	110,000

The cost of the machinery purchased on 2 May 2016 includes £10,000 spent on strengthening the factory floor to accommodate the new machinery.

The motor car purchased on 28 June 2016 for £13,200 was a new car and has a CO_2 emission rate of 69 grams per kilometre.

The machinery purchased on 3 July 2016 for £110,000 has an expected working life of 30 years.

Dividends received

During the period ended 31 December 2016 Crash-Bash Ltd received a dividend of £14,250 from a 100% owned subsidiary company, Safety Ltd and received dividends of £36,000 from Flat-Out plc, an unrelated company.

Required:

(a) Explain why Crash-Bash Ltd is treated as being resident in the UK. **(2 marks)**

(b) Calculate Crash-Bash Ltd's corporation tax liability for the nine-month period ended 31 December 2016. **(9 marks)**

(c) State the date by which Crash-Bash Ltd's self-assessment corporation tax return for the period ended 31 December 2016 should be submitted, and advise the company of the penalties that will be due if the return is submitted eight months late.

You should assume that the company pays its corporation tax liability at the same time that the self-assessment tax return is submitted. **(4 marks)**

(Total: 15 marks)

232 MOLTEN METAL PLC (ADAPTED) *Walk in the footsteps of a top tutor*

Molten-Metal plc is a manufacturer of machine tools. The following information is available for the year ended 31 March 2017:

Trading profit

The tax adjusted trading profit for the year ended 31 March 2017 is £2,090,086. This figure is **before** making any deductions required for:

(1) Interest payable.

(2) Capital allowances.

(3) Any revenue expenditure that may have been debited to the company's capital expenditure account in error.

Interest payable

During the year ended 31 March 2017 Molten-Metal plc paid loan stock interest of £22,500. Loan stock interest of £3,700 was accrued at 31 March 2017, with the corresponding accrual at 1 April 2016 being £4,200. The loan is used for trading purposes.

The company also incurred a loan interest expense of £6,800 in respect of a loan that is used for non-trading purposes.

Capital expenditure account

The following items of expenditure have been debited to the capital expenditure account during the year ended 31 March 2017:

1 May 2016   Purchase of a second-hand freehold office building for £378,000. This figure included £83,000 for a ventilation system and £10,000 for a lift. Both the ventilation system and the lift are integral to the office building.

During May 2016 Molten-Metal plc spent a further £97,400 on repairs. The office building was not usable until these repairs were carried out, and this fact was represented by a reduced purchase price.

26 June 2016	Purchase of machinery for £90,000. During June 2016 a further £7,000 was spent on building alterations that were necessary for the installation of the machinery.
8 August 2016	A payment of £41,200 for the construction of a new decorative wall around the company's premises.
27 August 2016	Purchase of movable partition walls for £22,900. Molten-Metal plc uses these to divide up its open plan offices, and the partition walls are moved around on a regular basis.
11 March 2017	Purchase of two motor cars each costing £17,300. Each motor car has a CO_2 emission rate of 120 grams per kilometre. One motor car is used by the factory manager, and 60% of the mileage is for private journeys. The other motor car is used as a pool car.

Written down value

On 1 April 2016 the tax written down value of plant and machinery in Molten-Metal plc's main pool was £87,800.

Interest receivable

Molten-Metal plc made a loan for non-trading purposes on 1 August 2016. Loan interest of £9,800 was received on 31 January 2017, and £3,100 was accrued at 31 March 2017.

The company also received bank interest of £2,600 during the year ended 31 March 2017. The bank deposits are held for non-trading purposes.

Quarterly instalment payments

Molten-Metal plc makes quarterly instalment payments in respect of its corporation tax liability. The first three instalment payments for the year ended 31 March 2017 totalled £298,200.

Required:

(a) Calculate Molten-Metal plc's corporation tax liability for the year ended 31 March 2017. **(13 marks)**

(b) Calculate the final quarterly instalment payment that will have to be made by Molten-Metal plc for the year ended 31 March 2017, and state when this will be due. **(2 marks)**

(Total: 15 marks)

233 STRETCHED LTD (ADAPTED)

Stretched Ltd has always prepared its accounts to 31 December, but has decided to change its accounting date to 31 March. The company's results for the 15-month period ended 31 March 2017 are as follows:

(1) The tax adjusted trading profit is £642,500. This figure is before taking account of capital allowances.

(2) Until January 2017 the company has never been entitled to capital allowances as all assets were leased. However, on 15 January 2017 the company bought office equipment for £57,500.

(3) There is a property business profit of £45,000 for the 15-month period ended 31 March 2017.

(4) On 15 April 2016 the company disposed of some investments, and this resulted in a chargeable gain of £44,000. On 8 February 2017 the company made a further disposal, and this resulted in a capital loss of £6,700.

(5) Dividend income of £30,000 was received on 10 September 2016.

(6) A qualifying charitable donation of £5,000 was made on 31 March 2017.

As at 1 January 2016 Stretched Ltd had unused trading losses of £330,000, and unused capital losses of £3,000.

In the year ended 31 December 2015 the company had taxable total profits of £300,000 and no dividend income.

Stretched Ltd has no related 51% group companies.

Required:

(a) **Calculate Stretched Ltd's corporation tax liabilities in respect of the 15-month period ended 31 March 2017, and advise the company by when these should be paid.** **(13 marks)**

(b) **State the advantages for tax purposes of a company having an accounting date of 31 March instead of 31 December.** **(2 marks)**

(Total: 15 marks)

234 STARFISH LTD (ADAPTED) *Walk in the footsteps of a top tutor*

Starfish Ltd, a retailer of scuba diving equipment, was incorporated on 15 October 2012, and commenced trading on 1 December 2012. The company initially prepared accounts to 31 March, but changed its accounting date to 31 December by preparing accounts for the nine-month period ended 31 December 2016. Starfish Ltd ceased trading on 31 March 2017, and a resolution was subsequently passed to commence winding up procedures.

Starfish Ltd's results for each of its periods of account up to 31 December 2016 are:

	Tax adjusted trading profit/(loss)	Bank interest	Qualifying charitable donations
	£	£	£
Four-month period ended 31 March 2013	(12,600)	600	(800)
Year ended 31 March 2014	64,200	1,400	(1,000)
Year ended 31 March 2015	53,900	1,700	(900)
Year ended 31 March 2016	14,700	0	(700)
Nine-month period ended 31 December 2016	49,900	0	(600)

The company's summarised statement of profit or loss for its final three-month period of trading ended 31 March 2017 is as follows:

	Notes	£	£
Gross profit			16,100
Expenses			
Depreciation		34,400	
Donations	1	1,650	
Impairment loss	2	2,000	
Other expenses	3	168,050	
		———	(206,100)
Loss before taxation			(190,000)

Note 1 – Donations

Donations were made as follows:	£
Donation to a political party	300
Qualifying charitable donation	1,350
	1,650

Note 2 – Impairment loss

On 31 March 2017 Starfish Ltd wrote off an impairment loss of £2,000 in respect of a trade debt.

Note 3 – Other expenses

Other expenses are as follows:

	£
Entertaining customers	3,600
Entertaining employees	1,840
Counselling services provided to employees who were made redundant	8,400
Balance of expenditure (all allowable)	154,210
	168,050

Note 4 – Plant and machinery

On 1 January 2017 the tax written down values of the company's plant and machinery were:

	£
Main pool	23,600
Special rate pool	13,200

On 10 January 2017 Starfish Ltd purchased a laptop computer for £3,120. This figure is inclusive of value added tax (VAT).

On 31 March 2017 the company sold all of the items included in the main pool for £31,200, and the laptop computer for £1,800.

The only item in the special rate pool was a car which had been acquired for £16,000 and which was sold on 31 March 2017 for £9,600. The car was used by the managing director, and 20% of the mileage was for private journeys.

Starfish Ltd is registered for VAT. All of the above figures are inclusive of VAT where applicable. None of the items included in the main pool was sold for more than its original cost, and all of the items in the main pool were standard rated.

Required:

(a)   Calculate Starfish Ltd's tax adjusted trading loss for the three-month period ended 31 March 2017.

Your computation should commence with the loss before taxation figure of £190,000, and should also list all of the items referred to in notes (1) to (4) indicating by the use of zero (0) any items that do not require adjustment.

(10 marks)

(b)   Assuming that Starfish Ltd claims relief for its trading losses on the most beneficial basis, calculate the company's taxable total profits for the four-month period ended 31 March 2013, the years ended 31 March 2014, 2015 and 2016 and the nine-month period ended 31 December 2016. (5 marks)

(Total: 15 marks)

235 HEAVY LTD (ADAPTED) *Walk in the footsteps of a top tutor*

Heavy Ltd runs a music publishing business. On 1 April 2016 Heavy Ltd acquired 100% of the ordinary share capital of Soft Ltd, a company that runs a music recording studio. Neither company has any other related companies.

Heavy Ltd has prepared accounts for the year ended 31 July 2017. The following information is available:

(1) The operating profit for the year ended 31 July 2017 is £433,100. Depreciation of £12,880 and a health and safety fine of £9,000 have been deducted in arriving at this figure.

(2) On 1 August 2016 the tax written down values of Heavy Ltd's plant and machinery were as follows:

	£
Main pool	900
Short life asset (1) – machine acquired May 2014	15,100
Short life asset (2) – plant acquired August 2014	13,200
Special rate pool	21,700

The following purchases and disposals of plant and machinery took place during the year ended 31 July 2017:

		Cost/(Proceeds)
		£
23 March 2017	Purchased office equipment	22,400
24 April 2017	Purchased new motor car	16,000
1 June 2017	Purchased computers	25,000
19 July 2017	Sold short life asset (2)	(4,600)
28 July 2017	Sold all the items included in the special rate pool	(12,300)

The motor car purchased on 24 April 2017 has CO_2 emissions of 70 grams per kilometre and is used by the managing director of Heavy Ltd, and 60% of the mileage is for private journeys.

The cost of the computers acquired on 1 June 2017 includes software costs of £5,000.

Short life asset (2) sold on 19 July 2017 originally cost £19,631.

(3) On 18 May 2017 Heavy Ltd sold a freehold office building to Soft Ltd for £113,600. The indexed cost of the office building on that date was £102,800.

(4) On 1 March 2017 Heavy Ltd sold half of its car park for £45,000. The company purchased the entire car park for £10,000 in May 2002. The market value of the remaining half of the car park on 1 March 2017 is £50,000.

(5) The company rents out a building that is now surplus to its requirements. It made a property business loss of £10,000 during the year to 31 July 2017 due to significant redecoration costs.

(6) During the year ended 31 July 2017 Heavy Ltd received the following dividends:

Company paying the dividend:	£
An unrelated UK company	27,000
Soft Ltd	6,300

Required:

Calculate Heavy Ltd's corporation tax liability for the year ended 31 July 2017.

The RPI for March 2017 is 265.9 and for May 2002 is 176.2.

Assume that tax rates and allowances for FY2016 continue into the future.   **(15 marks)**

236 SOFTAPP LTD (ADAPTED) *Walk in the footsteps of a top tutor*

 Timed question with Online tutor debrief

Softapp Ltd is a software developer. The company's summarised statement of profit or loss for the year ended 31 March 2017 is as follows:

	Notes	£
Operating profit	1	913,000
Other income		
Income from property	2	36,700
Loan interest receivable	3	8,100
Profit on disposal of shares	4	64,900
Finance costs		
Interest payable	5	(67,200)
Profit before taxation		955,500

Note 1 – Operating profit

Depreciation of £8,170 and amortisation of leasehold property of £2,500 have been deducted in arriving at the operating profit of £913,000.

Note 2 – Income from property

Since 1 November 2016, Softapp Ltd has let out one floor of a freehold office building which is surplus to requirements (see Note 5).

The income from property figure of £36,700 is made up of the following income and expenditure:

		£
23 October 2016	Advertising for tenants	(600)
25 October 2016	Security deposit of two months' rent	10,400
25 October 2016	Rent for the quarter ended 31 January 2017	15,600
1 November 2016	Insurance for the year ended 31 October 2017	(1,200)
2 February 2017	Rent for the quarter ended 30 April 2017	15,600
20 March 2017	Repairs following a flood	(12,800)
4 April 2017	Insurance claim in respect of the flood damage	9,700
		———
		36,700
		———

Note 3 – Loan interest receivable

The loan was made for non-trading purposes on 1 July 2016. Loan interest of £5,600 was received on 31 December 2016, and interest of £2,500 was accrued at 31 March 2017.

Note 4 – Profit on disposal of shares

The profit on disposal of shares is in respect of the sale of Softapp Ltd's entire (2%) shareholding in Networked plc on 28 February 2017. The disposal resulted in a chargeable gain of £61,300. This figure is after taking account of indexation.

Note 5 – Interest payable

The interest payable is made up as follows:

(1)   £42,200 in respect of the company's 4% debenture loan stock. Interest of £21,100 was paid on 30 September 2016 and again on 31 March 2017. The loan stock was used to finance the company's trading activities.

(2)   £25,000 in respect of a loan to acquire the freehold office building. The building has five floors, one of which is let out (see Note 2).

Additional information

Plant and machinery

The tax written down value of Softapp Ltd's plant and machinery as at 1 April 2016 was £Nil.

During October 2016 Softapp Ltd had an extension constructed adjacent to its existing freehold office building, which is used by the company's employees as a staff room.

The total cost is made up as follows:

	£
Integral to the building	
Building costs of extension	61,000
Heating system	93,600
Ventilation system	75,600
Not integral to the building	
Furniture and furnishings	38,400
Refrigerator and microwave cooker	1,400
	270,000

The full annual investment allowance is available to Softapp Ltd.

Subsidiary company

Softapp Ltd owns 100% of the ordinary share capital of Byte-Size Ltd.

Required:

Calculate Softapp Ltd's corporation tax liability for the year ended 31 March 2017 and state the date it is due for payment. Assume that Softapp Ltd was not a large company in the previous accounting period.

Your computation should commence with the operating profit figure of £913,000.

(15 marks)

 Calculate your allowed time, allocate the time to the separate parts................

237 E-COMMERCE PLC (ADAPTED) *Walk in the footsteps of a top tutor*

You are a trainee Chartered Certified Accountant, and your firm has recently completed its audit of E-Commerce plc's financial statements for the year ended 31 March 2017. The company runs an internet-based retail business.

E-Commerce plc prepared its own corporation tax computations for the year ended 31 March 2017, and your colleague has completed your firm's tax audit of these figures.

E-Commerce plc's original corporation tax computation, along with references to your colleague's queries, is as follows.

E-Commerce plc – Corporation tax computation for the year ended 31 March 2017

	Queries	£
Operating profit	1	2,102,300
Deduction for lease premium	2	(14,400)
Capital allowances	3	(209,200)
Trading profit		1,878,700
Property income	4	156,700
Loan interest receivable	5	42,400
Taxable total profits		2,077,800
Corporation tax (£2,077,800 at 20%)		415,560

Your colleague has raised some queries in regard to E-Commerce plc's corporation tax computation. Apart from any corrections arising from your colleague's queries, the corporation tax computation prepared by E-Commerce plc does not contain any errors.

Query 1 – Legal fees

E-Commerce plc has treated all of the company's legal expenditure as allowable when calculating its operating profit. However, legal expenses include the following:

(1)   Legal fees of £80,200 in connection with an issue of £1 preference shares.

(2)   Legal fees of £92,800 in connection with the issue of loan notes. The loan was used to finance the company's trading activities.

(3)   Legal fees of £14,900 in connection with the renewal of a 99-year lease of property.

(4)   Legal fees of £4,700 in connection with an action brought against a supplier for breach of contract.

(5)   Legal fees of £8,800 in connection with the registration of trade marks.

Query 2 – Deduction for lease premium

The amount assessed on the landlord has been correctly calculated, but the life of the lease should be 15 years and not the 12 years used by E-Commerce plc. The lease commenced on 1 April 2016.

Query 3 – Capital allowances

There are two issues here:

(1)   E-Commerce plc purchased four motor cars during the year ended 31 March 2017, and all four motor cars have been included in the plant and machinery main pool. Details are as follows:

	Cost £	CO_2 emission rate
Motor car [1]	20,300	122 grams per kilometre
Motor car [2]	24,900	114 grams per kilometre
Motor car [3]	62,100	245 grams per kilometre
Motor car [4]	19,800	73 grams per kilometre

(2)   Four years ago, E-Commerce plc purchased computer equipment on which a short-life asset election has been made. For the year ended 31 March 2017, the writing down allowance claimed on this equipment was £1,512, calculated at the rate of 18%. However, the computer equipment was actually scrapped, with nil proceeds, on 10 December 2016.

Query 4 – Property income

There are two issues here:

(1)   E-Commerce plc has claimed a deduction for repairs of £95,300 in respect of a warehouse which was purchased on 21 May 2016. The warehouse was purchased in a dilapidated state, and could not be let until the repairs were carried out. This fact was represented by a reduced purchase price.

(2)   E-Commerce plc did not receive the rent due of £16,200 in respect of this warehouse for the quarter ended 31 May 2017 until 1 April 2017. None of this amount has been taken into account in calculating the property business profit for the year ended 31 March 2017.

Query 5 – Loan interest receivable

The accrual at 31 March 2017 has been calculated at £4,800, but because of falling interest rates the accrual should actually be £3,500.

Other information

For the year ended 31 March 2016, E-Commerce plc had augmented profits of £1,360,000, and has forecast that its augmented profits for the year ended 31 March 2018 will exceed £2,000,000.

E-Commerce plc does not have any related 51% group companies.

Required:

(a)   Prepare a revised version of E-Commerce plc's corporation tax computation for the year ended 31 March 2017 after making any necessary corrections arising from your colleague's queries.

Note: Your calculations should commence with the operating profit figure of £2,102,300, and you should indicate by the use of zero (0) any items referred to in queries (1) to (5) which do not require adjustment.   (12 marks)

(b)   Explain why E-Commerce plc will not have been required to make quarterly instalment payments in respect of its corporation tax liability for the year ended 31 March 2017, but will have to do so for the year ended 31 March 2018.   (3 marks)

(Total: 15 marks)

238 LUCKY LTD *Walk in the footsteps of a top tutor*

Lucky Ltd was incorporated on 20 July 2016, and commenced trading on 1 December 2016. The following information is available for the four-month period 1 December 2016 to 31 March 2017:

(1) The operating profit for the four month period ended 31 March 2017 is £532,600. Advertising expenditure of £4,700 (incurred during September 2016), depreciation of £14,700, and amortisation of £9,000 have been deducted in arriving at this figure.

The amortisation relates to a premium which was paid on 1 December 2016 to acquire a leasehold warehouse on a 12-year lease. The amount of premium assessed on the landlord as income was £46,800. The warehouse was used for business purposes by Lucky Ltd throughout the period ended 31 March 2017.

(2) Lucky Ltd purchased the following assets during the period 20 July 2016 to 31 March 2017:

		£
19 August 2016	Computer	6,300
22 January 2017	Integral features	41,200
31 January 2017	Office equipment	32,900
17 March 2017	Motor car	12,800

The integral features of £41,200 are in respect of expenditure on electrical systems, a ventilation system and lifts which are integral to a freehold office building owned by Lucky Ltd.

The motor car has a CO_2 emission rate of 72 grams per kilometre.

(3) Lucky Ltd made a loan to another company for non-trading purposes on 1 February 2017. Loan interest income of £700 was accrued at 31 March 2017.

Required:

(a) State when an accounting period starts for corporation tax purposes. **(2 marks)**

(b) Calculate Lucky Ltd's corporation tax liability for the four month period ended 31 March 2017.

Note: Your computation should commence with the operating profit of £532,600, and should also indicate by the use of zero (0) any items referred to in the question for which no adjustment is required. **(11 marks)**

(c) Advise Lucky Ltd as to how long it must retain the records used in preparing its self-assessment corporation tax return for the four month period ended 31 March 2017, and the potential consequences of not retaining the records for the required period. **(2 marks)**

(Total: 15 marks)

RELIEF FOR TRADING LOSSES

239   HALF-LIFE LTD (ADAPTED)

Half-Life Ltd commenced trading on 1 April 2013 and ceased trading on 30 June 2017.

The company's results for all its periods of trading are as follows:

	y/e 31.3.14	y/e 31.3.15	y/e 31.3.16	p/e 30.6.16	y/e 30.6.17
	£	£	£	£	£
Tax adjusted profit/(loss)	224,000	67,400	38,200	(61,700)	(308,800)
Property income	8,200	12,200	6,500	4,400	0
Chargeable gains	0	0	5,600	0	23,700
Qualifying charitable donations	(1,200)	(1,000)	0	0	(700)

Required:

(a)   Assuming that Half-Life Ltd claims the maximum possible relief for its trading losses, calculate the company's taxable total profits for the years ended 31 March 2014, 2015 and 2016, the period ended 30 June 2016, and the year ended 30 June 2017.

Your answer should clearly identify the amounts of any losses and qualifying charitable donations that are unrelieved.   **(9 marks)**

(b)   State the dates by which Half-Life Ltd must make the loss relief claims in part (a).
                                                                                (2 marks)

(c)   Calculate the amount of corporation tax that will be repaid to Half-Life Ltd as a result of making the loss relief claims in part (a).

Assume that the corporation tax rate for FY 2016 applies throughout.   **(4 marks)**

                                                                        (Total: 15 marks)

240   VOLATILE LTD (ADAPTED)   *Walk in the footsteps of a top tutor*

Volatile Ltd commenced trading on 1 January 2012. The company's recent results are:

	y/e 31 Dec 2014	p/e 30 Sept 2015	y/e 30 Sept 2016
	£	£	£
Trading profit/(loss)	15,200	78,700	(101,800)
Property business profit	6,500	0	0
Chargeable gain/(loss)	0	(2,000)	11,700
Qualifying charitable donations	(1,200)	(1,000)	(800)

Required:

(a) State the factors that will influence a company's choice of loss relief claims.

You are not expected to consider group relief. **(2 marks)**

(b) Assuming that Volatile Ltd claims relief for its trading losses as early as possible, calculate the company's taxable total profits for the year ended 31 December 2014, nine month period ended 30 September 2015, and year ended 30 September 2016.

Your answer should also clearly identify the amount of any unrelieved trading losses as at 30 September 2016. **(8 marks)**

(Total: 10 marks)

241   RETRO LTD   *Walk in the footsteps of a top tutor*

Retro Ltd's summarised statement of profit or loss for the year ended 31 March 2017 is as follows:

	Note	£	£
Gross profit			127,100
Operating expenses			
Depreciation		27,240	
Gifts and donations	1	2,300	
Impairment loss	2	1,600	
Leasing costs	3	4,400	
Other expenses	4	205,160	
		———	(240,700)
Finance costs			
Interest payable	5		(6,400)
			———
Loss before taxation			(120,000)
			———

Note 1 – Gifts and donations

Gifts and donations are as follows:

	£
Gifts to employees (food hampers costing £60 each)	720
Gifts to customers (calendars costing £8 each and displaying Retro Ltd's name)	480
Political donations	420
Qualifying charitable donations	680
	———
	2,300
	———

Note 2 – Impairment loss

On 31 March 2017, Retro Ltd wrote off an impairment loss of £1,600 relating to a trade debt. This was in respect of an invoice which had been due for payment on 10 November 2016.

Note 3 – Leasing costs

The leasing costs of £4,400 are in respect of a motor car lease which commenced on 1 April 2016. The leased motor car has CO_2 emissions of 145 grams per kilometre.

Note 4 – Other expenses

The figure of £205,160 for other expenses includes a fine of £5,100 for a breach of health and safety regulations, and legal fees of £4,860 in connection with the defence of Retro Ltd's internet domain name. The remaining expenses are all fully allowable.

Note 5 – Interest payable

The interest payable is in respect of the company's 5% loan notes which were repaid on 31 July 2016. Interest of £9,600 was paid on 31 July 2016, and an accrual of £3,200 had been provided for at 1 April 2016. The loan notes were issued in order to finance the company's trading activities.

Additional information

Plant and machinery

On 1 April 2016, the tax written down value of the plant and machinery main pool was £39,300.

The following vehicles were purchased during the year ended 31 March 2017:

	Date of purchase	Cost	CO_2 emission rate
		£	
Motor car (1)	8 June 2016	14,700	124 grams per kilometre
Delivery van	3 August 2016	28,300	162 grams per kilometre
Motor car (2)	19 October 2016	12,400	74 grams per kilometre

Previous results

Retro Ltd commenced trading on 1 September 2014. The company's results for its two previous periods of trading are as follows:

	Year ended 31 August 2015	Period ended 31 March 2016
	£	£
Tax adjusted trading profit	56,600	47,900
Bank interest receivable	1,300	0
Qualifying charitable donations paid	(540)	(330)

Future results

Retro Ltd is expected to return to profitability in the year ended 31 March 2018 and to continue to be profitable in subsequent years.

Required:

(a)   Calculate Retro Ltd's tax adjusted trading loss for the year ended 31 March 2017.

Your computation should commence with the loss before taxation figure of £120,000, and should also list all of the items referred to in notes (1) to (5), indicating by the use of zero (0) any items which do not require adjustment.

(9 marks)

(b)   Assuming that Retro Ltd claims relief for its trading loss as early as possible, calculate the company's taxable total profits for the year ended 31 August 2015 and for the seven-month period ended 31 March 2016.   (4 marks)

(c)   Identify the amount of unrelieved trading loss which Retro Ltd will have at 31 March 2017, and state how this can be relieved.   (2 marks)

(Total: 15 marks)

WITH GROUP ASPECTS

242   MUSIC PLC (ADAPTED)

Music plc is the holding company for a group of companies. The group structure is as follows:

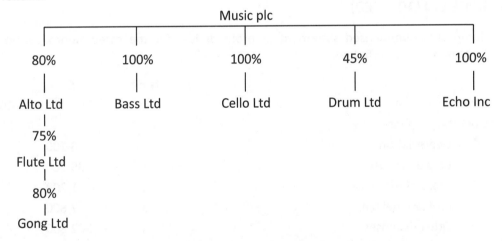

Music plc's shareholding in Bass Ltd was disposed of on 31 December 2016, and the shareholding in Cello Ltd was acquired on 1 January 2017. The other shareholdings were all held throughout the year ended 31 March 2017.

Echo Inc is resident overseas. The other companies are all resident in the United Kingdom.

For the year ended 31 March 2017 Music plc had a tax adjusted trading profit of £92,000. During the year Music plc received dividend income of £15,000 from an unconnected company, bank interest of £12,000 and a dividend of £5,400 from Bass Ltd.

As at 31 March 2016 Music plc had unused capital losses of £32,000. On 5 January 2017 the company sold a freehold office building, and this resulted in a further capital loss of £65,000.

Alto Ltd sold a freehold warehouse on 10 March 2017, and this resulted in a capital gain of £120,000. An election has been made so that the gain is treated as Music plc's gain.

Year ending 31 March 2018

Music plc is considering acquiring a property which it will rent out for £10,000 per annum. The company will take out a new non-trade related bank loan of £100,000 at a 10% interest rate to partly fund the acquisition. Legal fees in connection with acquiring the property will be £300.

Required:

(a) State, giving appropriate reasons, which companies in the Music plc group of companies form a group for capital gains purposes. **(5 marks)**

(b) Explain why Music plc has five related 51% group companies.

Your answer should identify the five related companies. **(5 marks)**

(c) Calculate Music plc's corporation tax liability for the year ended 31 March 2017. **(2 marks)**

(d) Explain how the interest costs, legal fees and rent receivable will be treated for tax purposes if Music plc acquires a property in the year ended 31 March 2018. **(3 marks)**

(Total: 15 marks)

243 JUMP LTD (ADAPTED)

Jump Ltd's summarised statement of profit or loss for the three-month period ended 31 March 2017 is as follows:

	Note	£	£
Revenue			264,900
Operating expenses			
Depreciation		8,100	
Employee costs	1	189,700	
Lease of motor car	2	1,200	
Professional fees	3	7,800	
Other expenses	4	202,800	
			(409,600)
Operating loss			(144,700)
Bank interest receivable			0
Loss before taxation			(144,700)

Note 1 – Employee costs

Employee costs are as follows:

	£
Employee training courses	3,400
Employee pension contributions paid	11,600
Cost of annual staff party (for eight employees)	1,500
Balance of expenditure (all allowable)	173,200
	189,700

Note 2 – Lease of motor car

The lease is in respect of a motor car with CO_2 emissions of 189 grams per kilometre.

Note 3 – Professional fees

Professional fees are as follows:

	£
Accountancy	2,200
Legal fees in connection with the issue of share capital	3,800
Legal fees in connection with the renewal of a 20-year property lease	1,800
	7,800

Note 4 – Other expenses

Other expenses are as follows:

	£
Entertaining UK customers	1,700
Entertaining overseas customers	790
Political donations	800
Balance of expenditure (all allowable)	199,510
	202,800

Additional information

Plant and machinery

On 1 January 2017, the tax written down values of Jump Ltd's plant and machinery were as follows:

	£
Main pool	12,100
Special rate pool	5,700

The following motor cars were sold during the three-month period ended 31 March 2017:

	Date of sale	Proceeds	Original cost
		£	£
Motor car [1]	7 January 2017	9,700	9,300
Motor car [2]	29 March 2017	6,100	13,200

The original cost of motor car [1] was added to the special rate pool when it was purchased, and the original cost of motor car [2] was added to the main pool when it was purchased.

Previous results

Jump Ltd's results for its two previous periods of trading are as follows:

	Year ended 31 May 2016	Period ended 31 December 2016
	£	£
Tax adjusted trading profit	78,600	42,400
Bank interest receivable	1,200	0

Group companies

Jump Ltd owns 80% of the ordinary share capital of Hop Ltd and 60% of the ordinary share capital of Skip Ltd.

Hop Ltd commenced trading on 1 August 2016, and for the eight-month period ended 31 March 2017 has taxable total profits of £63,000.

Skip Ltd has been trading for several years and has taxable total profits of £56,000 for the year ended 31 March 2017.

Required:

(a)　Calculate Jump Ltd's tax adjusted trading loss for the three-month period ended 31 March 2017.

　　Notes:

　　1　Your computation should commence with the operating loss figure of £144,700, and should list all of the items referred to in notes (1) to (4), indicating by the use of zero (0) any items which do not require adjustment.

　　2　You should assume that the company claims the maximum available capital allowances. **(10 marks)**

(b)　(1)　State the main factor which will influence Jump Ltd's choice of loss relief or group relief claims. **(1 mark)**

　　(2)　Advise Jump Ltd as to the maximum amount of its trading loss which can be relieved against its total profits for the year ended 31 May 2016 and the seven-month period ended 31 December 2016. **(2 marks)**

　　(3)　Advise Jump Ltd as to the maximum amount of its trading loss which can be surrendered as group relief. **(2 marks)**

(Total: 15 marks)

244   NEUNG LTD (ADAPTED) *Walk in the footsteps of a top tutor*

Neung Ltd is a UK resident company that runs a business providing financial services. The company's summarised statement of profit or loss for the year ended 31 March 2017 is:

	Notes	£
Operating profit	1	727,300
Income from investments		
Loan interest	2	37,800
Dividends	3	54,000
		————
Profit before taxation		819,100
		————

Note 1 – Operating profit

Depreciation of £11,830 and amortisation of leasehold property of £7,000 have been deducted in arriving at the operating profit of £727,300.

Note 2 – Loan interest receivable

The loan was made for non-trading purposes on 1 July 2016. Loan interest of £25,200 was received on 31 December 2016, and interest of £12,600 was accrued at 31 March 2017.

Note 3 – Dividends received

Neung Ltd has held shares in four UK resident companies for a number of years as follows:

	Percentage shareholding	Status
Second Ltd	25%	Trading
Third Ltd	60%	Trading
Fourth Ltd	100%	Dormant
Fifth Ltd	100%	Trading

During the year ended 31 March 2017 Neung Ltd received a dividend of £42,000 from Second Ltd, and a dividend of £12,000 from Third Ltd.

Fifth Ltd made a trading loss of £15,700 for the year ended 31 March 2017.

Additional information

Leasehold property

On 1 April 2016 Neung Ltd acquired a leasehold office building, paying a premium of £140,000 for the grant of a 20-year lease. The office building was used for business purposes by Neung Ltd throughout the year ended 31 March 2017.

Plant and machinery

On 1 April 2016 the tax written down values of Neung Ltd's plant and machinery were:

	£
Main pool	4,800
Short life asset	22,800
Special rate pool	12,700

The company purchased the following assets during the year ended 31 March 2017:

		£
19 July 2016	Motor car [1]	15,400
12 December 2016	Motor car [2]	28,600
20 December 2016	Ventilation system	262,000

The short life asset is a specialised piece of machinery which was purchased on 1 January 2016. Motor car [1] purchased on 19 July 2016 has a CO_2 emission rate of 212 grams per kilometre. Motor car [2] purchased on 12 December 2016 has a CO_2 emission rate of 118 grams per kilometre.

The ventilation system purchased on 20 December 2016 for £262,000 is integral to the freehold office building in which it was installed.

Year ended 31 March 2016

For the year ended 31 March 2016 Neung Ltd had taxable total profits of £600,000.

Required:

(a)   Calculate Neung Ltd's corporation tax liability for the year ended 31 March 2017.

You should assume that the whole of the annual investment allowance is available to Neung Ltd, that the company wishes to maximise its capital allowances claim, and that any favourable claims are made in respect of group losses.   **(11 marks)**

(b)   Explain, with supporting date(s) and amount(s), when Neung Ltd will be required to pay its corporation tax liability for the year ended 31 March 2017.   **(4 marks)**

(Total: 15 marks)

245   CLUELESS LTD (ADAPTED) *Walk in the footsteps of a top tutor*

(a)   You are a trainee accountant and your manager has asked you to correct a corporation tax computation that has been prepared by the managing director of Clueless Ltd, a company which manufactures children's board games.

The corporation tax computation is for the year ended 31 March 2017 and contains a significant number of errors:

Clueless Ltd – Corporation tax computation for the year ended 31 March 2017

	£
Trading profit (working 1)	453,782
Loan interest received (working 2)	32,100
Chargeable gain (working 3)	50,000
	———
	535,882
Dividends received (working 4)	28,700
	———
	564,582
	———
Corporation tax (£564,582 × 20%)	112,916
	———

Working 1 – Trading profit

	£
Profit before taxation	382,610
Depreciation	15,740
Donations to political parties	400
Qualifying charitable donations paid	900
Gifts to customers	
pens costing £40 each and displaying Clueless Ltd's name	920
food hampers costing £45 each and displaying Clueless Ltd's name	1,650
Capital allowances (working 5)	51,562
	———
Trading profit	453,782
	———

Working 2 – Loan interest received

	£
Loan interest receivable	32,800
Accrued at 1 April 2016	10,600
Accrued at 31 March 2017	(11,300)
	———
Loan interest received	32,100
	———

The loan was made for non-trading purposes.

Working 3 – Chargeable gain

The gain relates to the sale of a building to an unconnected party for £200,000 on 1 March 2017. The office had been acquired by Clever Ltd (a 100% UK subsidiary) for £70,000 on 1 April 2001. Clever Ltd had sold the building to Clueless Ltd on 1 June 2009 for £150,000, which was its market value at that date.

Working 4 – Dividends received

	£
From unrelated companies	20,700
From Clever Ltd (a 100% UK subsidiary company)	8,000
	———
Dividends received	28,700
	———

Working 5 – Capital allowances

	Main pool	Motor car	Special rate pool	Allowances
	£	£	£	£
TWDV brought forward	12,400		13,500	
Additions				
Machinery	42,300			
Motor car		11,800		
	———			
	54,700			
Annual investment allowance	(54,700)			54,700
Disposal proceeds			(9,300)	
			———	
			4,200	
Balancing allowance			(4,200)	(4,200)
			———	
WDA (18%)		(2,124) × 50%		1,062
	———	———		
TWDV carried forward	0	9,676		
	———	———		———
Total allowances				51,562
				———

Notes:

(1) The motor car has a CO_2 emission rate of 145 grams per kilometre. This motor car is used by the sales manager and 50% of the mileage is for private journeys.

(2) All of the items included in the special rate pool at 1 April 2016 were sold for £9,300 during the year ended 31 March 2017. The original cost of these items was £16,200.

Required:

(a) Prepare a corrected version of Clueless Ltd's corporation tax computation for the year ended 31 March 2017.

You should indicate by the use of zero any items in the computation of the trading profit for which no adjustment is required.

The RPI for March 2017 is 265.9, for June 2009 it is 213.4 and for April 2001 it is 173.1. (11 marks)

(b)   The managing director of Clueless Ltd understands that the company has to file its self-assessment corporation tax returns online, and that the supporting accounts and tax computations have to be filed using the inline eXtensible Business Reporting Language (iXBRL). The managing director is interested in the options regarding how the company can produce documents in this format.

Required:

(1)   State the date by which Clueless Ltd's self-assessment corporation tax return for the year ended 31 March 2017 should be filed.   (1 mark)

(2)   Explain the options available to Clueless Ltd regarding the production of accounts and tax computations in the iXBRL format.   (3 marks)

(Total: 15 marks)

246   LONG LTD AND ROAD LTD (ADAPTED)   *Walk in the footsteps of a top tutor*

(a)   Long Ltd owns 100% of the ordinary share capital of Road Ltd. Long Ltd and Road Ltd are both trading companies.

Long Ltd's shareholding in Road Ltd was acquired on 15 January 2016 when that company was incorporated. Long Ltd has prepared accounts for the year ended 31 March 2017, whilst Road Ltd has prepared accounts for the period 1 January 2017 (when the company commenced trading) to 31 March 2017.

The following information is available:

Long Ltd

(1)   The operating profit for the year ended 31 March 2017 is £384,400. Depreciation of £43,050, amortisation of £5,000 and leasing costs of £3,600 have been deducted in arriving at this figure. The amortisation relates to a premium which was paid on 1 August 2012 to acquire a leasehold office building on a 20-year lease. The amount of premium assessed on the landlord as income was £68,200. The office building was used for business purposes by Long Ltd throughout the year ended 31 March 2017. The leasing costs relate to a motor car with a CO_2 emission rate of 142 grams per kilometre, which was leased from 1 April 2016.

(2)   On 1 April 2016, the tax written down value of the plant and machinery main pool was £44,800. On 10 June 2016, Long Ltd purchased a lorry for £36,800 and a motor car for £15,700. The motor car has a CO_2 emission rate of 122 grams per kilometre. The motor car is used by the managing director of Long Ltd, and 40% of the mileage is for private journeys.

(3)   On 1 February 2017, Long Ltd disposed of a 2% shareholding in an unconnected company. The disposal resulted in a capital loss of £21,300.

Road Ltd

(1)   The operating loss for the three-month period ended 31 March 2017 is £26,100. Donations of £2,800 have been deducted in arriving at this figure. The donations consist of political donations of £400, and qualifying charitable donations of £2,400.

(2) On 3 October 2016, Road Ltd purchased a motor car for £11,600. The motor car has a CO_2 emission rate of 75 grams per kilometre.

(3) For the three-month period ended 31 March 2017, loan interest receivable was £4,300. The loan was made for non-trading purposes.

(4) On 18 March 2017, Road Ltd disposed of a 1% shareholding in an unrelated company. The disposal resulted in a chargeable gain of £29,800. This figure is after taking account of indexation.

Other information

Road Ltd is not expected to be profitable for the foreseeable future, and Long Ltd and Road Ltd claim maximum possible group relief where group relief is available.

Required:

On the assumption that any available reliefs are claimed as soon as possible, calculate the corporation tax liability of Long Ltd for the year ended 31 March 2017, and of Road Ltd for the three-month period ended 31 March 2017. **(12 marks)**

(b) Road Ltd's recently appointed bookkeeper understands that the company must report PAYE information to HM Revenue and Customs in real time. However, the bookkeeper does not know how PAYE real time reporting works in practice, having previously only produced payroll manually.

Road Ltd pays its employees at the end of each calendar month, with some employees receiving taxable benefits. Road Ltd has chosen not to tax the benefits through the payroll system.

Required:

Explain how and when Road Ltd will have to report real time PAYE information to HM Revenue and Customs, and state what forms, if any, will have to be provided to employees or submitted to HM Revenue and Customs following the end of the tax year. **(3 marks)**

(Total: 15 marks)

Section 5

PRACTICE VALUE ADDED TAX QUESTIONS

PRACTICE SECTION A OBJECTIVE TEST QUESTIONS

247 Fred began a trading as a sole trader on 1 January 2017 but did not register for VAT when he commenced to trade. He has made the following sales, all of which are standard rated:

	£
January 2017	2,000
February 2017	3,500
March 2017	4,000
April 2017	3,200
May 2017	1,400
June 2017	90,000
July 2017	5,000
August 2017	4,000

All of the sales in June 2017 relate to an order which was received on 1 June 2017 for goods to be delivered by 30 June 2017.

When must Fred start charging VAT to his customers?

A   1 June 2017

B   1 July 2017

C   30 June 2017

D   1 August 2017

248 Layla started trading on 4 January 2016.

Taxable supplies for 2016 are as follows:

3 months to 31 March	£3,000 per month
3 months to 30 June	£9,000 per month
3 months to 30 September	£30,000 per month
3 months to 31 December	£50,000 per month

What is the effective date of registration for VAT, assuming that Layla waits until her turnover exceeds the registration limit before registering?

A   1 February 2017

B   1 October 2016

C   1 July 2016

D   1 September 2016

249 Betty, a retailer, decides to voluntarily register for VAT.

Which TWO of the following statements, concerning supplies made to Betty before the date of VAT registration, are TRUE?

A   Betty can reclaim input VAT on a car that she purchased six months ago, which she still uses for both private and business purposes

B   Betty cannot reclaim input VAT on the petrol used in her car, for both private and business purposes, in the month prior to the date of VAT registration

C   Betty can reclaim input VAT on a van purchased for the business two years ago which she still uses in the business

D   Betty can reclaim input VAT on accountancy services she purchased one year ago in connection with setting up the business

E   Betty can reclaim input VAT on the cost of goods bought for resale two months ago, which she sold the week before registration

250 *September 2015 OT question*

Yui commenced trading on 1 April 2016, and registered for value added tax (VAT) from 1 January 2017. Her first VAT return is for the quarter ended 31 March 2017. During the period 1 April 2016 to 31 March 2017, Yui incurred input VAT of £110 per month in respect of the hire of office equipment.

How much input VAT in respect of the office equipment can Yui reclaim on her VAT return for the quarter ended 31 March 2017?

A   £660

B   £990

C   £330

D   £1,320

251 Fergus owns shares in a number of companies as set out below.

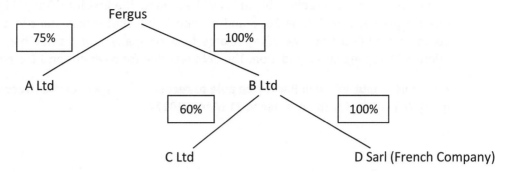

D Sarl's only place of business is in France.

Which of the above companies can be in a VAT group?

	Can be in VAT group
A Ltd	
B Ltd	
C Ltd	
D Sarl	

252 Vikram ceased trading on 17 June 2016.

By what date should he have notified HM Revenue & Customs that he had ceased to make taxable supplies?

A   17 June 2016

B   16 July 2016

C   30 July 2016

D   30 June 2016

253 Padma Ltd received an order for goods on 20 October 2016. The goods were delivered to the customer on 20 December 2016 and Padma Ltd sent the invoice for £1,000 on 15 January 2017, which the customer paid on 5 February 2017.

What is the tax point of the transaction for VAT?

A   20 October 2016

B   20 December 2016

C   15 January 2017

D   5 February 2017

254 Barney is VAT registered and only makes standard rated supplies. On 31 March 2017 he wrote off two irrecoverable debts in his VAT account. The first for £800 (VAT inclusive) was due for payment on 1 June 2016 and despite being chased has still not been paid. The second for £1,000 (VAT inclusive) relates to a company that Barney has recently been informed has gone into liquidation. The debt was due for payment on 1 December 2016.

How much input VAT will Barney be able to recover, in respect of the irrecoverable debts, in his VAT return for the quarter to 31 March 2017?

A   £160

B   £360

C   £300

D   £133

255 *June 2015 OT question*

Violet Ltd provides one of its directors with a company motor car which is used for both business and private mileage. For the quarter ended 31 March 2017, the total cost of petrol for the car was £600, of which 30% was for private use by the director. The relevant quarterly scale charge is £314. Both these figures are inclusive of value added tax (VAT).

What output VAT and input VAT entries will Violet Ltd include on its VAT return for the quarter ended 31 March 2017 in respect of the company motor car?

A   Output VAT of £52 and input VAT of £70

B   Output VAT of £0 and input VAT of £70

C   Output VAT of £0 and input VAT of £100

D   Output VAT of £52 and input VAT of £100

256 West Ltd is registered for VAT and makes standard rated supplies.

The company incurs the following costs:

(1)   £650 (VAT inclusive) on entertaining new suppliers based in France

(2)   £3,000 (VAT inclusive) on car leasing costs. The car has CO_2 emission of 120 g/km and is used by a director for both private (20% of the time) and business purposes.

How much input VAT can the company recover on the above costs?

A   £358

B   £250

C   £108

D   £608

257 Tobias is VAT registered and only makes standard rated supplies.

In the quarter to 31 March 2017 he had the following transactions:

(1)   Sales of £30,000 and purchases of goods for resale of £16,800. Both figures are VAT inclusive.

(2)   He gave samples of his products to a potential customer which he would normally sell for £100 (VAT exclusive).

How much VAT is payable by Tobias for the quarter ended 31 March 2017?

A   £2,640

B   £2,220

C   £2,660

D   £2,200

258 Blessing is VAT registered.

In the quarter to 31 March 2017 Blessing's accounts include the total cost of fuel for her car, which she uses 20% for private purposes, of £1,200 (VAT inclusive). The relevant VAT scale charge for the car is £408.

How much input VAT is reclaimable by Blessing, after adjusting for any output tax due, for the quarter ended 31 March 2017 in respect of the fuel for her car?

A   £200

B   £158

C   £132

D   £160

259 A less detailed VAT invoice can be provided when the consideration for the supply is less than how much?

A   £100

B   £200

C   £250

D   £500

260 Which of the following is not required on a less detailed VAT invoice?

A   Date of supply

B   Description of goods and services

C   Rate of VAT in force at time

D   Amount of VAT payable

261 Having always filed VAT returns on time, Chimney Ltd's VAT return for the quarter ended 31 October 2016 was submitted on 13 December 2016 along with the VAT due. For the quarter ended 31 January 2017 the return and VAT of £26,000 was filed on 23 March 2017.

What are the VAT consequences when the 31 January 2017 VAT return is filed late?

A   A surcharge liability period will run for the 12 months until 31 January 2018 but no penalty will be charged

B   A surcharge liability period will run for the 12 months until 31 January 2018 and a penalty of £520 will be charged

C   A surcharge liability period will run for the 12 months until 23 March 2017 but no penalty will be charged

D   A surcharge liability period will run for the 12 months until 23 March 2017 and a penalty of £520 will be charged

262 For the VAT quarter ended 30 June 2016 Beach Ltd has a taxable turnover of £380,000. It subsequently finds it has under-declared output tax of £8,000 on its VAT return for that quarter.

What of the following statements is correct?

A   Beach Ltd can correct the error on the next VAT return and will be charged a penalty for an incorrect VAT return only

B   Beach Ltd can correct the error on the next VAT return and will be charged a penalty for an incorrect return and default interest

C   Beach Ltd must separately notify HM Revenue & Customs of the error and will be charged a penalty for an incorrect return only

D   Beach Ltd must separately notify HM Revenue & Customs of the error and will be charged a penalty for an incorrect return and default interest

263 **For each of the following statements concerning the VAT cash accounting scheme select whether it is true or false:**

	True	False
Input tax cannot be claimed until the invoice is paid which delays recovery of input VAT		
Traders using the scheme do not have to pay output VAT to HMRC until they receive it from customers		
To join the scheme the trader's expected taxable turnover (excluding VAT) for the next twelve months must not exceed £150,000		
The cash accounting scheme cannot be used where a trader issues an invoice in advance of supplying goods		

264 Jano operates the annual accounting scheme. In the year ended 30 September 2015 he had a VAT liability of £3,600. In his year ended 30 September 2016 he estimated his VAT liability to be £4,115.

What is the amount of his balancing payment for the VAT year to 30 September 2016?

A   £875

B   £515

C   £411

D   £0

265 *Specimen paper June 2015 OT question*

For the quarter ended 31 March 2017, Zim had standard rated sales of £59,700 and standard rated expenses of £27,300. Both figures are inclusive of value added tax (VAT). Zim uses the flat rate scheme to calculate the amount of VAT payable, with the relevant scheme percentage for her trade being 12%.

How much VAT will Zim have to pay to HM Revenue and Customs (HMRC) for the quarter ended 31 March 2017?

A   £6,396

B   £3,888

C   £6,480

D   £7,164

266 Petr has standard rated sales of £80,000 excluding VAT, zero rated sales of £15,000 and exempt sales of £10,000 for the quarter ended 30 June 2016. He has standard rated expenses including VAT of £8,400. Petr uses the flat rate scheme for VAT and the flat rate for his business is 13%.

What is Petr's VAT liability for the quarter ended 30 June 2016?

A   £11,388

B   £13,650

C   £14,638

D   £15,730

267 A UK VAT registered trader making only standard rated supplies purchased goods worth £10,000 (VAT exclusive) from a VAT registered trader situated elsewhere within the European Union. The goods would be classed as standard rated if they were supplied in the UK. The standard rate in the EU country the good are supplied from is 5%.

What is the net effect on the VAT position of the UK trader?

A   £0

B   £2,000 to pay to HM Revenue & Customs

C   £2,000 to reclaim from HM Revenue & Customs

D   £500 to pay to HM Revenue & Customs

PRACTICE SECTION B OBJECTIVE TEST CASES

268 CANDY APPLE AND SUGAR PLUM (ADAPTED) *Walk in the footsteps of a top tutor*

 Timed question with Online tutor debrief

Candy Apple

Candy Apple began a trading business on 1 April 2016. Her sales since the commencement of trading have been as follows:

April to July 2016	£10,500 per month
August to November 2016	£14,000 per month
December 2016 to March 2017	£21,500 per month

These figures are stated exclusive of value added tax (VAT). Candy's sales are all standard rated and arise evenly over the month.

As her accountant you have advised Candy in writing that she should be registered for VAT, but she has refused to register because she thinks her net profit is insufficient to cover the additional cost which would be incurred.

Sugar Plum

Sugar Plum began trading on 1 April 2016 and registered for VAT on 1 May 2016 to avoid late registration penalties. The following information is available in respect of Sugar Plum's VAT for the quarter ended 31 July 2016:

(1) Invoices were issued for standard rated and zero rated sales of £53,700 and £23,100 respectively. These figures are exclusive of VAT.

(2) Sugar uses a room at her home as her office. The house has seven main rooms. The VAT charged on the electricity bill for the whole house for the quarter is estimated as £49.

During the quarter, Sugar also purchased several items of furniture for her office for a total of £1,500 exclusive of VAT. A 5% discount was applied to this amount as Sugar had purchased two items or more.

(3) Prior to starting business, Sugar engaged a consultancy firm to undertake some market research. Sugar paid the consultancy firm £250 on 1 August 2015 and £375 on 1 January 2016. Sugar also purchased £2,500 worth of inventory on 1 January 2016, of which £1,000 was unsold by 1 May 2016. These figures are exclusive of VAT.

1   **From what date was Candy Apple compulsorily required to charge VAT on her taxable supplies?**

   A   1 December 2016

   B   1 November 2016

   C   31 October 2016

   D   30 October 2016

2   **Which of the following is/are a consequence of late VAT registration?**

   (1)   A default surcharge penalty will be charged for late registration

   (2)   Candy must account to HM Revenue and Customs for output tax at 20/120 of the value of sales from the date that she should have been registered from

   (3)   Candy must issue VAT invoices charging her customers the VAT that she should have charged on sales from the date she should have been registered by

   A   (1) only

   B   (1) and (3)

   C   (2) only

   D   (2) and (3)

3   **What is the amount of output VAT payable by Sugar Plum in respect of her sales for the quarter ended 31 July 2016?**

   A   £15,360

   B   £10,740

   C   £4,620

   D   £8,950

4   **What is the amount of input VAT claimable by Sugar in respect of the electricity and furniture costs for the quarter ended 31 July 2016?**

   A   £292

   B   £334

   C   £245

   D   £307

5   **What is the amount of input VAT claimable by Sugar in respect of the consultancy fees and inventory costs incurred prior to the commencement of trade?**

   A   £625

   B   £200

   C   £325

   D   £275

 Calculate your allowed time, allocate the time to the separate parts.................

269 LITHOGRAPH LTD (ADAPTED)

Lithograph Ltd runs a printing business, and is registered for VAT. Because its annual taxable turnover is only £250,000, the company uses the annual accounting scheme so that it only has to prepare one VAT return each year. The annual VAT period is the year ended 31 March. Unless stated otherwise all of the figures below are exclusive of VAT.

Year ended 31 March 2016

The results for the year ended 31 March 2016 include the following:

(1)   Standard rated expenses of £28,000. This includes £3,600 for entertaining overseas customers.

(2)   On 1 May 2015 Lithograph Ltd purchased a motor car costing £18,400 for the use of its managing director. The manager director is provided with free petrol for private mileage, and the cost of this petrol is included in the standard rated expenses in Note (1). The car has CO_2 emissions of 200 g/km and the relevant annual scale charge is £1,608. Both figures are inclusive of VAT.

(3)   During the year ended 31 March 2016 Lithograph Ltd purchased machinery for £24,000, and sold office equipment for £8,000. Input VAT had been claimed when the office equipment was originally purchased.

Year ended 31 March 2017

In the year ended 31 March 2017 Lithograph Ltd wrote off two debts which were due from customers. The first debt of £4,800 was in respect of an invoice that was due for payment on 31 August 2016. The second debt of £6,400 was in respect of an invoice that was due for payment on 12 October 2016. Both these figures are VAT inclusive.

1   **How many payments on account (POA) of VAT would Lithograph Ltd have been required to pay in respect of the year ended 31 March 2016 and in which months would they have been payable?**

	Number of POAs	Months payable
A	9	April 2015 to December 2015
B	4	April, July, and October 2015 and January 2016
C	9	July 2015 to March 2016
D	4	July, August and November 2015, February 2016

2   **By reference to which VAT liability were the payments on account for the year ended 31 March 2016 calculated and by when must the annual VAT return for the year ended 31 March 2016 be submitted to HM Revenue and Customs?**

	VAT liability	Due date for return
A	Estimated for year ended 31 March 2016	7 May 2016
B	Actual for year ended 31 March 2015	30 May 2016
C	Estimated for year ended 31 March 2016	30 May 2016
D	Actual for year ended 31 March 2015	7 May 2016

3   **How much output tax is payable by Lithograph Ltd in respect of the items (1) – (3) included in the results for the year ended 31 March 2016?**

   A   £1,868

   B   £322

   C   £1,922

   D   £268

4   **How much input tax is reclaimable by Lithograph Ltd in respect of the items (1) – (3) included in the results for the year ended 31 March 2016?**

   A   £10,400

   B   £13,360

   C   £9,680

   D   £5,600

5   **How much VAT is reclaimable by Lithograph Ltd in the VAT year to 31 March 2017 in respect of the two impaired debts written off?**

   A   £1,867

   B   £2,240

   C   £960

   D   £800

270 **ANNE ATTIRE (ADAPTED)** *Walk in the footsteps of a top tutor*

Anne Attire runs a clothing manufacturing business. She is registered for VAT and is in the process of completing her VAT return for the quarter ended 31 May 2017.

Recently, she has had problems with customers taking a long time to pay. In order to improve cash flow she decided from 1 March 2017 to offer a discount of 5% for payment within 21 days of the invoice date.

The following information is available in respect of the quarter ended 31 May 2017 (all figures are exclusive of VAT):

(1)   Sales invoices totalling £100,000 were issued in respect of credit sales. These sales were all standard rated. During the quarter sales invoices totalling £40,000 were paid within the 21 day period. The invoice figures of £100,000 and £40,000 are stated before any deduction for the 5% discount.

(2) Included in purchase and expense invoices were the following which were received from VAT registered suppliers:

	£
Legal fees re dispute over land boundary	11,200
Purchase of delivery van -partly used privately by employee	6,000
Car leasing – car partly used privately by employee	2,000
	─────
	19,200
	─────

Anne pays all of her purchase and expense invoices two months after receiving the invoice.

(3) On 31 May 2017 Anne wrote off two impairment losses (bad debts) that were in respect of standard rated credit sales. The first impairment loss was for £300, and was in respect of a sales invoice due for payment on 15 April 2017. The second impairment loss was for £800, and was in respect of a sales invoice due for payment on 10 November 2016. Prompt payment discounts had not been offered in respect of these debts.

Anne does not use the cash accounting scheme.

Anne will soon be 60 years old and is therefore considering retirement. On the cessation of trading Anne can either sell the assets of her business on a piecemeal basis to individual VAT registered purchasers, or she can sell the entire business as a going concern to a single VAT registered purchaser. Anne expects that at the date of cessation the value of the assets on hand will be £12,500 for non-current assets (which includes £6,000 for a car which has been used partly for private purposes) and £6,100 for inventory. All figures are exclusive of VAT.

1   What output VAT figure will Anne include on the VAT return for the quarter ended 31 May 2017?

A   £20,000

B   £19,000

C   £7,600

D   £19,600

2   How much input tax, if any, is recoverable in respect of the purchase invoices set out in note (2)?

A   £1,200

B   £1,400

C   £3,640

D   £2,240

3   How much VAT can Anne reclaim in respect of impaired debts in the return for the quarter to 31 May 2017?

   A   £160

   B   £133

   C   £183

   D   £220

4   Assuming that Anne ceases trading and then sells the assets of her business on a piecemeal basis to individual VAT registered purchasers, how much VAT must be accounted for to HM Revenue and Customs by Anne on the cessation of trade?

   A   £2,520

   B   £1,220

   C   £3,720

   D   £2,100

5   Which of the following must apply for the sale of the entire business to be treated as a transfer of a going concern for VAT purposes, such that the transfer is not a taxable supply?

   (1)   All of the assets and liabilities of the business must be transferred

   (2)   The new owner must use the assets transferred in the same type of business as the seller

   (3)   The new owner must be an established VAT registered trader before the transfer

   (4)   There must be no significant break in the normal trading pattern of the business

   A   (1) and (2)

   B   (2) and (4)

   C   (1) and (3)

   D   (3) and (4)

271 ASTON MARTYN (ADAPTED) *Walk in the footsteps of a top tutor*

This objective test case question contains question types which will only appear in a computer-based examination, but this question provides valuable practice for all students whichever version of the examination they are taking.

Aston Martyn commenced self-employment on 1 November 2016 providing consultancy services to the motor industry. His sales revenue has been as follows:

		Standard rated £	Zero rated £
2016	November	2,300	–
	December	6,400	–
2017	January	20,900	4,800
	February	11,700	–
	March	16,100	–
	April	16,800	4,200
	May	4,200	–
	June	31,500	3,300
	July	44,600	6,600

Where applicable, the above figures are stated exclusive of value added tax (VAT).

Aston only supplies services and all of his supplies are to VAT registered businesses. Aston needs some advice on some administration aspects of VAT including VAT returns and invoices.

Aston is supplied with accountancy services by Financia SA, an accountancy business based in France (another European Union country). On 1 September 2017 Aston paid Financia SA £1,000 for the preparation of an overseas financial return which was completed by Financia SA on 30 September 2017.

Because of the complexity of the VAT legislation, Aston is concerned that despite his best efforts he will incorrectly treat a standard rated supply as zero rated, thus understating the amount of VAT payable. He wants to know about how he could correct any errors.

1   **By what date was Aston Martyn required to notify HM Revenue & Customs of his liability to register for VAT?**

A   30 May 2017

B   31 May 2017

C   30 July 2017

D   31 July 2017

2   **By what dates will Aston Martyn be required to submit his quarterly VAT returns and by what method should they be submitted?**

	Return date	Submission method
A	By end of month following end of quarter	Post
B	By 1 month and 7 days of end of quarter	Online
C	By 1 month and 7 days of end of quarter	Post
D	By end of month following end of quarter	Online

3   **Which FOUR of the following pieces of information is Aston Martyn REQUIRED to show on his new sales invoices in order for them to be valid for VAT purposes.**

    A   Customer's VAT registration number

    B   Invoice number

    C   The rate of VAT for the supply

    D   Invoice date

    E   Total price including VAT

    F   Aston Martyn's name and address

4   **In respect of the services provided to Aston by Financia SA, where is the place of supply and what is the time of supply?**

	Place	Time
A	France	1 September 2017
B	France	30 September 2017
C	UK	1 September 2017
D	UK	30 September 2017

5   **What is the maximum net error that Aston could correct on his next VAT return assuming a taxable turnover of £300,000?**

£ ☐

272   THE WHITLOCK SISTERS (ADAPTED) *Walk in the footsteps of a top tutor*

This objective test case question contains question types which will only appear in a computer-based examination, but this question provides valuable practice for all students whichever version of the examination they are taking.

Sisters Beth and Amy Whitlock trade as a partnership.

(1)   The partnership is registered for VAT and on 1 January 2017 it began using the flat rate scheme to calculate the amount of VAT payable. The relevant flat rate scheme percentage for the partnership's trade is 13%.

(2)   For the quarter ended 31 March 2017 the partnership had standard rated sales of £50,000 and exempt sales of £10,000. For the same period standard rated expenses amounted to £27,300. Both figures are stated inclusive of VAT.

(3)   The partnership has two private rooms in its premises that can be hired by customers. Such customers can book the rooms up to two months in advance, at which time they have to pay a 25% deposit.

An invoice is then given to the customer on the day after the room hire, with payment of the balance of 75% required within seven days. For VAT purposes, the renting out of the rooms is a standard rated supply of services.

1   How much VAT is payable by the partnership for the quarter ended 31 March 2017 if the flat rate scheme is used?

    A   £6,500

    B   £4,251

    C   £2,951

    D   £7,800

2   How much VAT would be payable by the partnership for the quarter ended 31 March 2017 if the flat rate scheme was NOT used?

£ [   ]

3   Which TWO of the following statements about the VAT flat rate scheme are CORRECT?

    A   To join the scheme expected taxable turnover (including VAT) for the next 12 months must not exceed £150,000

    B   The scheme can only be used by small unincorporated businesses

    C   A business must leave the scheme if total VAT inclusive turnover exceeds £230,000

    D   VAT must still be charged on standard rated sales invoices at the rate of 20%

4   What are the actual tax point dates in respect of the 25% deposit and 75% balancing payment in respect of the room hire?

Dates	Deposit	Balancing payment
When the deposit is paid		
Invoice date		
Day of the room hire		
When the balance is paid		

Beth and Amy are planning to make significant changes to the partnership's accounts payable and accounts receivable processes and plan to take key suppliers and clients out for dinner to explain the changes. The VAT inclusive cost of this will be as follows:

UK customers	£250
UK suppliers	£100
Overseas customers	£775
Overseas suppliers	£650

5   What is the amount of input VAT reclaimable on the proposed dinner expenses?

    A   £238

    B   £296

    C   £108

    D   £129

273   KNIGHT LTD (ADAPTED) *Walk in the footsteps of a top tutor*

Knight Ltd is a UK resident trading company. The following information is available in respect of Knight Ltd's value added tax (VAT) for the quarter ended 31 March 2017:

(1)   Output VAT of £38,210 was charged in respect of sales. This figure includes output VAT of £400 on a deposit received on 29 March 2017, which is in respect of a contract that is due to commence on 20 April 2017.

(2)   The managing director of Knight Ltd is provided with free fuel for private mileage driven in his company motor car. The relevant quarterly scale charge is £268. This figure is inclusive of VAT.

(3)   Input VAT of £12,770 was incurred in respect of sundry expenses. This figure includes the following input VAT:

	£
Entertaining UK customers	210
Entertaining overseas customers	139
Extending the office building in order to create a new reception area	3,300
Other sundry expenses (all recoverable)	9,121
	———
	12,770
	———

In the following quarter to 30 June 2017, the following information is available in respect of outstanding customer debts:

Customer	Invoice date	Payment due date	Output VAT
			£
Armour Ltd	1 November 2012	30 November 2012	640
Jousting Ltd	1 October 2016	1 November 2016	555
Marion Ltd	15 December 2016	31 January 2017	759

All of the above debts have been written off in Knight Ltd's accounts except for the debt due from Jousting Ltd, as Knight Ltd is still hopeful that the debt will be paid.

On 1 July 2017 Knight Ltd acquired 100% of the shares in Are Ltd and Can Ltd, which are both UK resident VAT registered companies. Knight Ltd will make standard rated supplies to both companies.

1   How much output tax is payable by Knight Ltd for the quarter to 31 March 2017?

A   £38,255

B   £37,855

C   £38,264

D   £37,864

2   How much input tax is recoverable in respect of the sundry expenses incurred in the quarter to 31 March 2017?

A   £9,260

B   £12,421

C   £12,560

D   £12,631

3   How much relief for impairment losses can Knight Ltd claim in respect of the quarter to 30 June 2017?

A   £1,195

B   £1,399

C   £640

D   £0

4   Which of the following statements concerning VAT groups is/are false?

(1)   If Knight Ltd forms a VAT group it will include both Are Ltd and Can Ltd

(2)   Standard rated supplies made by Knight Ltd to other VAT group members will be ignored for VAT purposes

(3)   Knight Ltd will be the representative member of the VAT group and will be required to submit one VAT return for the whole group

(4)   Each group member will remain liable for its share of the VAT payable

A   (1) only

B   (1), (3) and (4)

C   (2) and (4)

D   (2) and (3)

Knight Ltd was late in submitting the following VAT returns and in paying the related VAT:

Return period	VAT due
	£
3 months ended 31 December 2014	20,000
3 months ended 30 September 2016	30,000
3 months ended 30 June 2017	21,000

All of the company's other VAT returns have been submitted on time, and the related VAT liabilities have been paid on time.

5   What is the total amount of the default surcharge payable as a result of the late submission of the VAT return and late payment of VAT in respect of the 3 months ended 30 June 2017?

A   £400

B   £420

C   £2,100

D   £1,050

PRACTICE SECTION C CONSTRUCTED RESPONSE QUESTIONS

274 GARFIELD (ADAPTED) *Walk in the footsteps of a top tutor*

Garfield has been registered for valued added tax (VAT) since 1 April 2010. Garfield has previously completed his VAT returns himself, but for the quarter ended 31 March 2017 there are some items for which he is unsure of the correct VAT treatment.

Garfield's partly completed VAT computation for the quarter ended 31 March 2017 is shown below. All of the completed sections of the computation are correct, with the omissions marked as outstanding (O/S).

	Note	£
Output VAT		
Sales (all standard rated)		22,500
Discounted sale	1	O/S
Equipment	2	O/S
Fuel scale charge		60
Input VAT		
Purchases (all standard rated)		(11,200)
Motor car (purchased on 1 January 2017)		0
Equipment	2	O/S
Impairment losses	3	O/S
Entertaining – UK customers		0
– Overseas customers	4	O/S
Motor expenses	5	O/S
VAT payable		O/S

Unless otherwise stated, all of the figures in the following notes are stated exclusive of VAT.

Note 1 – Discounted sale

On 10 February 2017, a sales invoice for £4,300 was issued by Garfield in respect of a standard rated supply. To encourage this previously late paying customer to pay promptly, Garfield offered a 10% discount for payment within 14 days of the date of the sales invoice. The customer paid within the 14-day period.

This invoice has not been taken into account in calculating the output VAT figure of £22,500, and this is the only sale for which Garfield has offered a prompt payment discount.

Note 2 – Equipment

During the quarter ended 31 March 2017, Garfield acquired some new equipment at a cost of £12,400 from a VAT registered supplier situated in the European Union.

Note 3 – Impairment losses

On 31 March 2017, Garfield wrote off three impairment losses. Details are as follows:

Amount	Invoice date	Payment due date
£1,400	30 July 2016	29 August 2016
£2,700	12 September 2016	12 October 2016
£1,900	4 October 2016	3 November 2016

Note 4 – Entertaining

During the quarter ended 31 March 2017, Garfield spent £960 on entertaining overseas customers. This figure is inclusive of VAT.

Note 5 – Motor expenses

The motor car purchased on 1 January 2017 is used by Garfield 60% for business mileage. During the quarter ended 31 March 2017, Garfield spent £1,008 on repairs to the motor car and £660 on fuel for both his business and private mileage. Both of these figures are inclusive of VAT.

Additional information

Garfield does not use the cash accounting scheme, the annual accounting scheme or the flat rate scheme, but has read that the use of these schemes can be beneficial for small businesses such as his.

Garfield's VAT exclusive annual turnover is currently £450,000, and this is expected to steadily decrease over the coming years. He pays for most of his purchases and expenses on a cash basis, but allows many of his customers 30 days credit when paying for sales.

Required:

(a) Calculate the amount of value added tax (VAT) payable by Garfield for the quarter ended 31 March 2017. **(7 marks)**

(b) State which VAT schemes Garfield is currently permitted to use, and explain, with supporting reasons, which ONE of the available schemes would appear to be the most beneficial for him to use.

Notes:

1 Your answer should be confined to the information given in the question.

2 You are not expected to explain how any of the schemes operate. **(3 marks)**

(Total: 10 marks)

275 VICTOR STYLE (ADAPTED)

Victor Style has been a self-employed hairdresser since 1 January 2014.

His sales from the date of commencement of the business to 31 December 2016 were £5,800 per month.

On 1 January 2017 Victor increased the prices that he charged customers, and from that date his sales have been £9,500 per month. Victor's sales are all standard rated.

Concerned about the registration thresholds, Victor voluntarily registered for VAT on 1 January 2017.

As all of his customers are members of the general public, it was not possible to increase prices any further as a result of registering for VAT.

Victor's standard rated expenses are £400 per month.

Where applicable, the above figures are inclusive of VAT.

Required:

(a)   Calculate the total amount of VAT payable by Victor during the year ended 31 December 2017.   **(3 marks)**

(b)   Advise Victor why it would have been beneficial to have used the VAT flat rate scheme from 1 January 2017.

Your answer should include a calculation of the amount of VAT that Victor would have saved for the year ended 31 December 2017 by joining the scheme.

The flat rate scheme percentage for hairdressing for Victor in the year ended 31 December 2017 is 13%.   **(3 marks)**

(c)   Calculate the effect on Victor's net profit for the year ended 31 December 2017 as a consequence of the price increase on 1 January 2017 and subsequent VAT registration.   **(4 marks)**

(Total: 10 marks)

276   DENZIL DYER (ADAPTED)

Denzil Dyer has been a self-employed printer since 2008. He has recently registered for value added tax (VAT).

Denzil's sales consist of printed leaflets, some of which are standard rated and some of which are zero rated. He sells to both VAT registered customers and to non-VAT registered customers.

Customers making an order of more than £500 are given a discount of 5% from the normal selling price. Denzil also offers a discount of 2.5% of the amount payable to those customers that pay within one month of the date of the sales invoice.

All of Denzil's printing supplies are purchased from a VAT registered supplier. He pays by credit card and receives a VAT invoice. However, Denzil also purchases various office supplies by cash without receiving any invoices.

Denzil does not use the annual accounting scheme, the cash accounting scheme or the flat rate scheme.

Required:

(a)   Explain why it is important for Denzil to correctly identify whether a sale is standard rated or whether it is zero rated.   **(2 marks)**

(b)   Explain the VAT implications of the two types of discount that Denzil gives or offers to his customers.   **(2 marks)**

(c)   Advise Denzil of the conditions that will have to be met in order for him to recover input VAT.

You are not expected to list those goods and services for which input VAT is non-recoverable.   **(3 marks)**

(d)   State the circumstances in which Denzil is and is not required to issue a VAT invoice, and the period during which such an invoice should be issued.   **(3 marks)**

(Total: 10 marks)

277 SILVERSTONE LTD (ADAPTED) *Walk in the footsteps of a top tutor*

Silverstone Ltd is registered for value added tax (VAT), but currently does not use any of the special VAT schemes. The company has annual standard rated sales of £1,200,000 and annual standard rated expenses of £550,000. Both these figures are exclusive of VAT and are likely to remain the same for the foreseeable future.

Silverstone Ltd is up to date with all of its tax returns, including those for corporation tax, PAYE and VAT. It is also up to date with its corporation tax, PAYE and VAT payments. However, the company often incurs considerable overtime costs due to its employees working late in order to meet tax return filing deadlines.

Silverstone Ltd pays its expenses on a cash basis, but allows customers two months credit when paying for sales. The company does not have any impairment losses.

Silverstone Ltd is planning to purchase some new machinery at a cost of £22,000 (exclusive of VAT). The machinery can either be purchased from an overseas supplier situated outside the European Union, or from a VAT registered supplier situated in the European Union. Silverstone Ltd is not a regular importer and so is unsure of the VAT treatment for this purchase.

Required:

(a) Explain why Silverstone Ltd is entitled to use both the VAT cash accounting scheme and the VAT annual accounting scheme, and why it will probably be beneficial for the company to use both schemes. **(6 marks)**

(b) Explain when and how Silverstone Ltd will have to account for VAT in respect of the new machinery if it is purchased from:

(1) a supplier situated outside the European Union, or

(2) a VAT registered supplier situated elsewhere within the European Union. **(4 marks)**

(Total: 10 marks)

278 TARDY PLC *Walk in the footsteps of a top tutor*

You are a trainee Chartered Certified Accountant, and your firm has recently completed its audit of Tardy plc's financial statements for the year ended 31 March 2017. The company runs an internet-based retail business.

For the previous three value added tax (VAT) quarters, Tardy plc has been late in submitting its VAT returns and in paying the related VAT liabilities. The company is therefore currently serving a default surcharge period.

As part of your firm's tax audit for the year ended 31 March 2017, you have discovered that Tardy plc has been careless in incorrectly treating the supply of standard rated services received from VAT registered businesses situated elsewhere within the European Union. This careless incorrect treatment has resulted in an underpayment of VAT to HM Revenue and Customs of £8,200 for the year ended 31 March 2017.

Required:

(a)   Advise Tardy plc of the default surcharge implications if during the current default surcharge period it is late in paying a further VAT liability, and what the company will need to do in order to revert to a clean default surcharge record.   **(3 marks)**

(b)   Explain when and how a UK VAT registered business should account for VAT in respect of the supply of services received from VAT registered businesses situated elsewhere within the European Union.   **(3 marks)**

(c)   Explain why Tardy plc will be permitted to disclose the underpayment of VAT of £8,200 by entering this amount on its next VAT return, and state whether or not default interest will be due.   **(2 marks)**

(d)   Advise Tardy plc as to the maximum amount of penalty which is likely to be charged by HM Revenue and Customs in respect of the underpayment of VAT of £8,200, and by how much this penalty would be reduced as a result of the company's unprompted disclosure.   **(2 marks)**

(Total: 10 marks)

279   GLACIER LTD

Glacier Ltd runs a business providing financial services. The following information is available in respect of the company's value added tax (VAT) for the quarter ended 31 March 2017:

(1)   Invoices were issued for sales of £44,600 to VAT registered customers. Of this figure, £35,200 was in respect of exempt sales and the balance in respect of standard rated sales. The standard rated sales figure is exclusive of VAT.

(2)   In addition to the above, on 1 March 2017 Glacier issued a VAT invoice for £8,000 plus VAT of £1,600 to a VAT registered customer. This was in respect of a contract for financial services which will be completed on 15 April 2017. The customer paid for the contract in two instalments of £4,800 on 31 March 2017 and 30 April 2017.

(3)   Invoices were issued for sales of £289,100 to non-VAT registered customers. Of this figure, £242,300 was in respect of exempt sales and the balance in respect of standard rated sales. The standard rated sales figure is inclusive of VAT.

(4)   The managing director of Glacier Ltd is provided with free fuel for private mileage driven in her company motor car. During the quarter ended 31 March 2017, this fuel cost Glacier Ltd £260. The relevant quarterly scale charge is £408. Both these figures are inclusive of VAT.

For the quarters ended 30 September 2015 and 30 June 2016, Glacier Ltd was one month late in submitting its VAT returns and in paying the related VAT liabilities. All of the company's other VAT returns have been submitted on time.

Required:

(a)   Calculate the amount of output VAT payable by Glacier Ltd for the quarter ended 31 March 2017.   **(4 marks)**

(b)   Advise Glacier Ltd of the default surcharge implications if it is one month late in submitting its VAT return for the quarter ended 31 March 2017 and in paying the related VAT liability.   **(3 marks)**

(c)   State the circumstances in which Glacier Ltd is and is not required to issue a VAT invoice, and the period during which such an invoice should be issued.   **(3 marks)**

(Total: 10 marks)

280 SMART LTD *Walk in the footsteps of a top tutor*

Smart Ltd commenced trading on 1 September 2016. The company's sales for the first four months of trading were as follows:

2016		£
	September	26,000
	October	47,000
	November	134,000
	December	113,000

On 1 November 2016, the company signed a contract valued at £86,000 for completion during November 2016.

All of the above figures are stated exclusive of value added tax (VAT). Smart Ltd only supplies services and all of the company's supplies are standard rated.

Smart Ltd allows its customers 60 days credit when paying for services, and it is concerned that some customers will default on the payment of their debts. The company pays its purchase invoices as soon as they are received.

Smart Ltd does not use either the VAT cash accounting scheme or the annual accounting scheme.

Required:

(a) State, giving reasons, the date from which Smart Ltd was required to register for value added tax (VAT), and by when it was required to notify HM Revenue and Customs (HMRC) of the registration. **(3 marks)**

(b) State how and when Smart Ltd will have to submit its quarterly VAT returns and pay any related VAT liability.

Note: You are not expected to cover substantial traders or the election for monthly returns. **(2 marks)**

(c) State the circumstances when a VAT registered business like Smart Ltd, which is not using the VAT cash accounting scheme, would still have to account for output VAT at the time that payment is received from a customer. **(2 marks)**

(d) Advise Smart Ltd as to why it should be beneficial for the company to use the VAT cash accounting scheme. **(3 marks)**

(Total: 10 marks)

281   ZIM *Walk in the footsteps of a top tutor*

Zim has been registered for value added tax (VAT) since 1 April 2007.

The following information is available for the year ended 31 March 2017:

(1)   Sales invoices totalling £126,000 were issued, of which £115,200 were in respect of standard rated sales and £10,800 were in respect of zero rated sales. Zim's customers are all members of the general public.

(2)   On 31 March 2017, Zim wrote off two impairment losses which were in respect of standard rated sales.

The first impairment loss was for £780, and was in respect of a sales invoice which had been due for payment on 15 August 2016.

The second impairment loss was for £660, and was in respect of a sales invoice which had been due for payment on 15 September 2016.

(3)   Purchase invoices totalling £49,200 were received, of which £43,200 were in respect of standard rated purchases and £6,000 were in respect of zero rated purchases.

(4)   Rent of £1,200 is paid each month. During the year ended 31 March 2017, Zim made 13 rental payments because the invoice dated 1 April 2017 was paid early on 31 March 2017. This invoice was in respect of the rent for April 2017.

(5)   During the year ended 31 March 2017, Zim spent £2,600 on mobile telephone calls, of which 40% related to private calls.

(6)   During the year ended 31 March 2017, Zim spent £1,560 on entertaining customers, of which £240 was in respect of overseas customers.

All of the above figures are inclusive of VAT where applicable. The expenses referred to in notes (4), (5) and (6) are all standard rated.

Zim does not use either the cash accounting scheme or the flat rate scheme.

He has forecast that for the year ended 31 March 2018, his total sales will be the same as for the year ended 31 March 2017.

Required:

(a)   **Calculate the amount of value added tax (VAT) payable by Zim for the year ended 31 March 2017.**

You should indicate by the use of zero any items referred to in notes (1) to (6) where there is no VAT impact.   **(6 marks)**

(b)   **Explain why Zim will be permitted to use the VAT flat rate scheme from 1 April 2017, and state the circumstances in which he will have to leave the scheme.**

(2 marks)

(c)   Explain whether or not it would have been beneficial for Zim to have used the VAT flat rate scheme for the year ended 31 March 2017.

Notes:

1   You should assume that the relevant flat rate scheme percentage for Zim's trade would have been 12% throughout the whole of the year ended 31 March 2017.

2   Your answer for this part of the question should be supported by appropriate calculations.   **(2 marks)**

(Total: 10 marks)

Section 6

ANSWERS TO PRACTICE INCOME TAX AND NATIONAL INSURANCE QUESTIONS

PRACTICE SECTION A OBJECTIVE TEST QUESTIONS

INCOME TAX BASICS AND EMPLOYMENT INCOME

1

	Taxable	Exempt
£400 in shares in the company he works for	✓	
£1,000 in an Individual Savings Account		✓
£800 in a NS&I investment account	✓	
£500 purchasing a NS&I certificate		✓

Income generated from an Individual Savings Account and a NS&I certificate is exempt from income tax.

Income generated from shares (dividends) and from a NS&I investment account (interest) is subject to income tax.

2   B

	£
Personal allowance	11,000
Restriction (£110,200 − £800 − £100,000) = £9,400 ÷ 2	(4,700)
Restricted personal allowance	6,300

3   A

		£
Trading income		105,800
Dividend		1,500
Net income		107,300

	£	£
PA		11,000
Net income	107,300	
Less: Gross gift aid	(2,000)	
Adjusted net income	105,300	
Less: Income limit	(100,000)	
	5,300	
Reduction of PA (50% × £5,300)		(2,650)
Adjusted PA		8,350

4   A

5   D

			Non-savings income
			£
Rental income = net income			40,000
Less: PA			(11,000)
Taxable income			29,000
Income tax liability:			
Non-savings income – basic rate	29,000	× 20%	5,800
Less: Marriage allowance	1,100	× 20%	(220)
Income tax liability			5,580

6

	Qualifying interest	Not qualifying
Interest paid on a loan he incurred to purchase a laptop for use in his employment	✓	
Interest paid on the mortgage for his principal private residence		✓
Interest paid on an amount he borrowed to finance the acquisition of 2,000 shares in a quoted company		✓
Interest paid on a loan he took to invest capital in a partnership in order to become a partner	✓	

Tutorial note

Relief is given for interest paid on loans to finance expenditure for a qualifying purpose, which includes:

- *The acquisition of plant and machinery by an employed person for use in his employment.*

- *The purchase of shares in an employee-controlled trading company by a full-time employee.*

- *The purchase of a share in a partnership, or the contribution to a partnership of capital or a loan. The borrower must be a partner in the partnership.*

- *The purchase of plant and machinery for use in the partnership, by a partner.*

7   D

	£	£
Child benefit received		1,789
Trading income = Adjusted net income	53,000	
Less: Lower limit	(50,000)	
	3,000	
1% per £100 of £3,000 = 30%		
Child benefit tax charge = 30% of £1,789 (rounded down)		536

Tutor's top tips

The method for calculating the child benefit income tax charge is included in the tax rates and allowances provided to you in the examination.

8   B

	£	£
Child benefit received		1,076
		———
Trading income	56,500	
Less: Gross gift aid (£400 × 100/80)	(500)	
	———	
Adjusted net income	56,000	
Less: Lower limit	(50,000)	
	———	
	6,000	
	———	

1% per £100 of £6,000 = 60%

Child benefit tax charge = 60% of £1,076 (rounded down)   645

——————

9   A

	£	£
Child benefit received		1,789
		———
Employment income	55,000	
Bank interest	3,000	
	———	
Adjusted net income	58,000	
Less: Lower limit	(50,000)	
	———	
	8,000	
	———	

1% per £100 of £8,000 = 80%

Child benefit tax charge = 80% of £1,789 (rounded down)   1,431

——————

10   C

Tutor's top tips

The number of ties needed for an individual to be UK resident depending on the number of days spent in the UK in a particular tax year is included in the tax rates and allowances provided to you in the examination.

Both questions 10 and 11 could have been answered quickly and easily provided that you understood how to interpret the table!

11

	Resident	Not resident
Bao		✓
Min	✓	

Bao is treated as automatically non-UK resident, as he has spent less than 46 days in the UK in the tax year 2016/17 and has not been treated as UK resident in any of the three previous tax years (having spent less than 46 days in the UK each tax year).

Minh is treated as automatically resident in the UK as, although he has been here for less than 183 days, he works full time in the UK.

12

	Taxable	Exempt
NS&I investment account interest	✓	
Gilt edged security interest	✓	
NS&I savings certificate interest		✓

13   A

Accrued interest for the period 1 June 2016 to 28 February 2017 is £150 (£10,000 × 2% × 9/12).

Tutorial note

Gilts are subject to the accrued income scheme. On a disposal interest is effectively, allocated between the vendor and purchaser on the accruals basis in relation to their period of ownership.

14   D

	£
Interest received 30 June 2016 (£200,000 × 1% × 6/12)	1,000
Interest accrued (1 July 2016 - 30 November 2016)	
(£200,000 × 1% × 5/12)	833
Total interest income	1,833

Tutorial note

Gilt interest is assessed like other interest income on the receipts basis. However, under the accrued income scheme when gilts are sold interest is effectively allocated to the vendor and purchaser on the accruals basis up to the date of sale.

Matthew did not receive any interest on 31 December 2016 but will be taxed on £833 representing the interest accruing in the interest period for which he owned the gilts.

15   A

	Total	Non-savings Income	Savings Income
	£	£	£
Taxable income	13,075	1,200	11,875
Income tax liability:			
Non-savings income – basic rate	1,200	× 20%	240
Savings income – starting rate	3,800	× 0%	0
	5,000		
Savings income – nil rate band	1,000	× 0%	0
Savings income – basic rate	7,075	× 20%	1,415
	13,075		
Income tax liability			1,655

16   £2,220

	£
Dividends	43,600
Less: PA	(11,000)
Taxable income	32,600
Income tax liability:	
Dividend income – nil rate band (£5,000 × 0%)	0
Dividend income – basic rate band (£27,000 × 7.5%)	2,025
Dividend income - higher rate (£600 × 32.5%)	195
Income tax liability	2,220

Tutorial note

The dividend nil rate band is £5,000, this counts towards the basic and higher rate bands.

17   A

	£
Premium	82,000
Less: £82,000 × 2% × (15 – 1)	(22,960)
Property income	59,040

Alternative calculation = £82,000 × (51 – 15)/50 = £59,040

18   C

	£	£
Rent receivable		9,600
Less: Expenses		
Council tax	900	
Insurance (£540 × 6/12) + (£480 × 6/12)	510	
Refrigerator	870	
		(2,280)
Property income		7,320

Tutorial note

Property income is assessed on the accruals basis assuming a year end of 5 April. The deduction for insurance is calculated by reference to the cost related to the year ended 5 April 2017. A deduction can be taken for the cost of replacing furniture, furnishings, appliances (including white goods) and kitchenware provided for use in a dwelling.

19   £23,520

	£
Premium	42,000
Less: £42,000 × 2% × (23 − 1)	(18,480)
Property income	23,520

Alternative calculation = £42,000 × (51 − 23)/50 = £23,520

20   D

	£
Bonus – received 6 April 2016	2,800
Bonus – received 3 April 2017	3,300
Total bonus taxed in 2016/17	6,100

Tutorial note

Employment income is assessed on the receipts basis (i.e. income received in the tax year).

21   A

	£	£
Salary		55,000
Mileage allowance:		
Amount received (14,500 × 43p)	6,235	
AMAP rates:		
10,000 × 45p	(4,500)	
4,500 × 25p	(1,125)	
Excess mileage allowance		610
Employment income		55,610

22   £624

The assessable benefit is the excess of the childcare vouchers over the limit for a higher rate taxpayer – (£40 – £28) × 52 = £624. The other benefits are both exempt.

23   A

The original cost did not exceed £75,000, therefore it is not considered to be an 'expensive' accommodation. The only benefit is the basic charge based on the annual value of £2,600. Jo contributes more than the annual value (£250 × 12 = £3,000) and therefore the assessable benefit is nil.

24   D

CO_2 emissions = 188 g/km (rounded down to 185), available for 11 months

	%
Diesel	19
Plus: $(185 - 95) \times {}^{1}/_{5}$	18
Appropriate percentage	37

	£
Car benefit (£28,000 × 37% × 11/12)	9,497

25   B

Average method	£	£
Loan at start of tax year	100,000	
Loan at end of tax year	60,000	
	160,000	
Average loan (£160,000 ÷ 2)	80,000	
Assessable benefit (£80,000 × 3%)		2,400
Less Interest paid		
(£100,000 × 1% × 4/12)	333	
(£60,000 × 1% × 8/12)	400	
		(733)
		1,667

26   D

	£	£
Higher of:		
(i) MV at date of transfer	2,400	
	———	
(ii) Original cost	8,500	
Less: Annual value for 2014/15 and 2015/16		
for use of asset (£8,500 × 20% × 2)	(3,400)	
	———	
	5,100	5,100
	———	
Less: Employee contribution		(1,500)
		———
Taxable benefit		3,600
		———

Tutorial note

The benefit on 6 April 2016 when Ritvik purchased the home cinema system is the higher of the market value at the time of the purchase and the market value when it was first made available less amounts previously taxed.

The amount paid, by Ritvik for the asset, of £1,500 can be deducted in computing the benefit.

27   B

Tutorial note

Where an employee is reimbursed expenses by the employer, the amount received is taxable income. However, an exemption applies where the employee would be able to claim a tax deduction for the business related expenses under the rules set out above e.g. professional subscriptions.

The reimbursement of Albert's professional subscription fees is therefore exempt income.

INCOME TAX BASICS AND INCOME FROM SELF-EMPLOYMENT

28   £600

The £450 spent on food hampers needs to be added back as gifts of food are disallowable. Costs relating to the acquisition of a short lease are disallowable so £150 must be added back. The costs of renewing a short lease would be allowable.

Employee parking fines incurred on business and amounts spent on staff entertaining (regardless of the amount) are allowable deductions from trading profits.

Tutorial note

Annual events which cost the employer more than £150 per head are a taxable benefit for the employee, but the cost is still deductible for the employer.

29   B

Haniful is treated as making a sale to himself at selling price. As no adjustment has been made in the accounts to reflect the goods taken for personal use the full selling price must be added to the trading profits.

Tutorial note

If Haniful had already made an adjustment in the accounts to remove the cost of the goods taken out of the business (by adding back the cost of £850) then only the profit element of £250 would need to be added to the trading profits for tax purposes.

30   D

Firstly the amount taxable on the landlord as property income must be calculated:

	£
Premium	25,000
Less: £25,000 × 2% × (20 – 1)	(9,500)
Property income	15,500

Alternative calculation = £25,000 × (51 – 20)/50 = £15,500

Fleur can then take an annual deduction spread evenly over the period of the lease:

(£15,500 ÷ 20) = £775.

As Fleur acquired the lease on 1 January 2016 the full annual amount of £775 is deductible when calculating the tax adjusted trading profits for the year ended 31 December 2016.

31   C

	Main pool	Allowances
	£	£
TWDV b/f	6,200	
Addition: Computer	1,600	
	7,800	
Disposal	(9,800)	
	(2,000)	
Balancing charge	2,000	(2,000)
Total allowances	0	(2,000)

Tutorial note

In the period of account in which the business permanently ceases, the AIA, WDAs and FYAs are not available. Additions and disposals are added to/deducted from the relevant pool and a balancing charge or allowance is calculated.

32   C and F

Any asset with private use by the owner of the business will be allocated to a private use asset column rather than the main pool.

Cars with CO_2 emissions in excess of 130 g/km are allocated to the special rate pool rather than the main pool.

Long life assets (those with an expected life of over 25 years, with a total cost of £100,000 in a twelve month period) must be added to the special rate pool. Assets with an expected working life of less than 25 years are not treated as long life assets and will be added to the main pool.

33   B

A new car with CO_2 emissions up to 75 g/km qualifies for a first year allowance of 100% which is never time apportioned irrespective of the length of the period of account.

The tax written down value brought forward in the main pool will be entitled to WDA at 18% time apportioned for 8 months therefore:

	£	Main pool £	Allowances £
TWDV b/f		18,000	
WDA (18% × 8/12)		(2,160)	2,160
Addition (with FYA)			
Motor car	12,260		
FYA (100%)	(12,260)		12,260
		0	
TWDV c/f		15,840	
Total allowances			14,420

Tutorial note

In Section A, marks are not available for your workings. If you are confident with capital allowances you may find it quicker for straightforward questions such as this to calculate the allowances available for each pool without using the pro forma:

(£12,260 × 100%) = £12,260

(£18,000 × 18%) = £3,240 × 8/12 = £2,160

Total = (£12,260 + £2,160) = £14,420

34   D

In the final period of account, no AIA, WDA or FYA is available; only balancing adjustments arise.

	Main pool £	Allowances £
TWDV b/f	15,000	
Additions	4,500	
Disposals – pool items	(14,550)	
Disposals – laptop retained personally	(4,150)	
	800	
Balancing allowance	(800)	800

The laptop is treated as having been disposed of at market value.

35   £16,500

> **Tutorial note**
>
> *Jacinta started trading on 1 August 2016 and so the tax year 2016/17 is the first tax year of her trade.*
>
> *In the first tax year, the profits taxed will be the actual profits arising from the first day of trade up to the following 5 April.*
>
> *This is an eight month period and will include all the profits for the five months to 31 December 2016 and three months (1 January to 5 April 2017) from the next set of accounts.*
>
> *£10,500 + 3/12 × (£24,000) = £16,500.*

36   C

Lee ceased to trade on 31 January 2017 which falls into tax year 2016/17.

Up to that tax year Lee will have been taxed on the current year basis therefore in 2015/16, Lee will have been taxed on the profits of the accounting period ending in that year i.e. y/e 30 April 2015.

In the tax year in which he ceases to trade he will be taxed on any trading profits not taxed in previous years less his overlap profits that arose when he started his business, i.e.:

	£
y/e 31 April 2016	10,000
p/e 31 January 2017	14,000
Less: Overlap profits	(3,0000)
	———
Trading income assessment – 2016/17	21,000
	———

PARTNERSHIPS

37   D

y/e 31 December 2016	Total	Henry
	£	£
p/e 31 July 2016 (£120,000 × 7/12) = £70,000		
PSR (100:30)	70,000	21,000
p/e 31 December 2016 (£120,000 × 5/12) = £50,000		
Salary (£24,000 × 5/12)	10,000	10,000
PSR (100:20)	40,000	8,000
	———	———
Allocation of profit	120,000	39,000
	———	———

38   A

2015/16 – y/e 30 September 2016	Total	Albert	Jolene
	£	£	£
Salary	25,000	25,000	
Interest on capital			
(4% × £50,000/£40,000)	3,600	2,000	1,600
Balance (1:3)	51,400	12,850	38,550
Allocation of profit	80,000	39,850	40,150

39   B

y/e 31 December 2016	Total	Tim
	£	£
1.1.2016 – 31.5.2016 (£360,000 × 5/12) = £150,000		
Salary (£15,000 × 5/12)	6,250	6,250
PSR (1/6)	143,750	23,958
Allocation of profit	150,000	30,208

Tutorial note

You could have calculated the profit allocated to each of the three partners for the whole year ended 31 December 2016. However, only the profit allocated to Tim for the 5 months that he was a partner was required so it was not necessary to calculate how the remaining profit was allocated to the other two partners and would have wasted valuable time in the examination.

40   D

y/e 31 October 2016	Total	Fabiola
	£	£
1.6.16 – 31.10.16 (£240,000 × 5/12)		
PSR (1:5)	100,000	20,000
y/e 31 October 2017		
PSR (1:5)	300,000	60,000
2016/17 – First tax year		
Actual basis 1.6.16 – 5.4.17		
1.6.16 – 31.10.16		20,000
1.11.16 – 5.4.17 (£60,000 × 5/12)		25,000
Trading income assessment		45,000

TRADING LOSSES

41   A

Prior year loss relief claim

	£
Set against trading profits (unrestricted)	24,000
Set against non-trading profits (restricted to maximum)(note)	50,000
	———
Maximum loss relief claim	74,000
	———

Tutorial note

Only losses set against non-trading income of earlier years are restricted to the maximum amount; losses set against prior year trading profits are not restricted. The maximum amount is the greater of:

- *£50,000*

- *25% × Adjusted total income (ATI)*

  = (25% × £116,000) = £29,000

It is not strictly necessary to do this calculation in this case. This is because the maximum deduction will be £50,000 if ATI is < £200,000.

The cap on income tax reliefs is included in the tax rates and allowances provided to you in the examination.

---

42   £13,000

	2016/17
	£
Trading income	12,000
Less: Losses b/f	(12,000)
Dividends	9,000
Furnished holiday accommodation	4,000
NS&I certificate interest	exempt
	———
Net income	13,000
	———

Tutorial note

The trading loss of the tax year 2015/16 is carried forward to the tax year 2016/17 and offset against the first available trading profits from the same trade.

Profits from qualifying furnished holiday accommodation are not treated as trading income for the purposes of offsetting trading losses.

43   B

	2015/16	2016/17
	£	£
Trading income	55,000	0
Bank interest	14,000	14,000
	——————	——————
Total income	69,000	14,000
Less: Loss relief	(69,000)	(14,000)
	——————	——————
Net income	0	0
	——————	——————

Loss memorandum:

	£
Loss arising in 2016/17	90,000
Used in 2015/16 – Prior year	(69,000)
Used in 2016/17 – Current year	(14,000)
	——————
Loss carried forward to 2017/18	7,000
	——————

Tutorial note

A current and prior year loss relief claim is against total income in the tax years 2016/17 and/or 2015/16. It cannot be restricted to prevent the loss of the personal allowance.

The loss offset in the tax year 2015/16 is not restricted to £50,000 as the restriction only applies to losses offset against other income, not income from the same trade.

44 B

Tax year	Basis period	Available loss
		£
2014/15	1.11.14 – 5.4.15	
	(5/12 × £25,000)	10,417
		———
2015/16	y/e 31.10.15	25,000
Less: Used in 2014/15		(10,417)
		———
		14,583
		———

The loss arising in the tax year 2014/15 of £10,417 is a loss in the first four tax years of trading and can be offset against total income in the tax years 2011/12, 2012/13 and 2013/14 in that order.

45 C

		£
Available loss is lower of:		
(i)	Remaining trading loss following current year claim against total income (£45,000 - £8,000)	37,000
		———
(ii)	CY chargeable gains	32,000
	Less: CY capital losses	(4,000)
	Less: Capital losses b/f	(18,000)
		———
		10,000
		———
Available loss		10,000
		———

Tutorial note

The maximum amount of trading loss that can be offset against chargeable gains is the lower of:

(i)   the remaining loss, or

*(ii)   chargeable gains in the year after the deduction of current year capital losses and brought forward capital losses. Brought forward capital losses are **not** restricted to preserve the annual exempt amount in this calculation.*

*The maximum trading loss is then offset against current year chargeable gains, after current year capital losses but before brought forward capital losses. The offset of brought forward capital losses **is** restricted to preserve the annual exempt amount.*

46   A

Terminal loss	£	£
6 April before cessation to date of cessation		
6.4.16 – 30.9.16 (£24,000 × 6/8)		18,000
12 months before cessation to 5 April before cessation		
1.2.16 – 5.4.16 (£24,000 × 2/8)	6,000	
1.10.15 – 31.1.16 (£39,000 × 4/12)	(13,000)	
	———	
Profit – ignore	(7,000)	0
Plus: Overlap profits		12,000
		———
Terminal loss		30,000
		———

Tutorial note

A terminal loss is the loss of the last 12 months of trading. The result arising in the period from the 12 months before the date of cessation to 5 April 2016 is a profit. It is therefore ignored in the terminal loss calculation.

PENSIONS AND NIC

47   C

Tutorial note

Class 2 and class 4 national insurance contributions are paid by self-employed individuals.

48   C

	£
Employed – Class 1 (£27,940 (£36,000 – £8,060) × 12%)	3,353
Self-employed – Class 4 (£27,940 (£36,000 – £8,060) × 9%)	(2,515)
– Class 2 (52 × 2.80)	(146)
	———
	692
	———

49

	Paid by Hamid	Suffered by Hamid
Employee class 1 primary	✓	
Employer's class 1 secondary	✓	✓
Class 1A	✓	✓
Class 2	✓	✓
Class 4	✓	✓

Tutorial note

Hamid must pay class 2 and class 4 NICs in respect of his sole trader profits, employer's class 1 secondary NICs in respect of his employee's salary and class 1A NICs in respect of the company car benefit for the employee.

Although Hamid is required to pay over the employee class 1 primary NIC to HMRC, he will deduct this from the salary paid to his employee so it is not a cost that is suffered by him.

50   C

	£
(£43,000 – £8,060) × 12%	4,193
(£82,700 – £43,000) × 2%	794
	―――――
	4,987
	―――――

Tutorial note

Employment benefits are subject to class 1A NIC, not class 1 NIC.

51   A

	£
(£43,000 – £8,060) × 12%	4,193
(£63,000 – £43,000) × 2%	400
	―――――
Class 1 primary NICs	4,593
	―――――

52   B

	£
Class 1 employer's NICs	
(£50,600 − £8,112) × 13.8%	5,863

Working: Earnings liable to Class 1 NIC

	£
Salary	50,000
Excess mileage allowance (12,000 × (50p − 45p))	600
	50,600

Tutorial note

Occupational pension scheme contributions are not deductible from earnings for NIC purposes.

The excess mileage allowance above the AMAP of 45p per mile (regardless of the number of business miles) is subject to class 1 NICs.

---

53   B

	£
Class 1A NIC	
£2,700 × 13.8%	373

Working: Car benefit
CO_2 emissions = 109 g/km (rounded down to 105)

	%
Petrol	16
Plus: (105 − 95) × 1/5	2
Appropriate percentage	18

	£
Car benefit (£15,000 × 18%)	2,700

54   C and E

The annual summer event is a taxable benefit as the cost exceeds £150 per head, and the sports club membership fee is also a taxable benefit. As non-cash benefits they are subject to class 1A NIC.

Occupational pension scheme contributions paid by the employer, car parking spaces at or near the workplace and the provision of one mobile phone are all exempt benefits for NIC purposes.

The mileage allowance paid for normal commuting is a taxable cash benefit which is subject to class 1 NICs, not class 1A NICs.

55

	Class 2 NICs payable	Class 2 NICs not payable
Mohammed	✓	
Nicole		✓

Tutorial note

Mohammed will pay class 2 NICs for the tax year 2016/17 as his tax adjusted trading profit for the tax year is more than the small profits threshold of £5,965.

Nicole does not pay class 2 NICs for the tax year 2016/17 as she is above the state pension age.

56   A

	£
(£43,000 – £8,060) × 9%	3,145
(£68,000 – £43,000) × 2%	500
	———
Class 4 NICs	3,645
	———

57   C

	£
Trading profits	70,000
Less: trading loss b/f	(20,000)
	———
Assessable profits for class 4 NICs	50,000
	———

Tutorial note

If trading losses are carried forward they are offset against the first available trading income arising from the same trade.

A sole trader pays class 4 NIC on trading profits only, not on any other income.

58   £16,400

Isaac's income tax basic rate band will be extended by the grossed up contribution as follows:

£32,000 + (£40,000 × 100/80) = £82,000

Income tax of £16,400 (£82,000 × 20%) will be payable at the basic rate.

The contribution is lower than Isaac's relevant earnings for the year (£110,000) and therefore tax relief is available on the full amount.

Tutorial note

Issac's gross contributions will exceed the annual allowance threshold of £40,000 for the tax year 2016/17.

Therefore, although his basic rate band will be extended by his total gross contributions of £50,000, some tax relief may be clawed back via an annual allowance charge depending on the availability of unused allowances to carry forward from the previous three tax years.

---

59   C

2016/17

	£
2016/17 Annual allowance (W2)	20,000
Unused annual allowances b/f (W1)	32,000
	———
Maximum gross PPCs	52,000
	———

Workings

(W1) Unused annual allowances

	£
2013/14 (£50,000 – £23,000)	27,000
2014/15 (£40,000 – £40,000)	0
2015/16 (£40, 000 – £35,000)	5,000
	———
Unused annual allowances	32,000
	———

(W2) 2016/17 annual allowance

	£
Annual allowance 2016/17	40,000
Tapered for excess income:	
(£190,000 – £150,000)/2	(20,000)
	———
Reduction in annual allowance	20,000
	———

Tutorial note

Prior to the tax year 2014/15 the annual allowance was £50,000. This figure is given in the tax rates and allowances provided to you in the examination.

Unused annual allowances can be brought forward from the previous three tax years.

The annual allowance is tapered by £1 for every £2 of adjusted income in excess of £150,000 in the tax year 2016/17. The allowance cannot be tapered below the minimum amount of £10,000. Tapering was introduced in the tax year 2016/17 therefore earlier tax years are unaffected.

60 D

	£
Salary	50,000
Furnished holiday accommodation income	5,000
	_____
Relevant earnings	55,000
	_____

Tutorial note

Tax relief for both personal pension contributions and gift aid donations is made by extending the basic and higher rate bands by the gross contribution/donation.

There is no need to adjust relevant earnings for gift aid donations – this was included to mislead you!

61

	Fully tax relievable pension contributions	Not fully tax relievable pension contributions
Austin	✓	
Petra		✓

Austin's total gross pension contributions are £28,000 (£22,400 × 100/80). They are less than his relevant earnings of £51,200 and less than the annual allowance for the tax year 2016/17 of £40,000. His contributions are fully tax-relievable.

Petra's gross contributions of £62,500 (£50,000 × 100/80) exceed the annual allowance of £40,000 for the tax year 2016/17. She has no unused annual allowances brought forward as she was not a member of a pension scheme in previous years. She will obtain tax relief at source on the contributions, as they are less than her relevant earnings. However, part of the tax relief will be clawed back through an annual allowance charge.

Tutorial note

An employed individual can make pension contributions into either an occupational pension scheme or a personal pension scheme or both. Contributions will be fully tax-relievable provided total gross contributions do not exceed their total relevant earnings or the annual allowance.

62   £142,100

	£
Salary	145,000
Less: Occupational pension contributions (2% × £145,000)	(2,900)
	———
Net income	142,100
	———

Tutorial note

Employer pension contributions are an exempt benefit.

Tax relief for occupational pension scheme contributions is given at the employee's marginal rate of tax by deducting them from employment income.

Basic rate tax relief for personal pension scheme contributions is given at source. Tax relief at higher rates is given by extending the basic rate and higher rate tax bands.

63   C

2016/17

	£
Trading income	80,000
Annual allowance charge	10,000
	———
	90,000
Less: PA	(11,000)
	———
Taxable income	79,000
	———

Income tax liability	£
£79,000 × 20%	15,800
	———

Working: Extended basic rate band	£
Basic rate band	32,000
Gross personal pension contributions	50,000
	82,000

ADMINISTRATION AND ETHICS

64   D

Tutorial note

VAT is neither a capital nor a revenue tax. VAT is an example of a 'sales tax' suffered by consumers.

65   B

Tutorial note

The term tax evasion summarises any action taken to avoid or reduce tax by illegal means, for example providing HM Revenue and Customs with deliberately false information.

66   B and E

The other options refer to tax avoidance.

67   B

Tutorial note

Members should not disclose information about the client to third parties (including HMRC) unless they have authorisation from the client or there is a legal or professional right or duty to disclose (e.g. money laundering).

Where a money laundering report is made the client should not be informed as this may amount to tipping off, which is an offence.

68   B

A tax adviser must not assist a client to plan or commit any offence.

Tutorial note

A tax adviser may have a legal or professional right or duty to disclose information about a client without their authority (e.g. in the case of money laundering).

If the adviser becomes aware that a client has committed an offence they must discuss the irregularity with the client and ensure proper disclosure is made to HMRC).

A tax adviser has duties and responsibilities towards both his client and HMRC (e.g. they must ensure that all information provided to HMRC is accurate and complete).

69   B

70   C

Tutorial note

The taxpayer can amend the return within 12 months of the 31 January filing date. For the tax year 2015/16, amendments must therefore be made by 31 January 2018. HMRC must give written notice before commencing a compliance check. The written notice must be issued within 12 months of the actual date the return is filed with HMRC.

71

	Phillip	Harriet
31 January 2019		
31 January 2022		
31 January 2023	✓	✓

Taxpayers who are in business, which for this purpose includes the letting of a property, must keep their records until five years after the 31 January filing date (i.e. 31 January 2023 for a 2016/17 return).

72   D

Payments on account (POAs) for the tax year 2016/17 are based on the relevant amount for the tax year 2015/16.

= (£300 + £320) = £620

As this does not exceed £1,000, POAs are not required in the tax year 2016/17.

73   B

Tutorial note

The balancing payment is due on 31 January following the end of the tax year.

For the tax year 2016/17 this is 31 January 2018.

Where the balancing payment is made:

- *more than one month late, penalty = 5%*

- *more than six months late = an additional 5% is charged (total of 10%)*

- *more than 12 months late = a further 5% is charged (total of 15%).*

74   B

2016/17	**£**
Income tax liability	25,000
Less: PAYE	(5,400)
	———
Income tax payable (relevant amount)	19,600
Payments on account (POA)	(18,000)
CGT liability	5,000
	———
Balancing payment	6,600
	———

Tutorial note

CGT is payable in full on 31 January following the tax year and must therefore be included in the balancing payment.

75

	True	**False**
Belinda will have to pay interest on late paid tax from 31 January 2018 to 10 March 2018	✓	
Belinda will have to pay a £100 fixed penalty because the payment is late		✓
Belinda will have to pay a 5% penalty because the payment is more than 30 days late	✓	

The tax was due on 31 January 2018 and not actually paid until 10 March 2018.

Interest on late paid tax runs from the due date until the date of payment, therefore the first statement is true.

A 5% penalty is charged if the tax is paid more than 30 days late, therefore the third statement is true. Fixed penalties are only charged on the late submission of returns, not the late payment of tax.

76   £1,225

	£
Daily penalties as 3 months late -maximum 90 days (£10 × 90)	900
6 months late (£6,500 × 5%)	325
Maximum penalty	1,225

Tutorial note

The 2016/17 return was due on 31 January 2018 and was therefore filed more than 6 months but less than 12 months late.

77

	True	False
Under the Real Time Information PAYE system, Welan Ltd must submit income tax and NIC information in respect of the monthly salary payments to HM Revenue & Customs electronically by the 15th day of each month	✓	
Welan Ltd must pay the income tax and NIC due on the monthly salary payments to HM Revenue & Customs electronically by the 22nd of the month following the month the salaries are paid	✓	
Welan Ltd must provide each employee with a year-end summary form (P60) for the tax year 2016/17 by 6 July 2017		✓

An employer must provide an employee with a P60 by 31 May following the tax year (i.e. 31 May 2017 for the tax year 2016/17).

Tutorial note

Under the RTI PAYE system information must be submitted electronically to HMRC on or before the date of payment.

Employers with more than 250 employees must pay their PAYE payments electronically. The due date for electronic payments is 17 days after the end of the tax month (i.e. by the 22nd of the month following the month of payment).

PRACTICE SECTION B OBJECTIVE TEST CASES

INCOME TAX BASICS AND EMPLOYMENT INCOME

78   PHILIP & CHARLES (ADAPTED) *Walk in the footsteps of a top tutor*

Key answer tips

This case OT involves the income tax position for two individuals with different circumstances. It tests income tax, knowledge of NIC and pension contributions. All the topics are covered at a basic level and should therefore have been manageable.

1   B

	Total income £	Non-savings income £	Savings income £
Pension income	13,500	13,500	
Building society interest	14,600		14,600
Total income/Net income	28,100	13,500	14,600
Less: PA	(11,000)	(11,000)	
Taxable income	17,100	2,500	14,600

Income tax		£
£		
2,500 × 20% Non-savings		500
2,500 × 0% Savings		0
1,000 × 0% Savings		0
11,100 × 20% Savings		2,220
17,100		
Income tax liability		2,720

Tutorial note

Savings income falling in the first £5,000 of taxable income is taxed at the starting rate of 0%. In addition, basic rate taxpayers are entitled to a nil rate band of £1,000 for savings income. The starting rate band and the savings income nil rate band count towards the basic rate and higher rate thresholds.

2   C

	£	£
Personal allowance		11,000
Total income = net income	109,400	
Less: Gross gift aid	(800)	
	————	
ANI	108,600	
Less: Income limit	(100,000)	
	————	
Reduction of PA	8,600 × 50%	(4,300)
	————	————
Adjusted PA		6,700
		————

Tutorial note

1   *Charitable donations under gift aid are grossed up before being used in the adjusted personal allowance computation. The gross figure is given in the question so there is no need to gross up the figure given.*

2   *As the adjusted net income exceeds £100,000 the allowance is reduced by £1 for every £2 it exceeds the limit. Net income for these purposes is adjusted (i.e. reduced) for both gross gift aid and gross personal pension contributions made in the year.*

3   A

	£
(£43,000 − £8,060) = £34,940 × 9%	3,145
(£109,400 − £43,000) = £66,400 × 2%	1,328
	———
	4,473
	———

4 A

	£
Unused annual allowances:	
2013/14 (Not a member of a scheme)	0
2014/15 (£40,000 – £25,000)	15,000
2015/16	40,000
Total unused allowances b/f	55,000
Allowance for 2016/17	40,000
	95,000

Tutorial note

The total available annual allowance is the allowance for the tax year 2016/17 plus unused allowances from the previous three tax years, provided the individual was a member of a registered pension scheme in the tax year.

Tutor's top tips

Always check carefully whether you have been given payments gross or net.

5 B

Tutorial note

Statement (2) is incorrect because personal pension contributions do not affect taxable income. Instead basic rate tax relief is given at source and higher rate relief is given by extending the basic and higher rate bands by the amount of the gross contribution of £8,600 (£6,880 × 100/80).

Statement (3) is incorrect because HM Revenue and Customs would have contributed £1,720 i.e. the basic rate tax deducted at source (£6,880 x 20/80).

Statements (1) and (4) are correct because the basic rate band for 2016/17 is extended by the gross amount of the personal pension contributions (£6,880x100/80= £8,600). This reduces the income falling in the higher rate band by £8,600 such that this income will be taxed at 20% instead of 40% reducing the tax liability at the 40% rate by £3,440 (£8,600 x 40%).

79   KIM BAXTER (ADAPTED) *Walk in the footsteps of a top tutor*

Key answer tips

This case OT involves the employment income rules, including benefits and deductions of expenses. It also covers qualifying interest payments and the marriage allowance, which was introduced in Finance Act 2015 and is therefore very topical. Benefits are a highly examinable area and the detailed rules must be learnt.

1   D

	£
Interest payable at official rate (£14,600 × 3% × 10/12)	365
Less: Interest actually paid (£14,600 × 1% × 10/12)	(122)
Taxable benefit	243

Tutor's top tips

Where a benefit has only been available for part of the tax year, it must be time apportioned.

2   B

Ordinary commuting (i.e. travel between home and the permanent workplace) does not qualify for relief. The travel to a temporary workplace qualifies as it is for a period lasting less than 24 months.

Business mileage is therefore 10,500 miles (9,200 + 1,300)

Expense claim is therefore:

	£
10,000 miles at 45p	4,500
500 miles at 25p	125
	4,625

3 A

	£	£	£
Higher of:			
Market value when gifted		200	
		———	
Market value when first made available	800		
Less: Use of asset benefit:			
2015/16 (£800 × 20%)	(160)		
	———		
		640	
		———	640
Less: Price paid			(50)
			———
Taxable benefit			590
			———

4 £13,860

	Total
	£
Employment income = total income	25,000
Less: Relief for interest paid (Note)	(140)
	———
Net income	24,860
Less: PA	(11,000)
	———
Taxable income	13,860
	———

Tutorial note

The loan interest paid of £140 is eligible for relief since the loan was used by Kim to finance expenditure for a relevant purpose.

5

	Richard	Kim
Personal allowance reduced by £800		
Personal allowance reduced by £1,100	✓	
Personal allowance increased by £800		
Personal allowance increased by £1,100		
Income tax liability reduced by £160		
Income tax liability reduced by £220		✓

Tutorial note

The effect of the marriage allowance election is that the:

- *transferring spouse's PA is reduced by the fixed amount of £1,100 (for 2016/17)*

- *the recipient spouse's income tax liability is reduced by a maximum of £220 (£1,100 MA × 20% BR income tax)*

Note that there is no provision for transferring less than the fixed amount of £1,100.

INCOME TAX BASICS AND INCOME FROM SELF-EMPLOYMENT

80 FOO DEE (ADAPTED)

Key answer tips

This question covers both the rules for income from employment and self-employment.

It requires a simple adjustment of profit and capital allowances computation which should not have caused any problems if you remembered that it is a 9 month accounting period and therefore the maximum AIA and WDAs are time apportioned.

1   D

CO_2 emissions = 180 g/km, available 9 months

	%
Diesel	19
Plus: (180 − 95) × 1/5	17
	——
Appropriate percentage	36
	——

	£
List price of car	21,000
Less: Capital contribution	(2,000)
	——
	19,000
	——
Car benefit (£19,000 × 36% × 9/12)	5,130
	——

2   B

	£
Employer contribution to childcare costs (£55 × 39)	2,145
Employer pension contributions (6%)	0
	2,145

Tutorial note

Gastronomic Food plc's contribution towards Foo's mother looking after her two children is taxable in full as employment income assuming that her mother is not an approved childcare provider. The exemption of £55 per week (for a basic rate taxpayer) only applies where childcare vouchers are provided to employees for use with approved childcare providers.

3   C

Trading profit – 9 m/e 30 September 2017

	£
Net profit	130,854
Depreciation	3,500
Legal fees (capital re acquisition of restaurant)	1,400
Private accommodation (£12,800 × 1/4)	3,200
Trading profit before capital allowances	138,954

4   A

Capital allowances – nine months ended 30 September 2017

	Private use car £		Allowances £
Additions (no AIA)			
Car (76 – 130 g/km)	14,600		
WDA (18% × 9/12) (Note 2)	(1,971)	× 70%	1,380
TWDV c/f	12,629		
Total allowances			1,380

KAPLAN PUBLISHING

Tutorial note

1   The WDA is time apportioned by 9/12 as the accounting period is only 9 months long.

2   Capital allowances on car purchases are calculated based on CO_2 emissions.

     As the car purchased in this question has CO_2 emissions of between 76 – 130 g/km, it is eligible for a WDA at 18%. The WDA then needs to be adjusted for the short accounting period and for the private use by Foo Dee, as only the business use proportion of the allowance can be claimed.

5   B

Tutorial note

Foo starts to trade on 1 January 2017 in the tax year 2016/17. The basis period for the first tax year of trading (2016/17) is 1 January 2017 to 5 April 2017.

The time limit for notifying HM Revenue and Customs of chargeability is six months from the end of the tax year in which the liability arises i.e. 5 October 2017.

The filing date for the 2016/17 tax return is 31 January 2018.

PRACTICE SECTION C CONSTRUCTED RESPONSE QUESTIONS

INCOME TAX BASICS AND EMPLOYMENT INCOME

81   SALLY BURTON (ADAPTED)

Key answer tips

This question is a typical section C question requiring a calculation of income tax payable. However, due to the level of income, abatement of the personal allowance is necessary.

Always watch out for exempt income.

(a)   **Sally Burton**

Income tax computation – 2016/17

	Total	Non-savings income	Savings income
	£	£	£
Salary	90,000		
Car benefit (W1)	3,402		
Living accommodation (W2)	2,082		
	———		
Employment income	95,484	95,484	
Property income (W3)	7,690	7,690	
Gilt interest (W4)	333		333
Building society interest	1,917		1,917
	———	———	———
Total income	105,424	103,174	2,250
Less: PA (W5)	(8,288)	(8,288)	
	———	———	———
Taxable income	97,136	94,886	2,250
	———	———	———

Income tax		
£		£
32,000 × 20% (Non-savings income)		6,400
62,886 × 40% (Non-savings income)		25,154
500 × 0% (Savings income)		0
1,750 × 40% (Savings income)		700
———		
97,136		
———		———
Income tax liability		32,254
Less: PAYE		(30,000)
		———
Income tax payable		2,254
		———

Tutorial note

A nil rate band of £500 is available to higher rate taxpayers for savings income received during the tax year.

Workings

(W1) Car benefit

CO_2 emissions = 152 g/km (rounded down to 150), available for 10 months

	%
Petrol	16
Plus: $(150 - 95) \times \frac{1}{5}$	11
	——
Appropriate percentage	27
	——

	£
List price of car	17,118
Less: Capital contribution	(2,000)
	——
	15,118
	——
Car benefit (£15,118 × 27% × 10/12)	3,402
	——

Tutorial note

The maintenance costs are ignored as the car benefit covers all of the running expenses of the car. The provision of a car parking space near to the employer's premises is an exempt benefit

---

(W2) Living accommodation

	£
Annual value	1,632
Additional benefit for expensive accommodation	
(£120,000 (Note) – £75,000) × 3%	1,350
	——
	2,982
Less: Contributions to employer (£75 × 12 months)	(900)
	——
	2,082
	——

Tutorial note

The property was bought in 2008, which is more than 6 years before it was made available to Sally. Therefore in the calculation of the additional benefit, the cost must be replaced with the market value of the accommodation when the property was first made available.

(W3) Property income

	£
Premium	10,680
Less: £10,680 × 2% × (15 – 1)	(2,990)
	————
Property income	7,690
	————

Tutorial note

An alternative calculation of the assessment of the premium received on the granting of a short lease is as follows:

$P \times (51 – D)/50$

$= £10,680 \times (51 – 15)/50 = £7,690$

(W4) Gilt interest

Sally received interest of £1,000 (£100,000 × 2% × 6/12) on 31 March 2017. However, she will only include interest income of £333 (£1,000 × 2/6) in 2016/17 being the interest accrued in the interest period (1 October 2016 to 31 March 2017) for which she owned the gilts.

Tutorial note

Gilt interest is assessed like other interest income on the receipts basis. However, under the accrued income scheme when gilts are sold interest is effectively allocated to the vendor and purchaser on the accruals basis up to the date of sale.

Part of the price that Sally paid for the gilts represented accrued interest from 1 October 2016 to 31 January 2017 i.e. (£100,000 × 2% × 4/12 = £667).

The vendor will not receive any interest on 31 March 2016 but will be taxed on £667 representing the interest accruing in the interest period for which he owned the gilts. Sally received the interest of £1,000 on 31 March 2017 but is only taxed on £333. Thus the interest of £1,000 has been apportioned between the vendor and Sally (the purchaser).

(W5) Personal allowance

	£		£
PA			11,000
Less: Abatement			
Total income	105,424		
Income limit	(100,000)		
Excess	5,424	× 50%	(2,712)
Adjusted PA			8,288

82   VIGOROUS PLC (ADAPTED)

Key answer tips

This question required the calculation of three benefit packages for three employees. All of the key benefits that you need to be able to deal with in the F6 examination appear in this question!

Easy marks were available in part (b) for explaining how benefits are assessed.

However, careful calculation is required for the benefits as there are many places where calculations can go wrong. Remember to time apportion the calculation where the benefit is not available for all of the tax year, and don't forget to deduct any employee contributions paid.

The highlighted words in the written sections are key phrases that markers are looking for.

(a)   **Assessable benefits – 2016/17**

    Andrea Lean

	£
Car benefit (W1)	5,378
Fuel benefit (W1)	8,214
Living accommodation	
– Annual value	7,000
– Additional benefit (W2)	2,070
– Furniture (£6,000 at 20%)	1,200

Tutorial note

1   *The living accommodation cost in excess of £75,000 so there is an additional benefit.*

Since the property was purchased within six years of first being provided, the benefit is based on the cost of the property plus improvements prior to 6 April 2016 (see W2).

2   *The annual running costs are personally borne by Andrea and therefore are not included as a benefit. Had her employer paid the costs, a £4,000 benefit would arise which she would have reduced to £0 if she reimbursed the company directly.*

3   *The bouquet of flowers will be exempt under the trivial benefits exemption as it cost less than £50 and was not provided in recognition of services provided by Andrea.*

Workings

(W1) Car and fuel benefits

CO_2 emissions = 240 g/km, available all year

	%	
Petrol	16	
Plus: $(240 - 95) \times {}^1/_5$	29	
	——	
Appropriate percentage	45	Restricted to 37%
	——	

		£
Car benefit (£19,400 × 37%)		7,178
Less: Contributions (£150 × 12)		(1,800)
		———
		5,378
		———
Fuel benefit (£22,200 × 37%)		8,214
		———

(W2) Additional benefit for expensive accommodation

	£	
Cost of property (January 2012)	130,000	
Improvements before 6 April 2016	14,000	
	———	
	144,000	
Less: Limit	(75,000)	
	———	
	69,000	
	———	
Additional benefit	× 3%	£2,070
		———

Tutorial note

Improvements in May 2016 are not taken into account in calculating the benefit for 2016/17, as only improvements up to the start of the tax year are included.

However, they will be taken into account next year in calculating the benefit for 2017/18.

Ben Slim

	£
Beneficial loan (W1)	2,475
Relocation costs (£9,300 – £8,000) (Note 1)	1,300
Childcare vouchers ((£60 – £28) × 36) (Note 2)	1,152

Tutorial note

1   *Only £8,000 of relocation costs is exempt.*

2   *Ben is a higher rate taxpayer (salary of £60,000) so the payment of up to £28 per week for approved childcare is an exempt benefit.*

Working: Beneficial loan

Average method	£	
Loan at start of year	120,000	
Loan at end of year	100,000	
	———	
	220,000	
	———	
Average loan (£220,000 ÷ 2)	110,000	
	———	
Assessable benefit (£110,000 × 3% × 9/12)		£2,475
		———
Precise method		
(£120,000 × 3% × 5/12)	1,500	
(£100,000 × 3% × 4/12)	1,000	
	———	£2,500
		———

Ben will not elect for the precise method and in view of the small difference it is unlikely that HMRC will make the election so the benefit will therefore be £2,475.

Chai Trim

	£
Van benefit (£3,170 × 10/12) (Note 1)	2,642
Television (W)	330
Health club membership (Note 2)	150

Tutorial note

1   *The van was only available for ten months of the tax year 2016/17 so the fixed annual £3,170 benefit is time apportioned.*

2   *In-house benefits are valued at the marginal cost to the employer of providing the benefit. The taxable benefit in relation to the health club membership is therefore the direct costs of £150.*

Working: Benefit for the sale of the television

Greater of

		£	£
(i)	MV at date of transfer	250	
	Less: Amount paid	(150)	
		——	100
(ii)	Original cost	800	
	Less: Annual value for 2014/15 and 2015/16		
	(20% × £800 × 2 years)	(320)	
		——	
		480	
Less: Amount paid		(150)	
		——	330

Therefore the taxable benefit is £330.

(b)   **Income tax liability in respect of assessable benefits**

- An employer can choose to payroll most taxable benefits by including the taxable value of the benefits as taxable pay and deducting income tax under the PAYE system. It is then not necessary for the employer to complete a P11D.

- Benefits not payrolled will be included on a P11D and income tax is primarily collected under the self-assessment system.

- However, tax of less than £3,000 can be collected by an adjustment to an employee's tax coding for a subsequent tax year

- In addition, income tax on benefits reported on a P11D can be collected, for a subsequent tax year, through the PAYE system by a reduction in the employee's tax coding.

- Finally, tax on minor benefits may be paid under an employer's PAYE settlement agreement.

83   ALI PATEL (ADAPTED) *Walk in the footsteps of a top tutor*

Key answer tips

A common style question requiring the comparison of two remuneration packages and the impact on the income tax computation and national insurance liabilities.

Part (b) requires a decision to be made based on the net cash flow position after taking account of all costs including income tax and national insurance.

Tutor's top tips

Part (a) of this question involves some fairly straightforward income tax computations.

Don't forget that there is no car benefit if Ali uses his own car for business purposes!

You also need to calculate class 1 NICs. Remember that for the employee, only cash earnings are subject to national insurance.

(a)   **Income tax and class 1 NICs**

    (1)   **First remuneration package**

        Ali's income tax liability – 2016/17

	£
Salary (£29,000 + (£500 × 12))	35,000
Mileage allowance (W)	496
Employment income	35,496
Less: Personal allowance	(11,000)
Taxable income	24,496
Income tax liability (£24,496 × 20%)	4,899

        Employee class 1 primary NIC – 2016/17

(£35,000 – £8,060) × 12%	3,233

        Working: Mileage allowance

        The relocation is not expected to last for more than 24 months, so the branch office will be treated as a temporary workplace.

        Mileage for the year = (1,600 × 12) = 19,200 miles

Ali will therefore be taxed on the mileage allowance paid by Box plc as follows:

	£	£
Mileage allowance received (19,200 at 38p)		7,296
Authorised mileage allowance:		
10,000 miles at 45p	4,500	
9,200 miles at 25p	2,300	
	―――	(6,800)
Taxable benefit		496

Tutorial note

For NIC purposes only the excess mileage allowance above 45p per mile is subject to NIC. As Ali will be paid 38p per mile, none of the mileage allowance is charged to NIC.

(2)   **Second remuneration package**

Ali's income tax liability – 2016/17

	£
Salary	29,000
Living accommodation (W)	9,600
Property business profit	6,000
	―――
Total income	44,600
Less: Personal allowance	(11,000)
	―――
Taxable income	33,600
	―――

Income tax

£	
32,000 × 20%	6,400
1,600 × 40%	640
―――	
33,600	
―――	―――
Income tax liability	7,040
	―――

Employee class 1 primary NIC – 2016/17

(£29,000 – £8,060) × 12%	2,513
	―――

Working: Living accommodation

The benefit of living accommodation will be the greater of:

(i)	Annual value	£4,600
(ii)	Rent paid by the employer (£800 × 12)	£9,600

(b)   **Most beneficial remuneration package**

Tutor's top tips

When calculating the net disposable income think just in terms of cash and identify all cash coming in and all cash payments going out. Cash payments obviously include the tax liabilities calculated in part (a), but also include other expenses such as commuting costs.

Even if you made some mistakes in part (a), as long as you include your tax figures here in this part you will be awarded full marks.

The question specifically asks you to advise Ali as to which remuneration package is most beneficial, so make sure that you do this. A statement of which package should be accepted is therefore needed.

You will be given full marks here if your advice is consistent with your analysis, even if it is the wrong advice!

	Package (1) £	Package (2) £
Salary	35,000	29,000
Property business income	0	6,000
Mileage allowance received	7,296	0
Commuting costs	(1,800)	0
Class 1 NIC	(3,233)	(2,513)
Income tax	(4,899)	(7,040)
Net disposable income	32,364	25,447

Ali should choose the first remuneration package as he will be £6,917 (£32,364 – £25,447) better off.

84   PATIENCE (ADAPTED) *Walk in the footsteps of a top tutor*

Key answer tips

This question required the computation of income tax and capital gains tax for an individual including employment income, self–employment income and property income.

A calculation of the various types of income was necessary in order to complete the income tax computation.

There were two marks available for a basic capital gains computation on the disposal of the two rental properties.

Tutor's top tips

You are required to calculate employment income, self-employment income and property income for inclusion in the income tax computation. Start with your strongest of the three areas as it does not have to be completed in a set order.

Remember to clearly show your workings to enable the marker to award marks where mistakes have been made.

Patience – Income tax computation 2016/17

	£
Employment income	
Salary (£3,750 × 9)	33,750
Pension contributions – Patience (£33,750 × 6%)	(2,025)
– Employer	0
	————
	31,725
School place	540
Long-service award	0
Beneficial loan	0
Trading profit (W1)	16,100
Pensions (£1,450 + £6,000 + £3,300)	10,750
Property business profit (W3)	3,500
	————
Total income	62,615
Personal allowance	(11,000)
	————
Taxable income	51,615
	————

£		
36,500 (W4) at 20%		7,300
15,115 at 40%		6,046
————		
51,615		
————		————
Income tax liability		13,346
		————

Tutorial notes

(1)   *A non-cash long-service award is not a taxable benefit if it is for a period of service of at least 20 years, and the cost of the award does not exceed £50 per year of service.*

(2)   *There is no taxable benefit if beneficial loans do not exceed £10, 000 during the tax year.*

Workings

(W1) Trading profit

	£	£
Year ended 31 July 2016		14,800
Period ended 31 December 2016	6,900	
Balancing allowance (working 2)	(1,900)	
		5,000
		19,800
Relief for overlap profits		(3,700)
		16,100

(W2) Capital allowances

	Main pool	Allowances
	£	£
TWDV brought forward	2,200	
Addition – Laptop computer	1,700	
Proceeds (£1,200 + £800)	(2,000)	
Balancing allowance	(1,900)	1,900

Tutorial notes

1   *There is no annual investment allowance, 100% FYA or writing down allowance available in the final capital allowances computation. Additions are included in the relevant pool at cost. The disposal proceeds are deducted to calculate a balancing allowance/charge on all columns on cessation of trade.*

2   *The closing year basis period rules must be applied in the final tax year of trade. The final assessment includes any profits not yet assessed less overlap profits from commencement of trade.*

(W3) Property business profit

	£
Rent received (£3,600 + £7,200)	10,800
Expenditure (£4,700 + £2,600)	(7,300)
Property business profit	3,500

(W4) Tax band

	£
Property one – Disposal proceeds	
– Cost	
	40,600
Property two – Disposal proceeds	
– Cost	
	(5,700)
	———
Total chargeable gains	34,900
Annual exempt amount	(11,100)
	———
Taxable gains	23,800
	———
Capital gains tax: £23,800 at 28%	6,664
	———

Tutorial note

Gains on residential properties are taxed at higher rates than other gains, the rates are provided in the tax tables. Patience is a higher rate taxpayer so the gain is all taxed at 28%.

Examiner's report

This was the income tax question. It was well answered, and involved a taxpayer who had retired during the tax year, ceasing both employment and self-employment. The requirement was to calculate the income tax and capital gains tax liabilities for the tax year.

Two aspects to this question caused particular difficulty. Firstly, many candidates treated the pension income (state pension, employer's occupational pension scheme and a private pension) as exempt income. Secondly, the format in which information was given for two properties caused a certain amount of confusion, with the information relevant for income tax and the capital gains tax details being shown within the one table; candidates being required to separate out the relevant information for income tax and capital gains tax purposes. Here figures were often duplicated, with, for example, revenue expenditure being (correctly) deducted as an expense in calculating the property business profit, but then also (incorrectly) deducted in calculating chargeable gains.

ACCA marking scheme	
	Marks
Salary less employee pension contributions	1.0
Employer's pension contributions exempt	0.5
School place	1.0
Long service award	0.5
Beneficial loan	0.5
Trading profit year ended 31.7.16	0.5
Trading profit period ended 31.12.16	0.5
Deduct overlap profits	1.0
Capital allowances – TWDV b/f	0.5
Capital allowances – addition	0.5
Capital allowances – disposal proceeds	1.0
Capital allowances – balancing allowance	1.0
Property income – rental income	0.5
Property income – expenses	0.5
Pension income	1.0
Personal allowance	0.5
Extend BRB	1.0
IT	1.0
Gain on property 1	0.5
Gain on property 2	0.5
AEA	0.5
CGT at 28%	0.5
	———
Total	**15.0**
	———

85 SAMMI SMITH (ADAPTED) *Walk in the footsteps of a top tutor*

Key answer tips

This was a very unusual style of question for the F6 examination, which would probably challenge many students. However, we can expect more questions like this in the future.

The question required the comparison of two remuneration options, and consideration of the tax consequences from both the employee and the employer's perspective.

It therefore required four separate calculations (each option from each party's perspective), covering income tax, corporation tax and NICs.

The requirements here were very clear and easy marks could be gained from some very basic tax calculations, provided students were not scared off by the style of the question.

The final part of the question, which required the calculation of 'after tax net costs' of both options, may have thrown some students. It is helpful to sit back and think through all the tax and other cash consequences of both options before attempting to answer this part.

Tutor's top tips

The key when you are challenged by a style of question you have not seen before is not to panic!

In the more challenging questions the F6 examining team will often help you through the order in which they set out the requirements and by providing guidance within the requirements themselves. That is the case here, and if you consider the requirements carefully and work through them systematically you will find that the tax calculations themselves are actually very straightforward and it is possible to score very highly on parts (a) and (b).

A comparison of the choices of the provision of a car or remuneration to fund a car is a classic examination scenario. Bear in mind that you already know how to calculate the taxable benefit on a car, you know how to tax employee remuneration and you know the tax consequences for a company of providing a car to an employee or of paying salary to an employee. This question simply combines those calculations.

Ensure that you use clear headings, showing which calculation you are doing, so that the marker can more easily give you credit.

Part (c) may cause more difficulty as it is unfamiliar, but again not technically demanding. Ensure you pick up your figures from parts (a) and (b) as well as any other costs mentioned in the question.

(a) **Sammi Smith – Company car**

CO_2 emissions = 295 g/km, available all year

	%
Petrol	16
Plus: $(295 - 95) \times 1/5$	40
Appropriate percentage	56
Percentage restricted to	37

	£
List price of car	81,858
Car benefit (£81,858 × 37%)	30,287
Income tax at marginal rate (£30,287 × 40%)	12,115

There are no NIC implications for an employee in receipt of a non-cash benefit, such as a company car.

Sammi Smith – Additional remuneration

	£
Income tax at marginal rate (£24,870 × 40%)	9,948
NICs at marginal rate (£24,870 × 2%)	497
	———
Total tax cost	10,445
	———

Tutorial note

1   *The maximum amount for the car benefit percentage (37%) is not listed in the tax tables and must be learnt.*

2   *The list price of the car is £81,858 and this is used to calculate the car benefit.*

3   *There is no fuel benefit to calculate here as Sammi has not been provided with any private fuel.*

4   *It is not necessary to do a full income tax computation in order to calculate the income tax implications of either option. Instead you need to establish Sammi's marginal rate of tax, which is the rate at which additional income will be taxed. As Sammi already receives director's remuneration in excess of £45,000, she is already a higher rate taxpayer, and neither option will take her near the threshold for the reduction in the PA or for tax at the additional rate. Therefore her marginal rate of income tax is 40%.*

5   *Benefits are not subject to NICs for the employee unless they are readily convertible into cash (in which case they form part of earnings and are subject to class 1 NICs).*

6   *Sammi's marginal rate for NICs can be established in the same way as for income tax. As Sammi's remuneration is in excess of £45,000 she has already exceeded the upper earnings limit and any further income will be taxable at 2%.*

(b)   **Smark Ltd – Company car**

Tutor's top tips

This part is slightly more challenging than the previous part as the NICs payable by the company have an impact on the corporation tax payable. It is therefore important that you calculate the NICs before the corporation tax in both cases.

You should also be careful when considering whether all of the lease costs are an allowable deduction for corporation tax purposes.

	£
Annual lease cost	26,540
Disallowance – high emission car (£26,540 × 15%)	(3,981)
	———
	22,559
Class 1A NICs payable on car benefit (£30,287 × 13.8%)	4,180
	———
Total tax allowable costs	26,739
	———
Corporation tax reduction (£26,739 × 20%)	5,348
	———

Smark Ltd – Additional remuneration

	£
Additional remuneration	24,870
Employer's class 1 secondary NICs (£24,870 × 13.8%)	3,432
	———
Total costs	28,302
	———
Corporation tax reduction (£28,302 × 20%)	5,660
	———

Tutorial notes

1   Cars with CO_2 emissions in excess of 130 g/km are considered 'high emission' cars and 15% of the lease cost is disallowed.

2   Class 1A NICs are payable on the taxable benefit. You therefore need to use the figure you have calculated in part (a).

3   Once you have calculated the relevant allowable costs for tax purposes (including the class 1A NICs) you can calculate the reduction in the corporation tax liability.

(c)   **Most beneficial choice for Sammi Smith**

Tutor's top tips

This is the part of the question you may find most difficult, as rather than involving a tax calculation, you need to pull together the tax figures you have already calculated as well as the costs per the question to recommend which option Sammi and Smark Ltd will prefer.

You need to remember to include all the relevant costs in your calculations – the cost of providing the car or the remuneration, the IT costs, the NIC costs (for both Sammi and Smark Ltd) and the CT saving.

If you have made an error in your calculations earlier in the question, you will still get follow through marks provided you use your own figures correctly in this part.

- If Sammi is provided with a company car the only cost will be the additional income tax of £12,115.

- If Sammi chooses the director's remuneration the net after tax cost will be:

	£
Cost of leasing car	26,540
Additional tax cost	10,445
Additional remuneration	(24,870)
Net after tax cost	12,115

- The net costs are exactly the same; it therefore shouldn't matter to Sammi which option is chosen.

Most beneficial choice for Smark Ltd

- If Smark Ltd provide Sammi with a company car, the net after tax cost will be:

	£
Cost of leasing car	26,540
Additional NIC cost	4,180
Corporation tax saving	(5,348)
Net after tax cost	25,372

- If Smark Ltd provide Sammi with additional director's remuneration, the net after tax cost will be:

	£
Remuneration cost	24,870
Additional NIC cost	3,432
Corporation tax saving	(5,660)
Net after tax cost	22,642

- Smark Ltd would therefore prefer to provide Sammi with additional remuneration, as this option costs less overall.

Examiner's report

This question was generally answered quite badly, with the main problem being that candidates simply did not spend enough time thinking and planning their answers, but just plunged straight in performing every calculation that they could think of.

In part (a) the answer was in fact very straightforward, with a fairly simple car benefit calculation and then income tax and NIC calculations at the director's marginal rates of 40% and 2% respectively.

Far too many candidates calculated a fuel benefit despite being told that fuel was not provided for private journeys.

In part (b) many candidates stated that capital allowances would be available despite the motor car being leased.

Candidates often stated that the company's corporation tax liability would be increased rather than reduced as a result of the additional expenditure, and very few candidates appreciated that NIC was a deductible expense.

Part (c) was more difficult, although credit was given for any sensible approach such as comparing the tax liabilities under each alternative.

ACCA marking scheme		
		Marks
(a)	Company car	
	Car benefit	2.0
	Income tax	1.0
	NIC implications	0.5
	Additional director's remuneration	
	Income tax	0.5
	Class 1 NIC	1.0
		———
		5.0
		———
(b)	Company car	
	Class 1A NIC	1.0
	Allowable leasing costs	1.0
	Corporation tax saving	1.0
	Additional director's remuneration	
	Class 1 NIC	1.0
	Corporation tax saving	1.0
		———
		5.0
		———
(c)	Sammi	
	Director's remuneration – net cost	1.0
	Conclusion	1.0
	Smark Ltd	
	Director's remuneration – net cost	1.0
	Company car – net costs	1.0
	Conclusion	1.0
		———
		5.0
		———
Total		15.0
		———

86   LETICIA STONE *Walk in the footsteps of a top tutor*

Key answer tips

This question required the calculation of property losses – one for a furnished holiday letting property and one for the other let properties.

The calculations are not difficult provided you remember the following:

1   Property income is assessed on an accruals basis as if the individual had a trade with a 5 April year end.

2   Separate calculations are required for furnished holiday lettings, but all other property income and expenses are pooled into one calculation

3   One of the advantages of furnished holiday lettings is that they are entitled to capital allowances rather than replacement furniture relief.

Two easy marks were available in part (b) for explaining what an individual can do with property losses.

(a)   **Furnished holiday letting loss – 2016/17**

	£	£
Rent receivable (£425 × 22)		9,350
Loan interest	12,700	
Repairs (£12,200 – £10,900)	1,300	
Mileage allowance (W)	455	
Other expenses	3,770	
Capital allowances (£4,600 × 100% (AIA)	4,600	
	———	(22,825)
Furnished holiday letting loss		(13,475)

Working: Mileage allowance

The mileage that Leticia drove in respect of the property purchase is capital in nature, and therefore does not qualify.

Her mileage allowance is therefore:

(880 + 130) = 1,010 at 45p = £455

Tutor's top tips

You are told in the question that property one qualifies as a trade under the furnished holiday letting rules. Hence you will not receive any marks for writing out the conditions for a property to be a furnished holiday let and trying to apply them to any of the properties.

Property loss – 2016/17

	Notes	£	£
Premium received for sub-lease			45,000
Less: £45,000 × 2% × (5 – 1)			(3,600)
	1		41,400
Rent receivable	2		
– Property 2 (£2,160 × 4 × 11/12)	3		7,920
– Property 3 (£580 × 10)	4		5,800
– Security deposit	5		0
			55,120
Rent payable (£1,360 × 11)		14,960	
Impairment loss		580	
Loan interest		9,100	
Other expenses		36,240	
			(60,880)
			(5,760)
Furnished room (£3,170 – £4,840)	6		(1,670)
Property loss			(7,430)

Tutorial note

1   *An alternative calculation of the assessment of the premium received on the granting of a short lease is as follows:*

   P × (51 – D)/50

   = £45,000 × (51 – 5)/50 = £41,400

2   *Rents are assessed on an accruals basis. Therefore the rents receivable between 6 April 2016 and 5 April 2017 are required.*

3   *Property 2 is rented out for 11 months of the tax year, but the rents are quoted in the question on a quarterly basis. Therefore the annual rent needs to be calculated and 11/12ths of the annual rent is assessed in the tax year 2016/17.*

4   *Property 3 is only rented out for 10 months of the tax year, but the information is given in monthly terms, so the calculation is straightforward.*

5   *The security deposit relating to Property 3 is received in the tax year, but it relates to the tenancy of the property in 2017/18 (commencing 15 April 2017). Therefore it will not be assessed in the tax year 2016/17.*

6   *Leticia would elect to use the normal basis of assessment in respect of the furnished room since this allows a loss to be generated.*

(b)   **Relief for property losses**

- The furnished holiday letting loss will be carried forward and relieved against Leticia's future profits from furnished holiday lettings only.

- The property business loss will be carried forward and relieved against the first available future property business profits only.

Examiner's report

Part (a) of this question was very well answered, with no aspect causing significant problems.

However, several candidates did not claim capital allowances for the furnished holiday letting.

Although candidates were not penalised if they combined the property losses into just one calculation, not separating out the furnished holiday letting loss invariably meant that marks were then lost in part (b) as marks were not awarded for vague details on loss relief if it was not clearly stated as to which reliefs were available for which type of loss.

Note: *The examiner's report has been edited to remove comments on elements of the question that have been deleted due to changes in legislation.*

ACCA marking scheme		Marks
(a)	**Furnished holiday letting loss**	
	Rent receivable	0.5
	Loan interest	1.0
	Repairs	1.0
	Mileage allowance	1.5
	Other expenses	0.5
	Capital allowances	1.0
	Property loss	
	Lease premium received	1.0
	Rent receivable – Property 2	1.0
	– Property 3	1.0
	– Security deposit	0.5
	Rent payable	1.0
	Impairment loss	1.0
	Loan interest	0.5
	Other expenses	0.5
	Furnished room	1.0
		───
		13.0
		───
(b)	Furnished holiday letting loss	1.0
	Property loss	1.0
		───
		2.0
		───
Total		**15.0**
		───

87   RICHARD TRYER (ADAPTED) *Walk in the footsteps of a top tutor*

Key answer tips

This question requires a calculation of the income tax payable for a taxpayer who has correctly completed parts of his income tax computation, but left the following omissions:

1   Car and fuel benefits

2   Living accommodation

3   Property business profit

4   Income tax calculation

It is important not to be put off if a question is presented in a different format from those you have seen before; each one of these omissions tests areas that are commonly examined in F6.

Tutor's top tips

The best way to approach this question is the same as any other income tax computation question, by preparing an income tax computation in the normal columnar format. The F6 examining team has chosen to give you some of the information you need in the body of the incomplete income tax computation. You can score easy marks by using these figures in your own computation.

You do not have to use the layout presented in the question.

There is a lot of information in the question which you must read carefully. Pay special attention to dates given to see if income and benefits are available all year or must be time apportioned.

Richard Tryer

Income tax computation – 2016/17

	Total	Non-savings income	Savings income	Dividend income
	£	£	£	£
Employment income (W1)	66,030	66,030		
Property income (W4)	7,720	7,720		
Building society interest (per Q) (Note 1)	1,260		1,260	
Dividends (Note 1)	8,800			8,800
	83,810	73,750	1,260	8,800
Less: PA (per Q)	(11,000)	(11,000)		
Taxable income	72,810	62,750	1,260	8,800

£			
32,000	at 20% (per Q)		6,400
30,750	at 40%		12,300
62,750			
500	at 0%		0
760	(£1,260 – £500) at 40%		304
5,000	at 0%		0
3,800	(£8,800 – £5,000) at 32.5%		1,235
72,810			
Income tax liability			20,239
Less: PAYE (per Q)			(9,130)
Income tax payable			11,109

Tutorial note

1   There is no need to consider any potential issues in relation to the building society interest or dividend because the question states that the completed parts of the income tax computation are correct.

Workings

(W1) Employment income

	£
Salary (per question)	41,000
Car benefit (W2)	2,380
Fuel benefit (W2)	3,330
Living accommodation (W3)	13,200
Furniture (£12,100 × 20%)	2,420
Running costs	3,700
	———
Employment income	66,030
	———

(W2) Car and fuel benefits

CO_2 emissions = 119 g/km (rounded down to 115) and available all year.

	%
Petrol	16
Plus: (115 – 95)/5	4
	—
Appropriate percentage	20
	—

	£
List price of car	17,900
	———

	£
Car benefit (£17,900 × 20%)	3,580
Less: Contribution for private use	(1,200)
	———
Car benefit	2,380
	———
Fuel benefit	
(£22,200 × 20% × 9/12)	3,330
	———

Tutorial note

1   *Note that the fuel benefit is only given for part of the tax year (unlike the car itself which is available all year). Hence the fuel benefit must be time apportioned.*

2   *The cost of providing the fuel and the percentage that relates to private use is irrelevant for the purposes of calculating the fuel benefit.*

(W3) Living accommodation

- The benefit for the living accommodation is the higher of the annual value of £8,600 and the rent paid of £13,200 (£1,100 × 12).

- There is no additional benefit because Prog plc does not own the property.

Tutor's top tips

The F6 examining team has included the market value of the living accommodation. This is not needed to calculate the benefit because the property is rented by the employer and not owned.

This information is included to test that you understand this point, so do not fall into the F6 examining team's trap and try to use the market value.

(W4) Property income

	£	£
Premium received		12,000
Less: £12,000 × 2% × (30 – 1)		(6,960)
		5,040
Rent receivable (£830 × 4)		3,320
		8,360
Roof replacement	0	
Roof repairs (£8,600 – £8,200)	400	
Insurance (£480 × 6/12)	240	
		(640)
Property income		7,720

Tutorial note

The initial replacement cost of the shop's roof is not deductible. It is capital in nature, as the building was not in a usable state when purchased and this fact was reflected in the reduced purchase price.

Examiner's report

The question was generally well answered, and candidates obviously benefited from having a pro forma layout to follow.

Many candidates calculated an additional benefit for the living accommodation despite such a charge not being relevant where a property is rented.

Note: *The examiner's report has been edited to remove comments on elements of the question that have been deleted due to changes in legislation.*

ACCA marking scheme	
	Marks
Salary	0.5
Car benefit	2.0
Fuel benefit	1.5
Living accommodation	2.0
Furniture	0.5
Running costs	0.5
Assessment on premium	1.5
Rents receivable	1.0
Roof replacement	0.5
Roof repairs	1.0
Insurance	1.0
Building society interest & dividends	0.5
Income tax payable	2.5
	────
Total	**15.0**
	────

88 SAMSON AND DELILAH *Walk in the footsteps of a top tutor*

Key answer tips

This question is a classic example of a section C income tax question.

Part (a) requires the calculation of income tax for both a husband and wife, testing knowledge of both employment and trading income. Although there are tricky elements to deal with relating to the golf club membership and chauffeur, there are plenty of straightforward marks so it is important to manage your time well and get the easier marks.

Part (b) relates to tax planning between a married couple and the impact of transferring income-generating assets from one to the other. Think carefully before answering this type of requirement as it is possible to score marks easily here if you don't rush.

Tutor's top tips

Begin part (a) of this question by writing out separate income tax pro formas for Samson and Delilah. Work through the different types of income, inserting the more straightforward numbers first (such as the allowable deductions for Delilah's professional subscription and payroll giving). Where workings are required, attempt them after the easier numbers, and also make sure you leave time to calculate the income tax at the end!

(a)   **Samson – Income tax computation 2016/17**

	Total	Non-savings income	Savings income
	£	£	£
Employment income – Salary	112,000	112,000	
Building society interest (£9,600/2)	4,800		4,800
Total income = net income	116,800	112,000	4,800
Less: PA (W1)	(2,600)	(2,600)	
Taxable income	114,200	109,400	4,800

Income tax

£	
32,000 × 20% (non-savings income)	6,400
77,400 × 40% (non-savings income)	30,960
500 × 0% (savings income)	0
4,300 × 40% (savings income)	1,720

114,200

Income tax liability	39,080

Delilah – Income tax computation 2016/17

	Total	Non-savings income	Savings income
	£	£	£
Employment income:			
Salary	184,000	184,000	
Charitable payroll deductions (£250 × 12)	(3,000)	(3,000)	
Car benefit (W2)	24,192	24,192	
Chauffeur	9,400	9,400	
Professional subscription	(450)	(450)	
Golf club membership	0	0	
	214,142	214,142	
Trading profit	34,240	34,240	
(£85,600 (£93,600 – £8,000) × 40%)			
Building society interest (£9,600/2)	4,800		4,800
Total income	253,182	248,382	4,800
Qualifying interest paid	(6,200)	(6,200)	
Net income	246,982	242,182	4,800
Less: PA	(0)	(0)	
Taxable income	246,982	242,182	4,800

Income tax		£
£38,000 × 20% (W3) (non-savings income)		7,600
£118,000 × 40% (non-savings income)		47,200
		———
£156,000 (W3)		
£86,182 × 45% (non-savings income)		38,782
£4,800 × 45% (savings income)		2,160
		———
£246,982		
		———
Income tax liability		95,742
		———

Tutorial note

1   For an expense to be deductible from employment income it must be wholly, exclusively and necessarily incurred for the purposes of the employment. The golf club membership is not an allowable deduction despite being used to entertain customers as it not a **necessary** employment expense.

2   The loan interest paid of £6,200 is deductible because the loan was used by Delilah for a qualifying purpose.

3   The savings nil rate band is not available to additional rate taxpayers.

Workings

(W1) Personal allowance

			£
PA			11,000
Net income = ANI	116,800		
Less: Income limit	(100,000)		
	———		
Excess	16,800	× 50%	(8,400)
	———		———
PA			2,600
			———

Tutorial note

Delilah is not entitled to a personal allowance as her adjusted net income of £240,982 (246,982 – 6,000) exceeds the income limit plus twice the personal allowance (£122,000).

(W2) Car benefit

CO_2 emissions = 195g/km, available all year

	%
Petrol	16
Plus: $(195 - 95) \times 1/5$	20
	——
Appropriate percentage	36
	——
Car benefit ($£67,200 \times 36\%$)	£24,192

Tutorial note

1   Delilah's company car was available throughout the tax year 2016/17. The taxable benefit is not restricted for the period that she was unable to drive as the car remained available to her during this time.

2   The car benefit does not cover the cost of a chauffeur, so this is an additional benefit.

(W3) Extension of basic and higher rate bands

	£	£
Basic/higher rate band threshold	32,000	150,000
Plus: gross gift aid	6,000	6,000
	———	———
Extended basic/higher rate band	38,000	156,000

(b)   Samson's income tax saving

Tutor's top tips

You may have been unsure how to approach part (b). As it is only worth 2 marks there is clearly not time to recalculate the income tax liabilities for Samson and Delilah. However, it is quite easy to see the tax paid, and therefore saved, by Samson on the interest income from looking at your tax calculation in part (a). Don't forget however, to consider the implications of Samson's reduced income on the personal allowance.

Transferring the building society deposit account into Delilah's sole name would have saved Samson income tax of £2,680 (£1,720 + £960) in the tax year 2016/17. This is calculated as the tax paid on the savings income of £1,720 (part (a)) plus the reduction in tax paid on his non-savings income at 40% due to the increased personal allowance of £960 (£4,800 × 50% × 40%).

Tutorial note

Samson's PA is restricted to £2,600 as his ANI exceeds £100,000. Samson's taxable income in excess of £100,000 would normally be subject to a marginal tax rate of 60% income tax. This is made up of:

- *higher rate income tax = 40%*

- *lost PA (1/2 × 40%) = 20%*

Therefore, transferring income to his wife, would normally save Samson income tax at a rate of 60% i.e £2,880 (£4,800 × 60%).

However, in this instance Samson, as a higher rate taxpayer was entitled to a savings nil rate band of £500, thus reducing the tax paid on £500 of the savings income from 40% to 0%. The tax saved on transferring the interest income to Delilah is therefore reduced by the loss of the savings nil rate band and is £2,680 (£2,880 – (£500 × 40%)).

ACCA marking scheme		Marks
(a)	**Samson – income tax computation 2016/17**	
	Salary	0.5
	Interest	0.5
	Personal allowance	1.0
	Income tax at 20%	0.5
	Income tax at 0%	0.5
	Income tax at 40%	0.5
	Delilah – income tax computation 2016/17	
	Salary	0.5
	Interest	0.5
	Charitable payroll deductions	0.5
	Car benefit	1.5
	Chauffeur	0.5
	Professional subscription	0.5
	Golf club membership	0.5
	Trading profit	1.0
	Interest paid	1.0
	Personal allowance	0.5
	Extension of basic and higher rate bands	1.0
	Income tax at 20%	0.5
	Income tax at 40%	0.5
	Income tax at 45%	0.5
		13.0
(b)	Samson – income tax saving	2.0
Total		**15.0**

INCOME TAX BASICS AND INCOME FROM SELF-EMPLOYMENT

89 CAROL COURIER (ADAPTED)

Key answer tips

A straightforward purely computational question dealing with the income tax and national insurance consequences of being employed and self-employed.

Part (c) requires a comparison of the net disposable income arising from the two options.

(a) **Carol continues to be employed**

Carol's income tax liability – 2016/17

	£
Salary	37,500
Less: Pension contributions (£37,500 × 5%)	(1,875)
Employment income	35,625
Less: PA	(11,000)
Taxable income	24,625
Income tax liability (£24,625 × 20%)	4,925

Class 1 NICs – Employee's primary contributions

(£37,500 – £8,060) × 12%	3,533

(b) **Carol accepts self-employed contract**

Carol's income tax liability – 2016/17

	£
Income (£43,500 + £8,000)	51,500
Less: Expenses (£4,400 + £2,800)	(7,200)
Trading income	44,300
Less: PA	(11,000)
Taxable income	33,300
Income tax liability (£33,300 × 20%) (Working)	6,660

Class 4 NICs

(£43,000 – £8,060) × 9%	3,145
(£44,300 – £43,000) × 2%	26
	3,171

Class 2 NICs

(£2.80 for 52 weeks)   146
                                                                                               _____

Working: Extension of the basic rate band

	£
Basic rate band	32,000
Plus: Gross pension contributions	3,000
	_____
Extended basic rate band	35,000
	_____

All of Carol's taxable income of £33,300 falls into this extended basic rate band and is therefore taxed at 20%.

(c)   **Benefit of accepting self-employed contract**

	Employed	Self employed
	£	£
Salary	37,500	0
Trading income	0	44,300
Pension contributions paid (Note)	(1,875)	(2,400)
NIC – Class 1 and class 4	(3,533)	(3,171)
NIC – Class 2	0	(146)
Income tax	(4,925)	(6,660)
	_____	_____
Net disposable income	27,167	31,923
	_____	_____

It is therefore beneficial for Carol to accept the offer to provide delivery services on a self-employed basis as her net income will increase by £4,756 (£31,923 − £27,167).

Tutorial note

Carol will pay personal pension contributions net of basic rate tax. If self-employed she will therefore pay £2,400 (£3,000 × 80%).

Tutor's top tips

When calculating the net disposable income think just in terms of cash and identify all cash coming in and all cash payments going out.

Cash payments obviously include the tax liabilities but also include other expenses such as pension contributions.

90   IDRIS WILLIAMS *Walk in the footsteps of a top tutor*

Key answer tips

This question has been written to test the rules on the cash basis as well as the choice of accounting date.

Students should be familiar with the factors that influence the choice of accounting date and the advantages and disadvantages of choosing an accounting date early or late in the tax year.

The cash basis rules are examinable in F6 to a limited extent. This question tests all the rules which could be examined.

The highlighted words in the written sections are key phrases that markers are looking for.

Tutor's top tips

There are four marks available for part (a), therefore four clear points should be made.

(a)   **Advantages of a 5 April accounting date**

- If Idris chooses to prepare his accounts to 5 April, the application of the basis period rules will be simplified.

- Idris will not have any overlap profits on the commencement of trade. If he prepares his accounts to 30 June, nine months of overlap profits will arise and these would not be relieved until the cessation of trading.

Advantages of a 30 June accounting date

- If Idris prepares his accounts to 30 June the interval between earning profits and paying the related tax liability will be 9 months longer than with an accounting date of 5 April.

- An accounting date of 30 June would make it easier to implement tax planning measures as there is a longer period over which to plan.

(b)   (1)   **Tax adjusted trading profit – accruals basis – year ended 5 April 2017**

Tutor's top tips

This question does not specifically request that you start with the net profit figure and adjust for any disallowable items, but this is the most obvious approach to take.

Always show your workings if the figure you are adjusting for is not clear from the question.

When using the normal accruals basis no adjustment should be made for any receivables or payables.

	£	£
Net profit	20,175	
Food, utilities, etc. (personal use)	4,500	
Depreciation	1,250	
Motor expenses (£9,340 × 7,000/20,000)	3,269	
Capital allowances (W)		4,553
	———	———
	29,194	4,553
	(4,553)	———
Tax adjusted trading profit	24,641	
	———	

Tutorial note

The usual presentation of an adjustment of profits is produced above. However, an alternative method of calculating the same taxable trading profit figure is to reproduce the accounts just deducting the expenses which are allowable, as opposed to adding back those that are not allowable to the net profit. This alternative presentation is given below as it provides a more direct comparison of the difference in the treatment when the cash basis is used.

	£	£
Revenue		*49,910*
Food, utilities and other household goods (£17,660 – £4,500)		*(13,160)*
		———
		36,750
Depreciation	*0*	
Motor expenses (£9,340 × 13,000/20,000)	*6,071*	
Other expenses	*1,485*	
Capital allowances (W)	*4,553*	
	———	*(12,109)*
		———
		24,641
		———

Working: Capital allowances

	Main pool	Private use car	Allowances
	£	£	£	£
Additions (no AIA)				
Car (76 – 130 g/km)			9,000	
Additions (with AIA)				
Furniture	3,500			
Less: AIA	(3,500)			3,500
	———	0		
WDA (18%) (Note)			(1,620) × 65%	1,053
		———	———	
TWDV c/f		0	7,380	
		———	———	
Total allowances				4,553
				———

Tutorial note

Capital allowances on car purchases are calculated based on the CO_2 emissions.

As the car purchased in this question has CO_2 emissions of between 76 – 130 g/km, it is eligible for a WDA at 18%. The WDA then needs to be adjusted for the private use by Idris, as only the business use proportion of the allowance can be claimed.

The business mileage is 13,000 out of 20,000 miles (i.e. 65%).

   (2)   **Cash basis**

Idris is entitled to use the cash basis as his revenue is below the VAT registration threshold of £83,000.

Tutor's top tips

When operating the cash basis adjustments need to be made for any receivables and payables.

The F6 examining team has stated that where the cash basis is used you should assume that flat rate expenses are claimed for motor expenses and private use of business premises.

The motor expenses deduction is calculated using the HMRC approved mileage allowances. The private use of business premises flat rate adjustment covers the private use of food, utilities and other household goods and services.

Capital purchases are deductible in full in the year of purchase; however, no deduction is available for the purchase of a motor car as this is covered by the approved mileage allowance.

	£	£
Revenue (£49,910 – £10,275)		39,635
Less: Food, utilities, etc. (£17,660 × 95%)		(16,777)
		─────
		22,858
Plus: Flat rate private use adjustment		4,200
Less: Depreciation	0	
Capital expenditure	3,500	
Motor expenses (W)	5,250	
Other expenses (£1,485 – £400)	1,085	
	─────	(9,835)
		─────
Tax adjusted trading profit		17,223
		─────

Working: Motor expenses

Idris is entitled to claim a deduction for his business mileage of 13,000 miles at the approved mileage rates.

	£
10,000 miles at 45p	4,500
3,000 miles at 25p	750
	———
	5,250
	———

(3)   **More beneficial basis**

Using the cash basis will result in Idris being taxed on a lower amount in the tax year 2016/17, and is therefore preferable. The difference is £7,418 (£24,641 − £17,223).

91   SAM WHITE (ADAPTED) *Walk in the footsteps of a top tutor*

Key answer tips

A classic self-employed scenario. The adjustment of profits was straightforward, except that some may not have known what to do with the patent royalties. In fact, if you did nothing, that was the right thing to do!

Be careful with the calculation of the private use/business use proportion of the car and remember the impact private use has on both the adjustment of profits computation and capital allowances.

Tutor's top tips

The key to success when you are doing an adjustment of profits is to think about what, if anything, has already been included in the statement of profit or loss.

If an expense is disallowable and has been deducted, you need to add it back. If it hasn't been deducted you do nothing. Conversely, if an expense is allowable and has been deducted, you include it with a zero adjustment. If it hasn't been deducted, you need to deduct it.

Read the question carefully here! As the question just asks you to 'calculate', you do not need to explain why you are making adjustments, although you do need to make sure you label your answers so that the marker can see which expenses you are adding back or deducting. It is also important to include all the major items of expenditure in the question, showing a zero for the adjustment figure where the expenditure is allowable.

Always show your workings if the adjustment figure is not clear from the question.

Sam White – Trading profit for the year ended 5 April 2017

	£	£
Net profit	100,000	
Depreciation	7,600	
Motor expenses (£8,800 × 20%) (W1)	1,760	
Patent royalties (Note 1)	0	
Breach of contract fees (Note 2)	0	
Accountancy fees (Note 2)	0	
Personal capital gains tax advice	320	
Gifts to customers (£560 + £420) (Note 3)	980	
Use of office (£5,120 × 1/8)		640
Private telephone (£1,600 × 25%)		400
Own consumption (Note 4)	1,480	
Capital allowances (W2)		3,957
	112,140	4,997
	(4,997)	
Trading profit	107,143	

Tutorial note

1   *Patent royalties are allowed as a deduction when calculating the trading profit, because they are for the purposes of the trade. As they have already been deducted in arriving at the profit, no adjustment is required.*

2   *The fees incurred for accountancy and the breach of contract defence are allowable as incurred wholly and exclusively for the purposes of the trade.*

3   *Gifts to customers are an allowable deduction if they cost less than £50 per recipient per year, are not of food, drink, tobacco or vouchers exchangeable for goods and carry a conspicuous advertisement for the company making the gift.*

4   *Goods for own consumption must be treated as a sale at full market value. As no entries have been made in the accounts, the full sale proceeds are added back. Had the cost of the goods been accounted for already, only the profit element would need to be added back.*

Workings

(W1) Private/business mileage

	Total	Private	Business
Total miles	25,000		
Visiting suppliers	(5,000)		5,000
Allocate (25:75)	20,000	5,000	15,000
		5,000	20,000
(5,000/25,000)		20%	
(20,000/25,000)			80%

Tutor's top tips

A familiar full blown capital allowances computation is given in the workings to this answer to show clearly how the allowances are calculated.

However, where there are not many transactions it is perfectly acceptable to do one or two lines and just calculate the allowances available on each asset acquired rather than a full computation.

If you do this however, be careful and make sure you explain your calculations clearly.

(W2) Capital allowances

	Main pool £	Private use car £	Allowances £
TWDV b/f	14,800	20,200	
WDA (18%)	(2,664)		2,664
WDA (8%)(W1)		(1,616) × 80%	1,293
	———	———	
TWDV c/f	12,136	18,584	
	———	———	———
Total allowances			3,957
			———

Tutorial note

The motor car is a high emission car (CO_2 emissions exceed 130 g/km) and is eligible for a WDA at 8%.

Examiner's report

This question was very well answered by the majority of candidates.

The adjustments for use of office, business use of a private telephone and own consumption caused the most problems, with a number of candidates being unsure as to whether adjustments should be added or subtracted in order to arrive at the tax adjusted trading profit.

Note: *The examiner's report has been edited to remove comments on elements of the question that have been deleted due to changes to the examination format.*

ACCA marking scheme		
		Marks
Net profit		0.5
Depreciation		0.5
Motor expenses		1.5
Patent royalties		0.5
Professional fees		1.5
Gifts to customers		1.0
Use of office		1.0
Private telephone		1.0
Own consumption		0.5
Capital allowances	– Pool	1.0
	– Motor car	1.0
Total		**10.0**

92 GEORGE

Key answer tips

A classic examination question on self-employed versus employed which was not difficult, but presented in a scenario requiring the application of knowledge to the particular situation given.

This is a newer style of question for F6 students, comparing the income tax and NIC liabilities on the same amount of income for both an employee and a sole trader. This is useful preparation for those planning to move on to P6.

Tutor's top tips

It is important to learn the rules for determining whether an individual is self-employed.

However, it is not enough here to simply state those rules; instead they must be applied to the situation given.

The question requirement specifically asks only for those factors that indicate employment rather than self-employment.

The answer must therefore focus on those factors, not any factors you can remember and not those that would clearly suggest self-employment rather than employment.

Even without detailed knowledge of the rules here, common sense suggestions should enable students to pick up some marks.

(a)　**Factors indicating employment**

- The contract is for a relatively long period of time
- George is required to do the work personally
- Xpee plc exercises control over George via the weekly meetings and instructions
- George will not incur any significant expenses in respect of the contract
- George will only be working for Xpee plc.
- George is not taking any significant financial risk

Tutor's top tips

Part (b) involves straightforward income tax and NIC calculations, which you should be able to score well on, regardless of your answer to part (a).

Don't miss the opportunity to gain these easy marks by being put off by the first part of the question, or by running out of time.

(b)　**Income tax liability 2016/17**

	£
Income	40,000
Capital allowances (£3,600 × 100% AIA)	(3,600)
Trading profit	36,400
Personal allowance	(11,000)
Taxable income	25,400

Income tax

£	
25,400 at 20%	5,080

National insurance contributions 2016/17

(1)　Class 2 national insurance contributions will be £146 (52 × 2·80).

(2)　Class 4 national insurance contributions will be £2,551 (£28,340 (£36,400 – £8,060) at 9%).

(c)　(1)　If George is treated as employed in respect of his contract with Xpee plc, then the company will be required to deduct tax under PAYE every time that George is paid during 2016/17.

　　　　If treated as self-employed, George's income tax liability for 2016/17 would not be payable until 31 January 2018.

　　(2)　If George is treated as employed in respect of his contract with Xpee plc, then his class 1 national insurance contributions for 2016/17 will be £3,833 (£31,940 (£40,000 – £8,060) at 12%).

　　　　The additional amount of national insurance contributions which he will suffer for 2016/17 is therefore £1,136 (£3,833 – £146 – £2,551).

Tutorial note

For income tax purposes, capital allowances will reduce employment income in the same way that they are deducted in calculating the trading profit. However, there is no deduction for capital allowances when it comes to calculating class 1 national insurance contributions.

	ACCA marking scheme		
			Marks
(a)	The contract is for a long period of time		0.5
	Required to do the work personally		0.5
	Xpee exercises control over George		0.5
	George won't incur significant expenses		0.5
	Only working for Xpee		0.5
	No financial risk		0.5
			———
		Maximum	**2.0**
			———
(b)	**Treated as self employed**		
	Contract fee		0.5
	Capital allowances		1.0
	Personal allowance		0.5
	Income tax		0.5
	Class 2		0.5
	Class 4		1.0
			———
			4.0
			———
(c)	(1) If employed – PAYE		1.0
	Self- employed 31 January 2018		1.0
	(2) Class 1 employee		1.5
	Additional NIC		0.5
			———
			4.0
			———
Total			**10.0**
			———

Examiner's report

Part (a) required four factors which were indicators of the taxpayer being treated as an employee in relation to their contract rather than as self-employed. Most candidates missed the fact that the taxpayer would not incur any significant expenses in respect of the contract and would not be Examiner's report – F6 (UK) March 2016 3 taking any significant financial risk. Many candidates incorrectly gave the payment of tax under PAYE for the previous year as an indicator.

Part (b) required a calculation of the taxpayer's income tax liability and national insurance contributions if they were treated as self-employed in respect of the one-year contract. This was well answered, but many candidates produced extremely long answers for what should have been a simple set of workings. For example, the capital allowance was simply a 100% annual investment allowance on the purchase of a new asset and did not require a detailed capital allowances computation.

Part (c) required (1) an explanation why the taxpayer's income tax liability would be payable earlier if they were treated as being an employee instead of self-employed, and (2) a calculation of the additional amount of national insurance contributions which would be suffered. As regards the payment aspect, most candidates just referred to PAYE without any further relevant detail. Very few appreciated that the due date under the self-employed basis was simply 31 January following the tax year - payments on account not being required because the previous year's tax liability was collected under PAYE.

93 SOPHIA WONG (ADAPTED) *Walk in the footsteps of a top tutor*

Key answer tips

Part (a) is a relatively straightforward comparison of the tax cost of trading as either a sole trader or through a company.

The cost of trading as a sole trader is given in the question so detailed calculations are in fact only required for the cost of extracting profits from a company as either remuneration or dividends. The examining team provide a lot of guidance in the question; giving figures for the amount of salary and dividends to use in the calculations and telling you the calculations that are required in the notes to the requirement. So if you follow the instructions carefully the calculations are relatively easy.

Part (b) covered a topic that is no longer in the syllabus and has therefore been replaced with a new topic.

Tutor's top tips

Make sure you set out your answer clearly and logically, using headings so it is clear which calculations relate to each scenario.

In part (1) consider the implications, for both Sophia of receiving employment income and for the company of paying remuneration. Likewise in part (2) consider the implications for both parties of paying a dividend. Consider what tax consequences there may be, such as:

Is the payment tax deductible for the company?

Is it subject to NIC?

For each part work through the calculations specified in the notes to the requirements. And don't forget to summarise the total costs for each alternative and conclude on whether it is more or less than the cost of being self-employed – there are easy marks to be gained here.

(a) (i) **Profits withdrawn as director's remuneration**

- Employer's class 1 NIC will be = (£80,000 – £71,282) = £8,718

Tutorial note

If all of the profits of £80,000 are withdrawn as director's remuneration (including the employer's class 1 NIC) and the gross remuneration is £71,282 (per the question) then the employer's class 1 NIC must be the difference of £8,718.

The examining team has taken this 'short cut' approach, however if you were unsure of this approach you could prepare the usual NIC calculation as follows:

(£71,282 – £8,112) × 13.8% = £8,717 (£1 difference due to rounding)

The £3,000 NIC employment allowance is not available as Sophia is a director and the sole employee of the company.

- Sophia's income tax liability for 2016/17 will be:

	£
Director's remuneration	71,282
Less: PA	(11,000)
Taxable income	60,282
Income tax	

£	
32,000 × 20%	6,400
28,282 × 40%	11,313
60,282	
Income tax liability	17,713

- Sophia's employee class 1 NIC for 2016/17 will be as follows:

	£
(£43,000 – £8,060) × 12%	4,193
(£71,282 – £43,000) × 2%	566
	4,759

- There is no corporation tax liability for the new company as the profits are entirely withdrawn as director's remuneration.

- The total tax and NIC cost if all of the new company's profits are withdrawn as director's remuneration is as follows:

	£
Employer's NIC	8,718
Sophia's income tax	17,713
Sophia's employee NIC	4,759
	31,190

This is more than the cost on a self-employed basis of £25,231.

(ii) **Profits withdrawn as dividends**

- There will be no class 1 NIC.

- The corporation tax liability of the new company for the year ended 5 April 2017 will be £16,000 (£80,000 – £64,000).

Tutorial note

If all of the profits of £80,000 are withdrawn as dividends (after allowing for corporation tax) and the dividends are £64,000 (per the question) then the corporation tax liability must be the difference of £16,000.

The examining team has taken this 'short cut' approach, however if you were unsure of this approach you could prepare the usual corporation tax calculation as follows:

(£80,000 × 20%) = £16,000.

Remember that dividends are not tax deductible.

- The income tax liability of Sophia for the tax year 2016/17 will be:

	£
Dividends	64,000
Less: PA	(11,000)
Taxable income	53,000

Income tax		£
£		
5,000 × 0%		0
27,000 × 7.5%		2,025
21,000 × 32.5%		6,825
53,000		
Income tax liability		8,850

Tutorial note

The first £5,000 of dividend income is taxed at 0%, this counts towards the basic and higher rate bands.

- The total tax and NIC cost if all of the new company's profits are withdrawn as dividends are as follows:

	£
Corporation tax	16,000
Sophia's income tax	8,850
	24,850

This is £381 (£25,231 – £24,850) less than the cost on a self-employed basis.

(b) **Sophia Wong**

Capital gains tax liability – 2016/17

	Not qualifying for ER	Qualifying for ER
	£	£
Qualifying for entrepreneurs' relief (Note 1)		
Sale of business: Goodwill (£150,000 – £0)		150,000
Not qualifying for entrepreneurs' relief		
Necklace	11,153	
Chargeable gains	11,153	150,000
Less: Annual exempt amount (Note 2)	(11,100)	(0)
Taxable gains	53	150,000

	£
Capital gains tax liability	
Qualifying for ER (£150,000 × 10%)	15,000
Not qualifying for ER (£53 × 20%) (Note 3)	11
	15,011

Election

An election for entrepreneurs' relief must be submitted by 31 January 2019. (i.e. within 12 months of the 31 January following the tax year in which the disposal is made).

Tutorial note

1   *Where an individual sells the whole or part of a business which they have owned for at least 12 months they can elect for entrepreneurs' relief to apply such that the net chargeable gains (up to a lifetime maximum of £10 million) arising on the disposal are taxed at a lower rate of 10%.*

2   *The annual exempt amount is set against the chargeable gain from the sale of the necklace as it does not qualify for entrepreneurs' relief and therefore this saves CGT at the higher rate of 20% rather than 10%.*

3   *The gains qualifying for entrepreneurs' relief have to be taxed first and they utilise the remaining BR band of £12,000 (£32,000 − £20,000). Therefore the gain on the necklace is taxed at 20%.*

Examiner's report

Part (a) as a whole was very badly answered, often as a result of being attempted last with inadequate time remaining. Many students did not seem to notice that they had been given some of the information (employer's NIC when withdrawing profits as director's remuneration, and corporation tax when withdrawing profits as dividends) and wasted time trying to calculate the figures themselves.

As regards withdrawing profits as director's remuneration, very few candidates appreciated that there would be no taxable profit and hence no corporation tax liability. As regards withdrawing profits as dividends, far too many candidates did not appreciate that no NIC would be payable. Some candidates even attempted to answer this section with just one calculation combining the director's remuneration and dividend, and very few marks were available with this approach.

Part (b) has been replaced with a new question as the original topic is no longer in the syllabus. So the examiner's comments for this part are not relevant.

ACCA marking scheme			
			Marks
(a)	(1)	Profits withdrawn as director's remuneration	
		Employer's class 1 NIC	1.0
		Sophia's income tax liability	
		Personal allowance	0.5
		Tax at 20%	0.5
		Tax at 40%	0.5
		Sophia's employee class 1 NIC	1.5
		No corporation tax liability	1.0
		Summary of cost and conclusion	1.0
			———
			6.0
			———
	(2)	Profits withdrawn as dividends	
		No class 1 NIC	0.5
		Corporation tax liability	1.0
		Sophia's income tax payable	
		Personal allowance	0.5
		Tax at 0%	0.5
		Tax at 7.5%	1.0
		Tax at 32.5%	0.5
		Summary of cost and conclusion	1.0
			———
			5.0
			———
(b)		Gain on goodwill	0.5
		Gain on necklace - not qualifying for ER	0.5
		Annual exempt amount offset against gain on necklace	1.0
		CGT calculation	1.0
		Date of entrepreneurs' relief election	1.0
			———
			4.0
			———
Total			**15.0**
			———

94   FERGUS   *Walk in the footsteps of a top tutor*

Key answer tips

This question guides you through comparing whether a particular individual should remain self-employed or incorporate his business and be employed by his own company.

Note that no marks are available for considering issues other than the relevant taxes mentioned in the requirement. The notes at the end of the requirement give clear guidance on which taxes you need to calculate.

Make sure you follow the guidance given and give a clear conclusion that follows from your calculations.

Tutor's top tips

When asked to compare two situations from a tax perspective it is sensible to present your answer in a summary table supported by workings.

	Self-employed £	Incorporated £
Income tax payable by Fergus (W1)		8,225
Class 1 primary NICs – payable by Fergus (W2)		1,313
Class 1 secondary NICs – payable by the company (W2)		1,503
Corporation tax liability of the company (W3)		15,899
Total tax and NIC cost	33,631	26,940

Conclusion

If Fergus incorporated his business there would be an overall saving of tax and NIC of £6,691 (£33,631 – £26,940) compared to continuing on a self-employed basis.

Workings

(W1) Fergus – Income tax liability – 2016/17

	£
Director's remuneration	19,000
Dividends	40,000
Total income	59,000
Less: Personal allowance	(11,000)
Taxable income	48,000

Income tax

£		£
8,000	at 20%	1,600
5,000	at 0%	0
19,000	at 7.5%	1,425
32,000		
16,000	at 32.5%	5,200
48,000		
Income tax liability		8,225

(W2) National insurance contributions (NICs) – 2016/17

	£
Employee – class 1 primary NICs	
(£19,000 – £8,060) at 12%	1,313
Employer's – class 1 secondary NICs	
(£19,000 – £8,112) at 13.8%	1,503
Less: Employment allowance (tutorial note)	(0)
	1,503

Tutorial note

The employment allowance is not available in this scenario as Fergus is both a director and the sole employee of the company.

(W3) Corporation tax liability of the new limited company – year ended 5 April 2017

	£
Trading profit	100,000
Less: Director's remuneration	(19,000)
Employer's class 1 secondary NICs	(1,503)
Taxable total profits	79,497
Corporation tax at 20%	15,899

ACCA marking scheme	
	Marks
Income tax liability	
Director's remuneration	0.5
Dividend	0.5
PA	0.5
Income tax on other income at 20%	0.5
Income tax on dividend income at 0%	0.5
Income tax on dividend income at 7.5%	0.5
Income tax on dividend income at 32.5%	0.5
NICs	
Employee class 1	1.5
Employer class 1	1.5
No deduction for employment allowance	0.5
Corporation tax	
Trading profit	0.5
Deduction of director's remuneration	0.5
Deduction or employer's class 1 national insurance	0.5
Corporation tax at 20%	0.5
Total tax and NIC cost	0.5
Conclusion	0.5
Total	**10.0**

95   JOHN AND LIAN (ADAPTED) *Walk in the footsteps of a top tutor*

Key answer tips

Part (a) of the original question tested a topic which is no longer examinable. It has been replaced with a tax administration question covering the opening years of a business. The highlighted words in the written sections are key phrases that markers are looking for.

Part (b) also included a topic which is no longer examinable and this part has therefore been amended. This part now tests knowledge of the basis of assessment rules for a sole trader both on commencement and cessation of trade, including the related capital allowance rules.

(a)   **John Higgins – New business**

Tutor's top tips

For written parts, write short succinct sentences in bullet point form. Use precise language especially when explaining deadlines and time limits etc.

Bear in mind the mark allocation. In general, there is usually one mark allocated for each valid point made. Do not therefore dwell on any one point too much and keep an eye on the clock.

(1)   John must notify HM Revenue & Customs that he is chargeable to income tax in respect of his trading income by 5 October 2017 (i.e. 6 months from the end of the tax year in which the income tax liability arises).

(2)   John must keep all of the records (not just his business records) which support his 2016/17 tax return until 31 January 2023 (i.e. 5 years after the filing date for the return).

(3)   John will be required to make the first payment of tax in respect of his trading profits by 31 January 2018 (i.e. 31 January following the end of the tax year).

Tutorial note

1   The first tax year that John will be assessed to tax in respect of his business profits will be 2016/17 (i.e. the tax year in which trade commences).

2   John will not be required to make payments on account of his income tax liability for his first tax year (2016/17) as he did not have any income tax payable under self-assessment in the previous tax year as his income tax liability was settled at source under the PAYE system. He therefore makes just one payment for the tax year 2016/17 on the balancing payment due date.

(b)   **Lian Zhang – Assessable profits for the years 2014/15 to 2017/18**

Tutor's top tips

Deal with the information in strict date order, starting with the opening year rules, then CYB and finally the closing year rules.

Remember that all basis of assessment periods, other than in the first and final tax years must be of 12 months duration.

However, before you can calculate the closing year rules, you need to calculate the capital allowances for the 14 month closing period of account.

		£
2014/15	1 May 2014 to 5 April 2015	
	(£50,400 (W1) × 11/12)	46,200
2015/16	CYB	
	Year ended 30 April 2015 (W1)	50,400
2016/17	CYB	
	Year ended 30 April 2016 (W1)	37,200
2017/18	Period of cessation	
	Period ended 30 June 2017	
	Trading profit	61,500
	Less: Capital allowances (W2)	(4,400)
		57,100
	Less: Relief for overlap profits (W3)	(46,200)
		10,900

Tutorial note

1   *2014/15 is the first tax year of trading. Using the opening year rules the basis of assessment is the period from the date of commencement to the following 5 April.*

2   *There is a 12 month period of account ending in the second tax year (2015/16) and the profits for this period are therefore taxed under the current year basis in that tax year.*

3   *In the tax year 2016/17 the current basis applies.*

4   *2017/18 is the tax year of cessation. The basis period for the tax year 2017/18 runs from the end of the basis period for the previous tax year to the date of cessation (i.e. the 14-months to 30 June 2017). Overlap profits arising on commencement are relieved in the final tax year.*

5   *Over the life of a business the total profits of the business are taxed. Therefore you can check:*

Total profits: (£50,400 + £37,200 + £61,500 – £4,400) = £144,700

Assessments: (£46,200 + £50,400 + £37,200 + £10,900) = £144,700

Workings

(W1) Taxable trading profits

Year ended 30 April	2015	2016
	£	£
Trading profit	62,300	75,400
Less: Capital allowances	(11,900)	(38,200)
	————	————
Taxable trading profit	50,400	37,200
	————	————

(W2) Capital allowances

	Main pool	Allowances
	£	£
14 months ended 30 June 2017		
TWDV b/f	14,400	
Addition: Machine	12,000	
Disposal	(22,000)	
	————	
	4,400	
Balancing allowance	(4,400)	4,400
	————	————
Total allowances		4,400
		————

Tutorial note

1   *For an unincorporated trader (unlike companies), capital allowances are computed for the long period of account (i.e. in this case for the 14 months to 30 June 2017).*

A long period of account for sole traders is not split into the first 12 months and the balance period as it is for companies.

2   *In the period of account in which business is permanently ceased the AIA, WDAs and FYAs are not available. Additions and disposals are added to the relevant pool and a balancing charge or allowance is calculated.*

(W3) Relief for overlap profits

In 2015/16, there are overlap profits of £46,200 in respect of the 11-month period 1 May 2014 to 5 April 2015.

These are relieved in the final tax year of trade.

	ACCA marking scheme	
		Marks
(a)	Date re notification of chargeability	1.0
	Retention of records date	1.0
	First payment of tax date in opening year	1.0
		——
		3.0
		——
(b)	2014/15 assessment	1.0
	2015/16 assessment	0.5
	2016/17 assessment	0.5
	2017/18 assessment – Period of account 14 months long	1.5
	Taxable trading profits	1.0
	Capital allowances	2.0
	Overlap relief	0.5
		——
		7.0
		——
Total		**10.0**
		——

96   FANG, HONG AND KANG *Walk in the footsteps of a top tutor*

Key answer tips

A question covering three different scenarios all concerned with self-employed individuals.

Part (a) is a straightforward question involving the opening year basis of assessment rules and the deductibility of pre-trading expenditure for an individual starting a business. The highlighted words in the written sections are key phrases that markers are looking for.

Part (b) involves an established trader who has incurred trading losses. This is not a difficult question but involves a number of loss offsets and therefore needs to be approached in a methodical manner.

Part (c) involves a partnership where one of the partners is retiring. This is a commonly tested scenario and should not have caused any difficulties.

(a)   **Fang**

(1)   **Assessments**

		£
2014/15	Actual	
	(1 August 2014 to 5 April 2015)	
	(£45,960 × 8/12)	30,640
2015/16	CYB (Year ended 31 July 2015)	45,960
2016/17	CYB (Year ended 31 July 2016)	39,360

In 2015/16 there are overlap profits of £30,640 (i.e. the eight-month period 1 August 2014 to 5 April 2015).

(2)   **Pre-trading expenditure**

- The trading expenditure will be treated as incurred on 1 August 2014 provided it was incurred within the previous seven years and would have been allowable if the trade had already commenced.

- The computer equipment which Fang already owned will be an addition for capital allowances purposes based on its market value at 1 August 2014.

(b)   **Hong**

Tutor's top tips

There is a lot of information in this relatively short question which can appear daunting so it is important to approach the question in a methodical manner.

You are asked to calculate taxable income, taxable gains and the amount of trading loss carried forward – so layout your pro formas and start by filling in the easy numbers.

Then consider the trading losses – dealing with the earliest loss first. You are told how to offset the loss for the year ended 5 April 2017 in the question so you do not need to decide how best to use the loss – just follow the instructions!

Taxable income – 2015/16

	£
Trading profit	29,700
Less: Loss relief b/f	(2,600)
	———
	27,100
Property income	3,900
	———
Total income	31,000
Less: Loss relief – Prior year	(31,000)
	———
Net income	0
Less: Personal allowance	(wasted)
	———
Taxable income	0
	———

Taxable gain – 2015/16

	£
Chargeable gain	17,800
Less: Trading loss relief (W1)	(11,600)
	———
	6,200
Less: Capital loss b/f (Note)	(0)
	———
	6,200
Less: Annual exempt amount (part wasted)	(6,200)
	———
Taxable gain	0
	———

The trading loss carried forward is £3,200 (W2).

Tutorial note

Relief for trading losses against total income and net chargeable gains is 'all or nothing' (i.e. the relief cannot be restricted to preserve the PA for income tax or the AEA for CGT).

Capital losses brought forward however are not offset if they would result in wasting the AEA. Therefore, in this case, capital losses brought forward would not be utilised and would be carried forward to set against future net chargeable gains.

Workings

(W1) Trading loss relief

The trading loss relief claim against the chargeable gain = Lower of:

- Chargeable gain less capital loss brought forward

  = (£17,800 – £6,200) = £11,600, and

- Trading loss remaining = (£45,800 – £31,000) = £14,800

  Therefore, can only offset £11,600 against gains

(W2) Loss memorandum

	£
Loss – 2014/15	2,600
Less: Set off against trading profits – 2015/16	(2,600)
Loss – 2016/17	45,800
Less: Carry back against 2015/16 income	(31,000)
Loss relief extended to capital gains in 2015/16 (W1)	(11,600)
Loss carried forward	3,200

Tutorial note

The loss brought forward from the tax year 2014/15 must be set against the first available trading profits in subsequent years (i.e. 2015/16). The loss is offset before losses arising in later years.

The loss arising in the tax year 2016/17 can be offset against total income in the tax year (s) 2016/17 and/or 2015/16. Once a claim has been made to offset the loss against the total income of a particular tax year (e.g. 2015/16) a claim can also be made to offset any remaining trading losses against chargeable gains of the same tax year.

(c) **Kang, Ling and Ming**

Allocation of profits

	Total £	Kang £	Ling £	Ming £
Year ended 30 June 2015				
(£148,800 × 1/3)	148,800	49,600	49,600	49,600
Year ended 30 June 2016				
1 July 2015 to 31 October 2015				
(£136,800 × 4/12 × 1/3)	45,600	15,200	15,200	15,200
1 November 2015 to 30 June 2016				
(£136,800 × 8/12 × ½)	91,200	45,600	45,600	0
	136,800	60,800	60,800	15,200

Trading income assessments

	Kang £	Ling £	Ming £
2015/16			
Year ended 30 June 2015 – CYB	49,600	49,600	
Cessation rules:			
Year ended 30 June 2015			49,600
Period ended 31 October 2015			15,200
			64,800
Less: Relief for overlap profits			(29,400)
			35,400
2016/17			
Year ended 30 June 2016 – CYB	60,800	60,800	0

Tutorial note

The cessation rules apply to Ming for the tax year 2015/16 since she ceased to be a partner on 31 October 2015. Her basis period for the tax year 2015/16 runs from the end of the basis period for the tax year 2014/15 to the date of cessation (i.e. 1 July 2014 to 31 October 2015).

		ACCA marking scheme		
				Marks
(a)	(1)	2014/15 assessment		1.0
		2015/16 assessment		0.5
		2016/17 assessment		0.5
		Overlap profits		1.0
				──
				3.0
				──
	(2)	Pre-trading revenue expenditure		1.0
		Addition for capital allowance purposes at MV		1.0
				──
				2.0
				──
(b)		Taxable income		
		Trading profit		0.5
		Less trading losses b/f		0.5
		Property business profit		0.5
		Less loss of 2016/17 against total income		0.5
		PA = £0		0.5
		Taxable gain		
		Chargeable gain less loss relief		0.5
		AEA		0.5
		Trading loss c/f		0.5
		Maximum loss relief against chargeable gain		1.0
				──
				5.0
				──
(c)		Allocation of profits		
		Year ended 30.6.15		0.5
		Year ended 30.6.16		1.5
		Assessments		
		2015/16 – year ended 30.6.15		0.5
		2015/16 – plus period ended 31.10.15 for Ming		1.0
		Ming overlap relief		1.0
		2016/17		0.5
				──
				5.0
				──
Total				**15.0**
				──

97   NA STYLE (ADAPTED)   *Walk in the footsteps of a top tutor*

Key answer tips

This question is a classic self-employed individual scenario, testing opening year's basis of assessment and the compilation of an income tax computation. There is also an element of self-assessment at the end.

The first part is relatively easy to score highly on.

Part (b) was straightforward provided the self-assessment rules had been learnt and applied to the information given.

Tutor's top tips

Remember to read the requirement carefully.

This question has clear mark allocations, which should be used to allocate the time spent on each section. You need to adopt a logical approach, using the requirements to break down the information and plan your answer.

The first part just requires the application of the opening year rules to figures given in the question. It is possible to score very well on this sort of question, which is not technically difficult, as long as you do not panic.

Be sure to explain your answer; clearly showing the tax year, basis of assessment and calculation so that method marks can be given even if the maths goes awry!

Don't forget to highlight the overlap profits as they are specifically asked for and will therefore earn a mark.

(a) **Assessable trading profits – first four tax years**

Tax year	Basis of assessment	£
2013/14	Actual basis	
	(1 January 2014 to 5 April 2014)	
	(£25,200 × 3/6)	12,600
2014/15	First 12 months trading	
	(1 January 2014 to 31 December 2014)	
	£25,200 + (£21,600 × 6/12)	36,000
2015/16	Current year basis	
	(Year ended 30 June 2015)	21,600
2016/17	Current year basis	
	(Year ended 30 June 2016)	30,665

Overlap profits

Tax year	Profits taxed twice	£
2014/15	(1 January 2014 to 5 April 2014)	
	(£25,200 × 3/6)	12,600
2015/16	(1 July 2014 to 31 December 2014)	
	(£21,600 × 6/12)	10,800
		23,400

Tutorial note

The assessment for the tax year 2014/15 is the first 12 months of trading as the accounting period ending in that year is less than 12 months from the commencement of trading.

(b) (1) **Income tax computation – 2016/17**

Tutor's top tips

For part (b) a systematic approach is needed.

Remember not to ignore exempt income, as credit is given for stating that it is exempt, even though you do NOT include the figure in your computation.

Part (b)(2) goes on to require the balancing payment after taking account of payments on account (POAs) already paid, and then requires the POAs to be paid in the following year.

	£
Trading profit	30,665
Building society interest	700
Interest from ISA (exempt)	0
Interest from NS&I savings certificate (exempt)	0
Interest from government stocks	370
Dividends	8,200
Total income	39,935
Less: PA	(11,000)
Taxable income	28,935

Analysis of income (Note)

Dividends = £8,200;

Savings (£700 + £370) = £1,070;

Non-savings income (£28,935 − £8,200 − £1,070) = £19,665

Income tax		£
£		
19,665	× 20% (non-savings income)	3,933
1,000	× 0% (savings income)	0
70	× 20% (savings income)	14
5,000	× 0% (dividend income)	0
3,200	× 7.5% (dividend income)	240
28,935		
Income tax payable		4,187

Tutorial note

There is nothing wrong in presenting your computation in columnar form if you prefer to, however there is also no need to do so if you do not want to.

However, you do need to be able to break down the taxable income into the different types of income, namely: dividends, savings and non-savings income, in order to apply the correct rates of tax to each type of income.

Basic rate taxpayers are entitled to a £1,000 nil rate band for savings income.

A £5,000 nil rate band is also available to all taxpayers for dividend income.

(2)   **Tax payments**

- Na's balancing payment for the tax year 2016/17 due on 31 January 2018 is £987 (£4,187 – £3,200).

- Her payments on account for the tax year 2017/18 will be £2,094 and £2,093 (£4,187 × 50%). These will be due on 31 January 2018 and 31 July 2018.

Examiner's report

This question was very well answered, and there were many high scoring answers.

In part (a) some candidates lost marks because they did not show the relevant tax years in which profits were assessable.

As regards the balancing payment and payments on account, candidates were often not aware of the relevant dates.

Note: *The examiner's report has been edited to remove comments on elements of the question that have been deleted due to changes to the examination format.*

			Marks
ACCA marking scheme			
(a)	2013/14		1.0
	2014/15	– Assessment	1.0
		– Overlap profits	1.0
	2015/16	– Assessment	1.0
		– Overlap profits	1.0
	2016/17	– Assessment	1.0
			6.0
(b)	(1)	Income tax computation	
		Trading profit	0.5
		Building society interest	0.5
		Individual savings account	0.5
		Interest from NS&I savings certificate	0.5
		Interest from government stocks	0.5
		Dividends	0.5
		Personal allowance	0.5
		Income tax	2.5
			6.0
	(2)	Tax payments	
		Balancing payment	1.5
		Payments on account	1.5
			3.0
Total			**15.0**

98 SIMON HOUSE (ADAPTED) *Walk in the footsteps of a top tutor*

Key answer tips

A very familiar style question covering the badges of trade and requiring the calculation of the tax consequences of a transaction being deemed to be a trading transaction or a capital event.

Easy marks should have been picked up in this question.

The highlighted words in the written sections are key phrases that markers are looking for.

Tutor's top tips

*Usually these questions start with the requirement for you to list and then apply the badges of trade. However, this question is unusual in that it kindly gives you the badges of trade that it requires you to consider and asks you to explain the **meaning** of each for only 3 marks.*

It is fairly certain that half a mark will be allocated to each explanation and so therefore it is not possible, or necessary, to write huge amounts on any one explanation. Note also that it only requires an explanation of the badges of trade listed. Do not waste time explaining other badges of trade that are used by HM Revenue & Customs as you will not gain any extra marks.

Try to be clear, succinct and to the point and then move on!

(a) **Badges of trade**

- Trading is indicated where the property (subject matter) does not yield an ongoing income or give personal enjoyment to its owner.

- The sale of property within a short time of its acquisition is an indication of trading.

- Trading is indicated by repeated transactions in the same subject matter.

- A trading motive is indicated where work is carried out to the property to make it more marketable, or where steps are taken to find purchasers.

- A forced sale to raise cash for an emergency is an indication that the transaction is not of a trading nature.

- If a transaction is undertaken with the motive of realising a profit, this is a strong indication of trading.

(b) **Treated as carrying on a trade**

Tutor's top tips

If the transaction is treated as a trade transaction, a straightforward trading profit computation is required.

Simon is then liable to income tax and class 4 NICs on the trading profit and class 2 NICs as he will be self-employed.

Make sure you show your calculations for each liability clearly.

Income tax – 2016/17

	£	£
Income		260,000
Cost of property	127,000	
Renovation costs	50,600	
Loan interest (£150,000 × 6% × 4/12)(Note)	3,000	
Legal fees (£1,800 + £2,600)	4,400	
	———	(185,000)
Trading profit		75,000
Less: PA		(11,000)
Taxable income		64,000

£	
32,000 × 20%	6,400
32,000 × 40%	12,800
———	
64,000	
Income tax liability	19,200

Tutorial note

If treated as a trade, all costs incurred wholly and exclusively for the purposes of the trade are allowable deductions – including interest on the loan to purchase the house.

National insurance – 2016/17

	£
Class 2 NIC (18 weeks × £2.80)	50
Class 4 NIC	
(£43,000 – £8,060) × 9%	3,145
(£75,000 – £43,000) × 2%	640
	3,785

(c)   **Treated as a capital transaction**

Tutor's top tips

You should know that the consequences of applying the badges of trade are to determine whether or not the transaction is a trading one, or a capital event.

However, you did not necessarily need to remember that in this question as the examining team have kindly told you to what to do (i.e. calculate the capital gains tax liability).

Capital gains tax liability – 2016/17

		£	£
Proceeds			260,000
Less: Incidental costs – legal fees			(2,600)
			257,400
Less:	Cost	127,000	
	Enhancement expenditure	50,600	
	Loan interest (Note)	0	
	Incidental costs	1,800	
			(179,400)
Chargeable gain			78,000
Less: AEA			(11,100)
Taxable gain			66,900

£		
32,000 × 18%		5,760
34,900 × 28%		9,772
66,900		
Capital gains tax liability		15,532

Tutorial note

If it is treated as a capital transaction, no relief is available for the interest on the loan used to finance the transaction.

PPR and letting relief are not available as the property has never been his principal private residence.

Entrepreneurs' relief is not available as the house is an investment property, not a business.

The gain is taxed at 18% to the extent that it falls in the basic rate band and 28% on the excess as it arises on the disposal of a residential property. As Simon has no other income or gains, the first £32,000 is taxed at 18%.

Examiner's report

This question was very well answered, and often helped marginal candidates to achieve a pass mark.

In part (a) a number of candidates failed to score any marks because they did not state what did or did not indicate trading. For example, stating that the 'length of ownership' means how long an item has been owned did not score any marks. It was necessary to explain that the sale of property within a short time of its acquisition is an indication of trading.

Part (b) presented no problems for most candidates. In this type of question it is always best to produce full computations for each option. This will maximise marks if any mistakes are made.

It was pleasing to see that many candidates correctly restricted the class 2 NIC to 18 weeks' contributions.

ACCA marking scheme		Marks
(a)	The subject matter	0.5
	Length of ownership	0.5
	Frequency	0.5
	Work done	0.5
	Circumstances responsible for realisation	0.5
	Motive	0.5
		3.0
(b)	Income	0.5
	Cost of property	0.5
	Renovation costs	0.5
	Loan interest	1.0
	Legal fees	1.0
	Personal allowance	0.5
	Income tax liability	1.0
	Class 2 NIC	1.5
	Class 4 NIC	1.5
		8.0
(c)	Proceeds	0.5
	Cost	0.5
	Enhancement expenditure	0.5
	Incidental costs	0.5
	Loan interest	0.5
	Annual exempt amount	0.5
	Capital gains tax	1.0
		4.0
Total		**15.0**

99   TIM BURR (ADAPTED) *Walk in the footsteps of a top tutor*

Key answer tips

A short but complex question involving a new person joining a sole trade business part way through the accounting period and tax year, either as an employee or partner.

The employment NIC calculations were not straightforward as the annual thresholds need to be apportioned before they can be applied to the 4 months of earnings. In addition, the trading income assessments need to be very carefully calculated by allocating the partnership profits first, then applying the opening year rules.

The self-employment NIC calculations are however straightforward and should not cause difficulties.

Part (b)(2) requires figures brought forward from the previous part. However it is important to remember that full credit will still be given in this part even if the earlier part is calculated incorrectly.

(a)   **National insurance – if Hazel is employed**

Class 1 – primary employee contributions – paid by Hazel

(£3,300 – £672 (W)) × 12% × 4 months = £1,261

Class 1 – secondary employer contributions – paid by Tim

(£3,300 – £676) × 13.8% × 4 months = £1,448

As Hazel is the only employee the employer's class 1 secondary liability will be fully covered by the £3,000 employment allowance.

Working: Monthly earnings thresholds

Employee class 1 NIC

Primary earnings threshold (PET) = (£8,060 × 1/12) = £672

Upper earnings limit = (£43,000 × 1/12) = £3,583

Hazel's monthly earnings are £3,300 which falls in between these limits.

For each month that Hazel is employed, she is therefore liable to class 1 NICs at 12% on the excess over the PET of £672.

Employer's class 1 NIC

Secondary earnings threshold (SET) = (£8,112 × 1/12) = £676

Tim, as Hazel's employer, is liable to class 1 NICs at 13.8% on the excess over the SET of £676.

Hazel will be employed for 4 months of the tax year (December to March inclusive).

Tutor's top tips

Usually at F6, for simplicity, NICs are calculated on an annual basis using the annual limits. In this question however the individual has only been employed for four months in the tax year. Accordingly, the annual limits need to be time apportioned.

This is because NICs are actually calculated on an earnings period basis. This means that if an individual is paid monthly, the monthly limits are used (e.g. for employee class 1 NICs, £672 and £3,583). If they are paid on a weekly basis, the weekly limits are used. For employee class 1 NICs these are £155 (£8,060 × 1/52) and £827 (£43,000 × 1/52).

The examining team have confirmed that the alternative approach of using the annual earnings threshold and then taking 4/12ths of an annual NIC figure was acceptable in the examination.

(b)   (1)   **Trading income assessments**

Allocation of partnership profits

	Total £	Tim £	Hazel £
y/e 30.9.17			
1.10.16 to 30.11.16 (2 months)			
All profits to Tim	36,000	36,000	
1.12.16 to 30.09.17 (10 months)			
PSR (80%:20%)	180,000	144,000	36,000
	216,000	180,000	36,000
y/e 30.9.18			
PSR (80%:20%)	240,000	192,000	48,000

Applying basis of assessment rules

If Hazel joins the partnership on 1 December 2016, the opening year rules will apply to her profit share as follows:

Tax year	Basis of assessment	£	£
2016/17	Actual basis		
	(1.12.16 to 5.4.17)		
	(£36,000 × 4/10) (Note)		14,400
2017/18	First 12 months trading		
	(1.12.16 to 30.11.17)		
	10 m/e 30.9.17	36,000	
	y/e 30.9.18 × 2/12 (£48,000 × 2/12)	8,000	
			44,000

Tutorial note

The partnership profits should be allocated to the partners according to the partnership agreement in the accounting period.

The basis of assessment rules are then applied to each partner's share of profits separately.

Tim was a sole trader and becomes a partner. However he will continue to be assessed on a current year basis (CYB).

The commencement rules will apply to Hazel's share of profits for the tax year 2016/17 since she will join as a partner on 1 December 2016.

(2) **NICs – 2016/17**

Paid by Hazel – self employed

Class 2 NICs (Note 1) = (18 weeks × £2.80) = £50

Class 4 NICs (Note 2) = (£14,400 – £8,060) × 9% = £571

Paid by Tim

There are no NIC implications for Tim in relation to Hazel's trading income assessments (Note 3).

Tutorial note

1   *Class 2 NICs are £2.80 per week. If Hazel joins the partnership on 1 December 2016, she will be a partner for the period 1 December 2016 to 5 April 2017 which is 126 days (31 + 31 + 28 + 31 + 5), which is 18 weeks (126 days ÷ 7).*

2   *Class 4 NICs are calculated using the full annual lower profits limit (£8,060 in 2016/17), it is not time apportioned, as the opening year rules produce an assessment for the full tax year 2016/17.*

   This trading income assessment figure comes from the previous part. However, full credit would be given for this part even if the assessment was calculated incorrectly provided you calculated the NICs correctly based on your figure.

3   *The question asks for the NICs to be paid by Tim, but only in relation to Hazel's trading income assessment. The question specifically states that his own NICs are not to be calculated.*

Examiner's report

In part (a) it was pleasing to see several candidates correctly restricted NIC contributions to the four months of employment.

Although there were also many good answers to part (b), there were also a lot of candidates who wasted time by doing NIC calculations for both the taxpayer and the new person, or NIC calculations for both years, instead of just the one required.

Note: The examiner's report has been edited to remove comments on elements of the question that have been deleted due to changes to the examination format.

ACCA marking scheme		
		Marks
(a)	Monthly earnings thresholds	1.0
	Employee class 1 NIC	1.0
	Employer's class 1 NIC	1.0
	Employment allowance reduces class 1 secondary to £0	1.0
		────
		4.0
		────
(b)	Trading income assessments	
	2016/17	1.5
	2017/18	2.5
		────
		4.0
		────
	NIC re Hazel	
	Class 2 NIC	0.5
	Class 4 NIC	1.0
	Tim	0.5
		────
		2.0
		────
Total		**10.0**
		────

100 RICHARD FEAST (ADAPTED) *Walk in the footsteps of a top tutor*

Key answer tips

Part (a) is a fairly straightforward adjustment of trading profit computation, which should not have caused any problems.

Part (b) requires employer's NIC calculations for an employee. It was important to limit your answer to just the classes of NIC required.

Part (c) requires knowledge of basic self-assessment administration issues and should not have caused any problems. The highlighted words in the written sections are key phrases that markers are looking for.

(a)   **Trading profit – year ended 5 April 2017**

Tutor's top tips

This straightforward adjustment of profit computation is presented in a familiar format, with a statement of profit or loss followed by a number of notes.

As is common with this type of question you are instructed to start your computation with the net profit figure and list all items in the question, using a zero if no adjustment is necessary. Note that marks are available for correctly showing zero for a non-adjusting item, so do not lose easy marks by ignoring these items. Work methodically through the statement, referring to the notes where appropriate, and entering each item in your computation as you go.

Remember to adjust for private use by the proprietor, but not an employee.

	£
Net profit	32,200
Motor expenses – Richard (£4,710 × 70%)	3,297
Motor expenses – Chef	0
Parking fines	280
Property expenses (£16,200 × 1/5)	3,240
Decorating – Restaurant	0
– Apartment	1,320
Other expenses – Legal fees (capital)	2,590
	42,927
Less: Capital allowances (W)	(3,780)
Trading profit	39,147

Working: Capital allowances

	Main pool £	Private use car £	Business use %	Allowances £
Additions not qualifying for AIA:				
Private use car (76 – 130 g/km)		14,000		
Car (76 – 130 g/km)	16,800			
WDA (18%)		(2,520)	× 30%	756
WDA (18%)	(3,024)			3,024
TWDV c/f	13,776	11,480		
				3,780

Tutorial note

Both motor cars have CO_2 emissions between 76 and 130 grams per kilometre and therefore qualify for writing down allowances at the rate of 18%.

The private use of a motor car by an employee is irrelevant, since such usage will be assessed on the employee as a benefit.

(b)   Employer national insurance contributions

Tutor's top tips

This question only requires the calculation of the employer's NIC liabilities, so do not waste time calculating employee NICs.

Make sure that you clearly identify the different classes of NIC payable (i.e. class 1 and class 1A) and the different income on which they are charged.

	£	£
Employer's class 1 NIC		
(£46,000 – £8,112) × 13.8%	5,229	
Less: NIC employment allowance (Note)	(3,000)	
	———	2,229
Employer's class 1A NIC		
£2,856 (W1) × 13.8%		394
		———
Total NICs		2,623
		———

Tutorial note

As the chef is the only employee the employment allowance will be offset against the employer's class 1 NIC liability on his salary.

Workings

(W1) Car benefit

CO_2 emissions = 103 g/km (rounded down to 100g/km) available for the full tax year

	%
Petrol	16
Plus: $(100 - 95) \times 1/5$	1
	—
Appropriate percentage	17
	—
List price (same as cost)	£16,800
Car benefit ($£16,800 \times 17\%$)	£2,856

(c) **Self-assessment**

- Unless the notice to file a return is issued late, the latest date that Richard can file a paper self-assessment tax return for the tax year 2016/17 is 31 October 2017.

- However, he has until 31 January 2018 to file his self-assessment tax return for the tax year 2016/17 online.

Compliance checks

- If HM Revenue and Customs intend to carry out a compliance check into Richard's 2016/17 tax return, they will have to notify him within 12 months of the date that they receive the return.

- HM Revenue and Customs have the right to carry out a compliance check as regards the completeness and accuracy of any return, and such a check may be made on a completely random basis.

- However, compliance checks are generally carried out because of a suspicion that income has been undeclared or because deductions have been incorrectly claimed. For example, where accounting ratios are out of line with industry norms.

<table>
<tr><td colspan="4" align="center">**ACCA marking scheme**</td></tr>
<tr><td></td><td></td><td></td><td align="right">*Marks*</td></tr>
<tr><td>(a)</td><td colspan="2">Motor expenses – Richard</td><td align="right">1.0</td></tr>
<tr><td></td><td colspan="2">Motor expenses – Chef</td><td align="right">0.5</td></tr>
<tr><td></td><td colspan="2">Parking fines</td><td align="right">0.5</td></tr>
<tr><td></td><td colspan="2">Property expenses</td><td align="right">1.0</td></tr>
<tr><td></td><td colspan="2">Decorating – Restaurant</td><td align="right">0.5</td></tr>
<tr><td></td><td colspan="2">Decorating – Apartment</td><td align="right">0.5</td></tr>
<tr><td></td><td colspan="2">Legal fees – Purchase of property</td><td align="right">0.5</td></tr>
<tr><td></td><td colspan="2">Working – Capital allowances</td><td align="right"></td></tr>
<tr><td></td><td colspan="2">– Private use (PU) car – in own column</td><td align="right">0.5</td></tr>
<tr><td></td><td colspan="2">– Car 2 – in main pool</td><td align="right">0.5</td></tr>
<tr><td></td><td colspan="2">WDA on PU car</td><td align="right">1.0</td></tr>
<tr><td></td><td colspan="2">WDA on Car 2</td><td align="right">0.5</td></tr>
<tr><td></td><td></td><td></td><td align="right">———</td></tr>
<tr><td></td><td></td><td></td><td align="right">7.0</td></tr>
<tr><td></td><td></td><td></td><td align="right">———</td></tr>
<tr><td>(b)</td><td colspan="2">Employer's class 1 calculation</td><td align="right">1.0</td></tr>
<tr><td></td><td colspan="2">Deducting employment allowance</td><td align="right">0.5</td></tr>
<tr><td></td><td colspan="2">Class 1A calculation</td><td align="right">0.5</td></tr>
<tr><td></td><td colspan="2">Car benefit calculation</td><td align="right">1.0</td></tr>
<tr><td></td><td></td><td></td><td align="right">———</td></tr>
<tr><td></td><td></td><td></td><td align="right">3.0</td></tr>
<tr><td></td><td></td><td></td><td align="right">———</td></tr>
<tr><td>(c)</td><td>(i)</td><td>Paper return date</td><td align="right">1.0</td></tr>
<tr><td></td><td></td><td>Online return date</td><td align="right">1.0</td></tr>
<tr><td></td><td></td><td></td><td align="right">———</td></tr>
<tr><td></td><td></td><td></td><td align="right">2.0</td></tr>
<tr><td></td><td></td><td></td><td align="right">———</td></tr>
<tr><td></td><td>(ii)</td><td>Notify within 12 months of date received return</td><td align="right">1.0</td></tr>
<tr><td></td><td></td><td>Right to carry out compliance check on any return</td><td align="right">1.0</td></tr>
<tr><td></td><td></td><td>Generally carried out if suspicion of errors in return</td><td align="right">1.0</td></tr>
<tr><td></td><td></td><td></td><td align="right">———</td></tr>
<tr><td></td><td></td><td></td><td align="right">3.0</td></tr>
<tr><td></td><td></td><td></td><td align="right">———</td></tr>
<tr><td>**Total**</td><td></td><td></td><td align="right">**15.0**</td></tr>
<tr><td></td><td></td><td></td><td align="right">———</td></tr>
</table>

101   ALFRED KING *Walk in the footsteps of a top tutor*

Key answer tips

This question is in two parts. Part (a) carries the majority of the marks and requires a calculation of the balancing payment due under self-assessment. This therefore requires a calculation of the income tax payable, the class 4 national insurance contributions and a deduction of the payments on account.

The individual is a partner in a partnership and receives some dividend income.

There is a lot of work to be done here and it would be easy to overrun on time. Don't be daunted by the amount of work required though. It is important not to do more work than necessary and to plan the approach to your answer to ensure you work through it systematically.

Part (b) at the end could easily be neglected so it is important to leave time to answer this. It may provide a challenge, but there are 3 easy marks if a short amount of time is taken to think through the answer.

In the answer to part (b) the highlighted words are key phrases that markers are looking for.

(a)   **Balancing payment – 2016/17**

Tutor's top tips

In dealing with the trading income for a partnership you should adjust the profits first (which has already been done in this question), then deduct the capital allowances, which require calculation here. Finally you must allocate the profits amongst the partners, taking into account the change in partners during the period. It is not necessary to calculate the profit share allocated to the other partners in this question as you are only asked to calculate the income tax for one of them.

Remember to look out for any exempt income.

When calculating the balancing payment due you must remember to include class 4 NICs. The examining team has pointed out in the requirement that these must be taken into account.

Alfred has made charitable donations, via gift aid, which is paid net of tax and will extend the basic rate band.

Alfred King

Income tax computation – 2016/17

	Total	Non-savings income	Dividend income
	£	£	£
Trading profit (W1)	72,750	72,750	
Dividends (£3,320-£720) (Note)	2,600		2,600
	75,350	72,750	2,600
Less: Personal allowance	(11,000)	(11,000)	
Taxable income	64,350	61,750	2,600

£	
34,400 at 20% (W3)	6,880
27,350 at 40%	10,940
61,750	
2,600 at 0%	0
64,350	
Income tax payable	17,820
Class 4 NICs (W4)	3,740
	21,560
Less: Payments on account	(20,200)
Balancing payment	1,360

Tutorial note

The dividends from the ISA are exempt. The other dividends of £2,600 fall within the £5,000 dividend nil rate band.

Workings

(W1) Trading profit

	£
Trading profit	228,000
Capital allowances (W2)	(34,000)
	194,000

	£
Profit share	
6 April to 31 December 2016 (£194,000 × 9/12 × 1/3)	48,500
1 January to 5 April 2017 (£194,000 × 3/12 × ½)	24,250
	72,750

(W2) Capital allowances

	£	Main pool £	Allowances £
TWDV b/f		10,000	
Additions qualifying for AIA			
False ceiling	0		
Display units	15,100		
Tiled flooring	0		
Movable partitions	17,100		
	32,200		
Less: AIA (100%)	(32,200)	0	32,200
Less: WDA (18%)		(1,800)	1,800
TWDV c/f		8,200	
Total allowances			34,000

Tutorial note

Expenditure forming part of a building, such as the false ceiling and tiled flooring, does not qualify as plant. The display units and the movable partition walls are not treated as forming part of the shop building, as they perform a function in the trade and therefore qualify as plant.

(W3) Extended basic rate band

	£
Basic rate band	32,000
Plus: Gross gift aid donations (£1,920 × 100/80)	2,400
Extended basic rate band	34,400

(W4) Class 4 NICs

	£
(£43,000 – £8,060) × 9%	3,145
(£72,750 – £43,000) × 2%	595
	3,740

(b) Cost of employing one versus two employees

Tutor's top tips

This was a somewhat unusual requirement as it did not mention which tax you were being asked to consider. However, if you think about the scenario, which was the cost to a partnership of paying employees, the only tax cost suffered by the partnership is class 1 employer's NICs. Therefore you should calculate the cost of this tax under each of the two alternatives.

One full time employee

- If one full-time employee is employed on an annual salary of £22,000, then employer's class 1 NIC would be:

  (£22,000 – £8,112) at 13.8% = £1,917

- The total employment cost would be:

  (£22,000 + £1,917) = £23,917

Two part time employees

- If two part-time employees are employed on annual salaries of £11,450, then the total employer's class 1 NIC would be:

  (£11,450 – £8,112) at 13.8% = £461 × 2 employees = £922

- The total employment cost would be:

  (£11,450 × 2 employees) + £922 = £23,822

Examiner's report

Part (a) was generally satisfactorily answered, although many candidates wasted a considerable amount of time by providing detailed explanations and/or using far too many workings. The class 4 NIC calculation was sometimes omitted.

It was pleasing to see that part (c) was well answered by many candidates.

ACCA marking scheme			
			Marks
(a)	Trading profit		0.5
	Capital allowances	– TWDV brought forward	0.5
		– False ceiling	0.5
		– Display units	0.5
		– Tiled flooring	0.5
		– Movable partitions	0.5
		– AIA	0.5
		– WDA	0.5
	Profit share	– 6 April to 31 December	1.0
		– 1 January to 5 April	1.0
	Dividends		0.5
	Personal allowance		0.5
	Basic rate band extension		1.0
	Income tax liability		1.5
	Class 4 NICs		2.0
	Payments on account		0.5
			———
			12
			———
(b)	NICs for one full-time employee		1.0
	Total employment cost for one full-time employee		0.5
	NICs for two part-time employees		1.0
	Total employment cost for two part-time employees		0.5
			———
			3.0
			———
Total			**15.0**
			———

102 CHI NEEDLE (ADAPTED) *Walk in the footsteps of a top tutor*

Key answer tips

In this 10 mark question you are required to calculate income tax and national insurance contributions for a sole trader using the usual trading income rules and then to calculate the trading profit using the cash basis.

The two parts of the question are independent and can be answered in any order. If you feel more comfortable with one part than the other you may want to do this first.

The highlighted words in the written sections are key phrases that markers are looking for.

(a)   (1)   **Income tax liability – 2016/17**

Tutor's top tips

When allocating your time in the examination be guided by the number of marks available. This requirement is more straightforward than it may seem: the trading profit has been calculated for you, the notes relate to the cash basis adjustments required in part (b).

	£
Trading profit	52,400
Less: Personal allowance	(11,000)
Taxable income	41,400

£	
32,000 at 20%	6,400
9,400 at 40%	3,760
41,400	
Income tax liability	10,160

(2)   **National insurance contributions**

- Class 2 national insurance contributions – 2016/17

  = (£2.80 × 52 weeks) = £146

- Class 4 national insurance contributions – 2016/17

	£
(£43,000 – £8,060) × 9%	3,145
(£52,400 – £43,000) × 2%	188
	3,333

(b)   **Trading profit under the cash basis**

Tutor's top tips

The best approach to a cash basis question is to set out your answer using the same layout as the original calculation of profit. Although credit would be given for adjusting the profits as in a normal calculation of trading income, it is more confusing to approach a cash basis question in this way.

There are marks available for each item so make sure you pick up the easy marks for the revenue and expenses, which simply require the receivables and payables to be deducted from the accruals basis figures to calculate the cash basis figure.

The approved mileage rates are set out in the tax rates and allowances provided in the examination.

Trading profit for the year ended 5 April 2017 using the cash basis

	£	£
Revenue (£71,900 – £1,600)		70,300
Expenses		
Motor expenses (W)	5,300	
Other expenses (£8,200 – £900)	7,300	
Office equipment	4,020	
Capital allowances	0	
		(16,620)
Trading profit		53,680

Working – Allowable motor expenses

	£
10,000 miles at 45p	4,500
3,200 miles at 25p	800
	5,300

Tutorial note

1   *Capital allowances are not relevant for cash basis computations since purchases of equipment are deducted as an expense.*

2   *The running and capital costs of owning a motor car are replaced by the deduction based on approved mileage allowances.*

Examiner's report

Part (a) was generally well answered. For the first requirement, one common problem was making adjustments to the trading profit, despite being instructed to use this figure. Although this only resulted in a half mark being missed, it often wasted quite a lot of time with unnecessary workings.

Answers to part (b) were very mixed. For better prepared candidates, it was mainly the treatment of the capital expenditure that caused problems. Candidates that approached the calculation by attempting to adjust the trading profit (rather than preparing a revised profit computation) struggled.

Note: *The examiner's report has been edited to remove comments on elements of the question that have been deleted due to changes to the examination format.*

			ACCA marking scheme	*Marks*
(a)	(1)	Trading profit		0.5
		Personal allowance		0.5
		Income tax payable		1.0
				2.0
	(2)	Class 2 NICs		1.0
		Class 4 NICs		2.0
				3.0
(b)		Cash basis		
		Revenue		1.0
		Other expenses		1.0
		Office equipment		1.0
		Capital allowances		0.5
		Motor expenses		1.5
				5.0
Total				**10.0**

TRADING LOSSES

103 NORMA (ADAPTED)

Key answer tips

The first part required the computation of taxable income for five tax years before considering loss relief. Marks should have been gained here in laying out pro forma computations and filling in the easy numbers before applying the opening and closing year rules to establish the trading income assessments. A loss arises in the final tax year and so the trading income assessment in that year will be £0.

The second part involved consideration of the options available for loss relief, including a terminal loss.

It is important to communicate to the examining team that you know the loss relief rules; however you must apply the knowledge to the specific facts of the question.

The highlighted words in the written sections are key phrases that markers are looking for.

(a)   **Taxable income and gains before loss relief**

	2012/13	2013/14	2014/15	2015/16	2016/17
	£	£	£	£	£
Trading income (W)	25,250	17,000	16,900	8,835	0
Employment income (£11,400 × 10/12)					9,500
Interest income	2,400	2,400	2,400	2,400	2,400
Total income	27,650	19,400	19,300	11,235	11,900
Less: PA	(11,000)	(11,000)	(11,000)	(11,000)	(11,000)
Taxable income	16,650	8,400	8,300	235	900
Taxable gain				35,000	

Working: Trading income

Tax year	Basis of assessment	£	£
2012/13	Actual basis (1.5.12 – 5.4.13)		
	Period to 31.12.12	21,000	
	1.1.13 – 5.4.13 (£17,000 × 3/12)	4,250	
			25,250
2013/14	Year ended 31.12.13		17,000
2014/15	Year ended 31.12.14		16,900
2015/16	Year ended 31.12.15		8,835
2016/17	Year of cessation		
	Period to 31 May 2016	(11,000)	
	Less: Overlap profits (1.1.13 – 5.4.13) (£17,000 × 3/12)	(4,250)	
	Trading loss/Trading assessment	(15,250)	0

Tutorial note

If the trader does not have a 31 March (or 5 April) year end you should be looking for overlap relief.

The overlap relief increases the loss of the final tax year and is included in the calculation of the terminal loss.

(b)   **Options available to utilise loss arising in period ended 31 May 2016**

    (1)   **Relief against total income**

        The loss arising in the tax year 2016/17 can be set against total income in the tax year(s) 2016/17 and/or 2015/16, in either order.

        (1)   Setting the loss against total income of the tax year 2016/17 first (i.e. employment income and bank interest) would reduce total income to £0, would waste the personal allowance and save no tax (see Tutorial Note).

                The remaining loss of £3,350 (£15,250 – £11,900) could be offset against total income of the tax year 2015/16, wasting part of the personal allowance and saving no tax (see Tutorial Note).

        (2)   Setting the loss against total income of the tax year 2015/16 first would reduce total income to £0, would waste the personal allowance and save no tax.

                The remaining loss of £4,015 (£15,250 – £11,235) could be offset against total income of the tax year 2016/17, which would waste part of the personal allowance and save no tax.

Tutorial note

The rate of tax saving in the tax year 2015/16 on £235 and in the tax year 2016/17 on £900 is 0% because Norma's taxable income includes savings income which will fall into the first £5,000 of taxable income in those years.

    (2)   **Relief against chargeable gains**

        Alternatively, once a claim has been made to offset trading losses against total income in the tax year 2015/16, a claim can be made to offset any remaining losses against chargeable gains in 2015/16 instead of total income in 2016/17.

        Accordingly, the £4,015 loss remaining after the offset against total income in the tax year 2015/16 could be set against the chargeable gain arising in that year.

        Assuming that the current tax rates apply throughout this question, this will save tax at 10% on some of the gain and 20% on the remaining gain (see Tutorial Note).

Tutorial note

Currently, before loss relief, there is £31,765 (£32,000 – £235) of gain in the basic rate band and £3,235 (£35,000 – £31,765) in the higher rate band.

So using £4,015 of loss against the gain would save 20% on the top £3,235 of the gain, and 10% on £780 (£4,015 – £3,235).

(3) **Terminal loss relief**

The loss arising in the final 12 months of trading can be set against:

- available trading profits

- in the tax year of cessation, and

- the three preceding tax years

- on a last-in-first-out (LIFO) basis.

Calculation of terminal loss

			£
(1)	6 April before cessation to date of cessation		
	(6.4.16 – 31.5.16) (£11,000 loss × 2/5)		4,400
(2)	12 months before cessation to 5 April before cessation		

		£		
	1.6.15 – 31.12.15			
	(£8,835 profit × 7/12) .	5,154	Profit	
	1.1.16 – 5.4.16 (£11,000 loss × 3/5)	(6,600)	Loss	
		——		
		(1,446)	Net Loss	1,446
		——		

(3)	Overlap relief		
	1.1.13 – 5.4.13 (£17,000 × 3/12)		4,250
			——
Terminal loss			10,096
			——

Utilisation of terminal loss

Norma has no trading profits in the tax year 2016/17, the tax year of cessation.

The terminal loss can therefore be carried back against the trading profits arising in the preceding three years, on a LIFO basis, as follows:

	2013/14	2014/15	2015/16
	£	£	£
Trading income	17,000	16,900	8,835
Less: Terminal loss relief	(0)	(1,261)	(8,835)
	17,000	15,639	0
Interest income	2,400	2,400	2,400
Net income	19,400	18,039	2,400
Less: PA	(11,000)	(11,000)	(11,000)
Taxable income	8,400	7,039	0

The terminal loss reduces taxable income in the tax year 2015/16 to £0, wasting part of the personal allowance and saving no tax on £235.

The remaining loss of £1,261 (£10,096 – £8,835) is then offset against the taxable income in the tax year 2014/15, saving tax at 20% on £1,261.

Tutorial note

Taxable income before loss relief in 2014/15 of £8,300 comprises non-savings income of £5,900 (£16,900 – £11,000 PA) and savings income of £2,400. Tax on the loss of £1,261 is therefore saved at 20% on non-savings income.

104 LEONARDO *Walk in the footsteps of a top tutor*

Key answer tips

An opening year loss relief question, requiring a calculation of the assessments for the first few tax years and consideration of loss claims available.

Part (b) should have provided easy marks in stating due dates for making elections.

The highlighted words in the written sections are key phrases that markers are looking for.

(a)   **Assessments**

Tax year	Basis period		£
2013/14	Actual basis (1.9.13 – 5.4.14)	7/9 × £40,500	31,500
2014/15	First 12 months (1.9.13 – 31.8.14)	£40,500 – (3/12 × £54,000)	27,000
2015/16	CYB (y/e 31.5.15)	Loss	0
2016/17	CYB (y/e 31.5.16)	Loss	0
2017/18	CYB (y/e 31.5.17)		11,000

Tutor's top tips

As Leonardo will not be making any significant profits in the foreseeable future there is no point in carrying losses forward, therefore offset the losses as soon as possible.

Note the question does not require any calculation of tax savings, just computations to show how the loss would be utilised.

Loss memoranda

	£
Loss in 2015/16	
Loss in y/e 31.5.15	54,000
Less: Relief given in 2014/15 when applying the opening year rules (£54,000 × 3/12)	(13,500)
	40,500
Less: Special opening year loss relief – in 2013/14	(31,500)
– in 2014/15	(9,000)
	0

Loss in 2016/17

	£
Loss in y/e 31.5.16	27,000
Less: Special opening year loss relief in 2014/15 (£27,000 – £9,000)	(18,000)
Loss carried forward to 2017/18	9,000

Assessments after loss relief claims

	2013/14	2014/15	2015/16	2016/17	2017/18
	£	£	£	£	£
Trading income	31,500	27,000	0	0	11,000
Less: Loss relief b/f					(9,000)
	31,500	27,000	0	0	2,000
Less: Special opening year loss relief					
– 2015/16 Loss	(31,500)	(9,000)			
– 2016/17 Loss		(18,000)			
Net income	0	0	0	0	2,000

Tutorial note

*Under special opening year loss provisions, losses that arise in the **first four tax years** of a trade may be set off against:*

- *the total income*

- *of the three tax years preceding the tax year of loss*

- *on a first-in-first-out (FIFO) basis.*

*Losses should be dealt with in **chronological** order. Therefore the loss arising in the tax year 2015/16 is utilised before the loss arising in the tax year 2016/17.*

(b)   **Loss relief time limits**

Special opening year loss relief

For claims to carry back losses in the first four tax years of a trade against income of the three preceding tax years the claim must be made within 12 months from 31 January next following the tax year in which the loss was sustained.

- In the case of the loss sustained in the year ended 31 May 2015 (i.e. the loss in the tax year 2015/16), the claim must be made by 31 January 2018.

- In the case of the loss sustained in the year ended 31 May 2016 (i.e. the loss in the tax year 2016/17), the claim must be made by 31 January 2019.

Carry forward of losses

There is no specific statutory time limit on claims to carry forward losses against **future trading income.**

However, a claim to establish the amount of the loss to be carried forward must be made within four years from the end of the tax year in which the loss was sustained.

In the case of the loss sustained in the year ended 31 May 2016 (i.e. the loss in the tax year 2016/17) by 5 April 2021.

105 DEE ZYNE (ADAPTED) *Walk in the footsteps of a top tutor*

Key answer tips

An individual that is employed for part of the tax year, then sets up a business which is initially loss-making, is a common scenario in examination questions.

The calculation of the adjusted loss was straightforward provided you remembered to time apportion WDAs in the opening period of account.

Part (b) required consideration of alternative claims for Dee's trading loss, which is a common requirement in loss relief questions and you should therefore make sure that you are well prepared for this.

The highlighted words in the written sections are key phrases that markers are looking for.

Tutor's top tips

In this question, Dee has 5 April as her year end, so the capital allowances are calculated for the period ended 5 April 2017.

However, where a sole trader chooses a different year end, remember that the capital allowances are always calculated for the period of account before matching profits or losses to tax years.

(a)   **Tax adjusted trading loss – 2016/17**

	£
Trading loss	(11,440)
Patent royalties (Note)	(500)
Capital allowances (W)	(5,690)
	————
	(17,630)
	————

Tutorial note

The patent royalties were incurred for trade purposes and are therefore deductible in computing the tax adjusted trading loss. As the question says they have not been accounted for in arriving at the loss of £11,440, they must be adjusted for and will increase the loss.

Working: Capital allowances	£	Main Pool £	Car £	Allowances £
Additions (no AIA)				
Car (between 76 – 130 g/km)		10,400		
Car (> 130 g/km) (Note 1)			17,800	
Additions (with AIA)				
Computer	1,257			
Office furniture	2,175			
	3,432			
Less: AIA (Note 2)	(3,432)			3,432
		0		
Less: WDA (18% × 9/12)		(1,404)		1,404
Less: WDA (8% × 9/12) (Note 3)			(1,068) × 80%	854
TWDV c/f		8,996	16,732	
Total allowances				5,690

Tutorial note

1   *Capital allowances on purchases of cars are calculated based on their CO_2 emissions.*

   The car with CO_2 emissions of between 76 – 130 g/km is put in the main pool and is eligible for a writing down allowance at 18%.

   The car with CO_2 emissions of > 130 g/km is a private use car, has its own column and is eligible for a writing down allowance at 8%.

2   *The maximum AIA and the WDAs are time apportioned because Dee's period of account is only nine months' in length.*

   However, the maximum AIA of £150,000 (£200,000 × 9/12) exceeds the total qualifying expenditure and therefore all of the expenditure is eligible for relief.

3   *Only private use by the owner restricts capital allowances. Private use of the employee's motor car therefore does not affect the capital allowance claim, but will instead result in an assessable employment benefit for that employee.*

(b)   **Alternative uses of trading loss**

Tutor's top tips

When you are describing use of losses, you must be very specific about exactly what the loss can be set against, and when. For example, don't just say 'the loss can be set off in the current year'. Specify in which tax year that is, and state that the loss can be set against total income.

The examining team have stated that the use of section numbers is not required and is not encouraged at the expense of explaining the relief.

- The loss could have been claimed against total income for the tax year(s) 2015/16 and/or 2016/17.

- By claiming loss relief against her total income (£28,875) for the tax year 2016/17, Dee has relieved the loss entirely at the basic rate of 20% and reduced her income tax liability by £3,526 (£17,630 × 20%).

- If the loss is carried back to the tax year 2015/16 when Dee's total income was £80,000, Dee could relieve the loss entirely at the higher rate of 40% and reduced her income tax liability by £7,052 (£17,630 × 40%).

- The loss is incurred within the first four tax years of trading, so a claim for special opening year loss relief could have been made against total income for the three tax years 2013/14 to 2015/16, earliest first.

- As Dee's total income in the tax years 2013/14 to 2015/16 was £80,000, this would also have relieved the loss at the higher rate of 40%, and resulted in an income tax refund of £7,052 (£17,630 × 40%).

106 SAMANTHA FABRIQUE (ADAPTED)   *Walk in the footsteps of a top tutor*

Key answer tips

This is a losses question that requires you to choose the best use of the loss.

Given the information about gains it should be fairly obvious that you need to consider a claim against capital gains. However, remember that this only saves tax at 10% or 20% (for a higher rate taxpayer) and can only happen after a claim against total income has been made first in the same tax year.

Be careful to consider the loss relief restriction which applies to loss claims against total income other than the profits of the same trade. This restriction did not apply in the question as originally set, as these rules did not exist then.

Part (a) should have provided easy marks listing the factors a taxpayer takes into account when deciding what to do with a loss.

The highlighted words are key words or phrases that markers are looking for.

(a) **Factors influencing choice of loss relief claims**

- The rate of income tax or capital gains tax at which relief will be obtained, with preference being given to income charged at the higher rate of 40% or additional rate of 45%.

- The timing of the relief obtained, with a claim against total income/chargeable gains of the current tax year or preceding tax year resulting in earlier relief than a claim against future trading profits.

- The extent to which personal allowances, the capital gains annual exempt amount and the savings and dividend nil rate bands may be wasted.

Tutor's top tips

As long as you addressed the factors influencing the choice of relief, not what the relief options are, you should have scored well here.

(b)

Taxable income	2015/16	2016/17	2017/18
	£	£	£
Trading income	21,600	0	10,500
Interest	52,100	3,800	1,500
	73,700	3,800	12,000
Less: Loss relief		(0)	
– against trade profits (no restriction)	(21,600)		
– against other income (restricted)	(50,000)		
	2,100	3,800	12,000
Less: PA	(11,000)	(11,000)	(11,000)
Taxable income	0	0	1,000

Taxable gains	2015/16	2016/17	2017/18
	£	£	£
Chargeable gains	53,300	0	11,300
Less: Trading loss relief	(10,300)		
	43,000	0	11,300
Less: Capital loss b/f			(200)
	43,000	0	11,100
Less: AEA	(11,100)	(wasted)	(11,100)
Taxable gains	31,900	0	0

Tutorial note

The loss relief in the tax year 2015/16 against total income is restricted due to the cap on income tax reliefs. The losses offset against profits from the same trade are not restricted; therefore £21,600 of loss can be set against trading income. A further £50,000 of loss relief is available as this is the higher of £50,000 and 25% of total income (£73,700 × 25% = £18,425).

Although these two claims are both set off against total income in the computation, you may find it helpful to separate them out to ensure you relieve the correct amount of loss.

Key answer tips

Where loss questions require you to set off a loss against income and gains, make sure that you keep your income tax computation and CGT computation **separate**.

This is not only technically correct, but will also make it easier for you to see where best to set off the losses and apply your PA and AEA, and much easier for the marker to mark your answer!

The highlighted words are key words or phrases that markers are looking for.

Loss memorandum

	£
Loss in 2016/17	81,900
Less: Relief against total income	
2016/17 (no claim as income covered by PA)	(0)
2015/16 – total claim	(71,600)
	–––––––
Loss remaining	10,300
Less: Relief against chargeable gains	
2015/16	(10,300)
	–––––––
Loss carried forward	0
	–––––––

Utilisation of losses

Trading loss

Loss relief has been claimed:

- against total income for 2015/16,

- then against the chargeable gains of 2015/16.

This gives relief at the earliest date and at the highest rates of tax.

Capital loss

The capital loss for 2016/17 is carried forward and set against the chargeable gains for 2017/18.

The use of brought forward capital losses is restricted to the level that reduces gains down to equal the annual exempt amount (£11,300 – £200 = £11,100).

The balance of the loss £3,200 (£3,400 – £200) is carried forward against future gains.

Tutorial note

For the tax year 2015/16, if relief is claimed, the personal allowance is partially wasted in that year and the tax saving will be at 40% and 20% for income tax and 20% for capital gains.

Offsetting losses in the tax year 2016/17 however would utilise £3,800 of the loss, would waste the personal allowance and would not save any tax.

A claim against total income must be made before relief against chargeable gains can be considered.

Carrying all of the loss forward would use £10,500 of the loss in the tax year 2017/18 (as could only carry forward against future trading profits from the same trade), would waste most of the personal allowance and would save no tax.

The taxable income (before loss relief) of £1,000 represents savings income. All of the savings income falls in the nil rate starting rate band of £5,000 so no tax would be saved. The remaining loss would not be relieved until subsequent years.

The optimum relief is therefore to claim against total income for the tax year 2015/16, then against the chargeable gains of the tax year 2015/16, since this gives relief at the earliest date and at the highest rates of tax.

Examiner's report

This question was generally not answered well.

Although it was technically the most demanding question on the paper, requiring a bit more thought than the other four questions, it was quite short and should not have presented too many difficulties for reasonably well prepared candidates.

In part (a) many candidates explained the loss reliefs that were available rather than the factors that must be taken into account when deciding which loss reliefs to actually claim.

In part (b) it was extremely disappointing to see the vast majority of candidates include the capital gains in their computation of taxable income. The capital gains annual exempt amount was often then deducted against the combined figure of taxable income and taxable gains.

Many candidates claimed loss relief against the total income for the year of the loss despite this income clearly being covered by the personal allowance.

Very few candidates, even if they showed the capital gains separately, claimed loss relief against capital gains.

ACCA marking scheme			
			Marks
(a)		Rate of tax	1.0
		Timing of relief	1.0
		Personal allowance, annual exempt amount, nil rate bands	1.0
			3.0
(b)		Trading income	0.5
		Building society interest	0.5
		Loss relief against total income	2.0
		Personal allowance	0.5
		Capital gains	1.5
		Loss relief against capital gains	1.0
		Capital loss carried forward	1.0
		Explanation of most beneficial route	5.0
			12.0
Total			**15.0**

107 MICHAEL AND SEAN *Walk in the footsteps of a top tutor*

Key answer tips

Part (a) offered four easy marks to identify the reliefs available for individual savings accounts, pensions, gift aid, entrepreneurs' relief and capital allowances.

Part (b) was tricky and the hardest part of the whole examination. It involved opening and closing year losses.

Consideration of the optimum use of the losses was required together with the identification of the rates at which tax would be saved. A good knowledge of the loss relief rules and a lot of practice at application prior to sitting the examination was needed to score well on this part in the time given.

In order to score well in part (b) computations alone showing the different loss reliefs were not enough; explanations of how the reliefs work and advice on the most beneficial course of action were also needed.

The highlighted words are key words or phrases that markers are looking for.

Tutor's top tips

When you need to explain how tax policies can encourage individuals to take certain actions, always think about how those actions can save tax for the individual.

By opening an ISA, individuals can save income tax on the interest.

By saving money in a pension fund, individuals can save income tax by either reducing their employment income or extending their basic and higher rate bands.

By donating money to a charity, the individual can save income tax by either reducing their employment income (payroll deduction scheme) or extending their basic and higher rate bands (gift aid donations).

When the sole trader buys plant and machinery he gets capital allowances that reduce trading profits saving income tax.

(a)   **Government tax policies**

    (1)   **Individuals to save**

Saving is encouraged by offering individuals tax incentives such as tax-free individual savings accounts (ISAs) and tax relief on pension contributions. In addition the savings nil rate bands encourage basic and higher rate taxpayers to save by providing tax free savings income.

    (2)   **Individuals to support charities**

Charitable support is encouraged by giving individuals tax relief on donations made through the gift aid scheme or the payroll deduction scheme.

    (3)   **Entrepreneurs to build businesses and invest in plant and machinery**

Entrepreneurs are encouraged to build their own businesses through various capital gains tax reliefs such as entrepreneurs' relief.

Investment in plant and machinery is encouraged through capital allowances.

(b)   **Michael**

Tutor's top tips

It is difficult to comment on loss relief by just reading the scenario. Set up the income tax computations for each tax year involved, bringing in the figures given in the question.

This will give a clear picture of the position and will help to decide on the appropriate reliefs for the loss. It will also make it easier to comment on the tax savings and possible wastage of the personal allowance.

Loss relief available

1   **Special opening year loss relief**

The loss of £24,600 arising in the tax year 2015/16 can be claimed against total income for the three preceding tax years, earliest first, since it is incurred in the first four tax years of trading.

Amount of loss claim

The loss relief claim will therefore be £17,200 in the tax year 2012/13 and £7,400 (£24,600 – £17,200) in the tax year 2013/14.

Tax saving

For the tax year 2012/13 this will waste Michael's personal allowance, with the balance of the claim of £6,200 (£17,200 – £11,000) (W2) saving income tax at the basic rate of 20%.

For the tax year 2013/14 Michael has income of £8,000 (£51,000 – £11,000 – £32,000) subject to income tax at the higher rate of 40%, so the claim of £7,400 will save tax at the higher rate.

2   **Carry loss forward**

Alternatively, Michael could have carried the trading loss forward against future trading profits, but the trading profit of £7,100 for 2016/17 is less than the personal allowance, and therefore no tax is saved in that year. There is no information available regarding future trading profits.

Most beneficial

Claim special opening year loss relief.

Tutorial note

A standard loss relief claim against total income in the tax year of the loss (2015/16) and/or the preceding tax year (2014/15) is not possible since Michael does not have any income for either of these years.

Special opening year loss relief is one claim for all three years (if there is sufficient loss) on a FIFO basis, it is not possible to only claim in one year, and it is an 'all or nothing relief' (i.e. cannot restrict the offset to preserve the personal allowance).

Note that the limit on the amount of loss relief that can be deducted from other income in any tax year does not need to be considered in this question, as the loss is not sufficiently high for it to be an issue.

Workings

(W1) Opening year assessments

2015/16 – Actual basis

	£
1.7.2015 – 5.4.2016 Loss of £24,600	0

2016/17 – Current year basis

Year ended 5.4.2017	7,100

(W2) Taxable income for 2012/13 to 2015/16 (ignoring loss relief)

	2012/13	2013/14	2014/15	2015/16	2016/17
	£	£	£	£	£
Employment income	17,200	51,000	0	0	0
Trading income				0	7,100
Less: PA	(11,000)	(11,000)	0	0	(11,000)
Taxable income	6,200	40,000	0	0	0
Basic rate band		(32,000)			
Taxed at higher rate		8,000			

The loss carried back is offset against income before the personal allowance is deducted. This means that £11,000 of the loss each year does not actually save tax as it merely replaces the personal allowance. This working enables you to see how much of the loss actually saves tax and at what rate.

Sean

Amount of the loss

The unused overlap profits brought forward are added to the loss for the year ended 31 December 2016, so the total loss for the tax year 2016/17 is £26,700 (£23,100 + £3,600).

Loss relief available

1   **Terminal loss relief**

The whole of the loss can be claimed as a terminal loss since it is for the final 12 months of trading.

The claim is against trading income for the tax year of the loss and the three preceding tax years, latest first.

Amount of loss claim

The terminal loss claim will therefore be £3,700 in 2015/16, £18,900 in 2014/15 and £4,100 (£26,700 – £3,700 – £18,900) in 2013/14.

Tax saving

The property business profits are sufficient to utilise Sean's personal allowance for each year, so the loss relief claims will save income tax at the basic rate of 20%.

2   **Standard loss relief against total income**

Alternatively, Sean could have initially claimed loss relief against his total income for 2016/17 and/or 2015/16, but this would have wasted his personal allowance for either or both of those years.

Most beneficial

Claim terminal loss relief.

Tutorial note

A claim against future trading profits is not available since the business is ceasing and a trading loss can only be carried forward against future trading profits of the same trade.

A terminal loss claim is against trading profits only, on a LIFO basis, and is an 'all or nothing' relief (i.e. cannot restrict the offset to preserve the personal allowance).

The terminal is the loss of the last 12 months of trading. It is normally calculated as follows:

	£
6 April before cessation to the date of cessation	
Actual trading loss in this period (£23,100 × 9/12)	*17,325*
Overlap profits not yet relieved	*3,600*
12 months before cessation to 5 April before cessation	
Actual trading loss in this period (£23,100 × 3/12)	*5,775*
	———
Terminal loss	*26,700*
	———

However when the final period of account is 12 months long it is unnecessary to prepare this detailed working and it is acceptable to take the examining team's approach of simply adding the unused overlap profits to the trading loss for the final 12 month period.

Examiner's report

Part (a) was generally well answered, although candidates should note that where just one or two marks are available for a requirement then just a short sentence is required – not a detailed explanation.

Not surprisingly, part (b) was the section of the paper that caused the most problems.

For Michael, the claims should have been fairly straightforward given that he only had one source of income for each year. However, some candidates were not even aware that a claim could be made against total income.

For Sean, a few candidates suggested that the loss be carried forward despite the trade ceasing. In both cases, it was generally not appreciated that the most advantageous choice of loss relief claims would generally preserve the benefit of personal allowances.

ACCA marking scheme			Marks
(a)	(i)	Saving	1.0
	(ii)	Charitable support	1.0
	(iii)	Businesses	1.0
		Plant and machinery	1.0
			———
			4.0
			———
(b)	**Michael**		
	Relief against total income – opening year loss relief		1.0
	Amount of loss claims		1.0
	Rate of tax saved – 2012/13		1.0
	– 2013/14		1.0
	Carry forward		1.0
	Sean		
	Available loss		1.0
	Terminal loss relief		1.0
	Amount of loss claim		1.0
	Rate of tax saved		1.5
	Relief against total income		1.5
			———
			11.0
			———
Total			15.0
			———

PARTNERSHIPS

108 PETER, QUINTON AND ROGER (ADAPTED) *Walk in the footsteps of a top tutor*

Key answer tips

A loss making partnership presents a tricky problem and it is important to approach the computation in part (b) with care.

Firstly, profits/(losses) need to be allocated to each partner and then the opening year rules applied for each partner according to the date they joined the firm.

There are many loss relief options available. A brief mention of each is all you have time for in the examination. Be careful not to go into too much detail and there is no need to discuss the relative merits of each option in this question.

It is much better to mention all the reliefs available and applicable to the question succinctly than to talk about any one relief in great detail.

The highlighted words are key words or phrases that markers are looking for.

(a) **Basis of assessment – Joining partners**

- Each partner is treated as a sole trader running a business.

- The commencement rules therefore apply when a partner joins the partnership, with the first year of assessment being on an actual basis (i.e. date of commencement to the following 5 April).

(b)   **Trading income assessments**

	Peter	Quinton	Roger
	£	£	£
2013/14 Peter and Quinton Actual basis (1 January 2014 to 5 April 2014) (£40,000 × 1/2 × 3/12)	5,000	5,000	
2014/15 Peter and Quinton CYB (y/e 31 December 2014) (£40,000 × 1/2)	20,000	20,000	
Roger Actual basis (1 January 2015 to 5 April 2015) (£90,000 × 1/3 × 3/12)			7,500
2015/16 All partners – CYB (y/e 31 December 2015) (£90,000 × 1/3)	30,000	30,000	30,000

Tutorial note

The commencement rules apply to:

*   *Peter and Quinton from the tax year 2013/14, as the partnership started on 1 January 2014.*

*   *Roger from the tax year 2014/15, since he joined as a partner on 1 January 2015.*

(c)   **Possible methods of relieving trading loss for 2016/17**

*   Peter, Quinton and Roger each have a tax adjusted trading loss of £10,000 (£30,000 × 1/3) for the tax year 2016/17.

*   Peter resigned as a partner on 31 December 2016. His unrelieved overlap profits of £5,000 (1 January 2014 to 5 April 2014) will therefore increase his loss to £15,000 (£10,000 + £5,000).

*   **Carry forward relief:**

    Quinton and Roger can carry their share of the loss forward against their first available future trading profits arising in the same trade.

*   **Relief against total income:**

    Peter, Quinton and Roger can claim relief against their total income for the tax year(s) 2016/17 and/or 2015/16.

*   **Special opening year loss relief:**

    Peter, Quinton and Roger can carry back their share of the loss against their total income for the tax year(s) 2013/14 to 2015/16, earliest year first.

- **Terminal loss relief:**

    Peter can carry back his share of the loss of the last 12 months trading against his trading profits for the tax year 2015/16.

    He has insufficient losses to carry back the loss any further. If he had more losses, he could carry back the loss and make a claim in respect of the tax years 2014/15 and 2013/14, in that order.

Tutor's top tips

The requirement is to 'State the possible ways to relieve the losses'. Therefore there will be no marks for discussing in detail the relative merits of each claim and which would be the most beneficial.

Remember that it is much better to mention all the reliefs available and applicable to the question succinctly than to talk about any one relief in great detail.

---

109 AE, BEE, CAE, AND DEE (ADAPTED) *Walk in the footsteps of a top tutor*

Key answer tips

This question tests the basis of assessment rules, but with the application of the rules to partnerships, and includes the opening year rules and overlap profits.

A well prepared student should have been able to secure good marks on this question and each part is independent.

Part (b) of this question has been amended due to syllabus changes.

The highlighted words are key words or phrases that markers are looking for.

Tutor's top tips

Part (a) deals with both the partnership profit sharing rules together with straightforward opening year rules. Opening year rules can be tricky, but are commonly tested so you should make sure that you are prepared for a question on this topic.

(a)   **Ae, Bee & Cae**

Tax year	Basis of assessment	Ae	Bee	Cae
		£	£	£
2014/15	Actual basis 1 July 2014 to 5 April 2015 £54,000 × 9/12 × 1/2	20,250	20,250	
		————	————	
2015/16	CYB (y/e 30 June 2015) £54,000 × 1/2	27,000	27,000	
		————	————	
2016/17	CYB (y/e 30 June 2016) £66,000 × 1/2	33,000	33,000	
		————	————	
	Actual basis 1 July 2016 to 5 April 2017 £87,000 × 9/12 × 1/3			21,750
				————

Tutorial note

The commencement rules apply for Ae & Bee in the tax year 2014/15 and for Cae in the tax year 2016/17, as this is the tax year in which each partner started to trade.

In the case of Cae, the fact that the partnership had been trading in the years before is not relevant.

(b)   (1)   **Dee – Relief for losses**

Key answer tips

Part (b) has been rewritten due to syllabus changes since the question was originally set. It now tests the new cap on loss reliefs against total income and loss reliefs in a partnership.

Dee can claim relief against her total income in the tax year 2016/17 (the year of the loss), and/or the tax year 2015/16 (the previous tax year). As she has no trading profits in either year, any loss relief will be claimed against other income and the cap on income tax reliefs will apply. The maximum claim is therefore £50,000 in each year as this is greater than 25% of Dee's adjusted total income of £85,000 (i.e. 25% × £85,000 = £21,250). The remaining loss must then be carried forward for relief against her share of any future trading profit from the partnership.

It is likely that she will obtain relief for some of the carried forward loss in the tax year 2018/19 when she anticipates that the business will become profitable again. The fact that the business will then be a partnership does not prevent the future loss relief.

Loss memorandum

	£
Loss in 2016/17	165,000
Less: Relief against total income	
2016/17 (maximum)	(50,000)
2015/16 (maximum)	(50,000)
	———
Carried forward against future trading profits	65,000
	———

Tutorial note

It is assumed that the £5,000 loss for the tax year 2015/16 has been carried back to the tax year 2014/15 and set off against the savings income in that year.

Tutor's top tips

Since the question asked you to 'explain' the loss reliefs available, it is important to write narrative describing the loss reliefs as well as calculating the amount of loss relief that will be claimed.

(2) **Eae – relief for losses**

Eae will be entitled to claim relief for her share of the partnership's trading loss in the year ended 5 April 2018 as follows.

- The loss could be claimed against total income for 2017/18 (the tax year of the loss) and/or 2016/17 (the previous tax year).

- Since Eae has just joined the partnership, the loss is incurred within the first four tax years of trading from her perspective; therefore a claim for special opening year loss relief could be made against total income for the three tax years 2014/15 to 2016/17, starting with the earliest first.

Tutorial note

Since the question refers to a 'small' loss, it can be assumed that the cap on income tax reliefs is not relevant in this part.

Examiner's report

This question was extremely well answered by the majority of candidates, many of whom scored maximum marks.

One of the main problems in the answers of poorer candidates was not showing the appropriate tax years, thus losing a lot of marks throughout.

Note: *The final part of the examiner's report referred to the original part (b) which is no longer examinable following syllabus changes.*

					Marks
		ACCA marking scheme			
(a)	Ae, Bee & Cae – 2014/15				1.5
	– 2015/16				1.0
	– 2016/17 Ae & Bee				1.0
	– 2016/17 Cae				1.5
					5.0
(b)	(i)	Dee	– 2016/17 claim		1.0
			– 2015/16 claim		1.0
			– loss carried forward		1.0
	(ii)	Eae	– total income claim		1.0
			– opening years relief		1.0
					5.0
Total					**10.0**

---

110 AUY MAN AND BIM MEN (ADAPTED) *Walk in the footsteps of a top tutor*

Key answer tips

This question was unusual in that the scenario was a partnership. However, this should not have caused concern as there were many easy marks to be gained.

Part (a) may have caused some problems if the definition of residence status had not been learnt, however it was only worth 2 marks. The rules regarding the definition of residence have been amended since this question was set and are now more complicated.

Parts (b) and (c) involved preparing familiar adjustment of profits and capital allowances computations, followed by a straightforward allocation of profits between the partners and class 4 NIC calculations.

The highlighted words are key words or phrases that markers are looking for.

Tutor's top tips

Remember to read the requirement carefully.

This question has clear mark allocations, which should be used to allocate the time spent on each section. Don't overrun on parts which carry only a few marks.

The first part required the application of the residence status rules. Note that just stating the rules would not have gained full marks. You must apply the knowledge to the facts of the specific individuals.

(a)   **Residence status**

*   Auy will be treated as resident in the United Kingdom (UK) for the tax year 2016/17 as she was present in the UK for 190 days and therefore she meets the first automatic UK residency test (i.e. in the UK for at least 183 days in the tax year).

*   Bim will be treated as resident in the UK for the tax year 2016/17 as she was previously resident In the UK, was present here for between 91 and 120 days and she meets two of the sufficient ties tests.

     She has a home in the UK which she makes use of for 100 days during the tax year (the 'accommodation' test) and she has spent 90 days or more in the UK during both of the previous tax years (the 'days in UK' test).

Tutorial note

When considering residence it is important to approach a question systematically.

*You should firstly consider whether the individual meets one of the automatic non-residence tests. However, it is clear that these are not relevant here as the examining team has told you in the question that both individuals **are** resident in the UK.*

Secondly, you should consider whether the individual meets one of the automatic residence tests. This is the case for Auy in this question.

Finally, if neither of the automatic tests are applicable, you should consider how many days the individual has spent in the UK, whether they were resident in the UK within the previous three tax years, and how many of the sufficient ties tests are met. The table showing the number of ties which must be met is provided in the examination.

These rules are now more complex than they were when this question was originally set.

(b)   **Tax adjusted trading profit – year ended 5 April 2017**

Tutor's top tips

Part (b) gives you clear guidance on the approach that is needed for an adjustment of profits, and you should follow this – starting with the net profit and then making the necessary adjustments.

Work through the notes and the plant and machinery information in order. Ensure you have dealt with every single item, and shown, as stated in the requirement, nil in the profits adjustment where an adjustment is not necessary, as marks are given for this.

If you are not sure of how to deal with an item, make a sensible assumption and move on, but do not ignore it, or waste unnecessary time.

Note that as the question has asked you to 'calculate' the adjusted profits you do not need to explain each adjustment that you make, but you should show any workings.

	£	£
Net profit	87,780	
Depreciation	3,400	
Entertaining employees (Note 1)	0	
Appropriation of profit (Note 2)	4,000	
Capital allowances (W)		12,938
	―――――	―――――
	95,180	12,938
	(12,938)	―――――
	―――――	
Tax adjusted trading profit	82,242	
	―――――	

Tutorial note

1   *The only exception to the non-deductibility of entertainment expenditure is when it is in respect of employees.*

2   *Salaries paid to a partner are not allowable. They merely represent an agreed form of allocation of the partnership profits in the partnership agreement. Appropriations of profit (i.e. drawings such as partner's salaries) need to be added back to profit.*

Allocation of profits – year ended 5 April 2017

Tutor's top tips

Once the net profit of the partnership has been calculated, it must be allocated between the partners in accordance with the partnership agreement in force in the accounting period.

Note that full marks can be obtained for this part in showing clearly how you have allocated the amounts; even if your tax adjusted trading profit figure is incorrect.

	Total	Auy Man	Bim Men
	£	£	£
Salary	4,000		4,000
Interest (£56,000/£34,000 at 5%)	4,500	2,800	1,700
Balance (80%/20%)	73,742	58,994	14,748
	82,242	61,794	20,448

Trading income assessments – 2016/17

	£
Auy Man	61,794
Bim Man	20,448

Tutorial note

The profit share for each partner must now be assessed in the correct tax year. The basis of assessment rules need to be applied to determine in which tax year the profits are assessed.

However, in this question the partnership has a 5 April year end and therefore the rule is simple: the actual profits for the year ended 5 April 2017 will be assessed in the tax year 2016/17.

Working – Capital allowances

Tutor's top tips

A standard capital allowances computation is required; however it is slightly unusual in that the only transactions in the year involve cars. There are no other additions and therefore there is no AIA.

The rules for cars need to be known in detail and applied carefully here. Each of the cars has a different CO_2 emissions rate so these need to be considered carefully to determine the correct available capital allowances. Also watch out for 'private use' adjustments.

		Main pool	Motor car (1)	Special rate pool	Allowances
	£	£	£	£	£
TWDV b/f		3,100	18,000		
Additions (no AIA)					
Motor car (3)		14,200			
Motor car (4)				8,700	
		———	———	———	
		17,300	18,000	8,700	
WDA (18%)		(3,114)			3,114
WDA (8%)			(1,440) × 70%		1,008
WDA (8%)				(696)	696
Addition (with FYA)					
Motor car (2)	11,600				
FYA (100%)	(11,600) × 70%				8,120
	———	0			
		———	———	———	
TWDV c/f		14,186	16,560	8,004	
		———	———	———	———
Total allowances					12,938
					———

Tutorial note

1   *Capital allowances on car purchases are calculated based on the CO_2 emissions of the car as follows:*

  −   *New car with CO_2 emissions of ≤ 75 g/km:*
      eligible for a FYA of 100% (i.e. Motor Car (2))

  −   *CO_2 emissions of between 76 − 130 g/km:*
      put in main pool and eligible for a WDA at 18% (i.e. Motor Car (3))

  −   *CO_2 emissions of > 130 g/km:*
      put in special rate pool and eligible for a WDA at 8% (i.e. Motor Car (4))

  However, cars with an element of private use by a partner (i.e. owner of the business) are given a separate column and only the business use percentage of the allowances can be claimed.

  Note that motor car (2) is a de-pooled asset and in practice should be given a separate column and carried forward at a tax written down value of £0. When it is sold it will result in a balancing charge, but only the business proportion will be taxed.

2   *Motor car (1), which was owned at the beginning of the year, has CO_2 emissions of > 130 g/km and is therefore eligible for a WDA at 8%. This must then be adjusted for private use.*

(c)   **Class 4 national insurance contributions – 2016/17**

Tutor's top tips

Straightforward computations are required for this part.

Remember that full marks can be obtained for this part, even if your allocation of profit to the partners is incorrect, provided that you use the partners' profit allocations which you have calculated in part (b) as the basis of your national insurance calculations. Just make sure that you clearly show the method of calculation.

Auy Man

	£
(£43,000 – £8,060) × 9%	3,145
(£61,794 – £43,000) × 2%	376
	3,521

Bim Men

(£20,448 – £8,060) × 9%	1,115

ACCA marking scheme		
		Marks
(a)	Auy Man	1.0
	Bim Men	1.0
		2.0
(b)	**Trading profit**	
	Depreciation	0.5
	Entertaining employees	0.5
	Appropriation of profit	0.5
	Deduction of capital allowances	0.5
	Capital allowances – Main pool	1.0
	– Motor car (1)	1.5
	– Special rate pool	1.5
	– FYA	1.5
	Trading income assessments	
	Salary	0.5
	Interest on capital	1.0
	Balance of profits	1.0
		10.0
(c)	Auy Man	2.0
	Bim Men	1.0
		3.0
Total		**15.0**

111 DANIEL, FRANCINE AND GREGOR *Walk in the footsteps of a top tutor*

Key answer tips

This question comprises three separate parts, each related to a different area of income tax.

Part (a) tests the popular examination topic of basis periods.

Part (b) tests the calculation of a beneficial loan benefit. Employment benefits are a good opportunity for some easy marks, but care must be taken here as the loan is made part way through a tax year and the loan is not interest free.

Part (c) tests trading losses and you should think carefully before beginning to answer. The requirement asks you to calculate the remaining loss to carry forward and not net income after loss relief, as you may have been expecting.

Tutor's top tips

This question is made up of three separate scenarios which could be attempted in any order.

One strategy is to attempt the parts that you are most confident with first, ensuring you stick to the appropriate time allocation. Then use the remaining time for the question to attempt any parts that you are less confident about.

(a) **Daniel – Trading income assessment 2016/17**

	£
1 May 2016 to 31 October 2016	
(£96,000 × 1/4 × 6/12)	12,000
1 November 2016 to 5 April 2017	
(£180,000 × 1/4 × 5/12)	18,750
	———
	30,750
	———

Tutorial note

Daniel joined as a partner on 1 May 2016, so the commencement rules apply to him for the tax year 2016/17. The basis period is the 11 month period from 1 May 2016 to 5 April 2017 (using the actual basis).

(b) **Francine – Beneficial loan**

	£	£
Average method		
Loan on 1 August 2016		96,000
Loan at end of 2016/17 tax year		110,000
		———
		206,000
		———
Average loan (£206,000 ÷ 2)		103,000
		———
Taxable benefit (£103,000 × 3% × 8/12)		2,060
Less: Interest paid (£96,000 × 1.5% × 2/12)	240	
(£110,000 × 1.5% × 6/12)	825	
		(1,065)
		———
Taxable benefit		995
		———

Tutor's top tips

It is specifically stated in the question that the beneficial loan benefit should be calculated using the average method. It is important to follow this instruction as calculating an alternative benefit using the precise method will not score marks and will waste time that you could use elsewhere.

(c) **Gregor – Loss memorandum**

	£
Loss – 2016/17	68,800
Loss: Set off against total income 2015/16 (W1)	(20,600)
Loss: Set off against total income 2016/17 (W1)	(900)
Loss: Extended to chargeable gains 2016/17 (W2)	(14,500)
	———
Loss carried forward	32,800
	———

Workings

(W1) Income tax computations

	2015/16	2016/17
	£	£
Trading income	14,700	0
Property income	4,600	0
Interest income	1,300	900
Total income	20,600	900
Less: Loss relief – current year		(900)
– prior year	(20,600)	
Net income	0	0

Tutorial note

The property loss of £2,300 in the tax year 2016/17 is carried forward against future property income. It cannot be offset against 2016/17 total income nor carried back against any income from the tax year 2015/16.

(W2) Claim against chargeable gain

	2015/16	2016/17
	£	£
Current year chargeable gains	0	17,400
Less: Trading loss relief (W3)		(14,500)
		2,900
Less: B/f capital loss		(0)
Chargeable gain	0	2,900

Tutorial note

Gregor wishes to relieve his trading loss of £68,800 as early as possible so after a claim against total income is made in 2016/17, a claim against capital gains is made. The loss relief claim against the chargeable gain is restricted by the capital loss brought forward from 2015/16.

(W3) Trading loss relief against chargeable gains

The trading loss relief claim against the chargeable gain = Lower of:

- Chargeable gain less capital loss brought forward

  = (£17,400 – £2,900) = £14,500, and

- Trading loss remaining = (£68,800 – £20,600 – £900) = £47,300

Therefore the maximum loss that can be offset against chargeable gains is £14,500.

ACCA marking scheme		
		Marks
(a)	**Daniel – Trading income assessment 2016/17**	
	1 May 2016 to 31 October 2016	1.5
	1 November 2016 to 5 April 2017	1.5
		———
		3.0
		———
(b)	**Francine – Beneficial loan 2016/17**	
	Interest at official rate (average method)	1.5
	Interest actually paid	1.5
		———
		3.0
		———
(c)	**Gregor – Trading loss carried forward**	
	2015/16 – claim against total income	1.0
	2016/17 – claim against total income	1.0
	2016/17 – claim against chargeable gains	1.5
	Loss carried forward	0.5
		———
		4.0
		———
Total		**10.0**
		———

PENSIONS AND NIC

112 JOHN BEACH (ADAPTED) *Walk in the footsteps of a top tutor*

Key answer tips

Part (a) required the computation of the income tax liability of an employed individual with several employment benefits and both an occupational and personal pension scheme.

Straightforward marks were available for calculating the employment benefits. The pension scheme contributions were a little trickier and required knowledge of how tax relief is obtained for both types of contribution and the operation of the annual allowance, including tapering of the allowance for high earners.

The NIC computations in part (b) were relatively straightforward provided the key facts about national insurance contributions had been learnt.

Tutor's top tips

For part (a) a systematic approach is needed, taking one note at a time, and therefore breaking up the information given into smaller, manageable chunks.

Make the marker your friend, if you keep your calculations clear and easy to read you will score much higher marks. Always ensure your workings are clearly labelled.

(a)   **Income tax computation – 2016/17**

	£
Director's remuneration	141,000
Mileage allowance (W1)	1,425
	142,425
Occupational pension contributions (Note 1)	(28,000)
	114,425
Beneficial loan (W2)	890
Long service award (gold watch) – exempt	0
Total income = Net income)	115,315
Less: PA (W4)	(4,764)
Taxable income	110,551

Income tax	£
£	
34,843 × 20% (W5)	6,969
75,708 × 40%	30,283
110,551	
Income tax liability	37,252

Tutorial notes

1   Tax relief for contributions to occupational pension schemes is given by deduction from employment income. Contributions made by an employer are an exempt employment benefit.

2   Long service awards are exempt where there has been at least 20 years of service by the employee and where the cost is £50 or less for each year of service.

3   The personal allowance is not fully available as John's ANI exceeds the limit of £100,000 (see W4).

Workings

(W1) Mileage allowance

	£
Amount received by John (5,960 miles × 60p)	3,576
Less: Approved mileage allowance	
(4,270 + 510) = 4,780 miles × 45p	(2,151)
Taxable benefit	1,425

Tutorial note

Travel between home and office is ordinary commuting which does not qualify for tax relief.

(W2) Beneficial loan

Tutor's top tips

The question states that the average method is used to calculate the taxable benefit, so do not waste time also preparing calculations using the precise (or accurate) method which will score no marks.

John repaid £24,000 (£12,000 + £12,000) of the loan during the tax year 2016/17, so the outstanding balance at 5 April 2017 is £60,000 (£84,000 – £24,000).

The benefit calculated using the average method is:

	£
((£84,000 + £60,000) ÷ 2) × 3%	2,160
Less: Interest paid	(1,270)
Taxable benefit	890

(W3) Personal pension contributions

Tutor's top tips

You must calculate the amount of personal pension contributions paid by John in the tax year 2016/17 by reference to the available annual allowance. Read the question carefully as this provides some hints on how to approach the calculation.

Remember that ALL contributions count towards the available annual allowance. Once you have calculated the available annual allowance for the tax year 2016/17, you will need to consider the unused allowances from the three prior tax years. Although John's contributions will be the same in these prior years, you need to factor in that the annual allowance was £50,000 per annum prior to the 2014/15 tax year.

The annual allowance for the tax year 2016/17 is subject to tapering as John's adjusted income (i.e. net income plus employee's occupational pension contributions and employer's contributions) of £115,315 + £28,000 + £11,000 = £154,315 is above the income limit of £150,000.

	£	£
Annual allowance – 2016/17	40,000	
Less: 50% × (£154,315 – £150,000)	(2,157)	
		37,843
Unused allowances b/f from previous three tax years:		
2014/15 and 2015/16 ((£40,000 – £39,000) × 2)		2,000
2013/14 (£50,000 – £48,000)		2,000
Maximum annual allowance for 2016/17		41,843
Less: Employee occupational scheme contributions		(28,000)
Employer occupational scheme contributions		(11,000)
Remaining available annual allowance for 2016/17		2,843

John would therefore have made gross personal pension contributions (PPCs) of £2,843 in the tax year 2016/17.

Tutorial note

1 Both employee and employer pension contributions count towards the annual allowance.

2 Unused annual allowances can be carried forward for three years.

3 The annual allowance is the maximum gross amount that can be contributed into pension schemes in a tax year without incurring an annual allowance charge. The £2,843 is therefore the gross amount of contributions made by John into the personal pension scheme.

4 Higher and additional rate tax relief for personal pension scheme contributions is given by the extension of the basic and higher rate tax bands (W5).

5 Remember that the PPCs also affect John's adjusted net income (ANI) for the purposes of calculating the PA available.

(W4) Personal allowance

	£	£
Total income = net income	115,315	
Less: Gross PPCs (W3)	(2,843)	
ANI	112,472	
Personal allowance		11,000
Less: 50% × excess ANI (£112,472 − £100,000) × 50%		(6,236)
		4,764

(W5) Extension of basic and additional rate bands

	Basic rate	Additional rate
	£	£
Basic rate band threshold	32,000	150,000
Plus: Gross PPCs	2,843	2,843
Extended basic and additional rate bands	34,843	152,843

(b)   **National Insurance contributions – 2016/17**

Tutor's top tips

You are asked to calculate the class 1 national insurance contributions payable by both John Beach and Surf plc. Make sure you present your answer so that it is clear which contributions are paid by whom.

John Beach

- Class 1 employee's primary NICs payable:

    Cash earnings = (£141,000 salary + £1,425 mileage allowance) = £142,425

	£
(£43,000 – £8,060) × 12%	4,193
(£142,425 – £43,000) × 2%	1,988
	————
	6,181
	————

Tutorial note

Class 1 NICs are assessed on cash earnings without any allowable deductions. Accordingly pension contributions are ignored, and non-cash benefits are not subject to class 1 NICs.

Note that the taxable mileage allowance paid in respect of home to office travel is cash earnings and is subject to class 1 NIC.

Surf plc

- Class 1 employer's secondary NICs payable:

    Also payable on cash earnings of £142,425.

	£
(£142,425 – £8,112) × 13.8%	18,535
	————

Examiner's report

Part (a) was generally very well answered, and the only aspect that caused problems was the calculation of the personal pension contributions. A common mistake was to gross up the contributions.

Part (b) was well answered by the majority of candidates.

Note: *The examiner's report has been edited to remove comments on elements of the question that have been deleted due to changes to the exam format.*

ACCA marking scheme		
		Marks
(a)	Director's remuneration	0.5
	Mileage allowance received	0.5
	Authorised mileage allowance	1.0
	Taxable benefit on mileage	0.5
	Occupational pension contributions	1.0
	Outstanding balance on loan	1.0
	Loan interest at official rate	1.0
	Interest paid	0.5
	Long service award	0.5
	Personal allowance	1.0
	Income tax liability	1.0
	Unused annual allowance for 2016/17	1.5
	Total available annual allowance	1.0
	Extension of basic and higher rate bands	1.0
		12.0
(b)	Employee class 1 NIC	2.0
	Employer class 1 NIC	1.0
		3.0
Total		**15.0**

113 DUKE AND EARL UPPER-CRUST (ADAPTED)

Key answer tips

Part (a) involves a couple of income tax computations:

- one for a higher rate taxpayer with reduced personal allowances requiring the extension of the basic rate band for personal pension contributions

- the other is a basic rate taxpayer requiring no entries in the income tax computation in respect of pension contributions.

Parts (b) and (c) are wholly written, covering the rules on the pension contributions annual allowance.

The highlighted words are key words or phrases that markers are looking for.

(a)   **Duke Upper-Crust – Income tax computation – 2016/17**

	£
Employment income (£114,000 + £20,000)	134,000
Less: Adjusted PA (W1)	(11,000)
Taxable income	123,000

£		£
67,000 × 20% (W2)		13,400
56,000 × 40%		22,400
123,000		
Income tax liability		35,800

Net amount paid to pension company

All of Duke's pension contribution of £35,000 qualifies for tax relief as it is less than 100% of his earnings (£134,000).

He will therefore have paid £28,000 (£35,000 less 20%) to his personal pension company.

Workings

(W1) Adjusted personal allowance

	£	£
Personal allowance		11,000
Employment income = Total income		
= Net income	134,000	
Less: Gross PPC	(35,000)	
ANI	99,000	

The deduction of Duke's personal pension contribution brings his adjusted net income below £100,000 therefore the personal allowance is available in full.

(W2) Extension of basic rate band

	£
Basic rate band threshold	32,000
Plus: Gross PPC	35,000
Extended basic rate band	67,000

As taxable income of £123,000, is below the standard additional rate band of £150,000 it is not necessary to extend the higher rate band.

Earl Upper-Crust – Income tax computation – 2016/17

	£
Trading profit	34,000
Less: PA	(11,000)
	———
Taxable income	23,000
	———
Income tax liability (£23,000 × 20%)	4,600
	———

Tutorial note

As Earl is a basic rate taxpayer there is no need to extend his basic rate band for the pension contribution. Relief for allowable contributions is given at source.

Net amount paid to pension company

Only £34,000 (gross) of Earl's pension contribution of £40,000 qualifies for tax relief, since relief is only available up to 100% of his earnings.

The amount of tax relief is therefore £6,800 (£34,000 at 20%), which is given at source, and so Earl will have paid £33,200 (£40,000 – £6,800) to his personal pension company.

(b) **Effect of annual allowance**

- Although tax relief is available on pension contributions up to the amount of earnings for a particular tax year, there is no limit as to the amount of earnings that can qualify for tax relief. However, the annual allowance limit of £40,000 acts as an effective annual limit.

- Any tax relieved contributions paid in excess of the annual allowance are subjected to an additional tax charge for the tax year in which the contributions are paid. The tax charge is calculated at the taxpayer's marginal rate of tax.

- The annual allowance limit (£40,000 in the tax years 2014/15 to 2016/17) is increased by any unused annual allowance from the previous three tax years.

- For the tax year 2016/17 onwards the annual allowance limit of £40,000 is reduced by £1 for every £2 by which a taxpayer's adjusted income exceeds £150,000, down to a minimum of £10,000

- Prior to the tax year 2014/15, the annual allowance was £50,000, and therefore this is the amount that can be carried forward from the tax year 2013/14, subject to any reduction for contributions in these years.

(c)   **Maximum additional contributions**

- There is no restriction regarding the amounts that Duke and Earl could have contributed into a personal pension scheme for the tax year 2016/17.

- However, tax relief is available on the lower of:

  (i)   Gross contributions paid

  (ii)   Higher of:

  –   £3,600

  –   100% of relevant earnings

Duke

- Duke could therefore receive tax relief on additional contributions of up to £99,000 (£134,000 relevant earnings – £35,000 gross contributions paid).

- However, if his gross contributions in the tax year 2016/17 exceed £40,000 (annual allowance in 2016/17) plus unused annual allowances in the three previous tax years an annual allowance charge will arise.

- Duke's unused annual allowance in the tax year 2016/17 is £5,000 (£40,000 – £35,000). He has no unused annual allowance brought forward from the tax years 2015/16 and 2014/15 (£40,000 – £40,000). His unused annual allowance brought forward from the tax year 2013/14 is £10,000 (£50,000 – £40,000).

- The maximum additional amount that Duke could have contributed into a personal pension scheme in the tax year 2016/17 without incurring an annual allowance charge is £15,000 (£5,000 + £10,000).

Earl

- Earl has already made a pension contribution in excess of his earnings for the tax year 2016/17, and so any additional pension contribution would not have qualified for any tax relief.

Due date

- Pension contributions for the tax year 2016/17 would have had to have been paid between 6 April 2016 and 5 April 2017, as it is not possible to carry back contributions.

Tutor's top tips

Remember to state the due date of payment; an easy mark to gain, but easily lost if you are not efficient in making sure you address all parts of a question or run out of time.

This could have been answered early in the answer before getting involved with the computations, to make sure you gain the easy marks as quickly as possible.

---

114 VANESSA AND SERENE (ADAPTED) *Walk in the footsteps of a top tutor*

Key answer tips

This question is fairly straightforward, and asks for income tax and national insurance computations for a sole trader and an employee. It should be a good test of whether you have learnt the basics well.

The highlighted words are key words or phrases that markers are looking for.

Tutor's top tips

You should be able to score highly on part (a), although there were a few tricky points.

Where a sole trader has just purchased a single asset, there is no need to do a full capital allowances computation, as long as you show your workings. Remember that only the business proportion of the allowances can be claimed.

The car provided to Serene has CO_2 emissions between 51 g/km and 75 g/km and therefore a special rate applies. Note also that the question specifically says that the company did not provide Serene with any fuel for private journeys, so don't waste time calculating a fuel benefit! (See examiner's comments).

Watch out for the pension contributions:

*   *the contribution to the personal pension is paid net, and extra relief is given by extending the basic rate band by the gross amount*

*   *the occupational pension is paid gross, and is simply deducted from employment income.*

Try not to get these confused.

Remember that you will score full marks for the calculation of tax if you use the correct rates, even if your taxable income figure is wrong.

(a)　**Vanessa Serve**

Income tax computation – 2016/17

	Total	Non-savings income	Savings income
	£	£	£
Trading income	52,400		
Less: Capital allowances (W1)	(1,310)		
	51,090	51,090	
Interest received	1,100		1,100
Total income	52,190	51,090	1,100
Less: PA	(11,000)	(11,000)	
Taxable income	41,190	40,090	1,100
Income tax:			
On Non-savings income (W2)	38,400	× 20%	7,680
On Non-savings income	1,690	× 40%	676
	40,090		
On Savings income	500	× 0%	0
On Savings income	600	× 40%	240
	41,190		
Income tax liability and payable			8,596

Workings

(W1) Capital allowances

The car has CO_2 emissions of between 76 g/km and 130 g/km and is therefore eligible for a WDA at 18%.

Only the business proportion of the allowance can be claimed.

WDA = (£10,400 × 18%) × 14,000/20,000 = £1,310

(W2) Extension of basic rate band

	£
Basic rate band threshold	32,000
Plus: Personal pension contribution (gross)	6,400
Extended basic rate band	38,400

Serene Volley

Income tax computation – 2016/17

	£
Salary	26,400
Less: Pension contributions (£26,400 × 5%)	(1,320)
	25,080
Car benefit (W)	3,458
Employment income	28,538
Interest from NS&I Savings Certificate (exempt)	0
Total income	28,538
Less: Personal allowance	(11,000)
Taxable income	17,538
Income tax liability (£17,538 × 20%)	3,508
Less: PAYE	(3,016)
Income tax payable	492

Working: Car benefit

CO_2 emissions = 74 g/km, available all year

As the CO_2 emissions are between 51 – 75 g/km, the basic percentage of 11% is used.

However, as it is a diesel car, the appropriate percentage is 14%.

Car benefit (£24,700 × 14%) = £3,458

There is no fuel benefit as private diesel is not provided by the company.

(b)   **National Insurance**

Tutor's top tips

Remember that sole traders pay class 2 and 4 national insurance, whereas employees pay class 1 primary contributions.

As long as you calculate Vanessa's class 4 contributions correctly based on your adjusted trading income figure from part (a), you will be awarded full marks.

Vanessa Serve

	£
Class 2 NICs	
(£2.80 for 52 weeks)	146

Class 4 NICs

	£
(£43,000 − £8,060) × 9%	3,145
(£51,090 − £43,000) × 2%	162
	3,307

Serene Volley

Class 1 NICs

	£
(£26,400 − £8,060) × 12%	2,201

Tutorial note

Class 1 NICs are based on cash earnings, without any allowable deductions. Therefore, pension contributions are ignored, and benefits are not subject to employee class 1 NIC.

Benefits are assessed to class 1A NICs which are payable by the employer only, not the employee. However, the requirement is to calculate the NICs payable by the employee only, not the employer.

Examiner's comments

This question was generally very well answered.

In part (a) many candidates did not appreciate that interest from savings certificates is exempt from tax.

The contribution to the occupational pension scheme was often used to extend the basic rate tax band rather than being deducted in calculating employment income.

Many candidates wasted time in calculating a fuel benefit despite the question clearly stating that no fuel was provided for private journeys.

Note: *The examiner's report has been edited to remove comments on elements of the question that have been deleted due to changes to the examination format.*

ACCA marking scheme		
		Marks
(a)	**Vanessa Serve**	
	Trading profit	0.5
	Capital allowances	1.5
	Bank interest	0.5
	Personal allowance	0.5
	Extension of basic rate band	1.0
	Income tax	1.5
	Serene Volley	
	Salary	0.5
	Pension contributions	1.0
	Car benefit	1.5
	Interest from savings certificate	0.5
	Personal allowance	0.5
	Income tax	1.0
	PAYE	0.5
		–––––
		11.0
		–––––
(b)	**Vanessa Serve**	
	Class 2 NIC	1.0
	Class 4 NIC	1.5
	Serene Volley	
	Class 1 NIC	1.5
		–––––
		4.0
		–––––
Total		**15.0**
		–––––

115 ANN, BASIL AND CHLOE (ADAPTED)   *Walk in the footsteps of a top tutor*

Key answer tips

This question covers the pension relief available to three different individuals. This should be a straightforward question provided the rules had been learnt.

Relief for pension contributions is a key area of the syllabus that is tested regularly.

Note that this question has been adapted in light of the new syllabus and part (b) is a new addition to the question to test the annual allowance rules introduced in the pension legislation since the date of the sitting when this examination question was set.

The highlighted words are key words or phrases that markers are looking for.

Tutor's top tips

This question is classic in style with individuals in different situations contributing to a personal pension scheme.

The key is to:

- Remember the definition of 'relevant earnings'

- Compare the gross contributions paid with the 'relevant earnings' (or £3,600 if this is higher) to decide the maximum tax allowable amount

- Consider the annual allowance limit charge and tapering where necessary.

Note that the maximum contribution allowable for a person without any relevant earnings in the tax year (£3,600) and the annual allowance limit are given in the examination.

(a) (1) **Ann Peach**

Amount of pension contributions qualifying for relief

Ann can obtain relief for the lower of:

(1) Gross contributions of £42,000

(2) Higher of:

(i) £3,600

(ii) Relevant earnings of £38,000

Therefore, £38,000 will qualify for tax relief and her basic rate band is extended to £70,000 (W).

Her taxable income falls into the extended basic rate band and is therefore taxed at 20%.

Income tax liability

	£
Trading profit	38,000
Less: PA	(11,000)
Taxable income	27,000
Income tax liability (£27,000 × 20%) (W)	5,400

Working: Extension of basic rate band

	£
Basic rate band	32,000
Plus: Gross allowable pension contributions	38,000
Extended basic rate band	70,000

Tutorial note

The annual allowance charge is not applicable to Ann, as although she has made pension contributions in excess of £40,000, she has only received tax relief for contributions of £38,000. The annual allowance charge is intended to claw back tax relief for contributions in excess of the limit, which is not applicable here.

(2) **Basil Plum**

Amount of pension contributions qualifying for relief

Basil can obtain relief for the lower of:

(1) Gross contributions of £40,000

(2) Higher of:

    (i) £3,600

    (ii) Relevant earnings of £152,000

Therefore, £40,000 will qualify for tax relief and his basic rate band is extended to £72,000 (W2).

Tutorial note

Note that this scenario differs from the treatment for Ann (above) as Ann had contributed more than 100% of her relevant earnings into a scheme, whereas Basil has contributed less than 100% of his relevant earnings into the scheme.

Income tax liability

	£
Employment income	152,000
Less: PA (W1)	(5,000)
	————
Taxable income	147,000
	————

Income tax:	£
£	
72,000 × 20% (W2)	14,400
75,000 × 40%	30,000
————	
147,000	
————	
Income tax liability	44,400
	————

Workings

(W1) Personal allowance

Basil's adjusted net income is in excess of £100,000, therefore his personal allowance is restricted.

His ANI is calculated as follows:

	£
Employment income = Total income = Net income	152,000
Less: Gross PPC	(40,000)
ANI	112,000
Personal allowance	11,000
Less: 50% × excess ANI (112,000 – 100,000) × 50%	(6,000)
	5,000

(W2) Extension of basic rate band

	£
Basic rate band	32,000
Plus: Gross PPC	40,000
Extended basic rate band	72,000

(W3) Annual allowance

Basil's adjusted income for the purposes of tapering the annual allowance exceeds £150,000. His allowance is reduced by £1 for every £2 of adjusted income in excess of £150,000:

	£	£
Net income		152,000
Add: Employer's pension contributions		5,000
Adjusted income		157,000
Annual allowance – 2016/17	40,000	
Less: 50% × (£157,000 – £150,000)	(3,500)	
		36,500

Unused AA b/f from previous three tax years:

2014/15 and 2015/16	
((£40,000 – £40,000) × 2)	0
2013/14 (£50,000 – £40,000)	10,000
	———
Maximum annual allowance for 2016/17	46,500
Less: Employee pension scheme contributions	(40,000)
Employer pension scheme contributions	(5,000)
	———
Remaining annual allowance	1,500
	———

Basil's gross contributions combined with his employer's contributions are within the available annual allowance. Basil will not be subject to an annual allowance charge in the tax year 2016/17.

(3)   **Chloe Pear**

Amount of pension contributions qualifying for relief

Property income does not qualify as relevant earnings (unless it relates to qualifying furnished holiday accommodation).

Therefore, as Chloe has no relevant earnings, she will only receive tax relief on £3,600 of her pension contributions.

Her taxable income falls below the basic rate band even before extension due to pension contributions; therefore her income is taxed at 20%.

Income tax liability

	£
Property income	23,900
Less: PA	(11,000)
	———
Taxable income	12,900
	———
Income tax (£12,900 × 20%)	2,580
	———

(b)   **Consequences of Banana Bank plc contributing £100,000 into Basil's pension fund**

There is no limit on the amount that can be put into a personal pension fund by an individual and his employer.

However, there is a maximum amount of tax relief

• that the individual can obtain on their contributions into the scheme (i.e. the maximum contribution each year), and

• on the total contributions paid into a scheme by the individual and others on their behalf (i.e. the annual allowance).

If Basil's employer contributes into his personal pension scheme, the employer contributions are:

- a tax free benefit

- a tax allowable deduction in Banana Bank plc's corporation tax computation

- combined with Basil's contributions and compared to the annual allowance of £40,000 in the tax years 2014/15 to 2016/17 (£50,000 in the tax year 2013/14).

The annual allowance of £40,000 for the tax year 2016/17 is tapered where the individual's adjusted income is greater than £150,000, subject to a minimum of £10,000 where adjusted income is £210,000 or more.

Where the annual allowance is exceeded a tax charge is levied on the individual.

Basil has an annual allowance of £10,000 (the minimum allowance) for the tax year 2016/17 as his adjusted income is greater than £210,000. His adjusted income for the purposes of the annual allowance is as follows:

	£	£
Net income		152,000
Add: Employer's pension contributions		100,000
		———
Adjusted income		252,000
		———

Unused allowances from the previous three tax years can be carried forward.

In Basil's case the maximum contributions that can be made in the tax year 2016/17 without incurring the annual allowance charge is £20,000 (£10,000 + (£50,000 − £40,000) brought forward from the tax year 2013/14. Note that there is no unused allowance from the tax years 2014/15 and 2015/16 as actual contributions were the same as the annual allowance of £40,000 in that tax year.

Basil will therefore pay the annual allowance charge in the tax year 2016/17 on contributions of £120,000 (£40,000 + £100,000 − £20,000).

The tax charge is calculated at the taxpayer's marginal rate of tax. In Basil's case this is 40%, as the higher rate band is extended by his gross contribution in the tax year 2016/17 to £190,000 (£150,000 + £40,000).

Examiner's report

This question was reasonably well answered, although there were few first-rate answers.

For the first taxpayer the most common mistake was to extend the basic rate tax band by the amount of contributions rather than earnings.

For the second taxpayer the basic rate band was often extended by the amount of annual allowance rather than the contributions.

Very few candidates stated that the third taxpayer would have received tax relief up to £3,600 of her contributions.

Note: *This question has been adapted in light of the new syllabus and part (b) is a new addition to the question.*

ACCA marking scheme		
		Marks
(a)	**Ann Peach**	
	Taxable income	0.5
	Extension of basic rate band	1.0
	Income tax	0.5
	Amount qualifying for tax relief	1.0
		———
		3.0
		———
	Basil Plum	
	Taxable income	0.5
	Personal allowance	1.0
	Extension of basic rate band	1.5
	Income tax	1.0
	Amount qualifying for tax relief	1.0
		———
		5.0
		———
	Chloe Pear	
	Taxable income	0.5
	Income tax	0.5
	Amount qualifying for tax relief	1.0
		———
		2.0
		———
(b)	Employer contributions	
	No limit to contributions	0.5
	Limit to relief for individual	0.5
	Tax free benefit	0.5
	Tax allowable deduction for corporation tax	0.5
	Exceeding annual allowance	0.5
	Unused annual allowance for previous 3 years brought forward	0.5
	Basil's maximum contributions	1.0
	Charged at marginal rate	0.5
	Charged at 40% for Basil	0.5
		———
		5.0
		———
Total		**15.0**
		———

SELF-ASSESSMENT

116   PI CASSO (ADAPTED)

Key answer tips

The first part of this question involves detailed calculations to work out the income tax, class 4 NICs and CGT payable under self-assessment and when the payments are due.

The remaining two parts require wholly written answers on two common self-assessment topics.

These are marks which are easy to gain if you have done your work, but easy to lose if you do not invest the time in learning the self-assessment rules.

Part (a)(3) of the original question has been changed and part (4) has been deleted to reflect changes to the structure of the examination.

Part (b) i.e a new part that has been added to the original question to test the implications for tax planning for married couples of the new savings and dividend income nil rate bands.

The highlighted words are key words or phrases that markers are looking for.

(a)   (1)   **Due dates of payment of tax under self-assessment**

Due date	Tax year	Payment	£
31 July 2016	2015/16	Second payment on account (W1)	2,240
31 January 2017	2015/16	Balancing payment (W2)	6,126
31 January 2017	2016/17	First payment on account (W3)	1,860
31 July 2017	2016/17	Second payment on account (W3)	1,860
31 January 2018	2016/17	Balancing payment (W4)	146
31 January 2018	2017/18	First payment on account (W5)	1,860

Workings

(W1) Second payment on account – 2015/16

The second payment on account for the tax year 2015/16 is based on Pi's income tax and class 4 NIC liability for the tax year 2014/15 as follows:

	£
Income tax	3,240
Class 4 NICs	1,240
	———
	4,480
	———
Payments on account (50%)	2,240
	———

(W2) Balancing payment – 2015/16

	£
Income tax	4,100
Class 4 NICs	1,480
Class 2 NICs	146
Capital gains tax (see Tutorial Note)	4,880
	10,606
Less: POAs (£2,240 × 2)	(4,480)
Balancing payment	6,126

(W3) Payments on account – 2016/17

Pi will make a claim to reduce her total payments on account for the tax year 2016/17 as follows:

	£
Income tax	2,730
Class 4 NICs	990
	3,720
Payments on account (50%)	1,860

(W4) Balancing payment – 2016/17

	£
Income tax and class 4 NICs	3,720
Class 2 NICs	146
Capital gains tax	0
	3,866
Less: POAs (£1,860 × 2)	(3,720)
Balancing payment	146

(W5) First payments on account – 2017/18

The first payment on account for the tax year 2017/18 is based on Pi's income tax and class 4 NIC liability for the tax year 2016/17.

	£
Income tax	2,730
Class 4 NICs	990
	────
	3,720
	────
Payments on account (50%)	1,860
	────

Tutorial note

Class 2 NICs and capital gains tax are collected via self-assessment and are payable all in one payment on 31 January following the end of the tax year along with the balancing payment for income tax and class 4 NICs.

Payments on account are not required for class 2 NICs and CGT.

(2) **Reduction of payments on account to £0**

- If Pi's payments on account for the tax year 2016/17 were reduced to £0, then she would be charged late payment interest on the payments due of £1,860 from the relevant due date to the date of payment.

- A penalty will be charged if the claim to reduce the payments on account to £0 was made fraudulently or negligently.

(3) **Claim to reduce payment on accounts**

- Pi must submit a claim to reduce her payments on account for the tax year 2016/17 by 31 January 2018 (i.e. by 31 January following the tax year).

(b) **Turner and Andrea tax savings**

- Turner is an additional rate taxpayer in 2016/17. Therefore he does not have any savings nil rate band and has paid tax on his interest income at 45%.

- Andrea is a basic rate taxpayer in 2016/17. She did not use her savings nil rate band of £1,000 but had dividend income in excess of her £5,000 dividend nil rate band. She paid tax at 7.5% on the dividend income above £5,000.

- Their total tax liability for 2016/17 would have been reduced if:

  - Turner had transferred all of his interest income to Andrea. This would have utilised her savings nil rate band and the balance of the interest would have been taxed at 20% instead of 45%

  - Andrea had transferred £5,000 of dividend income to Turner to utilise his dividend nil rate band

- The total tax saving would have been:

	£
Interest income £1,000 × 45%	450
Interest income £4,000 × 25% (45% - 20%)	1,000
Dividend income £5,000 × 7.5%	375
	————
	1,825
	————

Examiner's report

This question was generally not well answered, and the impression given was that candidates had struggled with time management and had a lack of time remaining for this question.

Part (a)(1) caused the most problems, with the vast majority of candidates not being able to demonstrate how payments are calculated and paid under the self-assessment system.

In part (a)(2) most candidates appreciated that interest would be due, but very few mentioned the potential penalty that could be charged.

Note: *The examiner's report has been edited to remove comments on elements of the question that have been deleted due to changes to the examination format. Note that part (b) was not in the original question.*

ACCA marking scheme			
			Marks
(a)	(1)	Second payment on account for 2015/16	1.5
		Balancing payment for 2015/16	2.0
		Claim to reduce payments on account	1.0
		Payments on account for 2016/17	1.0
		Balancing payment for 2016/17	0.5
		First payment on account for 2017/18	1.0
			———
			7.0
			———
	(2)	Interest	1.0
		Penalty	1.0
			———
			2.0
			———
	(3)	Claim date	1.0
			———
(b)		Turner additional rate taxpayer	0.5
		No savings nil rate band	0.5
		Andrea basic rate taxpayer	0.5
		Unused savings nil rate band £1,000	0.5
		Dividends exceed £5,000 nil rate band	0.5
		Transfer all interest income to Andrea	0.5
		Transfer £5,000 dividends to Turner	0.5
		Calculation of tax saving	1.5
			———
			5.0
			———
Total			**15.0**
			———

117 ERNEST VADER (ADAPTED) *Walk in the footsteps of a top tutor*

Key answer tips

This is an unusual and tricky question requiring substantial written explanations and statements about ethical issues and self-assessment.

Detailed knowledge is required to score highly on this question; however the application of some basic common sense would also gain quite a few marks.

The highlighted words are key words or phrases that markers are looking for.

The legislation regarding the general anti-abuse rule and dishonest conduct by tax agents did not exist when this question was first written, and have been added since to test these areas. The original part (c) tested HMRC's information powers, which are no longer in the syllabus and this part has therefore been removed.

Part (d) has been amended to reflect changes to the examination structure.

Tutor's top tips

Remember to read the requirement carefully and allocate the time spent on each section.

Part (a) covers the classic topic of tax evasion and tax avoidance, but care must be taken to apply your knowledge to Ernest's particular problem. This part also tests awareness of the general anti-abuse rule.

Part (b) requires the application of common sense if the specific guidelines have not been learnt.

Parts (c) and (d) are straightforward if the self-assessment rules have been learnt, difficult if not learnt.

(a)   **Tax evasion and tax avoidance**

- Tax evasion is illegal and involves the reduction of tax liabilities by not providing information to which HMRC is entitled, or providing HMRC with deliberately false information.

- In contrast, tax avoidance involves the minimisation of tax liabilities by the use of any lawful means. However, certain tax avoidance schemes must be disclosed to HMRC.

- The general anti-abuse rule is a rule to counter artificial and abusive schemes where arrangements (which cannot be regarded as a reasonable course of action) are put in place deliberately to avoid tax.

- If Ernest makes no disclosure of the capital gain then this will be viewed as tax evasion as his tax liability for the tax year 2016/17 will be understated by £18,000.

(b) **Failure to disclose information to HMRC**

- How to deal with the failure to disclose is a matter of professional judgement, and a trainee Chartered Certified Accountant would be expected to act honestly and with integrity.

- Ernest should therefore be advised to disclose details of the capital gain to HMRC.

- If such disclosure is not made by Ernest, you would be obliged to report under the money laundering regulations, and you should also consider ceasing to act for Ernest.

- In these circumstances you would be advised to notify HMRC that you no longer act for him although you should not provide any reason for this.

(c) **Penalties for tax agent**

- A civil penalty may be payable by the firm if they have engaged in dishonest conduct, which may be the case if they have failed to supply the information HMRC have requested.

- The potential penalty is up to £50,000.

(d) **Interest payable**

- Late payment interest will run from the due date of 31 January 2018 to the payment date of 31 July 2018.

Examiner's report

This question was not well answered, with many candidates attempting it as their final question or omitting it altogether. This was disappointing given that several sections covered recent tax management changes which have been covered in my Finance Act articles.

In part (a) most candidates knew the difference between tax evasion and tax avoidance, but many failed to score an easy mark by not stating that the taxpayer's actions would be viewed as tax evasion.

Part (b) caused problems for most candidates but a common sense approach would have gained most of the available marks. Unfortunately, far too many candidates instead just incorrectly explained that it would be necessary to inform HMRC themselves.

The examiner's comments on the original parts (c) and (d) have been deleted as they are no longer relevant to the amended question.

ACCA marking scheme			
			Marks
(a)		Tax evasion	1.0
		Tax avoidance	1.0
		General anti-abuse rule	1.0
		Non-disclosure of disposal	1.0
			4.0
(b)		Professional judgement	1.0
		Advise disclosure	1.0
		Obligation to report	1.0
			3.0
(c)		Civil penalty for dishonest conduct	1.0
		£50,000 penalty	1.0
			2.0
(d)		Interest period	1.0
Total			**10.0**

118 SOPHIE SHAPE (ADAPTED)

Key answer tips

Occasionally the F6 examining team do include a section C question solely testing administration aspects of taxation such as this 10 mark personal tax question.

Parts (a) and (b) test the popular examination topic of payments on account. Part (c) tests tax return due dates for 1 mark. Part (d) tests compliance checks.

Provided you have revised the administration chapter, this question should be straightforward.

(a) **Schedule of tax payments**

Due date	Tax year	Payment	£
31 July 2017	2016/17	Second payment on account	
		£7,060 (£5,240 + £1,820) × 50%	3,530
31 January 2018	2016/17	Balancing payment	
		£13,436 (£6,100 + £1,910 + £146 + £5,280) − £7,060 (£3,530 × 2)	6,376
31 January 2018	2017/18	First payment on account	
		£8,010 (£6,100 + £1,910) × 50%	4,005

Tutorial note

1   The second payment on account for the tax year 2016/17 is based on Sophie's income tax and class 4 NIC liability for the tax year 2015/16.

2   The balancing payment for the tax year 2016/17 includes the class 2 NIC and capital gains tax liabilities for that year.

3   The first payment on account for the tax year 2017/18 is based on Sophie's income tax and class 4 NIC liabilities for the tax year 2016/17.

(b)   **Reduction of payments on account**

If Sophie's payments on account for the tax year 2016/17 were reduced to £0, then she would be charged interest on the payments due of £3,530 from the relevant due date to the date of payment.

A tax geared penalty will be charged as the claim to reduce the payments on account to £0 would appear to be made fraudulently or negligently.

(c)   **Filing a paper tax return**

Unless the return is issued late, the latest date when Sophie can file a paper self-assessment tax return for the tax year 2016/17 is 31 October 2017.

(d)   **Compliance check**

If HM Revenue and Customs (HMRC) intend to carry out a compliance check into Sophie's 2016/17 tax return they will have to notify her within 12 months of the date when they receive the return.

HMRC has the right to carry out a compliance check as regards the completeness and accuracy of any return, and such a check may be made on a completely random basis.

However, compliance checks are generally carried out because of a suspicion that income has been undeclared or because deductions have been incorrectly claimed. For example, where accounting ratios are out of line with industry norms.

Section 7

ANSWERS TO PRACTICE CHARGEABLE GAINS QUESTIONS

PRACTICE SECTION A OBJECTIVE TEST QUESTIONS

INDIVIDUALS – CAPITAL GAINS TAX

119   B and F

Qualifying corporate bonds, gilt-edged securities, a main residence (which has always been lived in by the owner) and all cars (regardless of any business use), are all exempt from CGT.

A painting is a non-wasting chattel. A non-wasting chattel is a chargeable asset unless it is bought and sold for less than £6,000 which is unlikely to be the case for a painting by a famous artist.

Assets used in the trade are still chargeable assets and will potentially realise a chargeable gain if they are sold at a profit. The wasting chattel rules do not apply to assets on which capital allowances have been claimed.

120   B

	£
Sale proceeds	340,000
Less: Selling costs	(2,500)
	———
Net proceeds	337,500
Less: Cost	(150,000)
	———
Chargeable gain	187,500
Less: AEA	(11,100)
	———
Taxable gains	176,400
	———
Capital gains tax liability (£176,400 × 28%)	49,392
	———

Tutorial note

Lexie has taxable income of £54,000 and is therefore a higher rate taxpayer. Her capital gains will therefore be subject to the higher tax rate for residential properties of 28%. Remember that higher rates of CGT apply when you are taxing a gain in relation to a residential property.

121 A

	£
Disposal proceeds	165,000
Less: Deemed acquisition cost	(115,000)
Chargeable gain	50,000
Less: Capital losses b/f	(5,000)
	45,000
Less: AEA	(11,100)
Taxable gains	33,900
Capital gains tax payable (£33,900 × 28%)	9,492

Tutorial note

A transfer between spouses is a no gain/no loss transfer. Sophia's deemed acquisition cost is equal to the deemed proceeds on the transfer from her husband. This is equal to his acquisition cost.

122 B

	£
Sale proceeds	425,000
Deemed cost of remainder (£300,000 – £112,500(W))	(187,500)
Chargeable gain	237,500
Less: AEA	(11,100)
Taxable gain	226,400

Working: Part disposal January 2012
Deemed cost of 10 acres disposed of:
£300,000 × £150,000/(£150,000 + £250,000)   £112,500

123 £2,000

	£
Painting 1	
Non-wasting chattel bought and sold for < £6,000	Exempt
Painting 2	
Sale proceeds	7,200
Less: Cost	(1,000)
	————
Chargeable gain	6,200
	————
Gain cannot exceed:	
5/3 × (£7,200 − £6,000)	2,000
	————
Total chargeable gain (£0 + £2,000)	2,000
	————

Tutorial note

The two paintings disposed of in this question are non-wasting chattels.

If non-wasting chattels are bought and sold for £6,000 or less they are exempt.

If bought for £6,000 or less but are sold for more than £6,000, the gain is restricted to:

5/3 × (gross proceeds − £6,000).

124 C

	£
Deemed sale proceeds	6,000
Less: Allowable selling costs (legal fees)	(300)
	————
Net sale proceeds	5,700
Less: Allowable expenditure	
Cost	(22,000)
Incidental costs of acquisition	(800)
	————
Allowable loss	(17,100)
	————

Tutorial note

The vase disposed of in this question is a non-wasting chattel.

If a non-wasting chattel cost more than £6,000 but is sold for £6,000 or less, the allowable loss is calculated using deemed gross sale proceeds of £6,000.

125 A

	£
Chargeable gain	23,700
Less: Current year capital losses	(10,400)
	————
	13,300
Less: Capital losses b/f (restricted)	(2,200)
	————
	11,100
Less: Annual exempt amount	(11,100)
	————
Taxable gains	0
	————

Capital loss c/f

	£
2015/16 Loss	6,000
Utilised – 2016/17	(2,200)
	————
Loss c/f	3,800
	————

Tutorial note

The offset of capital losses brought forward is restricted to preserve the annual exempt amount.

126 C

	£
Sale proceeds	28,800
Less: Allowable element of acquisition cost (W)	(12,600)
Chargeable gain	16,200

Working: Allowable element of acquisition cost

Remaining life at disposal = 9 years

Estimated useful life = 15 years

Allowable cost = £21,000 × 9/15 = £12,600

127 D

	£
Sale proceeds	44,000
Less: Allowable element of acquisition cost (W)	(14,000)
Chargeable gain	30,000

Working: Allowable element of acquisition cost

Remaining life at disposal = 8 years

Estimated useful life = 20 years

Allowable cost = £35,000 × 8/20 = £14,000

Tutorial note

A copyright is a wasting asset which is not a chattel as it is not tangible or movable.

The allowable expenditure on these assets is deemed to waste away over the life of the asset on a straight line basis.

Consequently, on a disposal the allowable cost is restricted to take account of the asset's natural fall in value.

128 D

	£
Sale proceeds	230,000
Less: Cost (W)	(152,000)
	————
Chargeable gain	78,000
	————
Working: Restored asset base cost	
Original cost	142,000
Plus: Restoration expenditure	70,000
Less: Insurance proceeds	(60,000)
	————
Revised base cost	152,000
	————

Tutorial note

Where insurance proceeds are received in respect of an asset that has been damaged there is a part disposal.

However, if all of the insurance proceeds are used in restoring the asset the taxpayer may claim to deduct the proceeds from the cost of the asset rather than be treated as having made a part disposal of the asset.

Remember to include the amount spent restoring the asset in the revised base cost.

129 B

	£
Original cost	73,000
Plus: Restoration expenditure	41,700
Less: Insurance proceeds	(37,200)
	————
Revised base cost	77,500
	————

130 £10,133

	£
Sales proceeds (W)	12,800
Cost (£4,000 × 10,000/15,000)	(2,667)
Chargeable gain	10,133

Working: Average of quoted prices

(120p + 136p) ÷ 2	128p

Sales proceeds = £12,800 (128p × 10,000)

Tutor's top tips

The share prices quoted in the question are given in pence, but you are required to provide your answer in pounds. Be careful when entering your answer that you have done this if the question requires you to!

131 B

	£
Gilts	Exempt
Martin plc shares:	
Proceeds – Market value	12,300
Less: Cost	(8,000)
Chargeable gain	4,300

Tutorial note

Where an asset is transferred to a connected party, market value is substituted for actual gross proceeds.

132

Share purchases

20,000 shares from the purchase on 1 June 2016

2,000 shares from the purchase on 1 October 2016

3,000 shares from the purchase on 23 October 2016

15,000 shares from the share pool as at 1 October 2016

17,000 shares from the share pool as at 1 October 2016

18,000 shares from the share pool as at 1 October 2016

20,000 shares from the share pool as at 1 October 2016

No further matches needed

No further matches needed

Matching order

Matched first	2,000 shares from the purchase on 1 October 2016
Matched second	3,000 shares from the purchase on 23 October 2016
Matched third	15,000 shares from the share pool as at 1 October 2016

Tutorial note

The matching rules require that shares disposed of by an individual are matched against shares acquired in the following order:

1   Shares purchased on the same day as the date of disposal; then

2   Shares purchased within the following 30 days; then

3   Shares in the share pool (made up of shares acquired before the date of disposal).

133   A

			£
Share pool (shares acquired pre 28 February 2017)			
Sale proceeds			42,500
Less: Cost (W)			(14,276)
Chargeable gain			28,224

Working: Share pool		**Number**	**Cost**
			£
April 1998	Purchase	9,000	27,050
April 2012	Purchase	2,600	9,750
		11,600	36,800
February 2017	Sale (4,500/11,600 × £36,800)	(4,500)	(14,276)
		7,100	22,524

134 C

The allowable cost of the shares disposed of in March 2017 is £50,000 (W)

Working: Share pool

		Number	Cost
			£
April 2005	Purchase	40,000	200,000
May 2008	Rights issue (1:4) @ £4 per share	10,000	40,000
		50,000	240,000
May 2012	Bonus issue (1:5)	10,000	0
		60,000	240,000
March 2017	Sale (12,500/60,000 × £240,000)	(12,500)	(50,000)
		47,500	190,000

135 C

The total consideration provided by Riley plc is:

	MV	Cost
	£	£
Cash (50,000 × £3)	150,000	50,000
Shares (50,000 × 2 × £1.20)	120,000	40,000
	270,000	90,000

Hunter has made a part disposal in relation to the cash consideration.

	£
Disposal proceeds (cash: 50,000 × £3)	150,000
Less: Original cost (£150,000/£270,000 × £90,000)	(50,000)
Chargeable gain	100,000

136 A

Zofia had periods of actual occupation before and after her absence so any period spent employed abroad would be classified as deemed occupation.

Therefore the entire eight year absence would qualify as deemed occupation.

Tutorial note

Only four years of the total eight year absence would qualify as deemed occupation if she was self-employed abroad or working elsewhere in the UK.

Only three years of the total eight year absence would qualify as deemed occupation if she was travelling, under the three years for any reason deemed occupation rule.

Occupation by a tenant is never deemed occupation by the homeowner.

137 B

	£
Chargeable gain before reliefs	120,000
Less: PPR relief (£120,000 × 6/10)	(72,000)
	48,000
Less: Letting relief (W)	(40,000)
Chargeable gain	8,000

Working: Letting relief

Lowest of:

1   Maximum = £40,000

2   PPR relief = £72,000

3   Gain on letting = £48,000

Tutorial note

PPR is available on 6/10 of the gain as Masuma has always occupied six out of the ten rooms in the house. Masuma cannot benefit from the rules of deemed occupation on the remaining four rooms as she has never used them as part of her main residence.

138 B

Ben will qualify for entrepreneurs' relief as he has worked for the company, and has owned at least 5% of the shares, for at least twelve months prior to the disposal.

139 B

	£
Qualifying for ER	
Gain on sale of business	13,250,000
Less: AEA	(11,100)
Taxable gain	13,238,900
Capital gains tax:	
£10,000,000 × 10%	1,000,000
£3,238,900 × 20%	647,780
	1,647,780

Tutorial note

Entrepreneurs' relief is available as Bhavin is disposing of his sole trade business that he has operated for at least 12 months prior to disposal.

Entrepreneurs' relief is subject to a lifetime limit of £10 million. Chargeable gains in excess of this are subject to capital gains tax at a rate of 20% as Bhavin is a higher rate taxpayer. Even if Bhavin had not utilised his basic rate band, the chargeable gains in excess of the £10 million lifetime limit would still all be taxed at 20% as the gains qualifying for entrepreneurs' relief are deemed to utilise any remaining basic rate band.

140 C and F

Only fixed (i.e. not movable) plant and machinery qualifies for rollover relief.

Shares are not qualifying assets.

Assets must be used for trading purposes to qualify for rollover relief.

Goodwill qualifies for rollover relief provided it is disposed of by a sole trader and not a company.

141 C

Disposal on 13 May 2016

Chargeable gain in 2016/17 = Lower of

(1) All of the chargeable gain = **£38,600**

(2) Sale proceeds not reinvested

(£184,000 – £143,000) = £41,000

As all of the gain is chargeable in the tax year 2016/17, no rollover relief claim is possible.

Accordingly, the base cost of the replacement asset is the actual cost of £143,000.

142 D

	£	£
Sale of warehouse		
Sale proceeds		270,213
Less: Cost	231,211	
Less: ROR on factory (Note)	(31,083)	
	————	(200,128)
		————
Chargeable gain		70,085
		————

Tutorial note

The proceeds from the sale of the factory were fully reinvested in the warehouse.

Therefore, the gain on the factory of £31,083 can be fully rolled over against the acquisition cost of the warehouse.

---

143 A and D

Unquoted shares in a trading company are qualifying assets for gift relief irrespective of the percentage shareholding.

Quoted shares are only qualifying assets if they are in the donor's personal trading company.

A company qualifies as a donor's personal trading company for the purposes of gift relief if at least 5% of the voting rights are held by the individual. However, unlike for entrepreneurs' relief, there is no minimum holding period and no requirement for the individual to work for the company.

Assets used by a donor's personal trading company are also qualifying assets for the purposes of gift relief but only if the company uses the asset in their trade.

COMPANIES – CHARGEABLE GAINS

144   A

	£
Sale of warehouse	
Sale proceeds	800,000
Less: Cost (£250,000 + £20,000)	(270,000)
	────────
Unindexed gain	530,000
Less: Indexation allowance (W)	
Cost (£270,000 × 0.242)	(65,340)
	────────
Chargeable gain	464,660
	────────

Working: Indexation factor

The indexation factor from December 2007 to May 2016 is:

(261.9 – 210.9)/210.9 = 0.242 (rounded to three decimal places)

145   C

	£
Land	
Sale proceeds	45,000
Less: Cost	(20,000)
	────────
Unindexed gain	25,000
Less: Indexation allowance (W)	
Cost (£20,000 × 1.590) – restricted (Note)	(25,000)
	────────
Chargeable gain	0
	────────
Warehouse	
Sale proceeds	75,000
Less: Cost	(80,000)
	────────
Unindexed loss	(5,000)
Less: Indexation allowance (Note)	0
	────────
Allowable loss	(5,000)
	────────

Working: Indexation factors

The indexation factor from May 1987 to October 2016 is:

(263.9 – 101.9)/101.9 = 1.590 (rounded to three decimal places)

Tutorial note

The indexation allowance cannot increase or create a loss.

146 £55,000

	£
Year ended 30 June 2016	
Capital loss	80,000
Offset against current year chargeable gain	(25,000)
	————
Loss carried forward	55,000
	————

Tutorial note

Capital losses can only be offset against chargeable gains arising in the same accounting period. Any remaining loss is then carried forward against future capital gains.

Capital losses cannot be offset against current year total profits nor carried back and offset against income or gains from previous accounting periods.

147 A

The indexed cost on the disposal of shares is £19,700 (see below).

Working: Share pool

		Number	Cost £	Indexed cost £
April 1993	**Purchase**	25,000	33,000	33,000
IA to June 2016	((262.3 – 140.6)/140.6) × £33,000			28,564
		————	————	————
		25,000	33,000	61,564
June 2016	**Sale**			
	(8,000/25,000 × £33,000/£61,564)	(8,000)	(10,560)	(19,700)
		————	————	————
		17,000	22,440	41,864
		————	————	————

148

	True	False
The £250,000 gain which could be deferred as a result of the acquisition of the machine will become chargeable on 1 October 2026		✓
The company must make a rollover relief election by 31 December 2020	✓	

The election must be made within four years of the later of the end of the accounting period in which the old asset is sold and the new asset is acquired.

Tutorial note

The deferred gain of £250,000 will become chargeable 10 years after the replacement asset is acquired (i.e. on 1 November 2025).

PRACTICE SECTION B OBJECTIVE TEST CASES

INDIVIDUALS – CAPITAL GAINS TAX

149   MICHAEL CHIN (ADAPTED)

Key answer tips

A typical examination question on capital gains tax with a series of disposals covering a variety of topics. Remember to use the market value as the proceeds in the computation of the gains when the disposal is a gift.

1   B

	£
Disposal of business	
Goodwill	60,000
Freehold property	64,000
Storage unit	(13,000)
	———
Net chargeable gains qualifying for entrepreneurs' relief	111,000
	———

Tutorial note

*The **net chargeable gains** on the disposal of an unincorporated business qualify for entrepreneurs' relief provided the business has been owned by the sole trader for 12 months prior to the disposal. The period of ownership of the individual assets is irrelevant.*

2   A

Ordinary shares in Minnow Ltd	£
Deemed proceeds = MV	180,000
Less: Cost	(87,500)
	————
	92,500
Less: Gift relief (W)	(74,000)
	————
Chargeable gain	18,500
	————

Working

The gift relief in respect of the ordinary shares in Minnow Ltd is restricted because the shares are in Michael's personal trading company (i.e. he owns > 5%) and the company has investment assets.

The proportion of gain eligible for gift relief is the proportion of chargeable business assets to chargeable assets, calculated as follows:

Gift relief = (£92,500 × £200,000/£250,000) = £74,000

Tutorial note

Gift relief is available as ordinary shares in an unquoted trading company are qualifying assets for gift relief purposes. However full relief is not available as the company holds investments.

3   D

	£	£
Painting		
Gross proceeds (£5,900 + £656)	6,556	
Less: Selling costs	(656)	
	———	
Net proceeds	5,900	
Less: Cost	(4,000)	
	———	
Gain	1,900	
	———	
Chargeable gain restricted to maximum of:		
5/3 × (£6,556 − £6,000)	927	927
	———	———

Tutorial note

It is important to be able to recognise when an asset is a chattel (i.e. tangible and movable) and therefore that the disposal is subject to special rules.

4   A

Tutorial note

It is important to be able to recognise when an asset is a chattel (i.e. tangible and movable) and therefore that the disposal is subject to special rules.

The necklace is a chattel that was bought and sold for less than £6,000 it is therefore an exempt chattel and the loss is not an allowable loss.

The boat is exempt as a wasting chattel and the gain is therefore not chargeable.

The machine is a wasting chattel, but as it has been used for trading activities the capital loss is not allowable as relief will be given through the capital allowances computation instead.

5   C

Loss left to c/f to 2016/17

	£
Capital loss – 2014/15	16,800
Less: Used in 2015/16 (W)	0
	———
Loss c/f to 2016/17	16,800
	———

Working – Capital loss brought forward

	£
Chargeable gain – 2015/16	17,100
Less: CY capital loss	(7,000)
	———
	10,100
Less: AEA (restricted)	(10,100)
	———
Taxable gain	0
	———

Tutorial note

The capital loss brought forward is not used in 2015/16, in order to preserve the annual exempt amount. Current year capital losses must be offset in full and cannot be restricted to preserve the annual exempt amount.

150   WILSON BIAZMA (ADAPTED)

Key answer tips

Q1 relates to the automatic UK residency tests. These and the other residency tests are not included in the tax rates and allowances provided to you in the examination. It is therefore important that you have a good knowledge of these.

The other questions relate to different aspects of capital gains tax including entrepreneurs' relief, rollover relief, the matching rules for share disposals and the calculation of a capital gains tax liability.

1

	Automatically UK resident	Not automatically UK resident
Wilson had close family in the UK in the tax year		✓
Wilson was in the UK for 180 days in the tax year		✓
Wilson worked in the UK in the tax year		✓
Wilson's only home during the tax year was in the UK	✓	
Wilson spent more time in the UK than any other country in the tax year		✓

Tutorial note

A person will be treated as automatically UK residence if they meet one of the following tests:

1   *They are in the UK for at least 183 days in the tax year.*

2   *Their only home is in the UK.*

3   *They work full time in the UK.*

2   C

Tutorial note

Entrepreneurs' relief is available on the goodwill as Wilson has disposed of a complete business which he has owned for at least one year.

Entrepreneurs' relief is not available on the freehold office building as this is the disposal of a single asset, not the whole or part of a business.

Entrepreneurs' relief is not available on the shares as STU plc is not Wilson's personal trading company (i.e. he doesn't own at least 5% of the shares).

3   £110,000.

	£
Disposal proceeds	246,000
Less: Cost	(104,000)
Capital gain before reliefs	142,000
Less: Rollover relief (W)	(32,000)
Chargeable gain	110,000

Working – Rollover relief

Rollover relief is not available in full because not all of the proceeds are reinvested.

The gain remaining chargeable is the lower of:

(i)   Total gain of £142,000, or

(ii)   Proceeds not reinvested (£246,000 – £136,000) = £110,000.

Rollover relief is therefore £32,000 (£142,000 – £110,000).

4   D

Tutorial note

When shares are disposed of they are matched against shares acquired of the same class in the following order:

- *Same day as the date of disposal.*

- *Within following 30 days.*

- *The share pool (shares acquired before the date of disposal are pooled together).*

5   A

	£	£
Gains not qualifying for entrepreneurs' relief	300,000	
Gains qualifying for entrepreneurs' relief:		500,000
Less: AEA	(11,100)	
Taxable gains	288,900	500,000
Capital gains tax:		
Qualifying gains (£500,000 × 10%)		50,000
Not qualifying gains (£288,900 × 20%)		57,780
CGT payable		107,780

Tutorial note

Wilson is a basic rate taxpayer for income tax purposes. Therefore gains up to the remaining basic rate band (£32,000 – £25,000) would usually be subject to CGT at a rate of 10%. However, the remaining basic rate band is first utilised by gains qualifying for entrepreneurs' relief and therefore in this scenario, only the gains qualifying for entrepreneurs' relief can be taxed at 10%.

Gains that qualify for entrepreneurs' relief will be taxed at 10% regardless of whether they fall into the basic rate or higher rate band.

151 BO (ADAPTED)

Key answer tips

This case covers an individual making disposals eligible for reliefs. The first two questions relate to a gift of a business asset and the application of gift relief, followed by a basic calculation of capital gains tax. The third question tests payment and claim dates – it is important to learn the administration rules and to be able to apply them to a given scenario. The fourth question looks again at gift relief, but this time where there is a sale at undervalue.

The last question relates to a separate individual and tests the rules regarding PPR relief.

1 **C**

The base cost of the son's 50,000 £1 ordinary shares in Botune Ltd is:

	£
MV of shares acquired	210,000
Less: Gift relief (W)	(116,000)
Base cost of shares	94,000

Working: Gift relief

This is a gift, and therefore the market value of the shares sold is used. Bo therefore has a chargeable gain of £116,000 (MV £210,000 – cost of £94,000).

Since no consideration has been paid for the shares, all of Bo's chargeable gain can be held over (i.e. deferred) with a gift relief claim.

2   C

	£
Chargeable gain	20,000
Less: AEA	(11,100)
	————
Taxable gain	8,900
	————

CGT payable:	£
Remaining BRB (£32,000 – £25,000) = £7,000	
£7,000 × 10%	700
£1,900 (£8,900 – £7,000) × 20%	380
	————
	1,080
	————

3   A

Tutorial note

Capital gains tax is due under self-assessment, with the balancing payment for income tax, on 31 January following the tax year i.e. 31 January 2018 for the tax year 2016/17.

A gift relief claim must be made within four years of the end of tax year of the gift i.e. 5 April 2021 for a disposal in the tax year 2016/17.

4   A

The consideration paid for the shares is less than the market value, but exceeds the allowable cost by £66,000 (£160,000 – £94,000). This amount will be immediately chargeable to capital gains tax.

The remaining gain of £50,000 (£116,000 – £66,000) can be deferred with a gift relief claim.

Tutorial note

With a sale at undervalue, the chargeable gain will still be calculated using the full market value of the asset i.e. £210,000 – £94,000 = £116,000.

However, any actual capital profit made by the owner at the time of the sale will be immediately chargeable. The remaining gain of £50,000 (£116,000 –£ £66,000) can be deferred with a gift relief claim.

5   D

Working: PPR relief

	Total months	Exempt months	Note	Chargeable months
1.10.04 to 30.9.06 (occupied)	24	24		
1.10.06 to 31.03.15	102	0	1	102
1.04.15 to 30.09.16	18	18		
	——	——		——
	144	42		102
	——	——		——

PPR exemption = (£172,000 × 42/144) = £50,167

Tutorial note

1   *The first 36 months of the 'unoccupied' period is a **not** a period of 'deemed occupation' because 36 months are allowed for no reason provided:*

-       *the property is actually occupied at some time before and at some time after the period of absence, and*

-       *there was no other PPR at that time.*

Bo did not reoccupy the property and therefore the exemption is not available.

2   *The last 18 months are always allowable provided the property was the taxpayer's PPR at some time.*

152 ALPHABET LTD (ADAPTED) *Walk in the footsteps of a top tutor*

Key answer tips

This is a familiar style capital gains tax question involving three individuals making disposals. All of them had shares in a company which is taken over.

Takeovers can be complicated where there is mixed consideration and many students may have been put off by the opening paragraph. However, in this question, there is no mixed consideration and it is quite straightforward.

They are disposing of their existing shares and have a choice of either cash or shares, but not a mixture of the two.

Of the three individuals, one chooses cash and therefore they just have a straightforward disposal of shares for cash.

The other two choose shares, which is just a share for share exchange with no capital gains tax consequences at that time. The new shares just 'stand in the shoes' of the old shares and are deemed to have been acquired at the same cost and at the same time as the original shares. They then dispose of some of the new shares.

For the first part, detailed knowledge of the entrepreneurs' relief conditions is required.

1   A

Bon

Bon acquired her shareholding and became a director on 1 February 2016, so the qualifying conditions were not met for the 12 months prior to the date of the takeover.

Cherry

Cherry owned 3,000 shares out of the 100,000 shares in the company, which is a 3% shareholding.

This is less than the minimum required holding of 5% to qualify for the relief.

Tutorial note

To qualify for entrepreneurs' relief, the company must be trading and the individual must:

- *Own 5% or more of the shares, and*

- *Work for the company, and*

- *Must satisfy both of these conditions for 12 months prior to the date of disposal.*

Note that the question specifically asks for whether the individuals meet the qualifying conditions in relation to their shares in Alphabet Ltd, i.e. before the date of the takeover.

Bon however, is also very unlikely to qualify for entrepreneurs' relief in respect of her shares in XYZ plc as it is reasonable to assume that her shareholding in XYZ plc, a quoted company, would not amount to at least 5% of the company's shares. In addition, there is no mention that she works for XYZ plc.

---

2   B

	£
Ordinary shares in Alphabet Ltd	
Disposal proceeds (60,000 × £6)	360,000
Cost (£50,000 + £18,600)	(68,600)
	———
Chargeable gain	291,400
	———

3   C

	£
Ordinary shares in XYZ plc	
Disposal proceeds (£7.14 × 10,000)(W)	71,400
Cost (£92,200 × 10,000/25,000)	(36,880)
	———
Chargeable gain	34,520
	———

Working: Valuation of quoted shares

The disposal is to a connected party (her brother) and market value is therefore used as the proceeds in the capital gains computation.

The shares in XYZ plc are valued using the mid-price (i.e. average) of the quoted prices in the Stock Exchange Daily Official List:

(£7.10 + £7.18) × 1/2) = £7.14

Total value is 10,000 × £7.14 = £71,400

Tutorial note

Following the takeover Bon received 25,000 ordinary shares in XYZ plc.

Where there is a share for share exchange, the cost of the original shareholding is treated as the cost of the new shareholding acquired on the takeover.

The cost of the new shares disposed of is therefore a proportion of the original cost of the Alphabet shares.

4   A

5   A

Tutorial note

Transfers on death are exempt disposals for CGT purposes. The daughter's cost of acquisition on a subsequent disposal is the probate value i.e. the market value of the shares at the date of death.

153   JORGE JUNG (ADAPTED)

Key answer tips

This is a fairly typical capital gains tax question involving a number of disposals. It tests the rules for wasting assets which are not chattels, the marginal rules for chattel disposals and part disposals. The last two questions then test gift relief and entrepreneurs' relief, and in particular look at the conditions for each relief to apply. It is important to learn these conditions, and the differences between them for each relief.

1   B

	£
Copyright	
Disposal proceeds	8,200
Less: Depreciated cost (£7,000 × 8/10)	(5,600)
Chargeable gain	2,600

Tutorial note

The copyright is a wasting asset. The cost of £7,000 must therefore be depreciated based on an unexpired life of ten years at the date of acquisition and an unexpired life of eight years at the date of disposal.

2   £667

	£
Painting	
Disposal proceeds	6,400
Less: Selling costs	(350)
Net proceeds	6,050
Less: Cost	(2,200)
Chargeable gain	3,850
Restricted to 5/3 × (£6,400 – £6,000)	667

Tutorial note

A painting is a non-wasting chattel that was sold for more than £6,000 but purchased for less than £6,000. The gain is restricted to 5/3 x (gross proceeds – £6,000).

3   C

	£
Land – part disposal	
Allowable cost	
£28,600 × (£92,000/(£92,000 + £38,000))	20,240
Legal fees	
£500 × (£92,000/(£92,000+£38,000))	354
Total cost	20,594

Tutorial note

The cost of the land for Jorge is £28,600 which is the value when his father died. Remember that where an individual inherits an asset the cost of acquisition is the market value at the date of death (i.e. the probate value). In addition he incurred £500 on legal fees defending his title to the land, which is an allowable cost of acquisition. His total base cost is therefore £29,100 (£28,600 + £500).

The proportion of the acquisition cost and the allowable cost of acquisition that can be deducted on the part disposal by Jorge are shown as separate calculations in the computation. It would be equally correct to show this as one calculation based on the total base cost of £29,100 as follows:

£29,100 × (£92,000/(£92,000 + £38,000)) = £20,594

4   C

Tutorial note

The company can be a quoted company provided that it is the individual's personal trading company (i.e. Jorge owns at least 5% of the voting rights).

If the company owns non-business assets a gift relief claim can be made but the relief will be restricted if the shares are in the individual's personal company.

There are no minimum ownership period requirements for gift relief.

5   A and C

Tutorial note

The individual can work part time for the company.

Jorge must own at least 5% of the shares of the company – but he can sell a smaller shareholding out of a shareholding of at least 5%.

154 ALBERT AND CHARLES (ADAPTED) *Walk in the footsteps of a top tutor*

Key answer tips

A typical capital gains question with two distinct parts.

The first part tests the rules for PPR relief and husband and wife transfers.

The second part involves the disposal of shares and tests the valuation of a gift, the share matching rules and the composition of the share pool.

1 B

One quarter of Albert's house was always used exclusively for business purposes, so the principal private residence relief is restricted to £462,825 (£840,000 – £222,900) × 3/4).

Tutorial note

*The last 18 months exemption does not apply to the whole house as one third has **always** been used for business purposes. If the business use had only been for part of the period of ownership the last 18 months would have applied to the whole house.*

2 A

The capital gains tax saving if 50% ownership of the house had been transferred to Victoria prior to its disposal would have been calculated as:

	£
Gains falling into the BRB for Victoria (£32,000 – £15,740) = £16,260	
– lower residential rate of CGT applied (£16,260 × 10% (28% – 18%))	1,626

Tutorial note

Transferring 50% ownership of the house to Victoria prior to its disposal would have enabled her remaining lower rate tax band of 18% for residential properties for 2016/17 to be utilised. There is no saving in respect of her annual exempt amount which has already been used by her other disposals in 2016/17. Remember to use the higher CGT rates of 18% and 28% when calculating tax on the disposal of residential properties.

Note that the tax saving could be calculated by computing the tax payable by Albert at 28%, and then compute the tax payable by Albert and Victoria sharing the gain equally.

However, with only 2 marks available, there is insufficient time to perform all of these calculations. Therefore, the examining team expects you to be able to see the effect of the planning on the computations and perform a two line short cut calculation.

3   D

Share pool	Number	Cost
		£
Purchase 1 March 2008	20,000	19,800
Purchase 20 July 2012	8,000	27,800
	28,000	47,600
Disposal 23 October 2016		
(£47,600 × 4,000/28,000)	(4,000)	(6,800)
Balance c/f	24,000	40,800

4   A

	£
Sale of painting – April 2017	
Deemed proceeds	6,000
Less: Cost of disposal	(300)
Net proceeds	5,700
Less: Cost	(13,000)
Allowable capital loss	(7,300)

Tutorial note

You were required to apply the rules for non-wasting chattels in this computation. In this situation the gross proceeds were <£6,000 and the cost was ≥£6,000. This requires the use of a deemed proceeds amount of £6,000 in the computation to determine the allowable capital loss.

5   C

Tutorial note

There is no requirement for an individual to work for the company in order to claim gift relief.

The donee paying for the asset does not prevent gift relief being available. However, if the amount paid exceeds the cost to the donor, the gift relief must be restricted so that any actual capital profit made by the donor at the time of the sale will be immediately chargeable.

COMPANIES – CHARGEABLE GAINS

155   HAWK LTD (ADAPTED) *Walk in the footsteps of a top tutor*

Key answer tips

The only capital gains relief available to companies is rollover relief and therefore it is not surprising to see it in this question as it is often tested in corporation tax questions.

1   C

	£
Indexation allowance	
On cost (July 1996 to April 2016)	
0.716 × £84,200 (£81,000 + £3,200)	60,287
On enhancement (May 2008 to April 2016)	
0.216 × £43,000	9,288
	———
	69,575
	———

2   C

Tutorial note

Assets which qualify for rollover relief are:

–   *Land and buildings used for the purposes of the trade*

–   *Fixed plant and machinery*

Goodwill is a qualifying asset for individuals but not for companies.

A vehicle is not fixed (i.e. immovable) plant and machinery.

3   B

Tutorial note

The gain rolled over is the indexed gain.

The reinvestment must take place by 30 April 2019 (i.e. three years after the date of sale).

4   B

The factory was sold for £496,160 (net of disposal expenses). Therefore this is the amount that Hawk Ltd will have to reinvest in order to claim the maximum possible amount of rollover relief.

Tutorial note

HM Revenue and Customs allow full rollover relief provided the net sale proceeds are reinvested in qualifying assets. It is not necessary to reinvest the gross sale proceeds.

5   A

Indexed cost of ordinary shares: £18,000/£30,000 × £12,280 = £7,368

Workings

(W1) Share pool – White plc	Number	Cost £	Indexed cost £
Purchase June 2000	3,000	8,000	8,000
Indexation to takeover – July 2016 (£8,000 × 0.535)			4,280
	3,000	8,000	12,280

(W2) Consideration received on takeover

	MV
	£
6,000 ordinary shares @ £3	18,000
6,000 preference shares @ £2	12,000
	———
	30,000
	———

156 ACEBOOK LTD (ADAPTED) *Walk in the footsteps of a top tutor*

Key answer tips

This is a standard chargeable gains question, based on a company having four capital transactions. The question covers the disposal of shares, a part disposal of land, the receipt and partial reinvestment of insurance proceeds on the destruction of an asset and the reinvestment of insurance proceeds following the damage of an asset.

The final two disposals may be difficult for students, who are perhaps less familiar with the rules regarding damage or destruction of an asset. However, the examining team has given a hint in the question, in saying that the company has made claims to defer the gains, and this information could be used to make a sensible assumption about the treatment of the insurance proceeds.

If you are ever unsure of how to deal with part of a question it is important to make a sensible guess and move on, rather than waste time, or potentially miss easy marks by not attempting to answer the part.

1   D

Tutorial note

Indexation allowance is not available on disposals of same day or previous 9 day purchases.

The indexation factor is not rounded to three decimal places in the share pool. However, note that in the F6 examination you may be provided with indexation factors in a share question, and in that case they will be rounded to three decimal places.

The indexation allowance cannot increase a loss nor turn a chargeable gain into an allowable loss.

The gain after indexation is deferred under rollover relief.

2   B

Share pool	Number	Cost	Indexed cost
		£	£
Purchase June 2007	24,000	25,200	25,200
Indexation to March 2016			
(£25,200 × 0.26)			6,552
Rights issue March 2016			
(24,000 × 1/5) = 4,800 × £4.30	4,800	20,640	20,640
	28,800	45,840	52,392

Tutorial note

A rights issue is simply a purchase of shares (usually at a price below market value) and is therefore an operative event (i.e. index up to the date of the rights issue, and then add in the number and cost of the shares).

3   D

	£
Allowable cost	
Indexed cost (Note 1)	
(£192,000/(£192,000 + £53,000)) × £196,000	153,600
Enhancement expenditure	
(£192,000/(£192,000 + £53,000)) × £29,400	23,040
	176,640

Tutorial note

This standard part disposal computation requires the appropriate proportion of the indexed cost to be calculated using the A/(A + B) formula.

The cost of clearing and levelling the land is enhancement expenditure. The cost relates to all four acres so again the standard part disposal computation requires the appropriate proportion of the enhancement expenditure to be calculated using the A/(A + B) formula.

Tutor's top tips

Part disposals are regularly examined, and it is important to learn the formula for calculating the cost and to know how to apply it. You should not be misled by the size or number of the parts bought and sold; it is the values which are used in the calculation.

4   A

Investment property 1	£
Insurance proceeds	189,000
Less: Indexed cost	(138,400)
	50,600
Less: Gain deferred (balancing figure)	(34,000)
Chargeable gain (proceeds not reinvested) = (£189,000 – £172,400)	16,600

Tutorial note

Where an asset is destroyed and the insurance proceeds are reinvested in a replacement asset within 12 months then the gain may be deferred against the cost of the replacement asset. Where the insurance proceeds are not fully reinvested then the amount which is not reinvested is chargeable immediately.

5   C

Revised base cost	£
Indexed cost at October 2016	216,500
Plus: Restoration expenditure	100,000
Less: Insurance proceeds	(100,000)
	216,500

Tutorial note

Where an asset is damaged and all of the insurance proceeds are used in restoring the asset an election can be made to deduct the proceeds from the cost of the asset rather than being treated as having made a part disposal of the asset.

PRACTICE SECTION C CONSTRUCTED RESPONSE QUESTIONS

INDIVIDUALS – CAPITAL GAINS TAX

157   DAVID AND ANGELA BROOK (ADAPTED)   *Walk in the footsteps of a top tutor*

Key answer tips

A classic question involving the calculation of capital gains tax liabilities of a husband and wife, with joint assets and assets held personally.

Tutor's top tips

Be careful to spot the exempt asset. You don't need to do any calculations for this asset; just say that it is exempt!

Predictably a husband and wife no gain/no loss transfer is included, with the subsequent disposal by the recipient spouse.

Remember also to consider entrepreneurs' relief on the disposal of shares.

David Brook

Capital gains tax liability – 2016/17

	£
Motor car (exempt)	0
House (W1)	31,439
Shares in Bend Ltd (W3)	0
Total chargeable gains	31,439
Less: AEA	(11,100)
Taxable gain	20,339
Capital gains tax (£20,339 at 18%)	3,661

Tutorial note

David has no taxable income. All of his gains therefore fall into his basic rate band and are taxed at the CGT rate applicable to gains on residential properties falling within the basic rate band. Entrepreneurs' relief is not available on any of his gains.

Angela Brook

Capital gains tax liability – 2016/17

	Residential property £	Other gains £
House (W1)	31,439	
Ordinary shares in Bend Ltd (W4)		26,400
	_____	_____
Total chargeable gains	31,439	26,400
Less: AEA	(11,100)	
	_____	_____
Taxable gain	20,339	26,400
	_____	_____

	£
Residential gains	
555 × 18% (W5)	100
19,784 × 28%	5,540
26,400 × 20%	5,280
	_____
46,739	
	_____
Capital gains tax liability	10,920
	_____

Tutorial note

The AEA should be offset against gains on residential property in priority to other gains in order to save the maximum amount of tax. In addition to this, gains on residential property should utilise any remaining basic rate band in priority to other gains.

Angela has taxable income that uses some of, but not all of, her basic rate band. The remaining basic rate band is £555.

There is no entrepreneurs' relief available on any of her gains therefore the 10% rate does not apply.

Workings

(W1) House

Tutor's top tips

If an asset is jointly owned by husband and wife, all you need to do is calculate the gain as usual and then split it 50:50.

Make sure you show your working for the calculation of principal private residence relief. Even if you can't count months, you will still be given marks for applying the correct principles!

	£
Disposal proceeds	381,900
Less: Cost	(86,000)
	295,900
Less: Principal private residence exemption (W2)	(233,021)
Chargeable gain	62,879

David and Angela will each be assessed on 50% of the chargeable gain:

Chargeable gain each = (£62,879 × 50%) = £31,439

(W2) Occupation of the house

The total period of ownership of the house is 240 months (189 + 51), of which 189 months qualify for exemption as follows:

		Total months	Exempt months	Chargeable months
1.10.96 to 31.3.00	(occupied)	42	42	
1.4.00 to 31.12.03	(working in UK)	45	45	
1.1.04 to 31.12.10	(occupied)	84	84	
1.1.11 to 31.03.15	(unoccupied)	51		51
1.04.15 to 30.9.16	(final 18 months)	18	18	
		240	189	51

PPR relief = (189/240 × £295,900) = £233,021

Tutor's top tips

Make sure that you include a brief explanation for the periods you allow as exempt due to the deemed occupation rules – as the examining team has said that such explanations are required to obtain maximum marks in these questions.

(W3) Shares in Bend Ltd – gift by David

Tutor's top tips

Remember that the market value at the time of the inter-spouse gift is a red herring and irrelevant. The transfer will be at no gain/no loss.

Transfers between husband and wife are no gain/no loss transfers.

David makes no gain and Angela takes over David's cost of £48,000.

(W4) Shares in Bend Ltd – Sale by Angela

	£
Disposal proceeds	62,400
Less: Cost (£48,000 × 15,000/20,000)	(36,000)
Chargeable gain	26,400

Tutorial note

It is not clear what percentage interest Angela has in Bend Ltd and whether it is her personal trading company (i.e. she holds 5% interest or more). However, even if she does hold at least 5%, entrepreneurs' relief is not available as Angela does not work for the company.

(W5) Remaining basic rate band

	£
Basic rate band	32,000
Less: Taxable income	(31,445)
Remaining basic rate band	555

Examiner's report

Although there were some very good answers to this question from well prepared candidates, it caused problems for many and was often the reason that they failed to achieve a pass mark.

One particular problem was that a lot of time was often spent performing unnecessary calculations for the exempt asset, and then not having sufficient time to deal with the chargeable assets.

Many candidates therefore did a lot of work for this question but scored few marks.

The jointly owned property caused particular difficulty. Only a few candidates correctly calculated the principal private residence exemption.

Some candidates did not allocate the resulting chargeable gain between the couple but instead deducted an annual exempt amount and calculated a separate tax liability.

Note: *The examiner's report has been edited to remove comments on elements of the question that have been deleted due to changes to the examination format.*

ACCA marking scheme		
		Marks
Jointly owned property – Motor car		0.5
– House	– Proceeds	0.5
	– Cost	0.5
	– Period of exemption	2.5
	– Exemption	1.0
	– Division of gain	0.5
David Brook – Bend Ltd		0.5
– Annual exempt amount		0.5
– Capital gains tax		0.5
Angela Brook– Bend Ltd – Proceeds		0.5
– Cost		0.5
– Annual exempt amount		0.5
– Capital gains tax		1.5
		——
Total		**10.0**
		——

158 BILL DING *Walk in the footsteps of a top tutor*

Key answer tips

This is a tricky question, examining the interaction between gift relief and entrepreneurs' relief. A good knowledge of the conditions for both reliefs and the way that they are applied is needed to score well here, and this should be a good test of whether you are well prepared for these topics!

In section (a) a father gifts shares qualifying for entrepreneurs' relief to his daughter, and they make a joint claim for gift relief. The daughter then sells the shares before 12 months have elapsed, meaning her disposal does not qualify.

In section (b) you are asked to not apply gift relief, in order for the father to benefit from entrepreneurs' relief on the full gain.

In section (c) you are asked to compare sections (a) and (b). This style of requirement has become a frequent feature of the F6 examination, so you should make sure that you are prepared for it.

(a)   **Bill and Belle make a joint claim for gift relief**

Bill

Capital gains tax liability – 2016/17

	£
Deemed proceeds (Market value)	260,000
Less: Cost	(112,000)
	148,000
Less: Gift relief (W)	(123,333)
Chargeable gain	24,667
Less: AEA	(11,100)
Taxable gain	13,567
Capital gains tax (£13,567 × 10%) (Note)	1,357

Working: Gift relief on shares in High Rise Ltd

Gift relief is available on these shares as they are in an unquoted trading company.

However, the gift relief in respect of the shares in High Rise Ltd is restricted because the shares are in Bill's personal trading company (i.e. he owns > 5%) and the company has investment assets.

The proportion of gain eligible for gift relief is the proportion of chargeable business assets to chargeable assets, calculated as follows:

Gift relief = (£148,000 × £150,000/£180,000) = £123,333

Belle

Capital gains tax liability – 2016/17

	£
Proceeds	265,000
Less: Cost (£260,000 – £123,333)	(136,667)
Chargeable gain	128,333
Less: AEA	(11,100)
Taxable gain	117,233
Capital gains tax (£117,233 × 20%)	23,447

Tutorial note

1   High Rise Ltd qualifies as Bill's personal company, as he holds at least 5% of the shares. As he has both worked for the company and held the shares for at least 12 months prior to disposal, entrepreneurs' relief is available.

2   High Rise Ltd also qualifies as Belle's personal company. However, she has not held the shares for 12 months and therefore does not qualify for entrepreneurs' relief.

3   As a joint claim for gift relief has been made, the cost for Belle is reduced by the amount of relief claimed.

(b)   **Bill and Belle do not make a joint claim for gift relief**

Bill

Capital gains tax liability – 2016/17

	£
Deemed proceeds (Market value)	260,000
Less: Cost	(112,000)
Chargeable gain qualifying for entrepreneurs' relief	148,000
Less AEA	(11,100)
Taxable gain	136,900
Capital gains tax (£136,900 × 10%)	13,690

Belle

Capital gains tax liability 2016/17

	£
Proceeds	265,000
Less: Cost	(260,000)
Chargeable gain	5,000
Less AEA	(5,000)
Taxable gain	0

(c) **Comparison capital gains tax payable under options (a) and (b)**

	Option (a) £	Option (b) £
Bill	1,357	13,690
Belle	23,447	0
Total	24,804	13,690

Conclusion of best option

- Total capital gains tax payable is £11,114 lower under option (b) (£24,804 – £13,690) as more of the gain is taxable on Bill, who pays tax at 10% as the disposal qualifies for entrepreneurs' relief.

- Bill however, may prefer option (a) as his own capital gains tax payable is £12,333 (£1,357 – £13,690) lower due to the claim for gift relief.

Tutor's top tips

In part (c) you are asked to summarise the capital gains tax liabilities that you have calculated in parts (a) and (b) and conclude on the most favourable option.

Provided that you use the capital gains tax figures that you have calculated in the earlier parts of the question, and come to a sensible conclusion, you will score marks here, even if your answers to parts (a) and (b) are incorrect.

159 JEROME (ADAPTED) *Walk in the footsteps of a top tutor*

Key answer tips

This question tests basic chargeable gains computations for individuals, along with a key relief: gift relief.

It also required calculations of the base costs for the recipients of the assets gifted in the tax year.

You do not have to deal with disposals in chronological order, the disposal of the bracelet was relatively straightforward and would have been a good place to start. You should be familiar with the chattels rules which apply to this disposal.

(a)

Tutor's top tips

Don't forget that disposals of assets between husband and wife and civil partners are automatically on a no gain/no loss basis. If you are provided with the market value or any actual proceeds they are merely there to distract you.

When dealing with a part disposal of land, the market value of the part disposed of and the remainder should be used to determine the cost for the computation. Don't be tempted to us the proportion of asset being disposed of i.e. 9/10 acres.

Jerome – Chargeable gains 2016/17

House

The gift of the house does not give rise to any gain or loss because it is a transfer between spouses.

Reward Ltd

	£
Deemed proceeds	98,400
Cost	(39,000)
	———
	59,400
Gift relief (W)	(50,600)
	———
Chargeable gain	8,800
	———

Working – Gift relief

Gift relief is restricted to £50,600 (£59,400 × £460,000/£540,000), being the proportion of chargeable business assets to chargeable assets.

Antique bracelet

	£
Disposal proceeds	12,200
Cost	(2,100)
Chargeable gain	10,100

This is lower than the maximum gain of £10,333
(5/3 × (12,200 – 6,000)).

Land

	£
Disposal proceeds	78,400
Cost (W)	(26,460)
Chargeable gain	51,940

Working – Cost

The cost relating to the nine acres of land gifted is £26,460 (£37,800 × £78,400/(£78,400 + £33,600)).

Tutorial note

The gift relief computation tested the restriction on gift relief that applies in a very specific scenario. When an individual makes a gift of shares in their personal company (i.e. owns ≥5% of the shares), the gift relief is restricted by reference to the proportion of the company's chargeable business assets to its chargeable asset.

The disposal of land is a part disposal requiring the application of A/(A+B) to the full cost of the land. Any cost not included in the computation is the base cost of the remaining land.

(b)　(1)　The house has a base cost of £112,800

　　　(2)　The 12,000 £1 ordinary shares in Reward Ltd have a base cost of £47,800 (£98,400 – £50,600).

　　　(3)　The bracelet has a base cost of £12,200.

　　　(4)　The nine acres of land have a base cost of £78,400.

Examiner's report

This question was on capital gains tax, and was generally very well answered. A taxpayer had made various gifts to family members during the tax year. These were (1) a no gain or loss gift of a house to their spouse, (2) a gift of shares in an unquoted trading company which qualified for gift relief, (3) the gift of a non-wasting chattel, and (4) a part disposal of land.

Part (a) required a calculation of the taxpayer's chargeable gains for the tax year. The only aspect which consistently caused problems was the gift relief, with relief being restricted to the proportion of the company's chargeable business assets to chargeable assets.

Part (b) required the base cost taken over by each recipient. Although relatively straightforward, this requirement often resulted in detailed, incorrect, workings. The gift to the spouse caused particular problems, with the base cost being the value at the time it was inherited by the taxpayer – not the value at the time of the gift.

ACCA marking scheme		Marks
(a)	No gain/no loss	0.5
	Reward shares proceeds	0.5
	Reward shares cost	0.5
	Gift relief – CBA/CA	1.5
	Antique bracelet proceeds	0.5
	Antique bracelet cost	0.5
	Max – 5/3 rule	1.0
	Land proceeds	0.5
	Land cost A/A+B	1.5
		7.0
(b)	House base cost	1.0
	Reward shares base cost	1.0
	Bracelet base cost	0.5
	Land base cost	0.5
		3.0
Total		**10.0**

160   GINGER AND NIGEL (ADAPTED) *Walk in the footsteps of a top tutor*

Key answer tips

This question tests two important capital gains tax reliefs: gift relief and entrepreneurs' relief.

Part (a) tested gift relief but in a slightly unusual way which required the application of the modified gift relief rules for sales at an undervaluation, and a calculation of the maximum number of shares that can be gifted without a capital gains tax liability arising.

If you are ever unsure of how to deal with part of a question it is important to make a sensible attempt and move on, rather than waste time, or potentially miss easy marks by not attempting to answer the part.

The highlighted words are key words or phrases that markers are looking for.

Part (b) compares the CGT payable by a husband or wife on the disposal of shares. Again easy marks were available for the basic gains computation in each case and the calculation of the difference in tax payable by the two individuals.

(a)   **Ginger**

Tutor's top tips

Remember that where there is a disposal at an undervalue (as opposed to an outright gift) then part of the gain may be chargeable now and cannot be held over (deferred).

The examining team has given you a hint in the question as to how to approach the answer by stating that Ginger has not utilised the annual exempt amount for the tax year 2016/17.

- The disposal is at an undervalue, so only the 'gift' element of the gain can be held over.

- The consideration paid for each share will be immediately chargeable to capital gains tax to the extent that it exceeds the allowable cost.

- The chargeable amount is therefore £1.61 (£4.00 – £2.39) per share.

- Ginger's annual exempt amount for the tax year 2016/17 is £11,100.

- She can therefore sell 6,894 shares (£11,100/£1.61) to her daughter without this resulting in any capital gains tax liability for the tax year 2016/17.

Tutorial note

This method may have proved quite challenging to some students. If you are unsure how to tackle the question, then make sure you write down what you do know.

One mark was available for simply stating how to calculate the gain on a transfer at an undervalue and another half mark for stating the amount of the annual exempt amount!

Proof of the calculation:

	£
MV of shares (6,894 × £6.40)	*44,122*
Less: Cost (6,894 × £2.39)	*(16,477)*
Capital gain	*27,645*
Less: Gift relief (6,894 × (£6.40 – £4.00))	*(16,546)*
Chargeable gain (6,894 × (4.00 – £2.39)) (excess actual proceeds received)	*11,099*
Less: Annual exempt amount	*(11,100)*
Taxable gain	*0*

(b)   **Innocent and Nigel**

Tutor's top tips

Clearly, the CGT is not going to be the same for both Innocent and Nigel, so you need to look out for the differences in their circumstances. You are given a lot of information concerning their total shareholdings and employment position. As this is different for each of them this should give you a hint that you should consider how this is relevant for determining their CGT liability.

- If Innocent makes the disposal, then her CGT liability for 2016/17 will be:

	£
Disposal proceeds	65,000
Less: Cost (2,000 × £1)	(2,000)
Chargeable gain	63,000
Capital gains tax (£63,000 × 10%)	6,300

Innocent pays CGT at 10% as the disposal qualifies for entrepreneurs' relief.

- If Nigel makes the disposal, then his CGT liability for 2016/17 will be:

	£
Disposal proceeds	65,000
Less: Cost (£46,200 × 2,000/3,000)	(30,800)
Chargeable gain	34,200
Capital gains tax (£34,200 × 20%)	6,840

Nigel pays CGT at 20% because he is a higher rate taxpayer and the disposal does not qualify for entrepreneurs' relief.

- The capital gains tax saving if Innocent makes the disposal rather than Nigel is therefore £540 (£6,840 – £6,300).

Tutorial notes

1   *A disposal by Innocent will qualify for entrepreneurs' relief as she is the managing director of Cinnamon Ltd, the company is a trading company, her shareholding of 20% (20,000/100,000) is more than the minimum required holding of 5% and she has held the shares for more than 12 months. The gain is therefore taxed at 10%.*

2   *A disposal by Nigel will not qualify for entrepreneurs' relief as he is not an officer or an employee of Cinnamon Ltd and his shareholding is only 3% (3,000/100,000). As Nigel is a higher rate taxpayer (taxable income £80,000) the gain is taxed at the higher rate.*

Examiner's report

Although there were a number of correct answers to part (a), it caused difficulty for many candidates. The main problem was not appreciating that the annual exempt amount should be used, despite a fairly heavy hint to this effect being given in the question.

Part (b) was another well answered section, with many candidates achieving maximum marks.

Note: The examiner's report has been edited to remove comments on elements of the question that have been deleted due to changes to the examination format.

ACCA marking scheme		Marks
(a)	Consideration paid in excess of cost is chargeable	1.0
	Chargeable amount per share	1.0
	Identifying available annual exempt amount	0.5
	Maximum number of shares that can be sold	1.5
		———
		4.0
		———
(b)	**Innocent**	
	Disposal proceeds	0.5
	Cost	1.0
	Capital gains tax	1.5
	Nigel	
	Disposal proceeds	0.5
	Cost	1.0
	Capital gains tax	1.0
	CGT saving	0.5
		———
		6.0
		———
Total		**10.0**
		———

161 MICK STONE (ADAPTED) *Walk in the footsteps of a top tutor*

Key answer tips

This 10 mark question requires the calculation of the chargeable gains arising from the disposal of two different assets by an individual.

In part (a) the calculations must be done assuming that no reliefs are available, and then part (b) requires an explanation of the capital gains tax reliefs that might be available for each disposal. You also need to state what further information you would require to decide if the reliefs are actually available, and whether there would be any restrictions on the amount of relief available. The highlighted words in the answer to part (b) below are key phrases that markers are looking for.

Tutor's top tips

As you read through the question and think about your answer, it makes sense to consider parts (a) and (b) at the same time. However, it is best to present your answer as two separate parts.

(a)   **Chargeable gains – 2016/17**

Tutor's top tips

If an item is not an allowable deduction (like the repair to the floor), then include it in your computation as £0 rather than just leaving it out. If you don't include the item the marker will not know if you have left it out deliberately or not so will not be able to give you a mark.

Freehold warehouse

		£
Disposal proceeds		522,000
Less: Cost		(258,000)
Enhancement expenditure	– Floor	(0)
Chargeable gain		264,000

Tutorial note

The cost of replacing the warehouse's floor is revenue expenditure and is therefore not deductible from proceeds when the warehouse is sold. As a repair, it would have instead been deductible from trading profits when the replacement was made.

Rolling Ltd

	£
Disposal proceeds	3,675,000
Less: Cost (W)	(537,600)
Chargeable gain	3,137,400

Working: Share pool

		Number of shares	Cost £
June 2007	Purchase	500,000	960,000
December 2012	Bonus issue (3:2)		
	(500,000 × 3/2)	750,000	0
		1,250,000	960,000
September 2016	Disposal		
£960,000 × (700,000/1,250,000)		(700,000)	(537,600)
Balance c/f		550,000	422,400

(b)   **Reliefs available**

Tutor's top tips

Think about the conditions for the relevant reliefs to help you decide what extra information you would require in order to establish whether the relief is available.

No calculations are required so do not waste time by including them.

Freehold warehouse

Possible relief

- Rollover relief may be available in respect of the chargeable gain arising on the disposal of the freehold warehouse.

Further information

- The acquisition date of the replacement warehouse is required, since relief will only be available if this is after 19 May 2015 (one year before the date of disposal).

The cost of the replacement warehouse is required, since relief will be restricted if the sale proceeds of £522,000 have not been fully reinvested.

Rolling Ltd

Possible relief

- Entrepreneurs' relief may be available in respect of the chargeable gain arising on the disposal of the shares in Rolling Ltd.

Further information

- Details of Rolling Ltd's share capital are required, since relief will only be available if Mick had the minimum required holding (and voting rights) of 5%.

- Details of any previous entrepreneurs' relief claims made by Mick are required, since there is a lifetime limit of £10 million of gains.

Examiner's report

Part (a) was extremely well answered, with many candidates attaining full marks. The only aspect that consistently caused problems was on the disposal of the freehold warehouse, where expenditure on repairing the floor following a flood should have been treated as revenue expenditure – and therefore not a cost in calculating the chargeable gain.

Part (b) caused a few more problems, with many candidates wasting time writing about reliefs that were not applicable.

ACCA marking scheme			
			Marks
(a)	Mick Stone – Chargeable gains		
	Freehold warehouse		
	Disposal proceeds		0.5
	Cost		0.5
	Revenue expenditure	– Floor	0.5
	Rolling Ltd		
	Disposal proceeds		0.5
	Share pool		
	Purchase		0.5
	Bonus issue		1.0
	Disposal		0.5
			———
			4.0
			———
(b)	Freehold warehouse		
	ROR may be available		1.0
	Acquisition date required		1.0
	Cost of replacement warehouse required		1.0
	Rolling Ltd		
	ER may be available		1.0
	Rolling Ltd's share capital required		1.0
	Previous ER claims required		1.0
			———
			6.0
			———
Total			**10.0**
			———

162 RUBY (ADAPTED) *Walk in the footsteps of a top tutor*

Key answer tips

This 10 mark question tests the calculation of CGT liability and the treatment of two alternative share disposals.

In part (a) you are required to perform a basic CGT liability calculation.

In part (b) you are required to consider the impact on the CGT liability of two alternative share disposals. This is an unusual approach by the F6 examining team but the calculations themselves are straightforward.

(a) **Ruby – Capital gains tax liability 2016/17**

	£
Chargeable gain on investment property	45,800
Less: Annual exempt amount	(11,100)
	34,700

£		
14,185	× 18% (W)	2,553
20,515	× 28%	5,744
34,700		

Capital gains tax liability	8,297

Working: Remaining basic rate band

	£
Basic rate band	32,000
Less: Taxable income	(17,815)
Remaining basic rate band	14,185

Tutor's top tips

Part (a) of this question is straightforward so you should aim to score well in this section.

Note that with only one disposal being made in the tax year, the full AEA is available to reduce the chargeable gain, and the remaining basic rate band can be used to tax some of the taxable gain at 18%.

Remember that different CGT rates apply to a gain on residential property. Gains in the basic rate band are taxed at 18%, rather than the 10% rate used for other gains.

(b) **Disposal of shareholding in Pola Ltd**

	Qualifying for ER £	Not qualifying for ER £
Ordinary shares in Pola Ltd (W1)	37,300	
Residential investment property		45,800
Less: Annual exempt amount	(0)	(11,100)
	————	————
Taxable gains	37,300	34,700
	————	————
(£37,300 at 10%)		3,730
(£34,700 at 28%)		9,716
		————
CGT liability		13,446
		————

Tutorial note

For the purposes of determining the rate of CGT payable the remaining basic rate band of £14,185 is set against the gain qualifying for entrepreneurs' relief of £37,300 even though this has no effect on the 10% rate. So CGT is payable at 28% on the full amount of the residential gain not qualifying for entrepreneurs' relief.

Disposal of shareholding in Aplo plc

	£	£
Ordinary shares in Aplo plc		
Sale proceeds	59,000	
Cost (W2)	(87,200)	
	————	
Capital loss		(28,200)
Chargeable gain on residential investment property		45,800
		————
Net chargeable gains		17,600
Annual exempt amount		(11,100)
		————
Taxable gains		6,500
		————
Capital gains tax liability		
(£6,500 at 18%)		1,170
		————

Workings

(W1) Chargeable gain on ordinary shares in Pola Ltd

	£
Sale proceeds	61,000
Cost	(23,700)
Chargeable gain	37,300

(W2) Cost of shares in Aplo plc

Average of the two quoted prices: (£2.12 + £2.24) × 1/2 = £2.18

£2.18 × 40,000 = £87,200

Examiner's report

Part (a) of the question was well answered, requiring a calculation of the taxpayer's capital gains tax liability for the tax year if the investment property was their only disposal in that tax year.

Part (b) The main problem here was that candidates did not appreciate that both disposals would impact on the capital gains tax payable in respect of the disposal of the investment property. The disposal of the shares in the unquoted trading company (qualifying for entrepreneur's relief) would utilise the remaining basic rate tax band, meaning that the 28% rate was now applicable. The capital loss arising on the disposal of the shares in the quoted trading company would be offset against the chargeable gain on the investment property. Another common problem was the 50p nominal value of the shares in the quoted trading company. This did not impact on the calculation of the capital loss, although many candidates incorrectly divided their cost figure by two.

ACCA marking scheme		
		Marks
(a)	**Ruby – Capital gains tax liability 2016/17**	
	Annual exempt amount	0.5
	Capital gains tax at 18%	1.0
	Capital gains tax at 28%	0.5
		2.0
(b)	**Disposal of shareholding in Pola Ltd**	
	Gain on shareholding in Pola Ltd	1.0
	Gain on residential property	0.5
	AEA	1.0
	Capital gains tax at 10%	1.0
	Capital gains tax at 28%	1.0
	Disposal of shareholding in Aplo plc	
	Cost of shares	1.0
	Gain on shareholding in Aplo plc	1.0
	Gain on residential property	0.5
	AEA	0.5
	Capital gains tax at 18%	0.5
		8.0
Total		**10.0**

163 DALJEET *Walk in the footsteps of a top tutor*

Key answer tips

This 10 mark capital gains tax question tests share disposals, entrepreneurs' relief and the calculation of after tax proceeds. You are required to consider two alternative disposals and decide which one results in higher after tax proceeds.

It is becoming more common for examination questions to require the consideration of alternatives and the comparison of different outcomes so it is important that you practise questions in this style before your examination.

Tutor's top tips

When calculating after tax proceeds, start with the gross proceeds received and deduct any expenses of sale. The most obvious deduction is the tax, but remember to look out for any incidental amounts such as the legal costs in relation to the cottage. This will also be payable out of Daljeet's proceeds, therefore reducing the after tax proceeds available.

(a)   **After-tax proceeds**

	ABC plc shares	**Holiday cottage**
Shares	£	£
Disposal proceeds	100,000	110,000
Less: Selling costs		(1,300)
Less: CGT (W1)(W3)	(3,176)	(9,128)
Net proceeds	96,824	99,572

Daljeet should sell the holiday cottage as this will generate the highest net proceeds.

Tutor's top tips

If a question requires you to make a conclusion based on your workings, there will be credit given for a sensible conclusion based on your workings, even if errors in your workings have led you to a different conclusion from the model answer.

(W1) Disposal of ABC Ltd shares

	£
Disposal proceeds	100,000
Less: Cost (W2)	(57,143)
Chargeable gain	42,857
Less: Annual exempt amount	(11,100)
Taxable gain	31,757
Capital gains tax (£31,757 × 10%)	3,176

Tutorial note

The disposal of the ABC Ltd shares qualifies for entrepreneurs' relief as for the 12 months prior to disposal, the following conditions are met:

- *ABC Ltd is a trading company,*
- *Daljeet is an employee of ABC Ltd, and*
- *Daljeet has a shareholding of ≥ 5%*

(W2) Cost of ABC Ltd shares – share pool

	Number	Cost
		£
Purchase 7 June 2011	1,000	60,000
Rights issue 7 June 2012		
(1,000 × 2/5) (£50 × 400)	400	20,000
	1,400	80,000
Disposal 31 December 2016		
(£80,000 × 1,000/1,400)	(1,000)	(57,143)
Balance c/f	400	22,857

(W3) Disposal of holiday cottage

	£
Disposal proceeds	110,000
Less: Selling costs	(1,300)
	————
Net disposal proceeds	108,700
Less: Cost	(65,000)
Repairs	0
	————
Chargeable gain	43,700
Less: Annual exempt amount	(11,100)
	————
Taxable gain	32,600
	————
Capital gains tax (£32,600 × 28%)	9,128
	————

Tutorial note

The repairs are not an allowable deduction in the CGT computation, as they are a revenue expense.

Daljeet is a higher rate taxpayer and no reliefs are available for this disposal, therefore the gain has been taxed at the higher rate for residential properties of 28%.

(b)   **Inheritance tax**

Inheritance tax is charged on a transfer of value of chargeable property by a chargeable person.   A transfer of value is a gift of any asset which results in a reduction in value of the donor's estate.

Daljeet is going to sell either the ABC Ltd shares, or the holiday cottage at arm's length and receive consideration in return. He does not intend to make a gift of either asset, so there is no transfer of value for inheritance tax purposes.

COMPANIES – CHARGEABLE GAINS

164 FORWARD LTD (ADAPTED)

Key answer tips

This question requires the calculation of the corporation tax liability of a company, however before that can be calculated two chargeable gains need to be calculated.

Remember that companies are entitled to an indexation allowance and that rollover relief for replacement of business assets is a key relief available for companies. No other reliefs are available. Note that the effect of reinvesting in a depreciating asset as in part (b) must be understood as this is an area that is often tested.

The highlighted words in the answer to part (b) below are key phrases that markers are looking for.

(a)   **Corporation tax liability – year ended 31 March 2017**

	£
Trading profit	78,000
Net chargeable gains	
(£30,000 (W1) + £39,064 (W3))	69,064
Taxable total profits	147,064
Corporation tax liability	
FY 2016 (£147,064 × 20%)	29,413
Due date	1 January 2018

Workings

(W1) Freehold office building

	£
Disposal proceeds	290,000
Less: Cost	(148,000)
Unindexed gain	142,000
Less: Indexation allowance	
(261.9 – 152.4)/152.4 = 0.719 × £148,000	(106,412)
Chargeable gain before reliefs	35,588
Less: Roll over relief (W2)	(5,588)
Chargeable gain	30,000

(W2) Rollover relief

The sale proceeds of the office building are not fully reinvested.

The chargeable gain which cannot be rolled over is calculated as follows:

	£
Disposal proceeds	290,000
Less: Reinvested in qualifying business asset	(260,000)
Sale proceeds not reinvested = chargeable now	30,000

The remaining gain of £5,588 (£35,588 − £30,000) can be deferred with a rollover relief claim.

(W3) Ordinary shares in Backward plc

	£
Disposal proceeds	62,500
Less: Cost (W4)	(12,895)
Unindexed gain	49,605
Less: Indexation allowance (£23,436 − £12,895) (W4)	(10,541)
Chargeable gain	39,064

Tutorial note

The gain cannot be rolled over into the acquisition of the shares in Sideways plc as shares are not qualifying assets for the purpose of rollover relief.

(W4) Share pool – Backward plc

		Number	Cost £	Indexed cost £
April 1990	Purchase	9,000	18,000	18,000
Indexation to November 2016 £18,000 × (264.3 − 125.1)/125.1 (do not round indexation factor)				20,029
				38,029
November 2016	Purchase	500	6,500	6,500
		9,500	24,500	44,529
November 2016 Cost × (5,000/9,500)	Disposal	(5,000)	(12,895)	(23,436)
Balance c/f		4,500	11,605	21,093

(b) **Reinvestment in leasehold office building**

- The freehold office building's sale proceeds of £290,000 will be fully reinvested, and so the whole of the gain of £35,588 is eligible for rollover relief.

- The leasehold office building is a depreciating asset, so its base cost will not be adjusted.

- The base cost of the 15 year lease will therefore be its actual cost of £300,000.

- The gain will be deferred until the earliest of:

  - ten years from the date of acquisition of the leasehold building,

  - the date that it is disposed of, or

  - the date that it ceases to be used for trading purposes.

165 LUNA LTD *Walk in the footsteps of a top tutor*

Key answer tips

As this question concerns chargeable gains for companies, be careful to ensure that your answer does not refer to individuals, an annual exempt amount or capital gains tax. A company pays corporation tax on its net chargeable gains and there is no annual exempt amount available for companies.

Part (a) is a deceptively straightforward written part about the indexation allowance and the fact that it cannot create nor increase a capital loss.

The highlighted words in the answer are the key phrases that markers are looking for.

Part (b) requires two calculations in relation to share disposals, which could be attempted in either order.

The first is a straightforward share disposal but potentially time consuming.

The second is more demanding and involves a takeover with mixed consideration, and a gain arising in respect of the cash received.

(a) **Indexation allowance**

Tutor's top tips

The requirement for part (a) is split into two parts so make sure your answer clearly sets out your explanation to each part separately.

- Where a company makes a capital loss, then no indexation allowance is available because it cannot be used to increase a loss.

- Where the indexation allowance is greater than a company's unindexed gain, then the gain is simply reduced to nil because the allowance cannot be used to create a loss.

(b)   **Chargeable gains – year ended 31 March 2017**

Tutor's top tips

In the absence of guidance on the split of marks you should assume equal weighting is given between the two disposals, and allocate your time accordingly.

It would be easy to spend too long on the first calculation you choose to tackle and miss easy marks on the second.

Pluto plc shares

	£
Disposal proceeds	53,400
Less: Cost (W1)	(13,800)
Unindexed gain	39,600
Less: Indexed allowance (£17,092 – £13,800) (W1)	(3,292)
Chargeable gain	36,308

Asteroid plc takeover – gain in respect of cash proceeds received

	£
Cash received on takeover	65,000
Less: Deemed cost (W2)	(19,500)
Chargeable gain	45,500

Tutorial note

On a takeover, no chargeable gain arises in respect of the £1 ordinary shares in Comet plc received as it is a paper for paper transaction. A new share pool is opened with the deemed cost calculated in respect of the shares on takeover as the base cost.

Workings

(W1) Share pool – Pluto plc

	Number	Cost £	Indexed cost £
Purchase June 2009	16,000	36,800	36,800
Add: Indexation to May 2011			
(£36,800 × (235.2 − 213.4)/213.4)			3,759
			40,559
Less: Disposal May 2011			
(£36,800/£40,559 × 10,000/16,000)	(10,000)	(23,000)	(25,349)
	6,000	13,800	15,210
Add: Indexation to November 2016			
(£15,210 × (264.3 − 235.2)/235.2)			1,882
			17,092
Less: Disposal November 2016	(6,000)	(13,800)	(17,092)

Tutorial note

Remember to index the share pool before each operative event (i.e. purchase and sale), and the indexation factor should not be rounded.

(W2) Asteroid plc – takeover consideration and allocation of original cost

Consideration received	MV of takeover consideration £	Allocation of indexed cost £
£1 ordinary shares in Comet plc		
(10,000 × £4.50)	45,000	
£33,000 × (£45,000/£110,000)		13,500
Cash		
(10,000 × £6.50)	65,000	
£33,000 × (£65,000/£110,000)		19,500
	110,000	33,000

Examiner's report

Part (a) All that was required here was a very short statement to the effect that the indexation allowance cannot increase or create a capital loss, but many candidates produced half-page explanations of everything to do with indexation and the use of capital losses.

Part (b) Answers to this section were very mixed. There were many good answers, but other candidates struggled with the workings of the share pool, and the basis of allocating the indexed cost following a takeover. This type of question is where revision question practice is essential, since it will mean that the various rules are understood and also that answers can be laid out as efficiently as possible. There is a standard approach to laying out the workings for a share pool, and candidates are advised to follow this to save confusion.

	ACCA marking scheme	Marks
(a)	Capital loss	1.0
	IA greater than unindexed gain	1.0
		2.0
(b)	**Pluto plc**	
	Disposal proceeds	0.5
	Share pool working	
	– purchase June 2009	0.5
	– indexation June 2009 – May 2011	1.0
	– disposal May 2011	1.0
	– indexation May 2011 – November 2016	1.0
	– disposal November 2016	0.5
	Asteroid plc	
	Disposal proceeds	1.0
	Indexed cost attributable to cash element	2.5
		8.0
Total		**10.0**

Section 8

ANSWERS TO PRACTICE INHERITANCE TAX QUESTIONS

PRACTICE SECTION A OBJECTIVE TEST QUESTIONS

166

	Exempt	Not exempt
On 7 May 2016 he gave 100,000 shares in Lahm Ltd to his wife. The shares have been valued at that date at £500,000	✓	
On 10 August 2016 he gave 50,000 shares in Hummells Ltd to a discretionary trust. The shares have been valued at that date at £75,000		✓
On 6 October 2016 he gave £2,000 to his son on the occasion of his marriage	✓	
On 9 February 2017 he gave £300 to his daughter		✓

The gift to Mario's wife is exempt as the inter spouse exemption applies.

A lifetime transfer up to £5,000 given from parent to child on the occasion of the child's marriage is exempt, so the gift of £2,000 to Mario's son is exempt.

The gift into the trust is a chargeable lifetime transfer and is therefore not exempt.

The gift to Mario's daughter is more than £250 and therefore the small gifts exemption does not apply.

167 D

The gift to Shola's daughter is a potentially exempt transfer. It is not chargeable during lifetime but it does utilise the annual exemption for the current year (2016/17) and the prior year (2015/16).

The gift to the trust is a chargeable lifetime transfer (CLTs). The lifetime inheritance tax on the CLT is £37,500 (W).

Working: CLT 29.12.2016

	£	£
Transfer of value		475,000
NRB at date of gift (2016/17)	325,000	
Less: GCTs in 7 years pre-gift (29.12.2009 – 29.12.2016)	(0)	
	———	(325,000)
		———
Taxable amount		150,000
		———
Lifetime IHT due (£150,000 × 25%) (donor pays tax)		37,500
		———

168 C

		CLT 20.05.2016
		£
Transfer of value		150,000
AE – Current year	(2016/17)	(3,000)
Previous year	(2015/16)	(3,000)
		———
Chargeable amount		144,000
NRB at date of gift		
2016/17	325,000	
Less: GCTs in 7 years pre-gift		
(20.05.2009 – 20.05.2016)	(274,000)	
	———	(51,000)
		———
Taxable amount		93,000
		———
Lifetime IHT due (donor pays tax)		
(£93,000 × 25%)		23,250
		———

169 A

	£	£
CLT 1.5.2016 (2016/17)		
Nil rate band – 2016/17		325,000
GCTs in previous 7 years (1.5.2009 – 1.5.2016)		
2015/16 – To Trust	200,000	
Less: Annual exemption – 2015/16 (W)	(2,000)	
2014/15 (W)	(3,000)	
	———	(195,000)
		———
Remaining nil rate band		130,000
		———

Working: 2015/16 annual exemption available

	£
2015/16 – Gift to nephew (PET but uses AEs)	2,000
Less: Marriage exemption	(1,000)
Less: Annual exemption (2015/16)	(1,000)
	0

170 A

Tutorial note

Option A describes the common inheritance tax planning technique of 'skipping a generation'. This technique can maximise the inheritance available to future generations as a charge to inheritance tax will only arise once, on the passing of the estate residue to Heng's grandchildren. If the residue had been left to Heng's children and they subsequently gifted the assets to their children, two charges to inheritance tax would arise.

This being said, skipping a generation would not reduce Heng's potential inheritance tax liability on death as legacies left to both children and grandchildren are equally chargeable to inheritance tax.

171

	Chargeable amount £
30 November 2009	**A** – £0
15 June 2010	**C** – £347,000

Date of death: 1.2.2017

7 years before: 1.2.2010

PET on 30 November 2009 is more than 7 years before death so no IHT payable on death.

	£
PET 15.6.2010	350,000
Less: Annual exemption – 2010/11	(3,000)
– 2009/10	(0)
Chargeable amount	347,000

Tutorial note

Although the PET made on 30 November 2009 does not become chargeable on death, it will still utilise the annual exemption for the tax year of the gift (2009/10). This annual exemption will therefore not be available to reduce the PET made in the tax year 2010/11 that becomes chargeable on death.

172 A

Tutorial note

The IHT payable on lifetime gifts as a result of death is always paid by the recipient of the gift. The extra tax is due six months after the end of the month of death.

173 A

	£	£
Gross chargeable amount		586,250
NRB (2016/17)	325,000	
Less: GCTs < 7 years before gift (10.11.2004 – 10.11.2011)	(0)	
	————	(325,000)
		————
Taxable amount		261,250
		————
IHT payable @ 40%		104,500
Less: Taper relief		
(10.11.2011 – 16.7.2016) (4 – 5 years before death) (40%)		(41,800)
		————
		62,700
Less: IHT paid in lifetime		(52,250)
		————
IHT payable on death		10,450
		————

174

	Inheritance tax payable
20 February 2006	
22 March 2009	
30 September 2015	✓
24 December 2016	

Date of death: 20.1.2017

7 years before: 20.1.2010

The gifts to the son and the discretionary trust are more than 7 years before death so no IHT is payable as a result of death.

The gift to the daughter is a PET which has become chargeable as a result of death. The available nil rate band is fully used by the CLT (gift to the trust) made in the 7 years before the date of the gift, so there will be an IHT liability on the gift to the daughter.

The gift to the wife is exempt under the inter spouse exemption.

175 B

Tutorial note

An endowment mortgage is not deductible since it is automatically repaid on the owner's death. Repayment and interest-only mortgages are deductible.

A verbal promise to pay a friend's debt is not legally enforceable and therefore not deductible.

Funeral expenses and credit card debts are deductible.

176 D

	£
Value of estate	890,000
Less: Legacy to wife	(260,000)
Legacy to brother	(120,000)
	510,000
Less: Inheritance tax payable	(276,000)
Residue of estate after inheritance tax	234,000

177 £495,000

	£
House (Note)	545,000
Life insurance policy (proceeds received)	350,000
	895,000
Less: Exempt legacy to wife	(400,000)
Gross chargeable estate	495,000

Tutorial note

Endowment mortgages are not deductible as they are automatically repaid on the owner's death.

178   C

	£	£
Gross chargeable estate		
House	400,000	
Less: Repayment mortgage	(85,000)	
	———	315,000
Chattels		70,000
Cash in ISA		20,000
		———
Chargeable estate		405,000
		———

Tutorial note

Gambling debts are not incurred for valuable consideration and are not deductible from the estate.

179   D

Date of death:	20.12.2016
7 years before:	20.12.2009

	£	£
Death estate		
Gross chargeable estate		1,101,000
NRB at death (2016/17)	325,000	
Less: GCTs in 7 years pre-death		
(20.12.2009 – 20.12.2016)	(124,000)	
	———	(201,000)
		———
Taxable amount		900,000
		———
IHT on chargeable estate (£900,000 × 40%)		360,000
		———

180   £114,000

	£
Value of estate before transfer (7,500 × £20)	150,000
Value of estate after transfer (4,500 × £8)	(36,000)
Transfer of value	114,000

181   H

		Additional tax on death		
		15 March 2017	**31 March 2017**	**30 April 2017**
Lifetime tax	**15 March 2013**			
	31 March 2013			
	30 April 2013		✓	

For a CLT made between 6 April and 30 September the lifetime inheritance tax is due by 30 April following the end of the tax year.

The additional tax due on CLTs as a result of death is due 6 months after the end of the month of death.

182

	Pays tax	**Suffers tax**	**Neither pays nor suffers tax**
Sister			✓
Daughter		✓	
Executor	✓		

Inheritance tax due on the death estate is paid by the executors but is suffered/borne by the residual legatee (i.e. the daughter).

183

	True	**False**
An advantage of giving an appreciating asset away during lifetime is that the increase in value up to the date of death will not be subject to inheritance tax	✓	
For capital gains tax purposes lifetime gifts are taxable but gifts on death are not	✓	
On a lifetime gift made more than three years before death, taper relief will reduce the amount of the gift chargeable to inheritance tax on death		✓

Taper relief reduces the **IHT payable on death** provided the donor survives for more than three years following the gift; it does not reduce the chargeable amount on death.

184   D

On Willow's death the available nil rate band (NRB) was £312,000 of which £124,800 was utilised by the legacy to her son. The amount left to Stanley was exempt under the inter spouse exemption. Therefore £187,200 (£312,000 – £124,800) of Willow's NRB was unused.

The unutilised proportion of the NRB is 60% ((£187,200/£312,000) × 100).

	£
Stanley: NRB on death	325,000
Proportion of Willow's unused NRB – elect to transfer to Stanley (£325,000 × 60%)	195,000
Total NRB available to Stanley	520,000

Tutorial note

*The amount of NRB that can be transferred to the surviving spouse is based on the **proportion** of the NRB unused on the first death. This proportion is applied to the NRB at the date of death of the surviving spouse.*

PRACTICE SECTION B OBJECTIVE TEST QUESTIONS

185   JIMMY (ADAPTED)   *Walk in the footsteps of a top tutor*

Key answer tips

This is a straightforward IHT question with two lifetime gifts, (one PET and one CLT) and a simple estate.

1   C

	PET 2 August 2012		CLT 14 November 2012	
	£	£		£
Transfer of value	5,000			800,000
Less: Marriage exemption	(2,500)			
AE – 2012/13	(2,500)			(500)
– 2011/12 b/f	(0)			(3,000)
Chargeable amount	0			796,500

Tutorial note

A lifetime transfer made 'in consideration of a marriage' (or registration of a civil partnership) is exempt up to the following maximum limits:

- £5,000 by a parent

- £2,500 by a grandparent or remoter ancestor

- £2,500 by a party to the marriage or civil partnership (e.g. from the groom to the bride)

- £1,000 by anyone else.

The annual exemption (AE):

- exempts the first £3,000 of lifetime transfers in any one tax year

- is applied chronologically to the first gift in the tax year, then (if there is any left) the second gift and so on

- must be applied to the first gift each year, even if the first gift is a PET and never becomes chargeable.

Any unused AE:

- may be carried forward to the next year

- however, it can be carried forward for one year only, and

- can only be used after the current year's AE.

- If other exemptions are available they are given before the AE.

2   C

Tutorial note

If the donor agrees to pay the tax:

- The gift is referred to as a net gift.

- As a result of the gift, their estate is being reduced by:

  – the value of the gift, and

  – the associated tax payable on the gift.

- Accordingly the amount of the gift needs to be 'grossed up' to include the tax that the donor has to pay.

- The appropriate rate of tax is therefore 25% (i.e. 20/80ths of the net gift).

The date of payment of lifetime IHT depends on the date of the gift:

Date of CLT	Due date of payment
6 April to 30 September	30 April in the following year
1 October to 5 April	Six months after the end of the month of the CLT

3 D

Tutorial note

Taper relief reduces the death tax payable, before the deduction of the lifetime tax paid. It does not reduce the taxable amount.

Jimmy survived between 4 and 5 years following his gift to the trust on 14 November 2012. Therefore taper relief will be applied to the inheritance tax due at a rate of 40%.

4 A

Death estate

	£
Property	260,000
Proceeds of life assurance policy	210,000
Gross chargeable estate	470,000

Tutorial note

The main residence is a chargeable asset for IHT purposes.

When the deceased has a life assurance policy on their own life, the proceeds of that policy are included in the death estate, rather than the market value of the policy at the date of death.

Debts are deductible from a death estate if they were outstanding at the date of death, and have been incurred for valuable consideration. A promise to pay money to another person e.g. Jimmy's godson, is not legally enforceable and therefore is not deductible from Jimmy's chargeable estate.

5   D

Tutorial note

Habitual lifetime gifts out of income are exempt under the normal expenditure out of income exemption.

Gifts are accumulated for seven years. Where the value of a gift, plus those accumulated in the previous seven years does not exceed the nil rate band, currently £325,000, then no IHT is payable. The availability of annual exemptions could mean that more than £325,000 is exempt over a seven year period.

The small gifts exemption is only available on lifetime gifts.

The value of a gift is frozen at the date of the gift. So any increase in the value of an appreciating asset up to the date of death is not taxed. If the gift is made more than seven years before death the gift will either be exempt if it is a PET or there will be no further IHT on death if it is a CLT.

186   NING GAO (ADAPTED)   *Walk in the footsteps of a top tutor*

Key answer tips

This inheritance tax case question covers a diverse range of topics. The first question tests the basic calculation of the value of a gift after exemptions. The second question tests the deductibility of debts in the death estate. The third question uses higher skills to identify the tax saving resulting from a further year between gifts and death.

The final two questions test the diminution in value principle and then the transfer of a spouse's unused nil rate band.

1   B

		£
Transfer of value		350,000
Less:	Marriage exemption	(5,000)
	AE 2009/10	(3,000)
	AE 2008/09 – already used.	0
Gross chargeable amount		342,000

2   A

Tutorial note

Debts are deductible if they:

*   *were outstanding at the date of death, and*

*   *had been incurred for valuable consideration, or were imposed by law (i.e. legally enforceable debts).*

3   D

The value of Ning's chargeable estate after the exempt legacy to her husband is £250,000 (£750,000 – £500,000). The nil rate band at death of £325,000 is fully used by the PET to the son of £342,000 which has become chargeable as a result of death within seven years. The IHT payable if Ning dies on 15 April 2016 is £100,000 (£250,000 × 40%).

If Ning had died a year later the PET would not have become chargeable and the nil rate band would have been available to fully cover Ning's death estate. The IHT payable on her estate would have been reduced by £100,000 to £0.

4   C

	£
Value of estate before transfer (5,500 × £25)	137,500
Less: Value of estate after transfer (4,125 × £12)	(49,500)
Transfer of value	88,000

Tutorial note

The transfer of value is the 'loss to the donor' or the 'diminution in the value' of the donor's estate.

In the case of shares, where a controlling shareholding has a higher value per shares than a minority holding, this will not be the same as the value of the asset received by the donee, which in this case would be £6,875 (1,375 × £5).

5   C

Tutorial note

*The executors of the **surviving** spouse or civil partner must claim the unutilised proportion of NRB by submitting the IHT return by the later of:*

- *2 years of the second death, or*

- *3 months of the executors starting to act.*

This increased NRB can be used against any lifetime gifts taxable as a result of the donor's death and the death estate. Note however, that it cannot be used against lifetime tax on chargeable lifetime transfers.

There is no requirement for the second spouse to die within a set time period after the first spouse.

187   TOM (ADAPTED) *Walk in the footsteps of a top tutor*

Key answer tips

This is a typical IHT question covering various aspects of lifetime gifts and then the death estate. The question doesn't test any peripheral topics and therefore should be relatively straightforward.

1   C

	£	£
Chargeable amount (after all exemptions)		450,000
NRB at date of gift	325,000	
Less: GCTs < 7 years before gift	(0)	
NRB available		(325,000)
Taxable amount		125,000
IHT payable × 25%		31,250
Gross chargeable amount (£450,000 + £31,250)		481,250

2   A

	PETs **20 Dec 2008**	CLT **20 Feb 2010**
	£	£
Transfer of value	5,900	
Less: AE – 2008/09	(3,000)	
– 2007/08 b/f	(2,900)	
Less: AE – 2009/10		(3,000)
– 2008/09 b/f		0

Tutorial note

The AE:

–   *exempts the first £3,000 of lifetime transfers in any one tax year*

–   *is applied chronologically to the first gift in the tax year, then (if there is any left) the second gift and so on*

–   *must be applied to the first gift each year, even if the first gift is a PET and never becomes chargeable.*

Any unused AE can only be carried forward one tax year.

---

3   A

4   A

	£
Racehorse	150,000
Cash	40,000
Main residence	850,000
Less: Repayment mortgage	(500,000)
	540,000

Tutor top tips

Gambling winnings and wasting chattels (e.g. a racehorse) are exempt assets for the purposes of capital gains tax. It is common for these types of assets to be included in a death estate in an examination question to test if you have remembered that there are no exempt assets for inheritance tax. Therefore, it is important that you have a clear understanding of what assets or income are exempt for each tax!

---

5   **B**

	£	£
Value of estate		2,250,000
NRB at death	325,000	
Less: GCTs in previous 7 years > £325,000 (Note)	(325,000)	
NRB available		(0)
Taxable amount		2,250,000
IHT × 40%		900,000

Tutorial note

There is no nil rate band remaining as the gross chargeable transfer on 20 February 2010, which is within the seven years before death, is greater than £325,000.

IHT as a result of death is due on the earlier of:

* *six months after the end of the month of death, or*

* *on delivery of the account of the estate assets to HMRC.*

188   AFIYA (ADAPTED) *Walk in the footsteps of a top tutor*

Key answer tips

This IHT question starts by looking at two lifetime gifts, (one PET and one CLT). It then moves on to consider what is included in the death estate. The last two questions cover the transfer of the unused nil rate band from the spouse and finally the due dates of lifetime tax and tax on the death estate.

1   **C**

Working: PET – 14 September 2011

	£
Value of shares held before the transfer (8,000 × £8)	64,000
Less: Value of shares held after the transfer (1,500 × £3)	(4,500)
Transfer of value	59,500
Less: AE – 2011/12	(3,000)
– 2010/11	(3,000)
Gross chargeable transfer	53,500

Tutorial note

The loss to the donor (or diminution in value) principle applies when calculating the transfer of value for IHT purposes. This is particularly relevant when valuing shares where a majority shareholding has a higher value per share than a minority shareholding in a company.

The transfer of value is the amount by which Afiya's estate has diminished and not the market value of the asset gifted.

Prior to the transfer Afiya had 8,000 shares (an 80% (8,000/10,000) shareholding) in the company and the shares are valued at £8 per share.

After the transfer Afiya owns 1,500 shares (a 15% shareholding) and the shares are valued at £3 per share.

2   A

Working: CLT – 27 January 2016

	£	£
Transfer of value (after all exemptions)		400,000
NRB at date of gift	325,000	
Less: GCTs in last 7 years (CLTs only)	(120,000)	
	————	(205,000)
		————
Taxable amount		195,000
		————
Lifetime IHT (donor pays tax)	(× 25%)	48,750
		————

Tutorial note

When calculating lifetime tax on a CLT, the available nil rate band is reduced by the value of CLTs in the previous seven years. PETs are ignored even if they subsequently become chargeable.

3   **A, B, D and E**

Tutorial note

Debts are only deductible if they were outstanding at the date of death and had been incurred for valuable consideration (i.e. not gambling debts) or were imposed by law.

Endowment mortgages are not deductible as the endowment element of the policy should cover repayment of the mortgage.

4   **A**

Husband's death estate

	£	£
NRB at death		312,000
Chargeable estate (£200 + £46,600)		(46,800)
Unused NRB		265,200
% of NRB at death £265,200/£312,000 = 85%		
Additional NRB (£325,000 × 85%)		276,250

Tutorial note

*The small gifts exemption only applies to **lifetime** gifts.*

5

Lifetime tax on gift to trust	**Tax on estate**
31 July 2016	31 May 2017

Tutorial note

The due date for the lifetime IHT on the CLT to the trust is due on 31 July 2016, being six months from the end of the month in which the gift was made.

The due date for the IHT on the estate is 31 May 2017, being six months after the end of the month in which Afiya died.

PRACTICE SECTION C CONSTRUCTED RESPONSE QUESTIONS

189 ETHEL AND BLU (ADAPTED) *Walk in the footsteps of a top tutor*

Key answer tips

This question has two distinct parts covering quite different topics. It is unlikely that IHT will be combined with the cash basis in the real examination; however this question provides useful revision of some elements of these topics.

Part (a) tested a topic which is no longer in the syllabus and has therefore been replaced with a question testing the cash accounting and flat rate basis rules. The highlighted words are key phrases that markers are looking for.

Part (b) was a very straightforward IHT question requiring the calculation of the lifetime and death tax on one CLT.

Tutor's top tips

You do not have to answer this question in the order set. Provided you start each part on a separate page and clearly indicate which part you are answering, you can answer in any order. Hence you might prefer to start with part (b) on IHT as this may be more familiar.

However, do take care when attempting a question out of order, as sometimes the answer to part (a) is required in part (b), and so on. This is clearly not the case in this question as each part involves a different individual.

(a) **Ethel Brown – Notes on cash accounting and flat rate expense adjustments**

    (1) **Business premises used partly for private purposes**

        • The total payments of £25,000 can be deducted from the trading profit but the flat rate private use adjustment of £7,800 must be added to the trading profit for tax purposes.

        • A net deduction from trading profits of £17,200 can therefore be claimed for tax purposes.

(2) **Car used for private and business purposes**

- The cash payments in respect of the purchase and running costs of the car totalling £17,000 (£14,000 + £3,000) are not deductible from the trading profit and capital allowances are not available.

- Instead a tax deduction for the car is allowed using the approved mileage allowances for the business mileage as follows:

	£
First 10,000 miles at 45p/mile	4,500
1,000 miles at 25p/mile	250
	———
Allowable deduction	4,750
	———

(3) **Kitchen equipment**

- A tax deduction can be claimed from the trading profits for the full cost of the kitchen equipment when the invoice is paid.

- No tax deduction is therefore allowed in the accounts for the year to 5 April 2017 but Ethel will obtain a tax deduction of £350 from trading profits in the following year to 5 April 2018.

Tutorial note

1   The question states that Ethel opts to use the cash basis and the flat rate expense adjustments. Note that the examining team have stated that whilst the use of flat rate expenses is optional it should be assumed in any question involving the cash basis that flat rate expenses are claimed.

2   Where a business premises is used partly for private purposes (e.g. a bed and breakfast or small care home), a private use adjustment must be made for tax purposes if the full cost of food, utilities and other household goods have been included in the accounts. The HMRC flat rate private use adjustments are based on the number of occupants and will be provided as part of the question in the examination. Any information regarding actual private expenses is irrelevant.

3   The flat rate expense adjustment in respect of cars is based on the HMRC approved mileage allowances. These are the same rates that are used to calculate the taxable benefit/allowable deduction where employees use their own cars for business purposes. The rates are given in the tax tables provided in the examination.

4   Under the cash basis a 100% trading deduction is given for the acquisition cost of items of plant and machinery (other than cars) rather than capital allowances.

(b) **Blue Reddy**

Inheritance tax computation

Lifetime tax on lifetime gift – 15 January 2017

	£	£
Value of shares held before the transfer (300,000 × £4)		1,200,000
Value of shares held after the transfer (100,000 × £2)		(200,000)
Transfer of value (Note 1)		1,000,000
Less: AE (ignore per question)		(0)
Chargeable transfer (Net)		1,000,000
NRB at time of gift	325,000	
GCTs in 7 years pre gift (15.1.2010 – 15.1.2017)	(0)	
		(325,000)
Taxable amount		675,000
IHT liability (£675,000 × 25%) (Note 2)		168,750
Gross chargeable transfer c/f (£1,000,000 + £168,750)		1,168,750

Additional death tax due on lifetime gift – 15 January 2017 (assuming death occurs 31 May 2021)

	£	£
Gross chargeable transfer		1,168,750
NRB at time of death	325,000	
GCTs in 7 years pre death (31.5.2014 – 31.5.2021)	(0)	
		(325,000)
Taxable amount		843,750
IHT liability (£843,750 × 40%)		337,500
Less: Taper relief		
(15.1.2017 – 31.5.2021) (4 – 5 years) (40%)		(135,000)
		202,500
Less: Lifetime IHT paid		(168,750)
Additional IHT payable on death		33,750

Tutorial note

1   The transfer of value is calculated by reference to the diminution in the value of the donor's estate. The value of the 40% shareholding transferred (i.e. 200,000 shares at £3 for a 40% shareholding) is irrelevant for IHT purposes. This is particularly relevant in this situation, where company shares are involved, where the diminution in value of Blu's estate from reducing his interest in the company from 60% to 20% (i.e. £1,000,000) is far greater than valuing a 40% shareholding in isolation (£600,000).

2   Remember that where the donor pays the tax the appropriate tax rate is 25% as their estate has been diminished not just by the gift but also by the IHT paid. The gross chargeable transfer is the value of the gift plus the tax paid.

Examiner's report

Candidates were helped in part (b) by being told to ignore annual exemptions, but many also ignored these instructions.

They were not penalised for this, but it made the calculations a bit more complicated than was necessary.

When calculating the additional liability arising on death many candidates had problems computing the amount of brought forward gross chargeable transfer, and taper relief was often calculated and deducted at the wrong point in the computation.

Candidates should also appreciate that examinations are not quite the same as real life.

With a six mark section it should be obvious that the value of the transfer was more than the nil rate band of £325,000 – many candidates calculating the transfer as (200,000 × £1) = £200,000. Using any of the other values would have enabled some marks to be obtained.

However, there were many perfect answers to part (b), with the six marks obtained often being the difference between a pass and a fail.

Note: The examiner's report has been edited to remove comments on elements of the question that have been deleted due to changes to the examination format.

ACCA marking scheme		Marks
(a)	**Business premises used for private purposes**	
	Food etc. payments deductible	0.5
	Less £7,800 flat rate private use adjustment	0.5
	Car	
	Payments re purchase and running costs not deductible	0.5
	No capital allowances available	0.5
	Calculation of deductible amount	1.0
	Equipment	
	Cost of acquisition 100% trading deduction	0.5
	Deductible when payment made i.e. following accounting period	0.5
		4.0
(b)	**Lifetime transfer**	
	Value transferred	2.0
	IHT liability	1.5
	Additional liability arising on death	
	Gross chargeable transfer	0.5
	IHT liability	0.5
	Taper relief	1.0
	IHT already paid	0.5
		6.0
Total		**10.0**

190 ROSIE AND TOM (ADAPTED) *Walk in the footsteps of a top tutor*

Key answer tips

This question involves two separate topics. The requirements and mark allocation are very clear. Make sure that you allocate your time in relation to the mark allocation. It is unlikely that IHT will be combined with pensions in the real examination; however this question provides useful revision of some elements of these topics.

Part (a) tests the income tax implications personal pension contributions. Relief for pension contributions is a key area of the syllabus that is tested regularly.

Part (b) is a straightforward IHT question testing the fundamentals of IHT. It deals with the lifetime tax payable on a chargeable lifetime gift.

The highlighted words are key phrases that markers are looking for.

(a)   **Rosie Rohan – Personal pension contributions**

Tutor's top tips

Read the question carefully – there are three parts to this requirement. You must deal with the amount of annual allowance available, how tax relief is given for contributions and the tax implications of making excess contributions. Make sure you address them all and do not spend too long on one part at the expense of another.

*Note that the question is concerned with **personal pension scheme** contributions and this will affect your answer on how tax relief is given for contributions.*

Also note that the amount of the annual allowance, minimum allowance and the income limit are given in the table of Tax Rates and Allowances provided in the examination.

Annual allowances

- Rosie was a member of a pension scheme for the tax year 2015/16, so the full annual allowance of £40,000 for that year is available.

- She has unused allowances of £83,000 for the tax year 2016/17 as follows:

		£
2013/14	(£50,000 – £41,000)	9,000
2014/15	(£40,000 – £16,000)	24,000
2015/16		40,000
2016/17	(W)	10,000
		83,000

Annual allowance	£	£
2016/17		40,000
Adjusted income	220,000	
Income limit	(150,000)	
Excess income	70,000	
50% × excess	35,000	
Less: 50% excess income	Restricted	(30,000)
Reduced allowance		10,000

Tutor's top tips

The annual allowance for the tax year 2016/17 is reduced by £1 for every £2 of adjusted income in excess of the income limit of £150,000. The minimum tapered annual allowance is £10,000, which is why the reduction was restricted when calculating Rosie's available allowance for the tax year 2016/17.

Tax relief

- Personal pension contributions are made net of basic rate tax.
- Higher and additional rate tax relief will be given by extending Rosie's basic and higher rate tax bands for the tax year 2016/17 by the gross amount of the pension contributions.

Excess contributions

- Rosie's contributions of £90,000 in 2016/17 exceed the available annual allowances of £83,000 by £7,000.
- If pension contributions are made in excess of the available annual allowances, then there will be an annual allowance charge.
- This charge will be subject to income tax at Rosie's marginal rate(s) of income tax.

(b)   **Tom Tirith**

Tutor's top tips

The only difference between the two computations in this part will be the rate of tax paid on the gift. Remember that if Tom pays the tax his estate will be reduced by the value of the gift and the associated tax – this is reflected in the rate of tax paid on the gift.

(1)   **Inheritance tax (IHT) paid by donee (the trust)**

	£	£
Value transferred		450,000
Annual exemption – 2016/17		(3,000)
– 2015/16		0
		————
Gross chargeable transfer		447,000
NRB at date of gift	325,000	
Less: GCTs < 7 years before gift	(0)	
	————	
NRB available		(325,000)
		————
Taxable amount		122,000
		————
IHT payable × 20%		24,400
		————

IHT paid by donor (Tom)

	£
Taxable amount (as above)	122,000
IHT payable × 25%	30,500
Gross chargeable transfer (£447,000 + £30,500)	477,500

Tutorial note

The potentially exempt transfer made on 20 December 2015 utilises the annual exemption for the tax year 2015/16 but does not use any of the nil rate band as Tom is still alive.

(2) **Effect of gift on 20 December 2015 being to a trust**

- If Tom had made a gift to a trust rather than to his daughter, it would have been a chargeable lifetime transfer rather than a potentially exempt transfer.

- No inheritance tax would be payable on the gift on 20 December 2015, as it is below the nil rate band for the tax year 2015/16.

- It would therefore reduce the nil rate band available for the chargeable lifetime transfer on 20 February 2017, resulting in more of the second gift being chargeable to inheritance tax in Tom's lifetime.

Examiner's report

Part (a) was generally well answered, with many candidates correctly calculating the amount of available annual allowances. However, it was often not appreciated that basic rate tax relief is given by contributions being made net, and also that an annual allowance charge is subject to tax at the taxpayer's marginal rate.

Most candidates answered part (b)(i) extremely well, often gaining all of the available marks. However, the PET was sometimes incorrectly included in the workings for the first requirement – not only losing marks, but also complicating the otherwise straightforward calculations.

Note: *The examiner's report has been edited to remove comments on elements of the question that have been deleted due to changes to the examination format.*

ACCA marking scheme			Marks
(a)	Rosie Rohan		
	Annual allowances		
	Full allowance for 2015/16 as member of pension scheme		0.5
	Calculation of total unused allowances		3.0
	Excess contributions		0.5
	Annual allowance charge		0.5
	Taxed at marginal rate of income tax		0.5
			───
			5.0
			───
(b)	Tom Tirith		
	(1)	Inheritance tax (IHT) paid by donee (the trust)	
		Annual exemption	0.5
		IHT liability	1.0
		IHT paid by donor (Tom)	
		IHT liability	0.5
		Gross chargeable transfer	1.0
			───
			3.0
			───
	(2)	Gift would be a CLT rather than a PET	0.5
		No IHT due as bellow NRB	0.5
		Reduces NRB available for second CLT and increases IHT	1.0
			───
			2.0
			───
Total			10.0
			───

191 PERE JONES (ADAPTED) *Walk in the footsteps of a top tutor*

Key answer tips

This 10-mark question involved knowledge of two taxes: inheritance tax (IHT) and capital gains tax.

Part (a) required a calculation of the IHT that would be payable on a PET and the estate, as a result of death. This involved a straightforward IHT computation with the only trickier points being remembering to include taper relief and including it in the correct place in the computation.

Part (b) required a calculation of an individual's capital gains tax liability. The key skill was in distinguishing between capital and revenue income/expenditure.

(a)   **Pere Jones**

Inheritance tax (IHT) arising on death

Lifetime transfer – 23 August 2011

	£	£
Value transferred		420,000
Less: Marriage exemption		(5,000)
Annual exemptions – 2011/12		(3,000)
– 2010/11		(3,000)
Potentially exempt transfer		409,000
NRB at death	325,000	
Less: GCTs in previous 7 years	(0)	
NRB available		(325,000)
Taxable amount		84,000
IHT × 40%		33,600
Less: Taper relief (23.8.2011 to 20.3.2017) (5 – 6 years) (60%)		(20,160)
Less: Lifetime IHT paid (£0 – as it is a PET)		(0)
IHT payable		13,440

Tutorial note

The gift is a potentially exempt transfer that becomes chargeable as a result of Pere dying within seven years of making it.

Pere died more than five but less than six years after the date of the gift so taper relief of 60% is available. The taper relief table is given in the Tax Rates and Allowances provided in the examination.

Death estate

	£
Value of estate	880,000
Less: Inter spouse exemption (£880,000 ÷ 2)	(440,000)
Chargeable estate	440,000
IHT liability at 40% (Note)	176,000

Tutorial note

There is no nil rate band available to set against the death estate as it has been fully utilised against the lifetime gift to Phil, which was within seven years of Pere's death.

(b) **Phil Jones**

Capital gains tax computation – 2016/17

	£
House	
Disposal proceeds	504,000
Less: Incidental costs of disposal	(8,600)
Net disposal proceeds	495,400
Less: Cost	(420,000)
Enhancement expenditure (boundary wall)	(5,300)
Replacement of chimney (Note 1)	0
Chargeable gain	70,100
Less: Annual exempt amount	(11,100)
Taxable gain	59,000
Capital gains tax liability	
(£59,000 × 28%) (Note 2)	16,520

Tutorial note

1 *The cost of replacing the property's chimney is revenue expenditure as the chimney is a subsidiary part of the house. The cost of the new boundary wall is capital expenditure as the wall is a separate, distinct, entity.*

2 *Phil is a higher rate taxpayer as he has earnings from employment of £80,000 in the tax year 2016/17. He therefore has no basic rate band remaining and all of his chargeable gain on residential property is taxable at the higher rate of 28%.*

Examiner's report

Part (a) was generally very well answered, with many candidates achieving maximum marks. The only aspect that consistently caused problems was taper relief, with either the incorrect rate being used or relief being given at the wrong point in the computation.

Note: *The examiner's report has been edited to remove comments on elements of the question that have been deleted due to changes to the examination format.*

ACCA marking scheme		Marks
(a) Lifetime transfer – 23 August 2011		
Marriage exemption		1.0
Annual exemptions 2011/12		0.5
2010/11		0.5
Potentially exempt transfer		0.5
Nil rate band		0.5
IHT liability at 40%		0.5
Taper relief		1.0
Death estate		
Spouse exemption		1.0
IHT liability at 40%		0.5
		6.0
(b) **Capital gains tax**		
Disposal proceeds		0.5
Cost		1.0
Enhancement expenditure		1.0
Incidental costs of disposal		0.5
Annual exempt amount		0.5
CGT at 28%		0.5
		4.0
Total		10.0

192 KENDRA OLDER *Walk in the footsteps of a top tutor*

Key answer tips

This question is primarily about inheritance tax, although you are also required to consider the capital gains tax implications of a gift in part (b). It can be daunting when a question requires you to think about two different taxes, and the best way to approach it is to decide on your answer for one tax, and then think about the second tax independently.

Part (b) is a written requirement. The highlighted words in the answer to part (b) are key phrases that markers are looking for.

(a) **Kendra Older – Inheritance tax arising on death**

Tutor's top tips

You may find it helpful to draw a timeline showing the lifetime gifts, the assumed date of death and the date seven years prior to death to help you visualise the scenario.

Lifetime transfer within seven years of death

Date of death:	31 March 2017
7 years before:	31 March 2010

Therefore only the PET on 5 October 2015 becomes chargeable on death.

PET – 5 October 2015

		£
Transfer of value		253,000
Less: Annual exemptions 2015/16		(3,000)
2014/15 b/f		(3,000)
		————
Gross chargeable transfer		247,000
NRB available (W1)		(185,000)
		————
Taxable amount		62,000
		————
IHT payable (£62,000 × 40%)		24,800
Less: Taper relief (< 3 years before death)		(0)
Lifetime IHT paid (£0 as a PET)		(0)
		————
		24,800
		————

Tutor's top tips

Do not be put off by the fact that the question includes the nil rate bands for the tax years 2009/10 and 2015/16. These are not needed in your answer.

The 2009/10 figure is not needed as the question states that there is no inheritance tax on the CLT on 20 June 2009 and we are given the gross chargeable transfer value of the gift.

The 2015/16 figure is not needed because the inheritance tax on a PET is always calculated using the nil rate band for the year of death (2016/17 in this case) and not the year of the gift. In this case the nil rate bands for the year of the gift and at death are the same, but this will not always be the case so you do need to remember this rule.

Death estate

	£	£
Property		970,000
Proceeds of life assurance policy		225,000
Gross chargeable estate		1,195,000
Less: Nil rate band on death (31 March 2017)	325,000	
GCTs in 7 years before death		
(31.3.2010 – 31.3.2017)	(247,000)	
		(78,000)
Taxable amount		1,117,000
IHT payable (£1,117,000 × 40%)		446,800

Tutorial note

The chargeable lifetime transfer made on 20 June 2009 is not relevant when calculating the inheritance tax on the death estate as it was made more than seven years before the date of Kendra's assumed death on 31 March 2017. Only the potentially exempt transfer made on 5 October 2015 is taken into account, and this utilises £247,000 of the nil rate band for the tax year 2016/17.

Working: Potentially exempt transfer

	£
Nil rate band on death (31 March 2017)	325,000
Less: GCTs in 7 years before gift	
(5.10.2008 – 5.10.2015)	
CLT – 20 June 2009	
Gross chargeable transfer value	(140,000)
Nil rate band available	185,000

Tutorial note

You are given the gross chargeable transfer value of the CLT on 20 June 2009. This figure is after the deduction of any exemptions. So this figure can simply be deducted from the nil rate band available to the PET without any further calculations.

(a)   Immediate lifetime gift of property

Tutor's top tips

It is important to leave sufficient time to address the written parts of questions. It is easy to get caught up with the computational parts, but often written elements provide easy marks.

This part is asking you to think about the advantages of a death gift compared to a lifetime gift. Lifetime gifts can be advantageous if the donor lives for 7 years after the PET is made as then no inheritance tax will be payable but this is not the case here.

With three marks available it is always best to aim to make three good points. However, in this question it may be difficult to think of three points to include and the mark scheme actually allocated 1.5 marks to the two main points.

- As the property is not expected to increase in value in the near future, there is no inheritance tax benefit in making a lifetime gift.

- Kendra would need to live for three more years for taper relief to be available.

- Also, a lifetime gift would result in a capital gains tax liability of £48,720 (£174,000 at 28%) in the tax year 2016/17, whereas a transfer on death would be an exempt disposal.

Examiner's report

Part (a) was generally very well answered. Some candidates did not appreciate that the chargeable gain was irrelevant to this section of the question given that the property was not disposed of. Also, the valuation of the life assurance policy sometimes caused problems, and one common mistake was to only include the difference between the open market value and the proceeds.

Very few candidates were able to correctly answer part (b), with the main problem being the lack of appreciation that there was no IHT advantage to making a lifetime gift. This was because Kendra would not live long enough to benefit from taper relief, and also because the property's value was not going to change. Even when CGT was mentioned, most candidates did not realise that holding the property until death would eliminate any liability.

			Marks
ACCA marking scheme			
(a)	PET – 5 October 2015		
	Transfer of value		0.5
	Annual exemptions – 2015/16		0.5
	– 2014/15		0.5
	Available nil rate band		
	Nil rate band on death		0.5
	CLT – 20 June 2009		0.5
	IHT payable		1.0
	Death estate		
	Property		0.5
	Proceeds of life assurance policy		1.0
	Nil rate band available		1.5
	Inheritance tax liability at 40%		0.5
			────
			7.0
			────
(b)	No IHT benefit		1.5
	CGT liability arises		1.5
			────
			3.0
			────
Total			**10.0**
			────

193 JAMES *Walk in the footsteps of a top tutor*

Key answer tips

Part (a) for six marks was a standard IHT question requiring the calculation of the tax payable on two lifetime gifts and the death estate as a result of the donor's death. This part also tested the knowledge of who is responsible for making the payments of IHT on both the lifetime gifts and the death estate.

Parts (b) and (c) involved basic IHT planning – this had to be applied to the scenario.

Tutor's top tips

The focus of this question was on lifetime gifts. Don't be put off by the fact there are three lifetime gifts made by the donor in the question.

Inheritance tax requires you to deal with the gifts in chronological order. Start with the earliest gift and apply any available exemptions. You can then consider which gifts will be subject to inheritance tax on the donor's death; any gifts more than seven years prior to the donor's death will not be subject to IHT on death.

(a)   **James – Inheritance tax arising on death**

Lifetime transfers within seven years of death
14 May 2015

		£
Value transferred		420,000
Annual exemptions	2015/16	(3,000)
	2014/15	(3,000)
		_____
Potentially exempt transfer		414,000
		_____

Inheritance tax liability	£296,000 (W) at nil%	0
	£118,000 at 40%	47,200
		_____
		47,200
		_____

James' daughter will be responsible for paying the inheritance tax of £47,200.

2 August 2015

	£
Chargeable lifetime transfer	260,000
	_____
Inheritance tax liability £260,000 at 40% (no nil rate band remaining)	104,000
	_____

The trust will be responsible for paying the inheritance tax of £104,000.

Death estate

	£
Chargeable estate	870,000
	_____
Inheritance tax liability £870,000 at 40% (no nil rate band remaining)	348,000
	_____

The personal representatives of James' estate will be responsible for paying the inheritance tax of £348,000.

Working – Available nil rate band

		£	£
Nil rate band			325,000
Chargeable lifetime transfer 9 October 2009			
Value transferred		35,000	
Annual exemptions	2009/10	(3,000)	
	2008/09	(3,000)	
		_____	
			(29,000)
			_____
			296,000
			_____

Tutorial notes

The gift in October 2009 was made more than seven years before the donor's death and as such there was no IHT due as a result of James' death. This was a gift into a trust however, which means it was chargeable to IHT immediately. As this gift was within 7 years of the next two lifetime gift, the nil rate band available to these gifts was reduced accordingly.

(b)   Skipping a generation avoids a further charge to inheritance tax when the children die. Gifts will then only be taxed once before being inherited by the grandchildren, rather than twice

(c)   (1)   Even if the donor does not survive for seven years, taper relief will reduce the amount of IHT payable after three years.

        (2)   The value of potentially exempt transfers and chargeable lifetime transfers are fixed at the time they are made.

        (3)   James therefore saved inheritance tax of £20,000 ((£310,000 − £260,000) at 40%) by making the lifetime gift of property.

Examiner's report

This question was on inheritance tax (IHT), and candidates found this to be a challenging area.

The requirement for part (a) was to calculate the IHT payable as a result of a taxpayer's death, and to state who was responsible for paying the tax. The taxpayer had made (1) a chargeable lifetime transfer (more than seven years before death), (2) a potentially exempt transfer and (3) another chargeable lifetime transfer. A quick review of the information given should have indicated that no lifetime tax would have been paid (this fact was actually stated in respect of the second chargeable lifetime transfer) and that taper relief was not relevant (given that none of the gifts were between four and seven years of death). However, many candidates dedicated a lot of time to establishing this. Candidates should read through the question carefully before they begin their calculations.

Part (b) required an explanation as to why it might have been beneficial if the taxpayer had left a portion of their estate to grandchildren rather than to children. This aspect was well answered, with most candidates appreciating the basic IHT planning of avoiding a double charge to tax.

The IHT planning in part (c) was less well understood. It was necessary to explain why it might be advantageous to make lifetime gifts even when such gifts are made within seven years of death. The main advantage here is that the value of the gift is fixed at the time it is made, so no IHT is payable on the increase in value between making the gift and the time of death. Taper relief may also be available.

ACCA marking scheme		Marks
(a)	PET – 14 May 2015	
	Annual exemptions – 2015/16	0.5
	– 2014/15	0.5
	Nil rate band £325,000	0.5
	Less: CLT – AEs	1.0
	IHT at 40%	0.5
	Daughter responsible	0.5
	CLT – 2 August 2015	
	Transfer of value	0.5
	IHT at 40%	0.5
	Trust responsible	0.5
	Death estate	
	IHT at 40%	0.5
	PRs responsible	0.5
		6.0
(b)	IHT planning	
	Skipping a generation reduces IHT	1.0
	Gifts only taxed once	1.0
		2.0
(c)	IHT saving	
	Taper relief after 3 years	0.5
	Gifts lock in value	0.5
	IHT saving	1.0
		2.0
Total		**10.0**

194 OPAL ELDER (ADAPTED)

(a) (1) **Chargeable estate**

	£	£
Property (£374,000 + £442,000)		816,000
Repayment mortgage		(160,000)
Endowment mortgage		(0)
		656,000
Motor cars		172,000
Investments (£47,000 + £36,000 + £69,000)		152,000
		980,000
Bank loan	22,400	
Legal fees	(0)	
		(22,400)
Chargeable estate		957,600

Tutorial notes

1   *There is no deduction in respect of the endowment mortgage as this will be repaid upon death by the life assurance element of the mortgage.*

2   *The promise to pay the nephew's legal fees is not deductible as it is not legally enforceable.*

(2)   **Inheritance tax on death estate**

		£
Chargeable estate		957,600
	£	
IHT liability	105,000 × 0% (W)	0
	852,600 × 40%	341,040
	957,600	341,040

The personal representatives of Opal's estate will be responsible for paying the inheritance tax

Working: Available nil rate band

		£
Nil rate band		325,000
Potentially exempt transfers	– 14 August 2007	(0)
	– 7 November 2016	(220,000)
		105,000

Tutorial note

The potentially exempt transfer on 14 August 2007 is exempt from inheritance tax as it was made more than seven years before 20 March 2017.

(b)   **If Opal lived seven years longer**

If Opal were to live for another seven years, then the potentially exempt transfer on 7 November 2016 would become exempt.

The inheritance tax payable in respect of her estate would therefore decrease by £88,000 (£220,000 at 40%).

195 MARCUS *Walk in the footsteps of a top tutor*

Key answer tips

Part (a) for three marks tests your knowledge of how the inheritance tax rules apply to married couples. It is important to be brief and to the point in this section, to maximise the time available to spend on the remainder of the question.

Part (b) also tests inheritance tax, this time in relation to the tax due on lifetime gifts as a result of the donor's death. This is a commonly tested scenario.

The highlighted words in the answer are key phrases that markers are looking for.

(a)   **Inheritance tax for married couples**

Tutor's top tips

Make sure that you pay close attention to the number of marks available for short written requirements such as these; one mark for part (1) suggests only a brief answer is required, whereas two marks for part (2) suggests that you need to state two special inheritance tax measures which are applicable to married couples.

(1)   Married couples (and registered civil partnerships) are not chargeable persons for inheritance tax (IHT) purposes, because each spouse (or civil partner) is taxed separately.

(2)   Gifts to spouses (and registered civil partners) are exempt from IHT. This exemption applies both to lifetime gifts and transfers on death.

Any unused nil rate band on a person's death can be transferred to their surviving spouse (or registered civil partner).

(b)   **Marcus – Additional IHT liability arising on death**

Tutor's top tips

It is important to read the information carefully. The examining team has indicated that the annual exemption should be ignored and the lifetime tax is given in the question. Make sure you do not waste time allocating annual exemptions or trying to recalculate the lifetime tax.

It has become more common in the F6 examination for a question to bring you in part-way through calculations you may be used to doing in full. You need to be prepared for this approach.

IHT on CLTs and PET becoming chargeable on death

14 January 2008

			£
Chargeable lifetime transfer			315,000
– more than seven years prior to death			

		CLT	PET
		03.02.14	**17.03.14**
	£	£	£
Transfer of value			
= chargeable amount (W)		395,000	570,000
Lifetime tax (paid by Marcus)		96,250	
		————	
Gross chargeable transfer		491,250	
NRB at death	325,000		
Less: GCTs in 7 years pre gift			
(03.02.07 – 03.02.14)	(315,000)		
	————		
		(10,000)	
NRB at death	325,000		
Less: GCTs in 7 years pre gift			
(17.03.07 – 17.03.14)			
(£315,000 + £491,250)	(806,250)		
	————		
			(0)
		————	————
Taxable amount		481,250	570,000
		————	————
IHT due on death × 40%		192,500	228,000
Less: Taper relief (3.2.14 – 10.3.17)			
(3 – 4 years) (20%)		(38,500)	
Less: IHT paid in lifetime		(96,250)	
		————	————
IHT payable on death		57,750	228,000
		————	————

Working: Transfer of value

	£
Value of shares held before the transfer (100,000 × £12)	1,200,000
Value of shares held after the transfer (70,000 × £9)	(630,000)
	————
Transfer of value	570,000
	————

Tutorial note

1   Although the CLT on 14 January 2008 was made more than seven years prior to Marcus's death, and is therefore not chargeable on death, it still reduces the nil rate band available to set against the CLT made on 3 February 2014 as it was made within seven years of that transfer.

2   Although no details are given, there would be no IHT liability in respect of Marcus's estate because this is left entirely to his spouse.

3   Prior to the transfer Marcus had 100,000 shares (a 100% holding) in the company and the shares are valued at £12 per share. After the transfer Marcus owns 70,000 shares (a 70% holding) and the shares are valued at £9 per share. The transfer of value is the amount by which Marcus' estate has diminished and not the market value of the asset gifted.

ACCA marking scheme		
		Marks
(a)	(1) Chargeable person	1.0
	(2) Special measures – Exempt transfers between spouses	1.0
	– Transferable NRB	1.0
		———
		3.0
		———
(b)	CLT – 14 January 2008	
	No further IHT	1.0
	CLT – 3 February 2014	
	GCT	1.0
	NRB	1.0
	IHT at 40%	0.5
	Taper relief	1.0
	IHT already paid	0.5
	PET – 17 March 2014	
	Value of shares held before the transfer	0.5
	Value of shares held after the transfer	1.0
	IHT liability	0.5
		———
		7.0
		———
Total		**10.0**
		———

Section 9

ANSWERS TO PRACTICE CORPORATION TAX QUESTIONS

PRACTICE SECTION A OBJECTIVE TEST QUESTIONS

CORPORATION TAX BASICS AND ADMINISTRATION

196

	Chargeable accounting period end
At the end of a company's period of account	✓
The end of the tax financial year	
Twelve months after the beginning of the accounting period	✓
The date the company begins or ceases to trade	✓

Tutorial note

A chargeable accounting period is the period for which a charge to corporation tax is made.

A company's period of account is the period for which it prepares accounts.

The tax financial year runs from 1 April to 31 March and is identified by the year in which it begins. The rate of corporation tax is fixed by reference to the financial year. A company may have a chargeable accounting period which straddles 31 March, for example if they prepare accounts for the year ended 31 December.

---

197 D

	Resident	Not resident
A Ltd, a company incorporated in the UK, with its central management and control exercised in the UK	✓	
B Ltd, a company incorporated overseas, with its central management and control exercised in the UK	✓	
C Ltd, a company incorporated in the UK, with its central management and control exercised overseas	✓	
D Ltd, a company incorporated overseas, with its central management and control exercised overseas		✓

198 B

Taxable total profits – y/e 31 March 2017

	£
Trading profit before capital allowances	100,000
Less: Capital allowances	(2,000)
	———
Tax adjusted trading profit	98,000
Interest receivable (£6,000 – £2,000 + £1,000)	5,000
	———
Total profits	103,000
Less: Qualifying charitable donations	(3,200)
	———
Taxable total profits	99,800
	———

Tutorial note

For the purposes of the F6 examination, dividends received are not taxable and therefore are not included in taxable total profits. However, dividends received from non-related companies are included in augmented profits which are used to determine whether the company is required to pay tax by instalments.

199 B

Taxable total profits – y/e 31 December 2016

	£
Tax adjusted trading profit	50,000
Property income	6,000
Interest income	2,000
Chargeable gain	12,000
Taxable total profits	70,000

Tutorial note

Interest income is taxable on an accruals basis (i.e. amount receivable for the accounting period) not on the receipts basis.

Taxable total profits should include a company's worldwide income (excluding dividends) and net chargeable gains.

Remember companies pay corporation tax on their chargeable gains and not capital gains tax.

200 D

Corporation tax liability – y/e 31 March 2017

	£
Tax adjusted trading profit	1,200,000
Property income	250,000
Total profits	1,450,000
Less: Qualifying charitable donations	(7,000)
Taxable total profits	1,443,000
Corporation tax liability (£1,443,000 × 20%)	288,600

201 A

Corporation tax liability – y/e 31 March 2017

	£
Tax adjusted trading profit	250,000
Chargeable gain	60,000
Total profits	310,000
Less: Qualifying charitable donations	(60,000)
Taxable total profits	250,000
Corporation tax liability (£250,000 × 20%)	50,000

202 D

Tax adjusted trading profit – y/e 30 June 2016

	£
Trading profit per the accounts	25,580
Staff entertaining	0
Leased car restriction (£2,000 × 15%)	300
Tax adjusted trading profit	25,880

Tutorial note

Where the CO_2 emissions of a leased car exceed 130 g/km 15% of the lease charges are disallowed.

Remember that there are no private use adjustments for a company. The lease payments are therefore allowed in full, irrespective of any private use, subject to the 15% restriction.

203 B

	£	Main pool £	Allowances £
y/e 31 March 2017			
TWDV b/f		35,000	
Less: WDA (18%)		(6,300)	6,300
Low emission car			
(CO$_2$ ≤ 75 g/km)	8,000		
Less: FYA (100%)	(8,000)		8,000
	———	0	
		———	
TWDV c/f		28,700	
		———	
Total allowances			14,300
			———

Tutorial note

Remember that there are no private use adjustments for a company. The employee who uses the car privately will have a taxable employment benefit instead.

204 A

Property income: y/e 31 December 2016

	£
Rent receivable (£15,000 × 7/12) + (£8,000 × 2/12)	10,083
Less: Expenses	
Replacing fitted units	(500)
	———
Property income	9,583
	———

Tutorial note

The cost of replacing the damaged fitted kitchen unit is an allowable expense as it is a repair to an asset (the fitted kitchen).

RELIEF FOR TRADING LOSSES

205 C

Loss memorandum

	£
Loss – y/e 31.3.2016	100,000
Less: Used in – y/e 31.3.16 (£12,000 + £15,000)	(27,000)
– y/e 31.3.17	(20,000)
Loss carried forward	53,000

Tutorial note

If a current year loss relief claim is made, trading losses are offset against total profits before deduction of qualifying charitable donations (QCDs).

Any remaining loss is then automatically carried forward and offset against the first available trading profits from the same trade.

206 A

Year ended 31 March	2016	2017
	£	£
Trading profit	40,000	0
Property income	15,000	21,000
Total profits	55,000	21,000
Less: Loss relief – current year		(21,000)
– carry back (£50,000 – £21,000)	(29,000)	
Total profits	26,000	0
Less: QCDs	(6,000)	Wasted
Taxable total profits	20,000	0

Tutorial note

A claim to carry back losses against total profits (i.e. before QCDs) of the previous year can only be made if a claim has been made to offset the loss against current year total profits first.

207 C

Loss memorandum

	£
Loss of year ended 31.3.2017	60,000
Less: Used in current year – y/e 31.3.2017	(5,000)
Less: Used in 12 month carry back	
– 9 m/e to 30.6.2016 (W)	(25,000)
– y/e 30.6.2015	
Lower of:	
(1) Total profits × 3/12 = (3/12 × 44,000) = £11,000	
(2) Remaining loss = £30,000	(11,000)
Loss carried forward	19,000

Working: Loss relief

	y/e 30 June 2015	9 m/e 31 March 2016	y/e 31 March 2017
	£	£	£
Trading profit	40,000	22,000	0
Interest income	4,000	3,000	5,000
Total profits	44,000	25,000	5,000
Loss relief:			
Current year			(5,000)
12 month carry back		(25,000)	
12 month carry back (£44,000 × 3/12)	(11,000)		
TTP	33,000	0	0

Tutorial note

A loss can be carried back against the total profits of the previous 12 months (provided a current year claim has been made first).

Where an accounting period falls partly into the 12 month carry back period the total profits must be time apportioned and only those falling in the 12 month carry back period can be relieved.

208 D

Loss memorandum

	£
Loss of year ended 31.3.2017	100,000
Less: Loss relief	
Current year	(14,000)
Terminal loss relief (Previous 3 years on LIFO basis):	
y/e 31.3.2016	(19,000)
y/e. 31.3.2015	(32,000)
y/e. 31.3.2014 (balance)	(35,000)
	————
Loss not utilised	0
	————

Working – Loss relief

Year ended 31 March	2014	2015	2016	2017
	£	£	£	£
Trading profit	45,000	32,000	10,000	0
Chargeable gain	5,000	0	9,000	14,000
	————	————	————	————
Total profits	50,000	32,000	19,000	14,000
Less: Loss relief				
Current year				(14,000)
Terminal loss relief (LIFO):				
First			(19,000)	
Second		(32,000)		
Third	(35,000)			
	————	————	————	————
Taxable total profits	15,000	0	0	0
	————	————	————	————

Tutorial note

A loss in the final 12 months of trading can be set against the total profits of the three preceding years on a LIFO basis, provided a claim has been made against current year total profits first.

209 B

Loss memorandum

	£
Loss of year ended 31.3.2016	65,000
Less: Loss relief	
Used in current year claim – y/e 31.3.2016 (W)	(20,000)
Carried forward – y/e 31.3.17 (W)	(35,000)
Loss not utilised as at 31.3.2017	10,000

Working – Loss relief

Year ended 31 March	2015	2016	2017
	£	£	£
Trading profit	16,000	20,000	25,000
Property income	5,000	0	10,000
Total profits	21,000	20,000	35,000
Less: Loss relief			
Current year		(20,000)	
Brought forward			(35,000)
	21,000	0	0
Less: QCDs	(800)	wasted	wasted
Taxable total profits	20,200	0	0

Tutorial note

A property loss is automatically (no choice available) set against the total profits (before QCDs) of the current year. Any unused loss is automatically carried forward against the first available future total profits (before QCDs).

Property losses cannot be carried back.

WITH GROUP ASPECTS

210 D

Tutorial note

Forty Ltd is not a 75% subsidiary of Thirty Ltd.

Accordingly, regardless of indirect percentage interests, Forty Ltd and Ten Ltd cannot form a group for group relief or chargeable gains purposes.

211 C

	Loss can be surrendered to
Chair Ltd	✓
Bin Ltd	
Paper Inc	
Cardboard Ltd	✓

A loss group consists of a company and directly/indirectly owned companies where there is a shareholding of at least 75%. Therefore, Bin Ltd is not in the loss group as Computer Ltd's direct shareholding is only 60%.

Computer Ltd has a direct holding of 75% in Chair Ltd and 100% in Paper Inc and an indirect 75% holding, through Paper Inc, in Cardboard Ltd (100% × 75%).

An overseas company can be part of the loss group structure but it cannot itself claim or surrender losses, so losses cannot be surrendered to Paper Inc.

212 B

Where the companies in a loss group have non-coterminous accounting periods, the available profits and losses must be time apportioned, to find the relevant amounts falling within the corresponding accounting period.

In this situation, the maximum loss that can be surrendered = lower of:

- Allowable loss in the surrendering (loss making) company for the corresponding accounting period = £25,000 (3/12 × £100,000).

- Taxable total profits in the claimant company for the corresponding accounting period = £40,000 (3/6 × £80,000).

213

	Capital gains group
Brazil Ltd	✓
Germany Ltd	✓
Holland Ltd	✓
Belgium Ltd	
Russia Ltd	✓

A capital gains group comprises the parent company and its 75% (direct or indirect) subsidiaries and also, the 75% subsidiaries of the first subsidiaries and so on. However the parent company must have an effective interest of over 50% in all group companies.

Brazil Ltd has a direct 100% holding in Germany Ltd and a direct 75% holding in Holland Ltd. Russia also forms part of the group as Brazil Ltd has an overall effective interest of over 50% (75% × 75% = 56.25%).

Belgium Ltd does not form part of the group as it is not a 75% subsidiary of Germany Ltd.

214 A

The deemed acquisition cost is £150,000.

This is made up of the original cost of the asset to Apple (£100,000) plus indexation allowance up to the date of the transfer (£50,000).

Tutorial note

When an asset is transferred between companies in a gains group the asset is deemed to be transferred at a price that gives rise to neither a gain or loss to the company transferring the asset.

The deemed transfer price becomes the deemed acquisition cost for the transferee.

215 C

There are 4 related 51% group companies (Telephone Ltd, Desk Ltd, Chair Ltd, and Window Ltd) for the purposes of adjusting the augmented profits threshold for the year ended 31 March 2017.

Related 51% group companies are those companies which are 51% subsidiaries of Telephone Ltd (i.e. Telephone Ltd owns, either directly or indirectly, more than 50% of the company's ordinary share capital).

The augmented profits threshold is adjusted for the number of related 51% group companies at the end of the previous accounting period. Therefore, Curtain Ltd is not included for the purposes of adjusting the limit for the year ended 31 March 2017.

Overseas companies are included but dormant companies are excluded.

216 D

Novak Ltd has two related 51% group companies (Roger Ltd and Rafael Ltd). The augmented profits threshold will therefore be £500,000 (£1,500,000/3).

Rafael Ltd is included as Novak Ltd indirectly owns > 51% of the shares (i.e. 80% × 70% = 56%). Andy Ltd is not included as Novak Ltd only owns (indirectly) 30.8% (i.e. 80% × 70% × 55%) of the company's shares.

217 A

Corporation tax liability – 8 m/e 31 March 2017

	£
Augmented profits threshold	1,500,000
Adjusted for 8 month accounting period and four related companies (Custard Ltd plus three 51% subsidiaries) £1,500,000 × 8/12 × 1/4	250,000

218 B

Augmented profits – y/e 31 January 2017

	£
TTP (£1,450,000 + £100,000)	1,550,000
Plus: Dividend income from non-group companies	20,000
Augmented profits	1,570,000

219 A

£5,940 (£4,680 + £1,260)

Tutorial note

Dividends received from related companies are excluded from augmented profits. As Luck Limited does not control the third company from which dividends of £1,260 are received, the two companies are not related 51% group companies.

220 B

£456,000/4 = £114,000

221   B

Tutorial note

If a period of account is split into two chargeable accounting periods, the related corporation tax return must be submitted within 12 months of the end of the period of account, not the end of the chargeable accounting periods.

222   A

Companies which are not large (i.e. augmented profits do not exceed £1,500,000) are required to pay their corporation tax 9 months and 1 day after the end of the chargeable accounting period.

W Ltd and Z Ltd both have a chargeable accounting period ending on 30 June 2016 so the due date for payment of corporation tax is 1 April 2017.

X Ltd's 15 month period of account contains two chargeable accounting periods for tax purposes, the year ended 30 June 2016 and the 3 months ended 30 September 2016. Therefore it also has a due date for payment of corporation tax of 1 April 2017 in respect of the year ended 30 June 2016.

Y Ltd's due payment date in respect of the year ended 31 March 2016 is 1 January 2017.

223   C

Tutorial note

Large companies are required to pay corporation tax in instalments from the CAP following the first CAP in which they are a large company.

A large company is one whose profits exceed the augmented profit threshold of £1,500,000. This limit must be divided by the number of 51% group companies.

Mammoth Ltd has one related 51% group company and therefore the relevant augmented profit threshold is £750,000 (£1,500,000/2). Mammoth's augmented profits exceed this threshold in the year ended 31 December 2015 and therefore quarterly instalment payments will be required from the year ended 31 December 2016.

224 B

Tutorial note

A large company is required to pay its final instalment of corporation tax by the 14th day of the 4th month after the end of the chargeable accounting period (CAP). Note that for a 12 month AP this is 16 months after the start of the AP.

Where a CAP is less than 12 months, the first instalment is due by the 14th day of the 7th month after the start of the CAP. Subsequent instalments are due at 3 monthly intervals thereafter, until the date of the final instalment is reached.

For an eight month CAP instalments of 3/8 × corporation tax liability are payable on 14 November 2016 (14th day of month 7 of the AP) and 14 February 2017 (3 months later). The final instalment of 2/8 × corporation tax liability is due on 14 April 2017 (the 14th day of the 4th month after the end of the CAP.

225 D

166,250 × 3% × 4/12 = £1,662 (period 1 April 2017 to 31 July 2017)

PRACTICE SECTION B OBJECTIVE TEST CASES

CORPORATION TAX BASICS AND ADMINISTRATION

226 GREENZONE LTD (ADAPTED) *Walk in the footsteps of a top tutor*

Key answer tips

This ten mark question concerns the adjustments to a company's tax adjusted trading profit, capital allowances computations and company payment dates.

1 C

	£
Repairs and renewals	
Repainting office building	0
New reception area (Note 1)	19,800
Entertaining expenses	
Entertaining UK customers (Note 2)	3,600
Entertaining overseas customers (Note 2)	1,840
	25,240

Tutorial note

1   The extension of the office building is not deductible, being capital in nature. The building has been improved rather than repaired.

2   For corporation tax purposes all entertaining expenditure is disallowed unless it relates to employees.

Top tutor tips

For VAT purposes, input VAT can be reclaimed on the expense of entertaining overseas customers, but not on the expense of entertaining UK customers. Because of this, students often get confused about whether the expense of entertaining overseas customers is an allowable deduction against trading profits for income tax and corporation tax. Remember, for income tax and corporation tax purposes, only employee entertaining is deductible.

2   A

	£
Gifts and donations	
Political donations	740
Non-qualifying charitable donations (Note 1)	0
Gifts to customers – Pens (Note 2)	660
– Clocks (Note 2)	910
	———
	2,310
	———

Tutorial note

1   The charitable donation is an allowable expense against trading profits as it is local and reasonable in size in relation to the business and is wholly and exclusively incurred for trading purposes (i.e. advertising).

2   Gifts to customers are only an allowable deduction if they cost less than £50 per recipient per year, are not of food, drink, tobacco or vouchers exchangeable for goods and carry a conspicuous advertisement for the company making the gift.

3   D

	FYA	Main pool	Allowances
		£	£
TWDV b/f		48,150	
Addition qualifying for 100% FYA			
Motor car (1)	10,800		
100% FYA	(10,800)		10,800
	———	0	
Addition not qualifying for AIA			
Motor car (2)		20,400	
		———	
		68,550	
Proceeds – Motor car (3)		(8,500)	
		———	
		60,050	
Less: WDA (18%)		(10,809)	10,809
		———	
TWDV c/f		49,241	
		———	———
			21,609
			———

Tutorial note

1   *Motor car (1) is a new car and has CO_2 emissions of 75 grams per kilometre or less and therefore qualifies for the 100% first year allowance (FYA).*

2   *Motor car (2) has CO_2 emissions between 76 and 130 grams per kilometre and therefore qualifies for writing down allowances at the rate of 18%.*

3   *The amount deducted on disposal of motor car (3) is restricted to the original cost figure of £8,500.*

4 A

6 months to 30.9.17	£	Special rate pool £	Allowances £
TWDV b/f		9,200	
Addition qualifying for AIA			
– special rate addition	150,000		
Less: AIA (Max £200,000 × 6/12)	(100,000)		100,000
	———		
Balance to special rate pool		50,000	
		———	
		59,200	
Less: WDA (8% × 6/12)		(2,368)	2,368
		———	
TWDV c/f		56,832	
		———	———
			102,368
			———

Tutorial note

The AIA and WDA must be adjusted to reflect the short accounting period of 6 months.

5 B

Tutorial note

Where the accounting period is less than 12 months:

- *First instalment due by: 14th day of 7th month after the start of the CAP (as normal).*

- *Subsequent instalments are due at 3 monthly intervals thereafter, until the date of the final instalment (see below) is reached.*

- *Last instalment due by: 14th day of 4th month after the end of the accounting period. Earlier instalments (as above) are only due if they fall before the date of the final instalment.*

RELIEF FOR TRADING LOSSES

227 LOSER LTD (ADAPTED)

Key answer tips

A fairly straightforward corporation tax loss question testing the different reliefs available.

1   A

Tutorial note

There is only one rate of corporation tax rate (20%) so this is not a relevant factor.

The timing of the relief obtained is relevant as a claim against total profits in the current year and previous 12 months will result in earlier relief than a claim to carry a loss forward, and such a claim will normally result in a tax repayment as well.

Losses may be lost on a cessation of trade if they have not previously been utilised, so this is a relevant factor.

The extent to which relief for qualifying charitable donations will be lost is relevant, since these cannot be carried forward.

2   B

	y/e 31.3.17	y/e 31.3.18
	£	£
Trading profit	0	60,000
Less: Loss b/f		(60,000)
Property income	5,600	3,000
	———	———
Total profits	5,600	3,000
Less: QCD relief	(1,100)	(1,300)
	———	———
Taxable total profits	4,500	1,700
	———	———

Loss working

	£
Trading loss for the y/e 31.3.17	78,300
Loss against future trading profits	(60,000)
	———
Unrelieved loss at 31.3.18	18,300
	———

3   D

	y/e 30.6.15	9 m/e 31.3.16	y/e 31.3.17
	£	£	£
Trading profit	15,700	24,300	0
Property profit	6,600	8,100	5,600
Total profits	22,300	32,400	5,600
Less: Loss relief			
– Current period			(5,600)
– 12 months c/b	(5,575)	(32,400)	
	16,725	0	0
Less: QCD relief	(800)	wasted	wasted
Taxable total profits	15,925	0	0

Loss working

	£
Trading loss for the p/e 31.3.17	78,300
Loss against total profits	
– Current period (p/e 31.3.17)	(5,600)
12 month carry back (p/e 31.3.16)	(32,400)
12 month carry back (y/e 30.6.15) (£22,300 × 3/12)	(5,575)
Unrelieved loss at 31.3.17	34,725

4   C

5   A

	y/e 30.6.13	y/e 30.6.14	y/e 30.6.15	9 m/e 31.3.16	y/e 31.3.17
	£	£	£	£	£
Trading profit	15,800	10,600	15,700	24,300	0
Property profit	5,200	1,200	6,600	8,100	5,600
Total profits	21,000	11,800	22,300	32,400	5,600
Less: Loss relief					
– Current period					(5,600)
– 36 months c/b	(5,250)	(11,800)	(22,300)	(32,400)	
	15,750	0	0	0	0
Less: QCD relief	(1,300)	wasted	wasted	wasted	wasted
Taxable total profits	14,450	0	0	0	0

Loss working

	£
Trading loss for the p/e 31.3.17	78,300
Loss against total profits	
– Current period (p/e 31.3.17)	(5,600)
36 month carry back:	
– p/e 31.3.16	(32,400)
– y/e 30.6.15	(22,300)
– y/e 30.6.14	(11,800)
– y/e 30.6.13 (£21,000 × 3/12)	(5,250)
Unrelieved loss at 31.3.17	950

Tutorial note

The whole of the trading loss for the final twelve months of trading can be relieved against total profits for the previous 36 months under the terminal loss relief rules.

WITH GROUP ASPECTS

228 DEUTSCH LTD (ADAPTED) *Walk in the footsteps of a top tutor*

Key answer tips

This corporation tax question involves a company with shareholdings in a number of other companies. Provided the relevant group definitions had been learnt there were easy marks available for identifying the related 51% group companies and calculating the maximum group relief claim.

1   B

Tutorial note

Two companies are related 51% group companies if:

–   One is a 51% subsidiary of the other, or

–   Both are 51% subsidiaries of a third company

A 51% subsidiary is one where more than 50% of the ordinary share capital is directly or indirectly owned.

It does not matter where a company is resident so overseas companies are included in the definition.

2   A

Tutor's top tips

Your first step should be to identify which companies are in a group relief group with Deutsch Ltd. You can then identify how much group relief is available.

- Deutsch Ltd cannot claim group relief from Eins Ltd as this company is not a 75% subsidiary. However, Drei Ltd and Deutsch Ltd are in a group relief group.

- The maximum amount of group relief that can be claimed is £64,700 being Drei Ltd's trading loss of £52,700 plus the unrelieved qualifying charitable donations of £12,000.

Tutorial note

- *The surrendering company may surrender any amount of its current period losses.*

- *There is no requirement for the surrendering company to relieve the loss against its own profits first.*

- *The losses which may be surrendered are trading losses, unrelieved QCDs and unrelieved property losses.*

3   D

	£
Sales proceeds	500,000
Less: Indexed cost	(285,200)
Chargeable gain	214,800
Less: Rollover relief	(174,800)
Gain chargeable (proceeds not reinvested £500,000 − £460,000)	40,000

4   A

Tutorial note

Berlin Ltd owns more than 75% of Zwei Ltd. The two companies therefore form a group for capital gains purposes.

Assets transferred within a gains group are automatically transferred at no gain/no loss (i.e. without a chargeable gain or allowable loss arising).

The transfer is deemed to take place at a price that does not give rise to a gain or a loss (i.e. the indexed cost at the date of the transfer).

The transferor's deemed proceeds figure is also the deemed cost of the acquiring company.

5   B

The claim for group relief should be made by Deutsch Ltd (the claimant company) on their corporation tax return by 31 March 2019 (within two years of the end of the chargeable accounting period).

The claim for rollover relief must be made within four years of the later of the end of the accounting period in which the asset is sold and replaced i.e. 31 March 2021.

Tutor's top tip

Time limits for claims and elections should represent easy marks provided that you have learnt them prior to the examination.

PRACTICE SECTION C CONSTRUCTED RESPONSE QUESTIONS

CORPORATION TAX BASICS AND ADMINISTRATION

229   ARABLE LTD (ADAPTED)

Key answer tips

The first part of this question deals with the calculation of corporation tax for a short accounting period. You should remember that the length of the period affects the calculation of the maximum AIA and the WDA for capital allowances.

The original question also tested other aspects of corporation tax, which are no longer examinable. These have been replaced by a new part (b) on the definition of a large company, which is important to learn as it determines the due date for the payment of corporation tax.

Other things to watch out for in this question are the effect of the short period on the lease premium deduction and the fact that the company has related 51% group companies, which affects the augmented profits threshold for determining whether the company is large.

The highlighted words in the written parts of the answer are key phrases that markers are looking for.

(a)   **Corporation tax computation – 9 months ended 31 December 2016**

	£	£
Trading profit		376,611
Deduction for lease premium (W1)	2,700	
Capital allowances – Plant and machinery (W2)	171,240	
	———	(173,940)
		202,671
Property income (W3)		49,700
Interest income – Loan interest (£6,000 + £3,000)		9,000
		———
Taxable total profits		261,371
		———
Corporation tax liability		
£261,371 × 20%		52,274
		———

Tutorial note

Dividends received are not subject to corporation tax. They are not therefore included in taxable total profits. They are however included in augmented profits (for the purposes of determining whether the company is' large') if they are received from unrelated companies (i.e. not related 51% group companies) (see part (b)).

Workings

(W1) Deduction for lease premium

The first office building has been used for business purposes, and so a proportion of the lease premium assessed on the landlord can be deducted.

Assessment on landlord:

	£
Premium received	75,000
Less: 2% × £75,000 × (15 – 1)	(21,000)
	———
Assessment on landlord (Note)	54,000
	———
Allowable deduction for 9 month period (£54,000 ÷ 15 × 9/12)	2,700
	———

Tutorial note

Alternative calculation of the assessment on the landlord:

£75,000 × (51 – 15)/50 = £54,000

(W2) Plant and machinery

	£	Main pool £	Special rate pool £	Allowances £
Additions (no AIA or FYA) (Note 1)				
Car (CO$_2$ between 76 – 130 g/km)		11,200		
Car (CO$_2$ > 130 g/km)			14,600	
Additions (with AIA) (Note 2)				
Delivery lorries	193,350			
Less: AIA (£200,000 × 9/12) (Note 2)	(150,000)			150,000
	———			
Transfer to pool		43,350		
		———		
		54,550		
WDA (18% × 9/12) (Note 2)		(7,364)		7,364
WDA (8% × 9/12) (Note 2)			(876)	876
Additions (with FYA) (Note 1)				
Car (CO$_2$ < 76 g/km)	13,000			
Less: FYA (100%)	(13,000)			13,000
	———	0		
		———	———	
TWDV c/f		47,186	13,724	
		———	———	
Total allowances				171,240
				———

Tutorial note

1   *Capital allowances on car purchases are calculated based on the CO_2 emissions of the car as follows:*

New cars with CO_2 emissions of < 76 g/km:
eligible for a FYA of 100%.

CO_2 emissions of between 76 – 130 g/km:
put in main pool, eligible for a WDA at 18%.

CO_2 emissions of > 130 g/km:
put in special rate pool, eligible for a WDA at 8%.

The appropriate rates are given in the tax rates and allowances.

2   *The maximum AIA and WDAs are time apportioned because Arable Ltd's accounting period is nine months long. The maximum AIA is £150,000 (£200,000 × 9/12).*

(W3) Property income

	£
Premium received for lease	50,000
Less: 2% × £50,000 × (5 − 1)	(4,000)
Assessment on premium received (Note)	46,000
Plus: Rent receivable (£14,800 × 3/12)	3,700
Property income	49,700

Tutorial note

Alternative calculation of the assessment on the lease:

£50,000 × (51 − 5)/50 = £46,000

(b)   **Large company**

A large company is defined as a company whose augmented profits in an accounting period exceed £1,500,000 (as adjusted for related 51% group companies and short accounting periods).

Arable Ltd's augmented profits for the nine-month period to 31 December 2016 are £281,371 (W1). As this is less than the adjusted augmented profits threshold of £375,000 (W2) then Arable Ltd is not large for the nine-month accounting period to 31 December 2016.

Workings

(W1) Augmented profits

		£
Taxable total profits		261,371
Plus: Dividends received		20,000
Augmented profits		281,371

(W2) Augmented profits threshold

		£
(£1,500,000 × 1/3 × 9/12)		375,000

The threshold is reduced for a nine month period and the three related group companies (i.e. Arable Ltd plus two related 51% group companies).

230 DO-NOT-PANIC LTD (ADAPTED)

Key answer tips

This 10 mark question involves a long period of account requiring knowledge of the rules of how to split income and gains between two chargeable accounting periods.

When the question was set, the capital allowance rules were different and more was involved in the calculation than under the current rules.

Corporation tax liabilities – Fifteen-month period ended 31 March 2017

	y/e 31.12.2016	p/e 31.3.2017
	£	£
Trading profit (12/15 : 3/15) (Note 1)	200,400	50,100
Less: Capital allowances (W1)	(18,000)	(24,000)
	182,400	26,100
Net chargeable gains		
(£42,000 – £4,250) (Note 2)	0	37,750
Interest income (W2)	18,000	1,000
Taxable total profits	200,400	64,850
Corporation tax		
£200,400/£64,850 × 20%	40,080	12,970
Total liability	£53,050	
Due dates of payment	1 Oct 2017	1 Jan 2018
Filing date of return	31 March 2018	31 March 2018

Tutorial note

Trading profits are allocated on a time basis: 12/15 to the year ended 31 December 2016 and 3/15 to the period ended 31 March 2017.

The capital loss of £4,250 for the year ended 31 December 2016 is carried forward and set against the first available future gains in the 3 months ended 31 March 2017.

The company is not a large company for corporation tax payment purposes (i.e. augmented profits < £1.5 million). The tax is therefore payable 9 months and 1 day after the end of the accounting period.

The filing date for both of the tax returns is 12 months after the end of the period of account.

Workings

(W1) Capital allowances

	£	Main pool £	Allowances £
Year ended 31 December 2016			
Addition qualifying for 100% FYA:			
New low emission car ($CO_2 \leq$ 75g/km)	18,000		
100% FYA	(18,000)		18,000
Total allowances			18,000
Period ended 31 March 2017			
Additions (with AIA)			
Equipment	24,000		
Less: AIA (Max £200,000 × 3/12)	(24,000)		24,000
		0	
TWDV c/f		0	
Total allowances			24,000

Tutorial note

The maximum AIA is time apportioned because the company's accounting period is three months long.

(W2) Interest income

	y/e 31.12.16	p/e 31.3.17
	£	£
Interest receivable	18,000	7,000
Interest payable	–	(6,000)
Interest income	18,000	1,000

Tutorial note

Interest receivable and payable on non-trading loan relationships are allocated to the accounting periods on the accruals basis.

Examiner's report

Depending on whether candidates appreciated that the period of account needed to be split into a twelve-month period and a three-month period, this question was either answered very well or quite badly.

Invariably many of the less well prepared candidates calculated corporation tax based on a fifteen-month period.

The due dates were often omitted or incorrect.

ACCA marking scheme		
		Marks
Trading profit		1.0
Capital allowances	– Year ended 31 December 2016	1.0
	– Period ended 31 March 2017	1.5
Capital gains		1.0
Interest income		1.5
Interest payable		1.0
Corporation tax	– Year ended 31 December 2016	0.5
	– Period ended 31 March 2017	0.5
Due dates		1.0
Filing dates		1.0
Total		**10.0**

231 CRASH BASH LTD (ADAPTED) *Walk in the footsteps of a top tutor*

Key answer tips

A standard corporation tax question requiring a capital allowances computation for plant and machinery followed by a corporation tax computation.

These areas are often tested and should not have caused many difficulties.

The original question also tested various overseas aspects of corporation tax, which are no longer examinable. This part has been replaced by a question on corporation tax administration, which is an area which is frequently tested and must be learnt.

The highlighted words in the answer are key phrases that markers are looking for.

Tutor's top tips

Be sure to read the requirement carefully and pay attention to the mark allocation.

Part (a) only requires two bullet points to be made, but remember to relate your answer to the specific information given in the question.

Part (b) is where the time should be spent, however, don't run out of time to attempt part (c) by spending too long here.

Part (c) deals with the implications of missing filing deadlines, and is a straightforward test of knowledge retention.

(a) **Residence status**

- Companies that are incorporated overseas are only treated as being resident in the UK if their central management and control is exercised in the UK.

- Since the directors are UK based and hold their board meetings in the UK, this would indicate that Crash-Bash Ltd is managed and controlled from the UK, and therefore it is resident in the UK.

(b)   **Corporation tax liability – period ended 31 December 2016**

Tutor's top tips

Remember to use your time effectively for this part.

Computations for capital allowances are required in workings before the corporation tax computation can be drawn up. Remember to reference your workings clearly to your main answer to the question.

Note that this question has been amended to reflect legislative and syllabus changes. The mark allocation in this answer has been adjusted accordingly.

	£	£
Trading profit per question		1,002,924
Advertising expenditure (Note 1)	12,840	
Capital allowances – Plant and machinery (W)	194,419	
	———	(207,259)
Tax adjusted trading profit/TTP		795,665
		———
Corporation tax		
(£795,665 × 20%)		159,133
		———

Tutorial note

1   *The advertising expenditure incurred during March 2016 is pre-trading revenue expenditure. Accordingly it is treated as incurred on the first day of trading (i.e. 1 April 2016) and is therefore an allowable deduction for corporation tax purposes.*

As no adjustment has been made for this expenditure yet, an adjustment is required.

2   *Dividends received are exempt from corporation tax and are therefore not included in taxable total profits.*

Working: Plant and machinery

	£	Main pool £	Allowances £
Additions (with AIA):			
Long life asset	110,000		
Less: AIA (Note 2)	(110,000)		110,000
Machinery (Note 3)	271,250		
Less: AIA (Maximum) (Note 2)	(40,000)		40,000
		231,250	
Less: WDA (Note 4)			
(£231,250 × 18% × 9/12)		(31,219)	31,219
Additions (with FYA):			
Car (CO_2 < 76 g/km)	13,200		
Less: FYA (100%)	(13,200)		13,200
		0	
TWDV c/f		200,031	
Total allowances			194,419

Tutorial note

1   *Capital allowances on car purchases are calculated based on the CO_2 emissions of the car. A new car with CO_2 emissions of < 76 g/km is eligible for a FYA of 100%.*

2   *The maximum annual investment allowance (AIA) is £150,000 (£200,000 × 9/12) because Crash-Bash Ltd's accounting period is nine months long. The AIA is allocated to the long life asset in priority to the general machinery as the long life asset is a special rate pool addition that otherwise would only qualify for WDA at 8%. The asset is treated as a long life asset as it has an expected working life of at least 25 years and the total cost is ≥£75,000 (£100,000 × 9/12). The £100,000 limit is reduced for short periods.*

3   *The cost of alterations to buildings needed for the installation of plant and machinery is deemed to be qualifying expenditure on plant and machinery.*

4   *The writing down allowance is similarly restricted to 9/12, however first year allowances are never restricted according to the length of the accounting period.*

(c)   **Implications of late filing and payment**

- Crash-Bash Ltd's self-assessment tax return for the period ended 31 December 2016 must be submitted by 31 December 2017.

- If the company submits its self-assessment tax return eight months late, then there will be an automatic fixed penalty of £200, since the return is more than three months late.

- There will also be an additional corporation tax related penalty of £15,913 (£159,133 × 10%) being 10% of the tax unpaid, since the self-assessment tax return is more than six months late.

Tutorial note

The tax geared penalty starts when 18 months or more have passed after the end of the return period (i.e. this is the same as saying 6 months or more after the filing date).

Examiner's report

Although the numerical aspects of this question were well answered, most candidates achieved lower marks for this question than for question one, despite this question being five marks longer.

In the first section of part (a) most candidates were not aware that the essential point regarding residence is where a company's central management and control is exercised.

Most candidates had little difficulty with the corporation tax computation, and there were many perfect answers to this part of the question.

Note: *The examiner's report has been edited to remove comments on elements of the question that have been deleted due to changes to the examination format.*

	ACCA marking scheme	
		Marks
(a)	Central management and control	1.0
	Board meetings held in the UK	1.0
		2.0
(b)	Trading profit	0.5
	Advertising expenditure	1.0
	P & M – AIA allocated to LLA in priority	1.5
	– Installation costs qualifying expenditure	1.0
	– Maximum AIA	1.0
	– Balance of P&M transferred to main pool	0.5
	– WDA	1.5
	– FYA (100%)	1.5
	Corporation tax calculation	0.5
		9.0
(c)	Due date	1.0
	Fixed penalty	1.5
	Corporation tax related penalty	1.5
		4.0
Total		**15.0**

232 MOLTEN METAL PLC (ADAPTED) *Walk in the footsteps of a top tutor*

Key answer tips

Part (a) requires a corporation tax computation including a partial adjustment of profits, an involved capital allowances computation and interest income.

Detailed knowledge of capital versus revenue expenditure, capital allowances and the treatment of interest is needed.

Part (b) tests the quarterly instalment system and is straightforward.

(a)   **Corporation tax computation – year ended 31 March 2017**

	£	£
Trading profit per question		2,090,086
Loan stock interest payable (W1) (Note 1)	22,000	
Repairs to office building (Note 2)	0	
Capital allowance – P & M (W2)	224,354	
		(246,354)
Tax adjusted trading profit		1,843,732
Interest income (W3)		8,700
TTP		1,852,432
Corporation tax (£1,852,432 × 20%)		370,486

Tutorial note

1   *Interest paid in respect of a loan used for trading purposes is deductible in calculating the trading profit.*

2   *The repairs to the office building are not deductible as revenue expenditure. They are treated as capital in nature, as the building was not in a usable state when purchased and this fact was reflected in the reduced purchase price.*

Workings

(W1) Interest payable

	£
Accrual b/f at 1 April 2016	(4,200)
Loan stock interest paid	22,500
Accrual c/f at 31 March 2017	3,700
	22,000

Tutorial note

The loan stock was issued to raise funds for a trading purpose; therefore the interest is an allowable deduction against trading profit, calculated on an accruals basis.

(W2) Plant and machinery

	£	Main pool £	Special rate pool £	Allowances £
TWDV b/f		87,800		
Additions not qualifying for AIA				
Motor cars (£17,300 × 2) (Note 1)		34,600		
Additions qualifying for AIA				
Integral features (Note 2)				
Ventilation system	83,000			
Lift	10,000			
	———			
	93,000			
Less: AIA (Note 3)	(93,000)			93,000
	———		0	
Other plant and machinery				
Machinery	90,000			
Building alterations (Note 4)	7,000			
Wall (Note 5)	0			
Partition walls (Note 5)	22,900			
	———			
	119,900			
Less: AIA (Note 3)	(107,000)			107,000
	———	12,900		
		———		
		135,300		
Less: WDA (18%)		(24,354)		24,354
		———	———	
TWDV c/f		110,946	0	
		———	———	
Total allowances				224,354
				———

Tutorial note

1   The motor cars have CO_2 emissions between 76 and 130 grams per kilometre, and therefore go in the main pool. They do not qualify for the AIA but do qualify for writing down allowances at the rate of 18%.

    The private use of a motor car is irrelevant for company capital allowances computations, since such usage will be assessed on the employee as an employment benefit.

2   The purchase of an office building itself is not eligible for plant and machinery allowances.

    However, the ventilation system and lift are both integral to a building and are eligible for plant and machinery allowances as special rate pool items.

3   It is beneficial to claim the AIA of £200,000 initially against the special rate pool expenditure, as it would otherwise only qualify for writing down allowance at the rate of 8%.

    Any remaining AIA, up to a maximum of £200,000 in total, is set against the plant and machinery expenditure and the balance is put in the main pool.

4   The building alterations were necessary for the installation of the machinery, and therefore qualify for capital allowances.

5   Walls are specifically excluded as qualifying for capital allowances, with the exception of partition walls which are movable and intended to be so moved. The partition walls perform a 'function' (enabling the office space to be changed and used efficiently) unlike the wall which is just decorative and is the 'setting' for the business.

(W3) Interest income

	£
Loan interest receivable (£9,800 + £3,100)	12,900
Bank interest receivable	2,600
	15,500
Less: Loan interest expense	(6,800)
Interest income	8,700

(b)   **Final quarterly instalment payment**

	£
Corporation tax liability	370,486
Less: Quarterly instalments paid	(298,200)
Final instalment payment	72,286
Due date:	14 July 2017

Examiner's report

This question was generally well answered, and there were many very good answers.

In part (a) there was no need to have separate computations for the trading profit and for taxable total profits, since it was quite straightforward to combine everything into one computation.

The accruals for the interest payable and interest income often caused problems, and many candidates did not appreciate that no adjustment to the trading profit was necessary in respect of any of the items debited to the capital expenditure account. The writing down allowance for a motor car with private use was often restricted, despite such an adjustment only being relevant for an unincorporated business.

Although most candidates correctly calculated the final quarterly instalment in part (b), the due date was generally not known.

Note: *The examiner's report has been edited to remove comments on elements of the question that have been deleted due to changes to the examination format.*

ACCA marking scheme		
		Marks
(a)	Trading profit	0.5
	Loan stock interest payable	1.5
	Repairs to office building	1.0
	P & M – Office building	0.5
	– Ventilation system and lift	1.0
	– AIA	1.0
	– Machinery	0.5
	– Building alterations	0.5
	– Wall	0.5
	– Partition walls	1.0
	– AIA	1.0
	– Main pool transfer	1.0
	– Main pool WDA	0.5
	Interest income	2.0
	Corporation tax liability	0.5
		———
		13.0
		———
(b)	Instalment payment	1.0
	Due date	1.0
		———
		2.0
		———
Total		**15.0**
		———

233 STRETCHED LTD (ADAPTED)

Key answer tips

This question deals with the rules for a 15 month period of account which must be split into two accounting periods of 12 months and 3 months.

For ease, use a columnar layout to do the corporation tax computations side by side. Don't forget to pick up the easy marks for stating the due dates of payment.

The highlighted words in the answer are key phrases that markers are looking for.

(a) **Corporation tax computations**

	y/e 31.12.16 £	p/e 31.3.17 £
Trading profit (12/15 : 3/15) (Note 1)	514,000	128,500
Less: Capital allowances (W1)	0	(50,338)
	514,000	78,162
Less: Loss relief b/f	(330,000)	0
	184,000	78,162
Property business profit (12/15 : 3/15) (Note 1)	36,000	9,000
Chargeable gains (£44,000 – £3,000) (Note 2)	41,000	0
Total profits	261,000	87,162
Less: QCD relief	0	(5,000)
Taxable total profits	261,000	82,162
Corporation tax £261,000/£82,162 × 20%	52,200	16,432
Due dates (W2)	1 Oct 2017	1 Jan 2018

Tutorial note

1   Trading profits and property business profits are allocated on a time basis: 12/15 to the year ended 31 December 2016 and 3/15 to the period ended 31 March 2017.

2   The capital loss of £6,700 for the period ended 31 March 2017 is carried forward, it cannot be carried back and set off against previous gains.

Workings

(W1) Capital allowances

	£	Main pool £	Allowances £
3 months ended 31 March 2017			
Additions (with AIA)			
Office equipment	57,500		
Less: AIA (Max £200,000 × 3/12)	(50,000)		50,000
	———	7,500	
Less: WDA (18%) × 3/12		(338)	338
		———	
TWDV c/f		7,162	
		———	———
Total allowances			50,338
			———

Tutorial note

The AIA and WDA must be time apportioned as the chargeable accounting period is only three months in length.

(W2) Payment dates

	y/e 31.12.16 £	p/e 31.3.17 £
Taxable total profits	261,000	82,162
Plus: Dividend income	30,000	0
	———	———
Augmented profits	291,000	82,162
	———	———
Augmented profits threshold (£1,500,000 × 3/12)	1,500,000	375,000
	———	———

The company is not a large company in either of the two accounting periods and was not a large company in the previous accounting period to 31 December 2015 (TTP and augmented profits £ 300,000). The tax is therefore due 9 months and one day after the end of the accounting period.

(b) **Advantages of 31 March year end**

- Being aligned with the financial year will make it easier for a company to calculate its corporation tax liability, since the same rates, reliefs and legislation will apply throughout the accounting period.

- For owner-managed companies, alignment with the income tax year (the odd five days can be ignored) will make it easier as regards calculating the most tax efficient method of extracting profits from the company.

234 STARFISH LTD (ADAPTED) *Walk in the footsteps of a top tutor*

Key answer tips

This question covers corporation tax aspects of a loss making company.

Part (a) involved a basic adjustment of profits computation with the standard requirement to calculate capital allowances. However, the period is loss-making and is the period of cessation. Particular care is therefore needed in the calculation of the capital allowances, especially as you are required to deal with the impact of VAT on the additions and disposals.

Part (b) was a little trickier as it involved the need to deal with two trading losses; an opening period loss and a terminal loss in the period of cessation. However, it is a company making the losses, not an individual and the loss relief rules for companies are much more straightforward. There are no special opening year and closing year rules to apply. The terminal loss can just be carried back 36 months rather than 12 months. Make sure you deal with the losses in strict date order.

It is therefore a fairly standard loss question which is largely computational and should not have been too difficult provided the approach to losses questions had been practised. For ease, a columnar format should be used to present the loss offset and remember to show your record of the losses and how they have been relieved in a working.

Tutor's top tips

This is a long time pressured question and you need to work through it methodically. The requirements are broken down into small parts which help you to structure your answer.

(a)   **Starfish Ltd**

   Tax adjusted trading loss – period ended 31 March 2017

	Notes	£	£
Loss before taxation			190,000
Depreciation		34,400	
Donation to political party		300	
Qualifying charitable donation	1	1,350	
Impairment loss		0	
Entertaining customers	2	3,600	
Entertaining employees	2	0	
Counselling services	3	0	
Capital allowances (W)			2,300
		–––––––	–––––––
		39,650	192,300
		(192,300)	–––––––
		–––––––	
Trading loss		(152,650)	
		–––––––	

Tutorial note

1   Qualifying charitable donations (QCDs) made by a company are allowable deductions, but not from trading profit. They are deductible from total profits in the main corporation tax computation. Therefore, in the adjustment of trading profits computation they need to be added back to trading profit.

2   The only exception to the non-deductibility of entertainment expenditure is when it is in respect of employees.

3   The costs of counselling services for redundant employees are allowable.

Working – Plant and machinery

	Notes	Main pool £	Special rate pool £	Allowances £
TWDV b/f		23,600	13,200	
Addition (£3,120 × 100/120)	1, 2	2,600		
		26,200		
Sale proceeds:	2			
Main pool (£31,200 + £1,800) × 100/120		(27,500)		
Motor car	3		(9,600)	
		(1,300)	3,600	
Balancing charge		1,300		(1,300)
Balancing allowance			(3,600)	3,600
TWDV c/f		0	0	
Total allowances				2,300

Tutorial note

1   The annual investment allowance and writing down allowances are not given for the period in which a trade ceases. Therefore the addition is simply added into the main pool.

2   The net cost (excluding VAT) of the addition is added to the main pool as input VAT is recovered on the purchase, and the net sale proceeds (excluding VAT) relating to the sale of main pool items is deducted.

3   Input VAT however would not have been recovered in respect of the motor car as it was not used exclusively for business purposes. Therefore, output VAT is not due on the disposal and the gross sale proceeds are deducted in the capital allowances computation.

Tutor's top tips

Once you have calculated your trading loss in part (a) you have to use it in the calculation of loss relief in part (b). Remember that even if your answer to part (a) is incorrect you will get marks for applying the rules correctly in part (b).

(b) **Starfish Ltd – Taxable total profits**

	4 m/e 31.3.2013	y/e 31.3.2014	y/e 31.3.2015	y/e 31.3.2016	9 m/e 31.12.2016	3 m/e 31.3.2017
	£	£	£	£	£	£
Trading profit	0	64,200	53,900	14,700	49,900	0
Less: Loss relief b/f		(12,600)				
	0	51,600	53,900	14,700	49,900	0
Bank interest	600	1,400	1,700	0	0	0
Total profits	600	53,000	55,600	14,700	49,900	0
Less: Loss relief						
– Current period	(0)					(0)
– Carry back	n/a	(13,250)	(55,600)	(14,700)	(49,900)	
	600	39,750	0	0	0	0
Less: QCD relief	(600)	(1,000)	wasted	wasted	wasted	wasted
TTP	0	38,750	0	0	0	0

Loss working

	£
Tax adjusted trading loss – 3 m/e 31.3.2017	152,650
Relief given in:	
– 3 m/e 31.3.2017	(0)
– 9 m/e 31.12.2016	(49,900)
– y/e 31.3.2016	(14,700)
– y/e 31.3.2015	(55,600)
– y/e 31.3.2014 (3/12 × £53,000)	(13,250)
Loss unrelieved	19,200

Tutorial note

1   *Starfish Ltd would not have made a loss relief claim against total profits for the period ended 31 March 2013 as this would have used £600 of the loss, but wasted the qualifying charitable donations (QCDs) for that period and saved no tax as the QCDs already cover the taxable profits.*

2   *The trading loss for the period ended 31 March 2017 is a terminal loss, and can therefore be relieved against total profits:*

   – *firstly for the period of the loss (£0 in this case), and then*

   – *carried back to the previous 36 months prior to the start of the loss-making period, on a LIFO basis.*

   As there is a 9 month CAP in the terminal loss carry back period, the loss can be carried back into the year ended 31 March 2014 computation, but can only be set against 3/12 of the total profits in that year.

3   *Note that the terminal loss is offset against total profits (i.e. before QCDs). The relief for QCDs is therefore wasted in each of the last four CAPs. The loss relief is an all or nothing claim and cannot be restricted to preserve relief for the QCDs.*

Examiner's report

Part (a) was very well answered, with many very good answers.

The only aspect consistently answered incorrectly was the treatment of a purchased asset. In the final capital allowances computation no allowances are given, so the addition should simply have been added to the main pool.

In part (b) many candidates overlooked the trading loss for the final period of trading.

Note: *The examiner's report has been edited to remove comments on elements of the question that have been deleted due to changes to the examination format.*

ACCA marking scheme		
		Marks
(a)	Depreciation	0.5
	Donations	1.5
	Impairment loss	1.0
	Entertaining customers	0.5
	Entertaining employees	0.5
	Counselling services	0.5
	P & M – WDV brought forward	0.5
	– Addition	1.5
	– Main pool proceeds	2.0
	– Special rate pool proceeds	1.0
	– Balancing adjustments	0.5
		10.0
(b)	Trading profit	0.5
	Relief for 2013 loss – Period ended 31 March 2013 (£0)	0.5
	– Carry forward	0.5
	Bank interest	0.5
	Relief for 2017 loss – Year ended 31 March 2014	1.0
	– Other periods	1.0
	Qualifying charitable donations	1.0
		5.0
Total		**15.0**

235 HEAVY LTD (ADAPTED) *Walk in the footsteps of a top tutor*

Key answer tips

This question required a straightforward corporation tax computation, and easy marks were available for a basic pro forma and straightforward adjustments to trading profits for depreciation and capital allowances.

Heavy Ltd

Corporation tax computation – year ended 31 July 2017

	£
Operating profit	433,100
Add back: Depreciation	12,880
Health and safety fine	9,000
	454,980
Less: Capital allowances (W1)	(76,370)
Trading profit	378,610
Chargeable gain (W2)	37,852

Total profits		416,462
Less: Property loss		(10,000)
TTP		406,462
Corporation tax		
(£406,462 × 20%)		81,292

Tutorial note

1   The sale of the office building does not give rise to a chargeable gain as it is an inter-group transfer of a capital asset to Soft Ltd, a 75% group company. The transfer is therefore a no gain/no loss event.

2   The UK dividends are exempt from UK corporation tax and are therefore excluded from TTP.

3   The property business loss is automatically set against total profits of the current period.

Workings

(W1) Capital allowances

	£	Main pool £	SLA (1) £	SLA (2) £	Special rate pool £	Allow-ances £
TWDV b/f		900	15,100	13,200	21,700	
Addition qualifying for AIA						
Office equipment	22,400					
Computers	25,000					
Less: AIA (100%)	(47,400)					47,400
		0				
Disposal proceeds				(4,600)	(12,300)	
		900	15,100	8,600	9,400	
Balancing allowance				(8,600)		8,600
Small pool WDA		(900)				900
WDA (18%)			(2,718)			2,718
WDA (8%)					(752)	752
Addition qualifying for FYA						
New low emission car ($CO_2 \leq 75$ g/km)	16,000					
Less FYA (100%)	(16,000)					16,000
		0				
TWDV c/f		0	12,382	0	8,648	
Total allowances						76,370

Tutorial note

1   The cost of software is specifically deemed to be plant and machinery for the purposes of capital allowances.

2   The balance on the main pool is less than £1,000 so a small pool writing down allowance equal to the unrelieved expenditure can be claimed.

3   Short life asset (1), being an item of plant and machinery, qualifies for a WDA at the rate of 18%. Short life asset (2) was disposed of in the year for proceeds less than its tax written down value and a balancing allowance therefore arises.

4   The motor car acquired on 24 April 2017 is a new low emission car (CO_2 emissions ≤ 75 g/km) and therefore qualifies for a 100% FYA. The private use of the motor car is irrelevant, since such usage will be assessed on the managing director as an employment benefit.

5   Although all of the items included in the special rate pool have been sold, there is no balancing allowance arising as the business is a continuing business which has not ceased.

(W2) Sale of car park

	£
Sale proceeds (March 2017)	45,000
Less: Cost (May 2002)	
£10,000 × (£45,000/(£45,000 + £50,000))	(4,737)
Unindexed gain	40,263
Less: Indexation allowance (W)	
Cost (£4,737 × 0.509)	(2,411)
Chargeable gain	37,852

(W3) Indexation factor

The indexation factor from May 2002 to March 2017 is:

(265.9 − 176.2)/176.2 = 0.509 (rounded to three decimal places)

Examiner's report

There were many very good answers.

The aspects that caused problems were not appreciating that:

1   There was no chargeable gain on a disposal of an office building to Soft Ltd because of the 75% group relationship.

2   The balance on the main capital allowances pool could be fully written off as it was less than £1,000.

3   There was no balancing allowance on the special rate pool despite all the items included therein having been sold.

Note: *The examiner's report has been edited to remove comments on elements of the question that have been deleted due to changes to the examination format.*

ACCA marking scheme	
	Marks
Operating profit	0.5
Depreciation	0.5
Health and safety fine	0.5
Capital allowances – Software qualifying expenditure	0.5
– AIA	1.0
– Main pool – small pool WDA	1.0
– SLA (1)	1.0
– SLA (2)	2.0
– Special rate pool	2.0
– Low emission car	2.0
No chargeable gain on transfer to Soft Ltd	1.0
Chargeable gain on part disposal of land	1.5
Offset of property business loss	1.0
Corporation tax	0.5
	——
Total	**15.0**
	——

236 SOFTAPP LTD (ADAPTED) *Walk in the footsteps of a top tutor*

Key answer tips

This question includes a wide range of corporation tax topics including an adjusted trading profit computation, capital allowances computation, property business income and loan relationships. Originally the question also included the profits of an overseas branch and the calculation of double tax relief, but these are no longer examinable and have therefore been replaced.

Unusually you are instructed to start your computation with the operating profit figure, rather than the more usual approach of starting with the net profit figure. This should not cause any problems but requires care and a slightly different approach.

Tutor's top tips

This corporation tax computation is presented in a familiar format, with a statement of profit or loss followed by a number of notes.

However, note that you are instructed to start your computation with the operating profit figure, rather than the more usual approach of starting with the net profit figure. When adjusting the operating profit for tax purposes note that you will not need to make the 'usual' adjustments for items which appear below operating profit in the statement of profit or loss. For example, you do not need to deduct loan interest receivable from the operating profit as it is not been included in the £913,000 figure.

As usual work methodically through the statement, referring to the notes where appropriate, and enter each item in your computation as you go.

The capital additions are slightly unusual but the examining team has given a big clue as to their treatment by indicating which are integral to the building. The question also requires the calculation of property business income from a list of receipts and payments. Care needs to be taken to only include those items which relate to the accounting period.

Corporation tax computation – year ended 31 March 2017

	£	£
Adjustment of profits:		
Operating profit	913,000	
Depreciation	8,170	
Amortisation	2,500	
Interest payable (W1)		(62,200)
Capital allowances (W2)		(201,620)
	————	————
	923,670	(263,820)
	(263,820)	————
	————	
Trading profit	659,850	
Property income (W3)	21,800	
Interest income (W4)	3,100	
Chargeable gain	61,300	
	————	
Taxable total profits	746,050	
	————	
Corporation tax liability (£746,050 × 20%)	149,210	
	————	
Due payment date (W5)	1 January 2018	

Workings

(W1) Loan interest payable for trading purposes

	£
Debenture interest	42,200
Freehold property (£25,000 × 4/5)	20,000
	————
	62,200
	————

Tutorial note

Interest paid in respect of a loan used for trading purposes is deductible in calculating the trading profit. Only four of the five floors of the office building are used for trading purposes. Therefore 4/5ths of the loan interest is deductible from trading profits.

The remaining 1/5th which relates to the floor which is let out is deductible from interest income under the loan relationship rules. Note that it is not deductible from property income.

(W2) Plant and machinery – Capital allowances

	£	Main pool £	Special rate pool £	Allowances £
TWDV b/f		0	0	
Additions qualifying for AIA				
Integral features (Note):				
Heating system	93,600			
Ventilation system	75,600			
	169,200			
Less: AIA (Max £500,000)	(169,200)			169,200
			0	
Additions qualifying for AIA				
Plant and machinery:				
Furniture and furnishings	38,400			
Refrigerator and cooker	1,400			
	39,800			
Less: AIA (remaining max)				
(£200,000 – £169,200)	(30,800)			30,800
		9,000		
Less: WDA (18%)		(1,620)		1,620
TWDV c/f		7,380	0	
Total allowances				201,620

Tutorial note

Note that there are no allowances available for the building costs, only integral features and plant and machinery purchases qualify.

The expenditure which is integral to the building is included in the special rate pool.

It is beneficial to claim the annual investment allowance of £200,000 initially against this expenditure, as it would otherwise only qualify for writing down allowance at the rate of 8%, instead of 18% in the main pool.

(W3) Property income

	£
Rent receivable (£15,600 + (15,600 × 2/3))	26,000
Security deposit	0
Less: Allowable expenses	
Advertising	(600)
Insurance (£1,200 × 5/12)	(500)
Repairs (£12,800 – £9,700)	(3,100)
Property income	21,800

Tutorial note

1   *Property income is calculated, like trading income, on the accruals basis. The rent receivable for the five months to 31 March 2017 is taxable (and not the actual rent received in the accounting period). Similarly, only the insurance payable for the 5 months to 31 March 2017 is deductible in the year to 31 March 2017.*

2   *A security deposit, less the cost of making good any damage, is returned to the tenant on the cessation of a letting. It is therefore initially not treated as income.*

3   *The insurance proceeds relate to the repair costs. As a tax deduction is available from trading profits for the repairs the associated insurance receipt is treated as taxable trading income.*

(W4) Interest income

	£
Loan interest receivable (£5,600 + £2,500)	8,100
Less: Non-trading loan interest payable on let property	
(£25,000 × 1/5)	(5,000)
Interest income	3,100

Tutorial note

Interest paid in respect of a loan used for non-trading purposes (i.e. letting), is deducted from interest income under the loan relationship rules. Note that it is not deductible from property income.

(W5) Payment date

Softapp Ltd has one related 51% group company, so the augmented profits threshold is reduced to £750,000 (£1,500,000 ÷ 2).

The company's augmented profits (same as TTP) are £746,050 and the company is therefore not a large company. As it was also not a large company in the previous accounting period the due date for the payment of tax is 9 months and one day after the end of the accounting period.

ACCA marking scheme	
	Marks
Trading income	
Operating profit	0.5
Depreciation	0.5
Amortisation	0.5
Chargeable gain	0.5
Corporation tax	0.5
Payment date	1.0
Debenture interest payable deduction	0.5
Freehold property interest payable deduction	1.0
Building costs – not a qualifying addition for capital allowances	0.5
Heating system – special rate (SR) addition	0.5
Ventilation system – SR addition	0.5
AIA firstly against SR additions	0.5
Furniture – main pool addition	0.5
Fridge and cooker – main pool addition	0.5
Balance of AIA	0.5
WDA on main pool	0.5
Rent receivable	0.5
Security deposit – not taxable income	0.5
Advertising	0.5
Insurance	1.0
Repairs net of insurance proceeds	1.0
Interest receivable	0.5
Interest payable re let property	1.0
Adjusted augmented profits threshold	0.5
Company not large in CY and PY	0.5
	——
Total	**15.0**
	——

237 E-COMMERCE PLC (ADAPTED) *Walk in the footsteps of a top tutor*

Key answer tips

Part (a) involves correcting an existing tax computation, rather than preparing the computation from scratch. This is a somewhat unusual presentation, although it is not dissimilar to that seen in a previous corporation tax question. Here, however, the question is made slightly more difficult as it also involves reversing the calculations which have already been done (incorrectly) to calculate the correct figures. This question was not popular with students, many of whom did not know how to tackle it. It is important however, to attempt every question in the examination and therefore you should set out the computation, including the figures you do know, attempt the workings for those you don't (making assumptions if necessary), and then go on to calculate the corporation tax liability, for which you will get follow through marks, even if parts of your answer are wrong. This part is also only for 12 marks, so you must make sure you don't overrun on time here.

Part (b) requires you to identify why the company would not pay instalments in the current year and why they would be due in the following year. This should be straightforward provided these aspects of administration have been learnt.

The highlighted words in the answer are key phrases that markers are looking for.

(a)   **Revised corporation tax computation – year ended 31 March 2017**

Tutor's top tips

In a challenging question such as this, it is important to maximise marks with a systematic approach and making sure you score all the easy marks (of which there are many).

Start by laying out your computation – inserting any obvious figures (such as those figures provided in the question which you know are correct) and leaving blank the more difficult ones. Then work through the gaps, doing straightforward workings on the face of the computation and more detailed ones in referenced workings underneath.

Where you are not sure you need to make a decision and move on, do not waste too much time on one small point.

For some of the figures, you need to reverse the calculations which have been carried out incorrectly (some of which are not shown in the question), before doing the revised calculations. This requires a good understanding of the way the calculations work, rather than just the ability to follow the pro forma and crunch the numbers. There are a number of ways these calculations could be presented, and this is discussed further in the tips below.

		£	£
Operating profit			2,102,300*
Legal fees	– Issue of preference shares (Note 1)	80,200	
	– Issue of loan notes (Note 2)	0	
	– Renewal of long lease (Note 3)	14,900	
	– Breach of contract (Note 4)	0	
	– Registration of trade marks (Note 5)	0	
		———	95,100
			———
			2,197,400
Deduction for lease premium (£14,400 × 12/15) (Note 6)			(11,520)
Capital allowances		209,200*	
Motor car [1] (Note 7)		0	
Motor car [2] (Note 7)		0	
Motor car [3] (£62,100 × 10% (18% – 8%) (Note 8)		(6,210)	
Motor car [4] (£19,800 × 82% (100% – 18%) (Note 9)		16,236	
Short-life asset (£1,512 × 82/18) (Note 10)		6,888	
		———	(226,114)
			———
Trading profit			1,959,766
Property income		156,700*	
Repairs (capital in nature)		95,300	
Rent accrual – March 2017 (£16,200 × 1/3) (Note 11)		5,400	
		———	257,400
Loan interest receivable		42,400*	
Accrual (£4,800 – £3,500) (Note 11)		(1,300)	
		———	41,100
			———
Taxable total profits			2,258,266
			———
Corporation tax (£2,258,266 at 20%*)			451,653
			———

*Figures provided in question

Tutor's top tips

Whilst it would be possible to calculate the capital allowances by doing a revised capital allowances computation, not all of the figures for that computation (such as the brought forward balance on the main pool) were provided in the question. Therefore it would be necessary to do significantly more workings (to establish the missing figures) if this approach were taken. It is therefore easier to simply correct the mistakes you are aware of via short workings as shown above.

Tutorial note

1   The issue of preference shares is not a trading expense and therefore the associated legal fees are not an allowable deduction.

2   Legal fees in relation to the issue of loan notes will be treated in the same way as the loan they relate to. Here the loan was for trading purposes, therefore the fees are a deductible trading expense.

3   Legal fees relating to a lease are only deductible if it is the **renewal** of a **short** (50 years or less) lease.

4   Legal fees for breach of contract are generally deductible, since they are likely to relate to a trading purpose.

5   Legal fees in relation to the registration of trademarks relate to the trade, and are therefore tax deductible.

6   Since it is only the life of the lease which was incorrect in the original calculation, this can be corrected by simply multiplying the figure given by the 12 years used originally and dividing by the correct figure of 15 years. It is not necessary to try to recalculate the deduction from scratch, and this would prove very difficult as the figure for the premium paid was not provided in the question.

7   Motor cars [1] and [2] have CO_2 emissions between 76 and 130 grams per kilometre, and qualify for writing down allowances at the rate of 18%. No adjustment is therefore required.

8   Motor car [3] has CO_2 emissions over 130 grams per kilometre, and therefore only qualifies for writing down allowances at the rate of 8%.

9   Motor car [4] has CO_2 emissions up to 75 grams per kilometre, and therefore qualifies for the 100% first year allowance.

10   The scrapping of the computer equipment is a disposal for capital allowances purposes. The company should therefore have received a 100% balancing allowance rather than a writing down allowance at the rate of 18%. The 82/18 adjustment represents the additional 82% (100% − 18%) of the brought forward TWDV which can be deducted.

11   Property and interest income must be dealt with on an accruals basis, therefore an adjustment is required for the rent due in respect of the period and the correct loan interest accrual.

(b) **Quarterly instalment payments**

Tutor's top tips

Being able to determine when corporation tax is payable is a common examination requirement, and it is important to learn the rules about which companies must pay by quarterly instalments and the exceptions from that system, which are relevant here.

- Large companies have to make quarterly instalment payments in respect of their corporation tax liability. A large company is one with augmented profits exceeding £1,500,000, adjusted for short accounting periods and related 51% group companies.

- However, a company is not required to make quarterly instalment payments in the first year that it is large.

  Therefore, E-Commerce plc will not have been required to make instalment payments for the year ended 31 March 2017 as it was not a large company in the year ended 31 March 2016.

  This is because the augmented profits of £1,360,000 were less than £1,500,000.

- For the year ended 31 March 2018, this exception will not apply. Therefore, E-Commerce plc will have to make quarterly instalment payments as its augmented profits will exceed £1,500,000.

Examiner's report

Part (a) was not particularly difficult, but the information was presented in a different format to previous questions of this nature. However, candidates would have benefited from knowing the pro forma layout.

The requirement was generally reasonably well answered and there were a few highly satisfactory answers. The deduction for the lease premium caused the most problems, with many candidates not appreciating that there was no need to recalculate the amount assessed on the landlord – thereby spending quite a bit of time unnecessarily.

Part (b) was also reasonably well answered, although to score full marks it was necessary for answers to be quite precise – not, for example, just mentioning large companies, without explaining what a large company is.

ACCA marking scheme

		Marks
(a)	Correct figures from return – operating profit, capital allowances, property profit, loan interest receivable	1.0
	Legal fees re preference shares	0.5
	Legal fees re loan notes	0.5
	Legal fees re renewal of lease	0.5
	Legal fees re breach of contract	0.5
	Legal fees re registration of trade marks	0.5
	Deduction for lease premium	1.0
	Capital allowances – motor car [1]	0.5
	– motor car [2]	0.5
	– motor car [3]	1.0
	– motor car [4]	1.0
	– short life asset	1.0
	Repairs disallowed	1.0
	Rent accrual	1.0
	Loan interest accrual adjustment	1.0
	Corporation tax liability	0.5
		———
		12.0
		———
(b)	Companies with augmented profits exceeding £1,500,000	1.0
	No instalments if not large in previous year	1.0
	No exception in year ended 31 March 2018	1.0
		———
		3.0
		———
Total		**15.0**
		———

238   LUCKY LTD   *Walk in the footsteps of a top tutor*

(a)   **The start of accounting period**

Key answer tips

This three part question on corporation tax is a classic section C corporation tax question.

Parts (a) and (c) test knowledge of administrative aspects of corporation tax.

Part (b) which is worth 11 out of the 15 marks available, is a straightforward corporation tax computation with marks available for adjustments to trading profit, capital allowances and the calculation of corporation tax.

The highlighted words in the answer are key phrases that markers are looking for.

Tutor's top tips

Parts (a) and (c) of this question could both be attempted before reading the scenario or carrying out the corporation tax computation in part (b). Answering both of these straightforward written parts first could help you manage your time, and ensure that you don't spend too long on part (b).

- An accounting period will normally start immediately after the end of the preceding accounting period.

- An accounting period will also start when a company commences to trade, or otherwise becomes liable to corporation tax.

Tutorial note

This is a common examination requirement and could be tested with either an objective test question or constructed response question, meaning it could feature in any one of the three examination sections.

(b) **Lucky Ltd – Corporation tax computation for the four-month period ended 31 March 2017**

Tutor's top tips

Begin part (b) by setting out the corporation tax pro forma then work through the information given, inserting the more straightforward numbers first (such as the interest income). Where a working is required (for example the capital allowances) attempt these after the easier numbers, but make sure you leave time to calculate the corporation tax!

	£	£
Operating profit per question		532,600
Advertising	0	
Depreciation	14,700	
Amortisation	9,000	
Deduction for lease premium (W1)	(1,300)	
Capital allowances (W2)	(80,291)	
		(57,891)
Tax adjusted trading profit		474,709
Interest income		700
Taxable total profits		475,409
Corporation tax (£475,409 at 20%)		95,082

Tutorial note

The advertising expenditure incurred during September 2016 is pre-trading expenditure. As it is incurred within seven years of the trade commencing, it is treated as being incurred on 1 December 2016. It is therefore deductible and no adjustment is required.

Workings

(W1) Deduction for lease premium

$£46,800/12 \times 4/12 = £1,300$

Tutorial note

The steps for calculating the allowable trading deduction for a lease premium paid by a company are as follows:

- ***Calculate the amount of the premium paid by the company that will be taxable for the landlord as property income.***

In this question the amount of premium assessed on the landlord as income has been given (£46,800) so do not waste time calculating this figure.

- ***The annual deduction available from trading profits is the property income on which the landlord taxed, divided by the number of years of the lease.***

In this question the annual deduction is 46,800/12 but since the lease was taken out on 1 December 2016 only 4/12 of this amount is deductible for the year ended 31 March 2017.

- ***Disallow any amortisation relating to the lease premium in the accounts.***

In this question the amortisation of £9,000 needs to be added back.

(W2) Capital allowances

4 m/e 31 March 2017	£	Main pool £	Special rate pool £	Allowances £
TWDV b/f		0	0	0
Additions qualifying for AIA				
Integral feature	41,200			
Less: AIA (100%)				
Max				
(£200,000 × 4/12 = £66,667)	(41,200)			41,200
	————		0	
Computer	6,300			
Office equipment	32,900			
	————			
	39,200			
Less: AIA (100%)				
(£66,667 − £41,200)	(25,467)			25,467
	————	13,733		
Less: WDA (18%) × 4/12		(824)		824
Addition qualifying for FYA				
Motor car	12,800			
Less: FYA (100%)	(12,800)			12,800
	————	0		
		————		
TWDV c/f		12,909		
		————		
Total allowances				80,291
				————

Tutorial notes

1   The computer purchased on 19 August 2016 is pre-trading expenditure as it was purchased within the seven years before the trade commenced. Therefore it is treated as purchased on 1 December 2016 for capital allowance purposes.

2   The motor car has CO_2 emissions up to 75 grams per kilometre, and therefore qualifies for the 100% first year allowance.

3   The expenditure which is integral to the building is included in the special rate pool.

4   It is beneficial to claim the annual investment allowance of £66,667 initially against special rate pool expenditure, as it would otherwise only qualify for 8% writing down allowance, whereas main pool expenditure will qualify for 18% writing down allowance.

(c)   **Retaining records**

Tutor's top tips

Due dates and time limits are easily tested in any of the three sections of the F6 examination. They are a source of easy marks provided you have learnt them!

- Lucky Ltd must retain the records used in preparing its self-assessment corporation tax return until six years after the end of the accounting period, which is 31 March 2023.

- A failure to retain records could result in a penalty of up to £3,000 per accounting period. However, the maximum penalty will only be charged in serious cases.

ACCA marking scheme		
		Marks
(a)	The start of accounting period	2.0
(b)	Lucky Ltd – Corporation tax computation for 4 m/e 31 March 2017	
	Advertising	0.5
	Depreciation	0.5
	Amortisation	0.5
	Deduction for lease premium	1.5
	Interest income	0.5
	Corporation tax	1.0
	Capital allowances	
	Integral feature	1.0
	Computer	0.5
	Office equipment	0.5
	AIA	2.0
	WDA	1.0
	Motor car	0.5
	FYA	1.0
		11.0
(c)	Retaining records	2.0
Total		**15.0**

RELIEF FOR TRADING LOSSES

239   HALF-LIFE LTD (ADAPTED)

Key answer tips

A loss question which is largely computational but it involves the use of a normal ongoing trading loss, and a terminal loss.

There are two consecutive losses, the first arising from a short three month period. The second is the terminal loss of the last twelve months trading.

Make sure you get the easy marks and give the dates required in part (b).

For ease, use a columnar format to present the loss offset in part (a) and remember to show your record of the losses and their usage.

The highlighted words in the answer are key phrases that markers are looking for.

(a)   **Taxable total profits**

	y/e 31.3.14	y/e 31.3.15	y/e 31.3.16	p/e 30.6.16	y/e 30.6.17
	£	£	£	£	£
Trading profit	224,000	67,400	38,200	0	0
Property income	8,200	12,200	6,500	4,400	
Chargeable gains			5,600		23,700
	———	———	———	———	———
Total profits	232,200	79,600	50,300	4,400	23,700
Less: Loss relief					
– p/e 30.6.16 loss			(50,300)	(4,400)	
– y/e 30.6.17 loss (W)	(174,150)	(79,600)			(23,700)
	———	———	———	———	———
	58,050	0	0	0	0
Less: QCD relief	(1,200)	wasted			wasted
	———	———	———	———	———
Taxable total profits	56,850	0	0	0	0
	———	———	———	———	———

Loss memorandum

	£	£
Loss for the period ended 30 June 2016	61,700	
Loss for the year ended 30 June 2017		308,800
Losses utilised:		
Current period claim		
– Period ended 30 June 2016	(4,400)	
12 month carry back claim		
– y/e 31 March 2016	(50,300)	
Current year claim		
– y/e 30 June 2017		(23,700)
36 month terminal loss carry back claim		
– y/e 31 March 2015		(79,600)
– y/e 31 March 2014 (W)		(174,150)
	———	———
Losses unrelieved	7,000	31,350
	———	———

Working: Terminal loss – set off in y/e 31.3.14

For the year ended 31 March 2014, loss relief is restricted to £174,150 (£232,200 × 9/12) as only 9 months of the year falls into the 36 months carry back period from the start of the final loss making accounting period.

Tutorial note

The trading loss for the period ended 30 June 2016 can be relieved against total profits of the current period and the previous 12 months.

The trading loss for the year ended 30 June 2017 can be relieved against total profits of the current year and the previous 36 months because it is a terminal loss.

Unrelieved qualifying charitable donations

Qualifying charitable donations of £1,000 for the year ended 31 March 2015 and £700 for the year ended 30 June 2017 are unrelieved.

(b) **Due date for loss relief claims**

- The loss relief claims against total profits in respect of the loss for the period ended 30 June 2016 must be made by 30 June 2018.

- The loss relief claims against total profits in respect of the loss for the year ended 30 June 2017 must be made by 30 June 2019.

(c) **Corporation tax repayments**

Year ended 31 March 2014

- Corporation tax of £34,830 (£174,150 at 20%) will be repaid in respect of the year ended 31 March 2014.

Year ended 31 March 2015

- Taxable total profits for the year ended 31 March 2015 were originally £78,600 (£79,600 – £1,000 QCD relief)

- Taxable total profits after loss relief is £0

- Corporation tax of £15,720 (£78,600 at 20%) will be repaid.

Year ended 31 March 2016

- Taxable total profits for the year ended 31 March 2016 were originally £50,300

- Taxable total profits after loss relief is £0

- Corporation tax of £10,060 (£50,300 at 20%) will be repaid.

Tutorial note

No tax is repayable in respect of the period ending 30 June 2016 or year ended 30 June 2017 as no tax will have been paid in respect of these periods. The company is not making instalments and the corporation tax return for both periods will show corporation tax payable of £0.

---

240   VOLATILE LTD (ADAPTED)   *Walk in the footsteps of a top tutor*

Key answer tips

A familiar style corporation tax losses question requiring relief to be claimed as soon as possible and a calculation of the loss left to carry forward.

The highlighted words in the answer are key phrases that markers are looking for.

Tutor's top tips

Part (a) requires a purely written answer highlighting the key factors that influence the choice of loss relief.

Only 2 marks are available, suggesting that 2 bullet points will suffice to answer this part.

This requirement is a common request in losses questions and you should learn the factors so that you can jot them down quickly in the examination.

(a)   **Factors influencing the choice of loss reliefs**

Cash flow

- The timing of the relief obtained is a key factor. A claim against total profits in the loss making period, then carry back will result in earlier relief than a claim against future trading profits.

Wastage of qualifying charitable donations

- The extent to which relief for qualifying charitable donations will be lost is another factor, since these cannot be carried forward.

Tutorial note

Remember that for companies, a carry back election cannot be made until the current year total profits have been relieved first.

(b)   **Taxable total profits**

	y/e 31 Dec 2014	9 m/e 30 Sept 2015	y/e 30 Sept 2016
	£	£	£
Trading profit	15,200	78,700	0
Property income	6,500	0	0
Chargeable gain (£11,700 – £2,000)	0	0	9,700
Total profits	21,700	78,700	9,700
Less: Loss relief (W)			
Current year			(9,700)
Carry back – 12 months	(5,425)	(78,700)	
	16,275	0	0
Less: QCD relief	(1,200)	wasted	wasted
Taxable total profits	15,075	0	0

Loss working

	£
Trading loss	101,800
Current year relief (Note)	(9,700)
Carry back relief (previous 12 months)	
– 9 m/e 30 September 2015	(78,700)
	13,400
– y/e 31 December 2014 (£21,700 × 3/12)	(5,425)
Unrelieved loss as at 30 September 2016	7,975

Tutorial note

For the year ended 31 December 2014 loss relief is restricted to the lower of:

(i)   *the proportion of the profits of that period of account that falls into the 12 months carry back period preceding 1 October 2015 (i.e. 3 months)*

= (£21,700 × 3/12) = £5,425

(ii)   *the remainder of the loss = £13,400*

Examiner's report

This question was not particularly well answered.

In part (a) far too many candidates explained the loss reliefs available rather than the factors influencing the choice of claims.

In part (b) many candidates approached this on a year by year basis, rather than one computation with a column for each of the periods. This not only wasted time in having to write out several computations, but also made it very difficult to calculate the correct loss relief claims.

Other common mistakes included treating the chargeable gains separately (rather than as part of the taxable total profits), and deducting qualifying charitable donations from trading profits rather than total income after loss relief.

ACCA marking scheme		Marks
(a)	Timing of relief	1.0
	Impact on qualifying charitable donations	1.0
		2.0
(b)	Trading profits	0.5
	Property business profits	0.5
	Chargeable gain	1.5
	Loss relief – Year ended 30 September 2016	1.0
	– Period ended 30 September 2015	1.0
	– Year ended 31 December 2014	2.0
	Qualifying charitable donations	1.0
	Unrelieved trading losses	0.5
		8.0
Total		**10.0**

241 RETRO LTD *Walk in the footsteps of a top tutor*

Key answer tips

This question on corporation tax losses starts with a requirement to calculate the amount of the corporation tax loss.

The remaining parts require consideration of how to relieve the loss and a calculation of the remaining loss to carry forward.

The highlighted words in part (c) are key phrases that markers are looking for.

Tutor's top tips

Make sure you follow the presentation instructions given. This is the standard approach the markers would expect to see in any adjustments to profit calculation.

(a) **Trading loss – year ended 31 March 2017**

	£
Loss before taxation	(120,000)
Depreciation	27,240
Gifts to employees (Note 1)	0
Gifts to customers (Note 2)	0
Political donations	420
Qualifying charitable donations	680
Impairment loss	0
Lease of motor car (£4,400 × 15%)	660
Health and safety fine	5,100
Legal fees – Internet domain name (Note 3)	0
Interest payable (Note 4)	0
Capital allowances (W)	(50,420)
	———
Trading loss	(136,320)
	———

Tutorial note

1   *Gifts to employees are an allowable deduction regardless of cost or the fact that the gift is food. This is because the gifts will be assessed on the employees as benefits of employment.*

2   *Gifts to customers are an allowable deduction if they cost less than £50 per recipient per year, are not of food, drink, tobacco or vouchers for exchangeable goods and carry a conspicuous advertisement for the company making the gift.*

3   *Legal fees incurred in defending the title to non-current assets (e.g. the domain name) are incurred for the purposes of the trade and are allowable trading expenses.*

4   *Interest on a loan used for trading purposes is deductible on an accruals basis.*

Working: Capital allowances

	£	Main pool £	Allowances £
TWDV brought forward		39,300	
Addition – Motor car (1)		14,700	
Additions qualifying for AIA			
Delivery van	28,300		
Less: AIA (100%)	(28,300)		28,300
	———	0	
		———	
		54,000	
Less: WDA (18%)		(9,720)	9,720
Addition qualifying for FYA			
Motor car (2)	12,400		
Less: FYA (100%)	(12,400)		12,400
	———	0	
		———	
TWDV carried forward		44,280	
		———	———
Total allowances			50,420
			———

Tutorial note

1   *Motor car (1) has CO_2 emissions between 76 and 130 g/km, and therefore qualifies for writing down allowances at the rate of 18%.*

2   *Motor car (2) has CO_2 emissions of less than 75 g/km, and therefore qualifies for the 100% first year allowance. In the absence of any other information always assume that cars purchased are new cars (not second hand).*

(b)   **Loss relief**

Tutor's top tips

It is more efficient to use a columnar format for loss relief questions.

A company cannot carry back losses unless they are offset against current year total profits first. However, only the carry back periods need to be shown in the answer as there is no other income in the loss-making period (year ended 31 March 2017) to set the losses against.

	Year ended	7 m/e
	31 August 2015	**31 March 2016**
	£	£
Trading profit	56,600	47,900
Bank interest	1,300	0
Total profits	57,900	47,900
Less: Loss relief – 12 month carry back (Note)		
– 7 m/e 31.3.16		(47,900)
– y/e 31.8.15 (£57,900 × 5/12)	(24,125)	
	33,775	0
Less: QCD relief	(540)	(wasted)
TTP	33,235	0

Tutorial note

Corporation tax losses can be carried back exactly 12 months before the start of the loss-making period.

If in the 12 month carry back period there has been a change in accounting date, and there is a short period of account, the loss can be carried back to two periods. The loss is carried back on a LIFO basis.

In this question, the loss is therefore carried back against the 7 m/e 31 March 2016 first, and then against the y/e 31 August 2015.

When carried back to the year ended 31 August 2015, the remaining loss can only be set against 5/12 of the total profits of that period.

(c)   **Loss carried forward**

Tutor's top tips

It would be equally acceptable to show the loss memorandum within your answer to parts (b) or (c).

- The amount of unrelieved trading loss at 31 March 2017 is £64,295 (W).

- The unrelieved trading loss can be carried forward and will be relieved against the first available trading profits of the same trade.

Working: Loss memorandum

	£
Loss in y/e 31 March 2017	136,320
Less: Current period	(0)
Carry back losses 12 months (LIFO basis)	
– 7 m/e 31 March 2016	(47,900)
– 5 m/e 31 August 2015	(24,125)
	———
Loss c/f	64,295
	———

Examiner's report

Part (a) Most candidates had little difficulty with this section. One poor practice was the use of notes and explanations. It was a simple matter, as per the model answer, to just list all the items of expenditure (and show whether or not an adjustment was required), so the use of notes (such as for the gifts and donations) was completely unnecessary and against the guidance given in the note to the requirement. Since the requirement was for a calculation, explanations are not required, and result in wasted time. As regards the capital allowances, many candidates did not appreciate that the delivery van qualified for the 100% annual investment allowance – instead including it in the special rate pool.

Part (b) There were many perfect answers to this section, although disappointingly a few candidates tried to time-apportion profits using the opening year rules.

Part (c) This section caused few problems, although many candidates did not mention that the carry forward would be against the first available profits.

		Marks
	ACCA marking scheme	
(a)	**Adjustment to profits**	
	Depreciation	0.5
	Gifts to employees	0.5
	Gifts to customers	0.5
	Political donations	0.5
	Qualifying charitable donations	0.5
	Impairment loss	0.5
	Lease of motor car	1.0
	Health and safety fine	0.5
	Legal fees – Internet domain name	0.5
	Interest payable	0.5
	Capital allowances	
	TWDV b/f	0.5
	Additions qualifying for AIA - delivery van	0.5
	AIA – 100%	0.5
	Addition – motor car (1)	0.5
	WDA – 18%	0.5
	Addition qualifying for FYA – motor car	0.5
	FYA – 100%	0.5
		───
		9.0
		───
(b)	Trading profits	0.5
	Bank interest	0.5
	Loss relief	1.0
	Restriction of relief to 5m/e 31 August 2015	1.0
	QCD	1.0
		───
		4.0
		───
(c)	Amount of unrelieved trading loss	1.0
	Loss c/f	1.0
		───
		2.0
		───
Total		**15.0**
		───

WITH GROUP ASPECTS

242 MUSIC PLC (ADAPTED)

Key answer tips

In this question there are 10 marks for written explanations of the gains group and related 51% group company rules. It is important to state the basic rule and then apply to the facts of the question. Be careful with the overseas company, which is included but unable to enjoy the benefits of gains group status.

The highlighted words in the answer are key phrases that markers are looking for.

(a)   **Capital gains group**

- Companies form a capital gains group if at each level in the group structure there is a 75% shareholding, provided the parent company has an effective interest of more than 50%.

- Alto Ltd, Bass Ltd, Cello Ltd, Echo Inc and Flute Ltd are all 75% subsidiaries, and Music plc has an effective interest of 60% (80% × 75%) in Flute Ltd. All of these companies therefore form a capital gains group.

- However, Bass Ltd and Cello Ltd will only be included in respect of assets acquired or disposed of whilst they were members of the group.

- Drum Ltd and Gong Ltd are not included as Drum Ltd is not a 75% subsidiary, and Music plc's effective interest in Gong Ltd is only 48% (80% × 75% × 80%).

- Although Echo Inc is included in the definition of the capital gains group, companies that are resident overseas are not able to take advantage of the provisions applicable to a capital gains group.

(b)   **Related 51% group companies**

- Music plc directly owns at least 51% of the shares in Alto Ltd, Bass Ltd, Cello Ltd and Echo Inc. They are therefore related 51% group companies.

- Flute Ltd is also a related 51% group company as Music Ltd indirectly owns at least 51% of the company i.e. 80% × 75% = 60%.

- Gong Ltd is not a related 51% group company as Music Ltd owns (indirectly) less than 51% of the company i.e. 80% × 75% × 80% = 48%.

- Drum Ltd is not a related 51% group company since Music plc's effective interest in this company is only 45%.

- For these purposes, it does not matter where a company is resident. Echo Inc is therefore included despite being resident overseas.

- Companies related for part of the accounting period, such as Bass Ltd and Cello Ltd, count as 51% related companies for the whole of the period.

(c)   **Corporation tax liability – year ended 31 March 2017**

	£
Trading profit	92,000
Interest income	12,000
Net chargeable gains (W)	23,000
Taxable total profits	127,000
Corporation tax (£127,000 × 20%)	25,400

Tutorial note

The capital gain of £120,000 is included in Music plc's taxable total profits since an election has been made with Alto Ltd to transfer the gain to Music plc. Music plc's capital losses may be set against this gain.

Working: Net chargeable gain

	£
Net chargeable gain in the year (by election)	120,000
Less: Capital losses in the year	(65,000)
	_____
	55,000
Less: Capital losses b/f	(32,000)
	_____
Net chargeable gain	23,000
	_____

(d) **Bank loan**

Under the loan relationship rules, loans used for non-trade purposes are deductible from interest income. If the loan was used to acquire a property which was to be rented out (i.e. a non-trade purpose), the interest would not be deducted from trading income, nor property business income (as for individuals), but from the company's interest income.

Legal fees

Legal fees incurred in relation to the purchase of a capital asset are not deductible from the company's trading profits. They will be deductible in the chargeable gain computation when the building is ultimately sold.

Rent receivable

The rent receivable from letting the property to a tenant will be included on an accruals basis, net of any allowable deductions, in taxable total profits as property income.

243 JUMP LTD (ADAPTED)

Key answer tips

The first part of this question involves a standard adjustment of profit computation where the company is loss making.

The second part is more difficult and requires detailed group relief knowledge and the calculation of the maximum surrender possible to a subsidiary that commenced trading during the year. The usual principles apply but the TTP and loss must be time apportioned for the period the subsidiary is part of the loss relief group.

Tutorial note

An adjustment to profits calculation is required and the fact that the company is making a loss should not change your approach in any way.

Just start with a negative figure for the loss, then make the same adjustments as you would make if it were a profit and lay out your answer in the same way.

Remember that it is important to list all the major items indicated in the question requirement, showing a zero (0) for expenditure that is allowable. This is because credit will be given for showing no adjustment where none is needed.

List the adjustments in the order they appear in the question.

If required, also add notes to show why you have not adjusted for an item, or why you have added it back. However, lengthy explanations are not required where the requirement is just to 'calculate' the adjusted profits, rather than to explain them.

Always show your workings if the figure you are adjusting for is not clear from the question.

(a)   **Jump Ltd – Trading loss for the three-month period ended 31 March 2017**

	£
Operating loss	(144,700)
Depreciation	8,100
Employee training courses (Note 1)	0
Employee pension contributions (Note 2)	0
Staff party (Note 3)	0
Lease of motor car (£1,200 × 15%) (Note 4)	180
Accountancy (Note 5)	0
Legal fees – Issue of share capital (Note 6)	3,800
– Renewal of short lease (Note 7)	0
Entertaining UK customers (Note 8)	1,700
Entertaining overseas customers (Note 8)	790
Political donations	800
Capital allowances (net balancing charge)	3,330
Trading loss	(126,000)

Tutorial note

1   *The cost of employee training courses is wholly and exclusively for trade purposes and therefore allowable.*

2   *Employer's pension contributions are allowable on a paid basis.*

3   *The only exception to the non-deductibility of entertainment expenditure is when it is in respect of employees. The £150 limit does not apply to employers, this limit relates to employment income only.*

4   *The leased car has emissions of >130g/km hence 15% of the expense has been disallowed.*

5   *Audit and accountancy fees are allowable, as they are incurred wholly and exclusively for the purposes of the trade.*

6   *Legal fees in connection with the issue of share capital are not allowable, being capital in nature.*

7   *The cost of renewing a short-lease (less than 50 years) is specifically allowable as a trading expense.*

8   *The only exception to the non-deductibility of entertainment expenditure is when it is in respect of employees.*

9   *Political donations are specifically disallowable.*

Working – Capital allowances

	Main pool	Special rate pool	Allowances
	£	£	£
TWDV brought forward	12,100	5,700	
Proceeds – Motor car [1]		(9,300)	
– Motor car [2]	(6,100)		
		————	
		(3,600)	
Balancing charge		3,600	(3,600)
	————	————	
	6,000	0	
WDA – 18% × 3/12	(270)	————	270
	————		
TWDV carried forward	5,730		
	————		
Overall balancing charge			(3,330)
			————

Tutorial note

The proceeds for motor car [1] are restricted to the original cost figure of £9,300. Note that a balancing charge can arise on the main and special rate pools at any time but a balancing allowance on these pools can only arise on the cessation of trade.

(b)   (1)   The main factor which will influence Jump Ltd's choice of loss relief or group relief claims is the timing of the relief obtained, with an earlier claim generally being preferable.

Tutorial note

Another possible factor is the extent to which relief for qualifying charitable donations will be lost. However, this is not relevant given that Jump Ltd has not made any charitable donations.

(2)   The maximum loss relief claim for the seven-month period to 31 December 2016 is £42,400, being the total profits for this period

The loss relief claim for the year ended 31 May 2016 is restricted to £33,250 ((£78,600 + £1,200) × 5/12).

(3)   The maximum amount of trading loss which can be surrendered to Hop Ltd is £23,625, being the lower of Hop Ltd's taxable total profits (£63,000 × 3/8 = £23,625) and Jump Ltd's loss of £126,000.

Skip Ltd is not a 75% subsidiary of Jump Ltd, so no group relief claim is possible.

Examiner's report

Part (a) was generally well answered; requiring a calculation of the company's tax adjusted trading loss. Candidates need to appreciate that where a profit adjustment involves a loss, then they must clearly show whether adjustments are added or deducted – in particular, capital allowances which in this case were deducted due to there being an overall balancing charge. Some candidates did not appreciate that where disposal proceeds exceed a pool's brought forward written down value, then there will be a balancing charge.

Part (b) required candidates to (1) state the main factor influencing the choice of a company's loss relief or group relief claims, (2) advise the company as to the maximum amount of trading loss which could be relieved against total profits for previous periods, and (3) advise the company as to the maximum amount of trading loss which could be surrendered as group relief. For (1), a number of candidates gave the rate of corporation tax as the main factor, despite the single 20% rate of tax. For (3), it was often not appreciated that a 75% shareholding is necessary in order for a group relief claim to be possible.

	ACCA marking scheme	Marks
(a)	Depreciation	0.5
	Employee training	0.5
	Employee pension contributions	0.5
	Staff party	0.5
	Lease	1.0
	Professional fees	1.5
	Entertaining	1.0
	Political donations	0.5
	Capital allowances add back	0.5
	TWDV b/f	0.5
	Motor car (1)	1.0
	Motor car (2)	0.5
	Balancing charge	0.5
	WDA at 18% × 3/12	1.0
		10.0
(b)	Main factor	1.0
	Max relief 6 months ended 31.12.16	0.5
	Loss relief year ended 31.5.16	1.5
	Maximum surrender to Hop	1.5
	Skip not in group	0.5
		5.0
Total		**15.0**

244 **NEUNG LTD (ADAPTED)** *Walk in the footsteps of a top tutor*

Key answer tips

This corporation tax question is a classic question, testing the calculation of a corporation tax liability. There is also a small element of corporation tax groups and group relief for losses.

The bulk of the marks available are for a short adjustment of profits calculation, a fairly detailed capital allowances computation, the calculation of taxable total profits and then the calculation of the corporation tax liability. The question originally contained some overseas income and branch losses, however these aspects are no longer in the syllabus and have been replaced by a trading loss in a group company and the due date for payment of the tax. This is a relatively straightforward group relief scenario.

You must also be careful to remember the implications of the related group companies on the due date for payment of tax.

Tutor's top tips

This question can appear daunting on first reading; however it is possible to score very well on this sort of question as long as you do not panic over the group parts where you may be less confident.

(a)   **Neung Ltd – Corporation tax liability – year ended 31 March 2017**

Tutor's top tips

It is important to take a logical step by step approach here. Think through which calculations you will need to do in workings and in particular make sure that your workings for the capital allowances are clearly laid out (on a new sheet of paper) and well referenced.

Remember to consider how to deal with the group loss.

	£
Trading profit (W1)	524,466
Interest income (£25,200 + £12,600)	37,800
Taxable total profits before group relief	562,266
Less: Group relief	(15,700)
Taxable total profits after group relief	546,566
Corporation tax liability:	
£546,566 × 20%	109,313

Tutorial note

Fifth Ltd's trading loss is available to Neung Ltd as it is a 100% subsidiary and therefore in a group relief group. Since the only other company in the group (Fourth Ltd) is dormant, the whole loss should be surrendered to Neung Ltd.

Workings

(W1) Trading profit

	£
Operating profit	727,300
Depreciation	11,830
Amortisation	7,000
Less: Lease deduction (W2)	(4,340)
Capital allowances (W3)	(217,324)
Trading profit	524,466

(W2) Lease deduction

	£
Premium paid	140,000
Less: £140,000 × 2% × (20 – 1)	(53,200)
Assessment on landlord	86,800
Allowable deduction per year (£86,800 ÷ 20)	4,340

Tutorial note

Since the property is used for business purposes, a deduction is allowed for the revenue element of the lease premium (which is the amount assessable on the landlord), spread over the life of the lease.

Alternative calculation of the assessment on the landlord:

£140,000 × (51 – 20)/50 = £86,800

(W3) Capital allowances

	£	Main pool £	Short life asset £	Special rate pool £	Allowances £
TWDV b/f		4,800	22,800	12,700	
Additions (no AIA)					
Motor car (1)				15,400	
Motor car (2)		28,600			
Additions (with AIA)					
Ventilation system	262,000				
Less: AIA	(200,000)				200,000
				62,000	
		33,400	22,800	90,100	
WDA (18%)		(6,012)			6,012
WDA 18%			(4,104)		4,104
WDA (8%)				(7,208)	7,208
TWDV c/f		27,388	18,696	82,892	
Total allowances					217,324

Tutorial notes

1   Capital allowances on car purchases are calculated based on the CO_2 emissions of the car as follows:

        –   New car with CO_2 emissions of ≤ 75 g/km:

            eligible for a FYA of 100% (none in this question)

        – CO_2 emissions of between 76 – 130 g/km:

            put in main pool and eligible for a WDA at 18% (i.e. Motor Car (2))

        – CO_2 emissions of > 130 g/km:

            put in special rate pool and eligible for a WDA at 8% (i.e. Motor Car (1))

2   The short life asset is an item of machinery and is eligible for a WDA at 18%.

3   The ventilation system is an integral feature of the freehold office building and is therefore included in the special rate pool. The AIA should always be given against special rate pool expenditure in priority to any other expenditure as it is only eligible for allowances at 8%.

(b)   **Payment of corporation tax liability**

Neung Ltd is a large company in the year ended 31 March 2017 as its augmented profits of £588,566 (W1) exceed the adjusted threshold of £500,000. Neung Ltd was also a large company in the previous year to 31 March 2016 as its taxable total profits were £600,000. Neung Ltd is therefore required to pay its corporation tax by instalments as follows:

	£
14 October 2016 (£109,313/4)	27,328
14 January 2017	27,328
14 April 2017	27,329
14 July 2017	27,328
	109,313

(W1) Augmented profits

	£
Taxable total profits after group relief	546,566
Plus: Dividend received from non-related companies	42,000
Augmented profits	588,566

Neung Ltd has two related 51% group companies (Third and Fifth) therefore there are three related 51% group companies in total.

The adjusted augmented profits threshold of £1,500,000 is therefore £500,000 (£1,500,000/3).

Tutorial note

The dividend received from Second Ltd is added to TTP to determine the augmented profits but the dividend received from Third Ltd is not included as the company is a related 51% group company.

Neung Ltd only owns 25% of Second Ltd so it is not a related 51% group company. Fourth Ltd is also excluded as it is dormant.

Examiner's report

This question was generally well answered, and there were many very good answers.

The only aspect which consistently caused problems was the asset that was integral to a building. Although candidates correctly claimed the annual investment allowance against this expenditure, many candidates then claimed the 40% first year allowance on the balance of expenditure, rather than adding it into the special rate pool. [Note that the 40% FYA is no longer available so this would no longer be a potential issue in this question].

Several candidates treated the lease premium as income rather than as a deduction.

Candidates should try to use a new page for large capital allowances computations.

Note: *The examiner's report has been edited to remove comments on elements of the question that have been deleted due to changes to the examination format.*

	ACCA marking scheme		
			Marks
(a)	Operating profit		0.5
	Depreciation		0.5
	Amortisation		0.5
	Lease premium – Assessable amount on landlord		1.5
	– Deduction		0.5
	Capital allowances	– AIA	1.0
		– Main pool	1.5
		– Short life asset	1.0
		– Special rate pool	1.5
	Loan interest		1.0
	Group relief		1.0
	Corporation tax		0.5
			———
			11.0
			———
(b)	Payment dates		1.0
	Amounts		0.5
	Augmented profit		1.0
	Augmented profits threshold		1.5
			———
			4.0
			———
Total			**15.0**
			———

245 CLUELESS LTD (ADAPTED) *Walk in the footsteps of a top tutor*

Key answer tips

Part (a) requires the computation of a company's corporation tax liability including an adjustment of trading profits calculation. The information is presented in a slightly unusual format as an existing corporation tax computation that contains numerous errors. However this should not prove a problem for the well prepared student.

Part (b) deals with the administrative aspects of corporation tax. There is an easy mark in part (1). However, part (2) may cause some students problems if they have not learnt this topic. As all companies must now file their tax returns electronically it is an important and topical area.

The highlighted words in the answer are key phrases that markers are looking for.

Tutor's top tips

Do not be put off by the different format in which the information is presented. Set up your corporation tax computation as usual and work through each of the workings in the question dealing with each piece of information as you go. Remember to indicate by the use of zero any items in the computation of trading profit for which no adjustment is required.

Note that the company has a wholly owned subsidiary, Clever Ltd. Remember that dividends received are not included in taxable total profits, regardless of the relationship with the paying company. However, remember there are special rules where members of a capital gains group transfer assets between each other.

(a)   **Corporation tax computation – year ended 31 March 2017**

	£
Trading profit (W1)	355,488
Loan interest receivable	32,800
Chargeable gain (W3)	92,458
	———
Taxable total profits	480,746
Less: QCD relief	(900)
	———
Taxable total profits	479,846
	———
Corporation tax liability	
(£479,846 × 20%)	95,969
	———

Tutorial note

Loan interest income is assessed on the amount receivable in respect of the accounting period.

Workings

(W1) Trading profit

	£
Profit before taxation	382,610
Depreciation	15,740
Donations to political parties	400
Qualifying charitable donations	900
Gifts to customers – pens	0
Gifts to customers – food hampers	1,650
	————
	401,300
Less: Capital allowances (W2)	(45,812)
	————
Trading profit	355,488
	————

Tutorial note

1   *Donations to political parties are a disallowable trading expense. Qualifying charitable donations are a disallowable trading expense but are deductible from total profits.*

2   *Gifts to customers are an allowable deduction if they cost less than £50 per recipient per year, are not of food, drink, tobacco or vouchers for exchangeable goods, and carry a conspicuous advertisement for the company making the gift.*

(W2) Capital allowances

	£	Main pool £	Special rate pool £	Allowances £
TWDV b/f		12,400	13,500	
Additions not qualifying for AIA				
Motor car			11,800	
Additions qualifying for AIA				
Machinery	42,300			
Less: AIA	(42,300)			42,300
		0		
Less: Disposal proceeds			(9,300)	
			16,000	
Less: WDA (18%)		(2,232)		2,232
Less: WDA (8%)			(1,280)	1,280
TWDV c/f		10,168	14,720	
Total allowances				45,812

Tutorial note

1   *The motor car has CO_2 emissions over 130 grams per kilometre and therefore qualifies for writing down allowances at the rate of 8%. The private use of a motor car by an employee is irrelevant, since such usage will be assessed on the employee as a benefit.*

2   *A balancing allowance only arises on the main and special rate pools on the cessation of trade, even where all of the assets in the relevant pool have been disposed of.*

(W3) Chargeable gain

Clueless Ltd owns 100% of Clever Ltd and together they form a capital gains group. The transfer from Clever Ltd to Clueless Ltd takes place at no gain/no loss as follows:

	£
Cost (April 2001)	70,000
Plus:IA (April 2001 to June 2009)	
(213.4 − 173.1)/173.1 = 0.233 × £70,000	16,310
Deemed proceeds	86,310

When Clueless Ltd sells the building outside of the group, its deemed cost is £86,310. The chargeable gain is:

	£
Proceeds (March 2017)	200,000
Less: Deemed cost	(86,310)
	————
Unindexed gain	113,690
Less: IA (June 2009 to March 2017)	
(265.9 – 213.4)/213.4 = 0.246 × £86,310	(21,232)
	————
Chargeable gain	92,458
	————

(b) **Self-assessment return**

Tutor's top tips

For written parts, write short succinct sentences in bullet point form and bear in mind the mark allocation for each sub-section. In general, there is usually one mark allocated for each valid point made. Do not therefore dwell on any one part too much and keep an eye on the clock. The highlighted words indicate those that the marker will be looking for.

(1) **Filing date**

Clueless Ltd's self-assessment tax return for the year ended 31 March 2017 must be submitted by 31 March 2018.

(2) **Options for iXBRL format**

If Clueless Ltd has straightforward accounts, it could use the software provided by HM Revenue and Customs. This automatically produces accounts and tax computations in the iXBRL format.

Alternatively, other software that automatically produces iXBRL accounts and computations could be used.

A tagging service could be used to apply the appropriate tags to the accounts and tax computations, or Clueless Ltd could use software to tag documents itself.

Examiner's report

Part (a) was generally very well answered. The only aspect that consistently caused problems was the loan interest with very few candidates appreciating that this is assessed on a receivable basis.

In part (b) it was surprising that only a few candidates were aware of the filing date for a self-assessment corporation tax return, with far too many candidates giving a 31 January date. Despite being covered in the Finance Act 2011 article, hardly any candidates were able to provide relevant details regarding the production of accounts and computations using iXBRL.

Note: The examiner's report has been edited to remove comments on elements of the question that have been deleted due to changes to the examination format.

ACCA marking scheme			
			Marks
(a)		Loan interest	0.5
		Qualifying charitable donations	0.5
		Corporation tax	0.5
		Trading profit	
		Depreciation	0.5
		Donations to political parties	0.5
		Qualifying charitable donations	0.5
		Gifts to customers – pens – no adjustment	0.5
		Gifts to customers – food hampers	0.5
		Capital allowances deducted	0.5
		Capital allowances	
		TWDVs brought forward	0.5
		AIA on machinery	1.0
		Motor car addition in special rate pool	0.5
		Disposal proceeds in special rate pool	0.5
		WDA on main pool at 18%	0.5
		WDA on special rate pool at 8%	0.5
		Chargeable gain	
		Deemed proceeds on no gain/no loss transfer	1.5
		Chargeable gain on disposal outside of group	1.5
			———
			11.0
			———
(b)	(i)	Submit by 31 March 2018	1.0
			———
	(ii)	HMRC software	1.0
		Other software producing iXBRL accounts	1.0
		Tagging service/software to tag documents	1.0
			———
			3.0
			———
Total			**15.0**
			———

246 LONG LTD AND ROAD LTD (ADAPTED)   *Walk in the footsteps of a top tutor*

Key answer tips

This question, about a group of two companies, is split into two unrelated areas.

Part (a) requires you to calculate the corporation tax liability for each of the companies. There are capital and trading losses to deal with.

Part (b) has two requirements: firstly to explain the reporting of real time PAYE information to HM Revenue and Customs ('HMRC'); and secondly to state which forms must be provided to employees or submitted to HMRC following the end of the tax year. The highlighted words in the answer to part (b) below are key phrases that markers are looking for.

Tutor's top tips

It is easy to overrun on part (a), so you could consider answering part (b) before part (a) to make sure that you do not run out of time to answer both parts of the question.

(a)   **Corporation tax computations**

Tutor's top tips

When you read the information you see that one company has a capital loss and one has a trading loss. The requirement states that reliefs must be claimed as soon as possible so you will need to consider how relief can be taken for these losses.

You were told the amount of premium assessed on the landlord as income, not the premium itself, so all that is needed to calculate the tax allowable amount is to divide this figure by the number of years in the lease.

Long Ltd – Corporation tax computation – year ended 31 March 2017

	£
Operating profit	384,400
Depreciation	43,050
Amortisation	5,000
Lease of motor car (£3,600 × 15%) (Note 1)	540
Less: Deduction for lease premium (£68,200 ÷ 20) (Note 2)	(3,410)
Less: Capital allowances (W)	(47,690)
	————
Trading profit	381,890
Net chargeable gain (£29,800 – £21,300) (Note 3)	8,500
	————
Total profits	390,390

Less: Group relief – from Road Ltd (Note 4)		
Lower of:		
Road Ltd's loss	£34,900	
3/12 of Long Ltd's profit (£390,390 × 3/12)	£97,598	(34,900)
		————

	£
Taxable total profits	355,490
	————
Corporation tax liability	
(£355,490 at 20%)	71,098
	————

Tutorial note

1   The leased motor car has CO_2 emissions of more than 130 grams per kilometre, so 15% of the leasing costs are disallowed.

2   The office building has been used for business purposes. Therefore the proportion of the lease premium assessed on the landlord as property income can be deducted from trading income, spread over the life of the lease.

3   A joint election can be made so that Long Ltd is treated as having made Road Ltd's capital gain. It would be equally beneficial for a joint election to be made so that Road Ltd is treated as having made Long Ltd's capital loss. In the examination equal marks would be awarded for either treatment.

4   Group relief is not restricted as Road Ltd's available loss is less than 3/12ths of Long Ltd's taxable total profits.

Road Ltd

Trading loss – period ended 31 March 2017

	£
Operating loss	(26,100)
Donations	2,800
Capital allowances (£11,600 × 100%)	(11,600)
	_____
Surrendered as group relief	(34,900)
	_____

Tutorial note

1   The motor car is purchased on 3 October 2016 before trade commences, so is treated as incurred on the first day of trading – 1 January 2017. The motor car has CO_2 emissions up to 75 grams per kilometre and therefore qualifies for the 100% first year allowance. First year allowances are never time apportioned.

2   It is beneficial for Road Ltd to surrender its trading loss to Long Ltd as this will use the loss as soon as possible.

Road Ltd

Corporation tax computation for the period ended 31 March 2017

	£
Interest income	4,300
Less: Qualifying charitable donations	(2,400)
Taxable total profits	1,900
Corporation tax (£1,900 at 20%)	380

Tutorial note

The qualifying charitable donations cannot be surrendered as group relief as they are fully relieved against Road Ltd's interest income.

Working – Plant and machinery – Long Ltd

	£	Main pool £	Allowances £
TWDV b/f		44,800	
Addition not qualifying for AIA			
Motor car		15,700	
Addition qualifying for AIA			
Lorry	36,800		
Less: AIA	(36,800)		36,800
	———	0	
		60,500	
Less: WDA (18%)		(10,890)	10,890
TWDV carried forward		49,610	
Total allowances			47,690

Tutorial note

The motor car has CO_2 emissions between 76 and 130 grams per kilometre, and therefore qualifies for writing down allowances at the rate of 18%.

When dealing with a company there is never any private use adjustment. The private use of the motor car will be assessed on the managing director as an employment benefit.

(b)   **PAYE real time reporting**

Tutor's top tips

Use headings to separate the two parts of your answer which makes it easier to mark.

Real time PAYE information

- Real time PAYE information must be filed electronically, so Road Ltd will have to either run payroll software or use the services of a payroll provider.

- Road Ltd will have to send real time PAYE information to HMRC electronically by the end of each calendar month (the time when employees are paid).

Forms

- Form P60 must be provided to employees following the end of the tax year.

- Form P11D detailing the benefits provided to the employees must be submitted to HMRC following the end of the tax year, with a copy provided to the employees.

- Form P11D (b) should be submitted to HMRC detailing class 1A national insurance contributions.

Examiner's report

Part (a) was generally well answered. The only aspect that consistently caused problems was Road Ltd, where candidates often incorrectly increased the loss for donations, and decreased it for capital allowances. In some cases, the loss was simply treated as a profit.

Part (b), perhaps not surprisingly, was not generally well answered. In many cases, the only form mentioned was form P45 which is no longer relevant. Candidates often explained PAYE in general terms, rather than answering the requirements of the question.

			Marks
		ACCA marking scheme	*Marks*
(a)		Long Ltd – Corporation tax computation	
		Depreciation	0.5
		Amortisation	0.5
		Lease of motor car	1.0
		Deduction for lease premium	1.0
		Net chargeable gain	1.5
		Group relief from Road Ltd	1.5
		Corporation tax	0.5
		TWDV brought forward	0.5
		Lorry	0.5
		AIA	0.5
		Motor car	0.5
		WDA – 18%	0.5
		Road Ltd – Trading loss for the period	
		Donations	0.5
		Capital allowances	1.0
		Road Ltd – Corporation tax computation	
		Interest income	0.5
		Qualifying charitable donations	0.5
		Corporation tax	0.5
			12.0
(b)		PAYE real time reporting	
		File electronically	1.0
		Timing	0.5
		P60	0.5
		P11D	0.5
		P11D(b)	0.5
			3.0
Total			**15.0**

ANSWERS TO PRACTICE VALUE ADDED TAX QUESTIONS

PRACTICE SECTION A OBJECTIVE TEST QUESTIONS

VALUE ADDED TAX

247 A

Under the future prospects test, Fred is required to register for VAT when taxable supplies in the next 30 days in isolation are expected to exceed £83,000.

Fred had grounds for expecting this to be the case on 1 June 2017 when he received an order to supply £90,000 of goods by 30 June 2017. Registration is effective from the start of the 30 day period so Fred must start charging VAT from 1 June 2017.

248 B

Taxable supplies for 7 m/e 31 July 2016 are £66,000 and for 8 m/e 31 August 2016 taxable supplies are £96,000. Layla therefore exceeds the registration limit of £83,000 by the end of August 2016.

Layla must notify HM Revenue & Customs by 30 September 2016 and she will be registered from 1 October 2016.

249 B and C

VAT cannot be reclaimed on cars which are used for private purposes.

VAT can normally be reclaimed on fuel used partially for private purposes (although output VAT will be due based on the fuel scale charge). However, the fuel has been consumed prior to the date of registration and therefore the input tax cannot be reclaimed. Input tax can only be reclaimed on goods if they are still on hand (or not consumed) at the date of registration.

Pre-registration input VAT can only be reclaimed on services if they were supplied within six months of registration.

Pre-registration input VAT can be reclaimed on goods acquired for the business provided they are on hand (i.e. in inventory) at the date of registration.

250 B

	£
1.7.16 – 31.12.16: Pre-registration (6 × 110)	660
1.1.17 – 31.3.17: Post-registration (3 × 110)	330
	_____
Total input tax recoverable	990
	_____

Tutorial note

Pre-registration input VAT relating to services can only be recovered if it was incurred in the six months prior to registration.

251

	Can be in VAT group
A Ltd	✓
B Ltd	✓
C Ltd	✓
D Sarl	

Companies that are under common control (>50%) can be in a VAT group provided they all have a place of business in the UK. All of the companies are under the common control of Fergus, but D Sarl cannot be a member of the group as it does not have a place of business in the UK.

252 B

A VAT registered trader must notify HM Revenue and Customs within 30 days of ceasing to make taxable supplies.

253 B

The basic tax point is the date the goods are delivered. This is only overridden if a tax invoice is issued or payment is made before the basic tax point or an invoice is issued within 14 days after the basic tax point.

254 D

Quarter ended 31 March 2017

	£
Input tax:	
Relief for impairment losses (£800 × 1/6)	133

Tutorial note

Relief for impairment losses is only available where at least six months has elapsed since the debt was due for payment and the seller has written the debt off in their VAT account.

The VAT on the £1,000 debt (net of any recovery from the liquidator) can be recovered in the quarter to 30 June 2017.

255 D

Input VAT: £600 × 20/120 = £100

Output VAT: £314 × 20/120 = £52

256 B

Recoverable input VAT

	£
Entertaining new suppliers	0
Car leasing (£3,000 × 1/6 × 50%)	250
	250

Tutorial note

VAT can only be recovered on entertaining staff and overseas customers.

Where any car, which has some private use, is leased only 50% of the input VAT can be recovered. The level of the car's CO_2 emissions is irrelevant.

257 D

Quarter ended 31 March 2017

	£	£
Output tax:		
Sales (£30,000 × 1/6)	5,000	
Samples	0	
	———	5,000
Input tax:		
Purchases (£16,800 × 1/6)		(2,800)
		———
VAT payable		2,200
		———

Tutorial note

Business samples are not treated as taxable supplies and therefore no output VAT is payable in respect of them.

258 C

Quarter ended 31 March 2017

	£
Output tax:	
Fuel scale charge (£408 × 1/6)	68
Input tax:	
Fuel (£1,200 × 1/6)	(200)
	———
VAT reclaimable	(132)
	———

259 C

260 D

261 B

This is the second time the return is late. On the first offence a surcharge liability period (SLP) would start, which would end on 31 October 2017 (the 12-month anniversary of the VAT period to which the default relates.

The second offence is the first default in the SLP, the SLP is extended to 31 January 2018 and a 2% penalty of £520 (£26,000 × 2%) is charged.

262 A

The error is smaller than the greater of £10,000 or 1% of turnover (£3,800) and can therefore be corrected on the next quarter's VAT return. Any error that can be corrected on the next return will not attract an interest charge.

263

	True	False
Input tax cannot be claimed until the invoice is paid which delays recovery of input VAT	✓	
Traders using the scheme do not have to pay output VAT to HMRC until they receive it from customers	✓	
To join the scheme the trader's expected taxable turnover (excluding VAT) for the next twelve months must not exceed £150,000		✓
The cash accounting scheme cannot be used where a trader issues an invoice in advance of supplying goods	✓	

To join the scheme a trader's taxable turnover (excluding VAT and sales of capital assets) for the next twelve months must not exceed £1,350,000.

264 A

There will have been nine payments at 10% of last year's liability in months 4 to 12 totalling £3,240 (9 × 10% × £3,600).

This year's liability is £4,115 leaving a balance left to pay of £875 (£4,115 – £3,240).

265 D

£59,700 × 12% = £7,164

266 D

The flat rate scheme applies a percentage to the VAT inclusive total turnover including zero rated and exempt sales. Expenses are not deductible.

Standard rated sales = (£80,000 + 20% VAT) = £96,000.

Total VAT inclusive turnover = (£96,000 + £15,000 + £10,000) = £121,000

This is multiplied by the flat rate percentage to calculate the VAT due to HMRC

(£121,000 × 13%) = £15,730

267 A

The UK trader accounts for output VAT of £2,000 as the goods would be standard rated if supplied in the UK. The UK trader can claim back input VAT of £2,000 on the same return as the goods are used by a trader that only makes taxable supplies. The net effect on VAT payable is therefore nil.

PRACTICE SECTION B OBJECTIVE TEST CASES

268   CANDY APPLE AND SUGAR PLUM (ADAPTED) *Walk in the footsteps of a top tutor*

Key answer tips

This question is really two separate questions and tests knowledge of a number of VAT issues.

There were some easy marks to be gained in the first part for a relatively straightforward compulsory registration computation and knowledge of the implications of late registration.

The second part of the question is purely computational and tests your knowledge of output and input VAT, including the rules for pre-registration input VAT.

1   A

Candy was liable to compulsory register for VAT when her taxable supplies during any 12 month period exceeded £83,000.

This happened on 31 October 2016 when taxable supplies amounted to £84,000 (£10,500 + £10,500 + £10,500 + £10,500 + £14,000 + £14,000 + £14,000).

Candy was required to notify HMRC within 30 days of the end of the month in which the threshold was exceeded (i.e. 30 November 2016) and was registered from and required to charge VAT on taxable supplies from the first day of the second month after her taxable supplies rose above the threshold (i.e. from 1 December 2016).

2   C

Tutorial note

A late registration penalty may be charged. A default surcharge penalty applies for filing a return and paying the related VAT late.

Output VAT must be accounted for to HM Revenue and Customs from the date that she should have been registered. Sales from the date of compulsory registration are treated as VAT inclusive (even though VAT was not actually charged to customers). Candy can try to recover the VAT that she should have charged from customers but is not required to do so by HM Revenue and Customs and indeed it may not be possible.

3 **B**

	£
Output VAT	
Standard rated sales (£53,700 × 20%)	10,740
Zero rated sales (£23,100 × 0%)	0
	─────
	10,740
	─────

4 **A**

	£
Input VAT	
Electricity (£49 × 1/7)	7
Furniture (£1,500 × 95% × 20%)	285
	─────
	292
	─────

Tutorial note

Where services are used partly for private and partly for business use, an apportionment is made to calculate the recoverable input VAT.

5 **D**

	£
Pre-registration input VAT	
Consultancy fees (£375 × 20%)	75
Inventory (£1,000 × 20%)	200
	─────
	275
	─────

Tutorial note

Pre-registration Input VAT can be reclaimed on:

- *services supplied within the six months prior to registration, and*

- *inventory acquired for business purposes in the four years prior to registration that has not been sold at the time of registration.*

269 LITHOGRAPH LTD (ADAPTED)

Key answer tips

The first two questions in this case test your knowledge of the VAT annual accounting scheme.

The other three questions require fairly standard calculations of output VAT and input VAT, including relief for impaired debts.

1 C

Lithograph Ltd will have made nine payments on account, and these will have been paid in the months of July 2015 to March 2016, being months 4 to 12 of the annual VAT return period.

2 B

The payments on account are 10% of the VAT payable for the previous year i.e. the year ended 31 March 2015.

The annual VAT return is due 2 months after the end of the VAT period i.e. 30 May 2016.

3 A

	£
Output VAT	
Motor car scale charge (£1,608 × 20/120)	268
Office equipment (£8,000 × 20%)	1,600
	─────
	1,868
	─────

Tutorial note

For transactions quoted inclusive of VAT, the VAT is calculated as 20/120 (or 1/6).

4   A

	£
Input VAT	
Expenses (£28,000 × 20%)	5,600
Machinery (£24,000 × 20%)	4,800
	———
	10,400
	———

Tutorial note

Input VAT on business entertainment is not recoverable unless it relates to overseas customers.

Input VAT cannot be recovered in respect of the motor car as this is not used exclusively for business purposes.

5   D

	£
Recoverable VAT	
Impaired debt 1 (£4,800 × 1/6)	800
Impaired debt 2 – not recoverable	0
	———
	800
	———

Tutorial note

Relief for impaired debts is available where the claim is made more than six months from the time that payment was due, and the debt has been written off in the company's books.

The VAT on the second impaired debt cannot be recovered until the VAT return for the year ended 31 March 2018.

270 ANNE ATTIRE (ADAPTED) *Walk in the footsteps of a top tutor*

Key answer tips

The first three questions in this case look at different aspects of the VAT return and cover discounts, the recoverability of input VAT and impairment loss relief. The last two questions look at the cessation of a business and the different treatments depending whether it is sold as a going concern or not.

1 D

	£
Output VAT	
Invoices issued (£100,000 × 20%)	20,000
Adjustment for prompt payment discount:	
(£40,000 × 5% × 20%)	(400)
	———
	19,600
	———

Tutorial note

If a discount is offered, then VAT must be calculated on the amount that the customer actually pays.

For prompt payment discounts the supplier will not know, when the invoice is raised, whether the customer will qualify for the discount by paying within the required timescale. The supplier must therefore charge VAT on the invoice on the full price and either:

– *issue a credit note if the discount is taken or*

– *show full details of the terms of the prompt payment discount and include a statement that the customer can only recover input tax based on the amount paid to the supplier. If the discount is taken the supplier must then adjust their records to account for output tax on the amount received.*

2 C

	£
Input VAT	
Legal fees (£11,200 × 20%)	2,240
Delivery van (£6,000 × 20%)	1,200
Car leasing (£2,000 × 50% × 20%)	200
	———
	3,640
	———

Tutorial note

1   There is no distinction between capital and revenue expenditure for VAT purposes. The input tax on the capital related legal fees is therefore recoverable.

2   Input tax incurred on motor cars is not recoverable unless there is 100% business use or the car is leased, in which case 50% of the input tax is recoverable where there is some private use.

3   A delivery van is not a motor car and the input tax is therefore fully recoverable.

3   A

Tutorial note

Relief for an impairment loss is not given until six months from the time that payment is due. Therefore relief can only be claimed in respect of the invoice due for payment on 10 November 2016.

Amounts due from customers are recorded inclusive of VAT. However the question clearly states that all figures are VAT exclusive unless stated otherwise.

4   A

	£
Input VAT	
Non-current assets (£12,500 – £6,000) × 20%)	1,300
Inventory (£6,100 × 20%)	1,220
	2,520

Tutorial note

Upon the cessation of trading Anne will cease to make taxable supplies, so her VAT registration will be cancelled on the date of cessation or an agreed later date.

Output VAT will be due in respect of the value of the non-current assets at the date of deregistration on which VAT has been claimed (output VAT is never charged on a car which has been used partly for private purposes as input VAT is not recoverable on its purchase). Output VAT is not due if it totals no more than £1,000.

5   B

Tutorial note

If all of the conditions below are satisfied, then the sale/transfer:

* *will not be treated as a taxable supply*
* *no output tax will therefore be charged on the assets transferred by the seller, and*
* *no input tax is recoverable by the purchaser.*

Conditions:

* *The business is transferred as a going concern.*
* *There is no significant break in the trading.*
* *The same type of trade is carried on after the transfer.*
* *The new owner is or is liable to be registered for VAT, immediately after the transfer.*

271   ASTON MARTYN (ADAPTED) *Walk in the footsteps of a top tutor*

Key answer tips

This question focuses on various aspects of VAT administration, including when a business should notify the need to register for VAT, when returns are required, the necessary contents of a VAT invoice and VAT errors. It includes a question on EU supplies, which is unusual as it relates to the supply of services rather than goods.

1   A

Tutorial note

Aston would have been liable to compulsory registration for VAT when his taxable supplies at the end of any month exceeded £83,000 for the previous 12-month period (or since the commencement of trade if less than 12 months). Taxable supplies include zero rated supplies.

This occurs on 30 April 2017 when taxable supplies amounted to £83,200 (£2,300 + £6,400 + £25,700 + £11,700 + £16,100 + £21,000).

The notification date is 30 days after the end of the month in which the threshold is exceeded.

He will be registered from the first day of the second month after his taxable supplies rose above the threshold.

Therefore, Aston should have notified HMRC within 30 days (i.e. by 30 May 2017) and registration will have been effective from 1 June 2017 or from an agreed earlier date.

2   B

3   B, C, D and F

4   C

Tutorial note

As a business to business service the supply is treated as made in the UK I.e. where the customer is established).

The time of supply is the earliest of the date that the service is completed or the date it is paid for.

The VAT charged at the UK VAT rate should be declared on Aston's VAT return as output VAT, but will then be reclaimed as input VAT on the same VAT return.

This is known as the reverse charge procedure.

5   **£10,000**

      Working:

                                                                    £

      De minimis limit is greater of :
      (i)   £10,000
      (ii)   (1% × £300,000) = £3,000
      Maximum net error   10,000

Tutorial note

Errors below the de minimis limit can be corrected on the next VAT return.

The de minimis limit is the greater of £10,000 and 1% of turnover (subject to an upper limit of £50,000).

272   THE WHITLOCK SISTERS (ADAPTED)   *Walk in the footsteps of a top tutor*

Key Answer Tips

The first two questions test the straightforward computation of the VAT payable using the flat rate scheme percentage, and then the VAT that would have been payable if the normal basis had been used, and should have provided easy marks to a well prepared student.

Be careful to read the question carefully though to ascertain whether the figures given are inclusive or exclusive of VAT.

The third question tests more of the details regarding the flat rate scheme – this sort of question can only really be answered if the rules have been learnt.

The final two questions test tax points in respect of services.

1   D

Using the flat rate scheme to calculate its VAT liability the partnership will have paid VAT of £7,800 (£50,000 + £10,000) × 13% for the quarter ended 31 March 2017.

Tutorial note

Under the flat rate scheme, VAT is calculated by applying a fixed percentage to the turnover figure inclusive of VAT and including any exempt or zero rated supplies. Expenses and purchases are not relevant.

2   £3,783

If the partnership had used the normal basis it would have paid VAT of £3,783 ((£50,000 – £27,300) = £22,700 × 20/120).

Tutorial note

1   Calculate the VAT element of VAT inclusive prices using either 1/6 or 20/120 of the VAT inclusive price.

2   Output tax is not charged on exempt supplies.

3   C and D

Tutorial note

*To join the scheme expected taxable turnover (**excluding** VAT) for the next 12 months must not exceed £150,000.*

The scheme can be used by both small unincorporated and incorporated businesses

4

Deposit	Balancing payment
When the deposit is paid	Invoice date

The basic tax point date (BTP) is the date when the service is completed, which will be the date that the room is used, i.e. the day of the room hire.

In respect of the 25% deposit the BTP is overridden by a payment before the BTP and that payment date becomes the actual tax point.

In respect of the 75% balancing payment the BTP is not overridden by either a payment or an invoice being issued before the BTP. However, as the invoice is issued within 14 days of the BTP, the invoice date becomes the actual tax point.

Tutorial note

For services, the basic tax point (BTP) is the date the service is provided/completed.

The actual tax point (ATP) can be either before or after the BTP.

The ATP will be before the BTP if:

- *An invoice is issued before the BTP, or*

- *A payment is received before the BTP (as in this case with the deposit payments).*

The ATP will be after the BTP if:

- *An invoice is issued within 14 days of the BTP, or*

- *The business has an agreement with HMRC for a different date (typically businesses agree a month end invoicing policy so that the invoice date is usually the ATP).*

5   D

Tutorial note

*Input VAT incurred on business entertaining cannot be recovered, with the exceptions of staff entertaining and entertaining overseas **customers**.*

273   KNIGHT LTD (ADAPTED) *Walk in the footsteps of a top tutor*

Key Answer Tips

This question covers a variety of VAT topics. Firstly it deals with the VAT return looking at output VAT and then input VAT separately. The third question looks at impairment loss relief, and tests the detailed rules regarding what is recoverable. The fourth question tests the rules regarding VAT groups. Finally, the fifth question relates to the default surcharge penalty and the specifics of when it is charged as well as the relevant rates.

1   A

	£
Output VAT	
Sales (Note 1)	38,210
Fuel scale charge (£268 × 20/120) (Note 2)	45
	_____
	38,255
	_____

Tutorial note

1   *The tax point for the deposit is the date of payment, so no adjustment is required to the output VAT figure of £38,210.*

2   *The fuel scale charge is quoted inclusive of VAT. The VAT element can be calculated as 20/120 of the scale figure, or as a short cut, you can use 1/6.*

2   C

Working: Input tax – Sundry expenses

	£
Other sundry expenses (all recoverable)	9,121
Entertaining UK customers (Note 1)	0
Entertaining overseas customers (Note 1)	139
New reception area (Note 2)	3,300
	_____
	12,560
	_____

Tutorial note

1   Input VAT on business entertainment is not recoverable unless it relates to the cost of entertaining staff or overseas customers.

2   Input tax is recoverable on the extension (capital expenditure). There is no distinction between capital and revenue for VAT purposes.

3   D

Tutorial note

Relief is only available for the impairment loss provided that both six months has passed from the time that payment was due and the debt has been written off in the seller's accounts.

Claims must be made within four years and six months of the payment being due.

4   B

Tutorial note

Are Ltd and Can Ltd can form a group with Knight Ltd for VAT purposes as they are under the control of Knight Ltd and all of the companies are UK resident. However, eligible companies are not automatically included in the group. Either Are Ltd or Can Ltd may be excluded.

There will be no need to account for VAT on goods and services supplied between group members. Such supplies will simply be ignored for VAT purposes.

The group must appoint a representative member which will be responsible for completing one VAT return for the group. However, the representative member could be any of the group companies.

Each group member is jointly and severally liable for the VAT payable by the whole group, not just its share.

5 B

Tutorial note

The late submission for the quarter ended 31 December 2014 is irrelevant, as it was followed by the submission of four consecutive VAT returns on time.

The late payment for the quarter ended 30 September 2016 results in the issue of a surcharge liability notice for the period up to 30 September 2017.

The late payment of VAT for the quarter to 30 June 2017 occurs during the surcharge period. Therefore, there will be a surcharge of £420 (£21,000 × 2%).

In addition, the surcharge period will be extended to 30 June 2018.

The surcharge of £420 is payable as it exceeds the de minimis amount of £400.

PRACTICE SECTION C CONSTRUCTED RESPONSE QUESTIONS

274 GARFIELD (ADAPTED) *Walk in the footsteps of a top tutor*

Tutor's top tips

Read the question carefully – there are two parts to this requirement. The first requirement is computational, requiring the VAT payable for a specific quarter.

The second part of the requirement asks you to state the potential VAT schemes available in this scenario. It asks for an explanation of which scheme would be suitable, which involves applying your knowledge to the situation in hand. Don't waste time explaining how the different schemes work as there are no marks available in relation to this as stated in the notes.

The highlighted words in the answer are key phrases that markers are looking for.

(a)   **Garfield – Value added tax (VAT) return for the quarter ended 31 March 2017**

	£
Output VAT	
Sales	22,500*
Discounted sale (£4,300 × 90% × 20%)	774
Equipment (£12,400 × 20%)	2,480
Fuel scale charge	60*
Input VAT	
Purchases	(11,200)*
Motor car	0*
Equipment	(2,480)
Impairment losses (£1,400 × 20%)	(280)
Entertaining – UK customers	0*
– Overseas customers (£960 × 20/120)	(160)
Motor expenses (£1,668 (£1,008 + £660) × 20/120)	(278)
VAT payable	11,416

*Figures provided in question.

Tutorial notes

(1)   *Relief for an impairment loss is only available if the claim is made more than six months from the time when payment was due. Therefore, relief can only be claimed in respect of the invoice due for payment on 29 August 2016.*

(2)   *Input VAT on business entertainment is recoverable if it relates to the cost of entertaining overseas customers.*

(b)   (1)   Given Garfield's current annual turnover of £450,000, he can use the cash accounting scheme and the annual accounting scheme, but not the flat rate scheme.

(2)   The cash accounting scheme would appear to be the most beneficial scheme for Garfield to use.

(3)   The scheme will provide automatic VAT relief for the impairment losses which he is incurring.

(4)   Where credit is given to customers, output VAT could be accounted for later than at present.

(5)   The recovery of input VAT on most purchases and expenses will not be affected as Garfield pays for these on a cash basis.

Tutorial notes

(1) *The annual turnover limit for both the annual accounting scheme and the cash accounting scheme is £1,350,000, but for the flat rate scheme it is £150,000.*

(2) *Although the annual accounting scheme would mean only having to submit one VAT return each year (reducing the risk of late return penalties), payments on account are based on the VAT payable for the previous year. From a cash flow viewpoint, this is not beneficial where turnover is decreasing.*

Examiner's report

Part (a) required a calculation of the amount of VAT payable for the quarter. A partly completed VAT computation was provided, so copying this out was the obvious starting point. However, some candidates amended the given figures despite being told that these were correct. It is important to read the question carefully in order to avoid unnecessary complications. The only point which consistently caused problems was the impairment losses, with the impairment loss figure itself being included rather than the VAT thereon.

Part (b) required candidates to state which VAT schemes the taxpayer was currently permitted to use, and then to explain which scheme appeared to be the most beneficial. Provided candidates appreciated that the flat rate scheme was not available, they generally answered this section quite well. This demonstrates the need to relate answers to the information given rather than just writing everything known on a particular subject. The scheme qualifying conditions were not required.

ACCA marking scheme		Marks
(a)	Output VAT on discounted sale	1.0
	Output VAT on equipment sold	1.0
	Input VAT on equipment	0.5
	Input VAT on impaired debts	1.0
	Input VAT on overseas customers	1.0
	Input VAT on motor expenses	1.5
	Inclusion of amounts provided in the question	1.0
		7.0
(b)	Can use cash and annual schemes – not flat rate	1.0
	Cash accounting is beneficial	0.5
	Automatic impairment relief	0.5
	Delays output VAT recognition on credit sales	0.5
	Input VAT recovery mostly unaffected	0.5
		3.0
Total		10

275   VICTOR STYLE (ADAPTED)

Key answer tips

This is a question covering the common issues of registration and the flat rate scheme and also asks for the effect of registration on profit. This is unusual because traders usually pass on the cost of VAT to their customers, but in this case the question clearly states that it was not possible to raise prices as a consequence of becoming registered.

Provided you work carefully through the numbers, this should be a straightforward question.

(a)   **VAT payable – y/e 31 December 2017**

- Output VAT will be £19,000 (£9,500 × 12 = £114,000 × 20/120) since Victor must absorb this himself rather than pass it on to his customers.

- Input VAT will be £800 (£400 × 12 = £4,800 × 20/120).

- The total VAT payable by Victor during the year ended 31 December 2017 is therefore £18,200 (£19,000 – £800).

(b)   **Flat rate scheme**

- The main advantage of the flat rate scheme is the simplified VAT administration. Victor will calculate his VAT liability by simply taking a percentage of his turnover rather than having to calculate output tax and input tax separately.

- If Victor had used the flat rate scheme from 1 January 2017, then he would have paid VAT of £14,820 (£114,000 × 13%) during the year ended 31 December 2017.

- This is a saving of £3,380 (£18,200 – £14,820) for the year.

Tutorial note

In the first 12 months of VAT registration, HMRC allow a 1% reduction in the appropriate percentage for that trade group. However, knowledge of this is not required in the examination.

Therefore, you will be given the rate that should apply in the first 12 months and you do not need to deduct 1%, just use the rate given.

(c)   **Reduction in net profit**

- If Victor had not increased his prices, his net profit for the year ended 31 December 2017 based on the information given would have been £64,800 (£5,800 – £400 = £5,400 × 12).

- As a result of increasing his prices, Victor's net profit will be as follows:

	£
Sales (£114,000 – £18,200)	95,800
Less: Expenses (£4,800 – £800)	(4,000)
Net profit	91,800

- This is an increase in net profit of £27,000 (£91,800 – £64,800).

Tutor's top tips

If the flat rate scheme had been used from 1 January 2017 there would have been an increase in net profit of £30,380 (£27,000 + £3,380).

276 DENZIL DYER (ADAPTED)

Key answer tips

A question ranging over a number of VAT issues. Make sure you consider each part and write enough for each part.

Remember also to relate your answer to the specific circumstances of the business.

Numbered points or bullet points are the best way to make your answer 'marker friendly'.

(a) **Identification of the type of supply**

- Output VAT is only due in respect of standard rated supplies. Incorrectly classifying a supply as zero rated would not remove Denzil's liability to pay the output VAT which is calculated on the actual price charged. This would then be an additional cost to the business.

- The type of supply, whether standard rated or zero rated, has no effect on the recovery of input VAT for Denzil.

(b) **VAT implications of discounts**

- Where a discount of 5% is given for an order of more than £500 then output VAT is simply calculated on the revised, discounted, selling price.

- As regards the 2.5% discount offered for prompt payment, output VAT is calculated on the amount that the customer actually pays.

- For prompt payment discounts the supplier will not know, when the invoice is raised, whether the customer will qualify for the discount by paying within the required timescale. The supplier must therefore charge VAT on the invoice on the full price and either issue a credit note if the discount is taken or adjust their records to account for output tax on the amount received when the invoice is paid.

(c)   **Conditions for the recovery of input VAT**

- The supply must be made to Denzil since he is the taxable person making the claim.

- The supply must be supported by evidence, normally in the form of a VAT invoice. Denzil will therefore not be able to recover any input VAT in respect of the purchases of office supplies for cash, where there is no invoice.

- Denzil must use the goods or services supplied for business purposes, although an apportionment can be made where supplies are acquired partly for business purposes and partly for private purposes.

(d)   **Circumstances for issuing VAT invoices**

- Denzil must issue a VAT invoice when he makes a standard rated supply to one of his VAT registered customers.

- A VAT invoice is not required if the supply is zero rated or the supply is to a non-VAT registered customer (e.g. a member of the public) then an invoice need not be issued unless the customer requests.

- A simplified invoice can be issued if the supply is less than £250.

- A VAT invoice should be issued within 30 days of the date that the supply of services is treated as being made.

277   SILVERSTONE LTD (ADAPTED) *Walk in the footsteps of a top tutor*

Key answer tips

This is a classic 10 mark VAT question. A number of easy marks are available for the key facts and advantages of the VAT cash accounting and annual accounting schemes, provided they are related to the particular circumstances of Silverstone Ltd.

Part (b) covers the overseas aspects of VAT which is relatively straightforward provided the rules have been learnt.

Tutor's top tips

Part (a) – Read the requirement carefully – you are required to explain why the company can use the schemes and why they will be beneficial. Make sure that you take account of and refer to the specific circumstances of the company and do not just write about the schemes in general.

In part (b) use headings in your answer so that it is clear which points relate to each type of supplier and remember to deal with both when and how to account for the VAT for each supplier.

(a)   **Cash accounting scheme and annual accounting scheme**

- Silverstone Ltd can use both schemes because its expected taxable turnover for the next 12 months does not exceed £1,350,000 exclusive of VAT.

- In addition, for both schemes the company is up to date with its VAT payments, and for the cash accounting scheme it is up to date with its VAT returns.

- With the cash accounting scheme, output VAT will be accounted for two months later than at present since the scheme will result in the tax point becoming the date that payment is received from customers.

- The recovery of input VAT on expenses will not be affected as these are paid in cash.

- With the annual accounting scheme, the reduced administration in only having to file one VAT return each year should save on overtime costs.

(b)   **Supplier situated outside the European Union**

- Silverstone Ltd will have to pay VAT of £4,400 (£22,000 at 20%) to HM Revenue and Customs at the time of importation.

- This will then be reclaimed as input VAT on the VAT return for the period during which the machinery is imported.

- **Supplier situated elsewhere within the European Union**

- VAT will have to be accounted for according to the date of acquisition. This will be the earlier of the date that a VAT invoice is issued or the 15th day of the month following the month in which the machinery comes into the UK.

- The VAT charged of £4,400 will be declared on Silverstone Ltd's VAT return as output VAT, but will then be reclaimed as input VAT on the same VAT return. This is known as the reverse charge procedure.

Examiner's report

The first requirement was reasonably well answered, although candidates had a tendency to write everything they knew about the two schemes rather than tailoring their answers to the information given in the question.

The second requirement caused more problems, and there was little appreciation that the two alternatives would effectively leave Silverstone Ltd in the same overall financial position.

		ACCA marking scheme	
			Marks
(a)		Both schemes – Expected taxable T/O for next 12 mths ≤ £1,350,000	1.5
		And up to date with VAT payments and returns	1.5
		Cash accounting – output tax accounted for 2 months later	1.0
		Cash accounting – input tax recovery not affected	1.0
		Annual accounting – reduced admin (only one return a year)	1.0
			——
			6.0
			——
(b)	(1)	Supplier situated outside the European Union	
		Pay at time of importation	1.0
		Reclaim as input tax on VAT return in period in which imported	1 0
	(2)	Supplier situated elsewhere within the European Union	
		Date of acquisition	1.0
		Include as output and input tax on same return	1.0
			——
			4.0
			——
Total			**10.0**
			——

278 TARDY PLC *Walk in the footsteps of a top tutor*

Key answer tips

This question has four requirements covering various administrative aspects including default surcharges, accounting for supplies of services from the EU, disclosure of VAT errors, default interest and penalties for errors. All these aspects should be manageable provided you have learnt the detailed administration rules. However, make sure you are guided by the marks available, that you answer the specific question asked and that you base your answer on the facts in the question, not everything you know about VAT!

In the answers the highlighted words are key phrases that markers are looking for.

(a) **Default surcharge**

Tutor's top tips

There are two separate requirements here – to advise of the implications of a further late payment and what the company needs to do to revert to a clean record. You must make sure you deal with both.

Default surcharges are tested relatively frequently. The key points to grasp are that there is no penalty on the first default, penalties are payable on subsequent defaults and each default will trigger an extension of the default surcharge period.

The rates of penalties do need to be learnt as they are not provided in the tax tables.

Make sure you make three clear points to get the three marks available.

- Tardy plc has already defaulted twice during the current default surcharge period, so a further default will result in a surcharge of 10% of the amount of VAT outstanding.

- In addition, the default surcharge period will be extended to the 12-month anniversary of the VAT quarter to which the default relates.

- In order to revert to a clean default surcharge record, Tardy plc will need to submit four consecutive VAT returns on time and also pay the related VAT liabilities on time.

(b) **Supply of services within the EU**

Tutor's top tips

*This part also has two requirements, **when** and **how** the VAT should be accounted for. It would be easy to miss the first part of this requirement, which is actually about tax points, rather than EU supplies. Note that the question relates to services, not goods, and therefore the tax point rules are different.*

The second requirement requires an explanation of the reverse charge procedure, by which VAT is accounted for in the country where the services are carried out.

- VAT should be accounted for on the earlier of the date when the service is completed and the date the service is paid for.

- Output VAT at the UK VAT rate should be declared on the UK business's VAT return.

  This will then be reclaimed as input VAT on the same VAT return, so the effect will be VAT neutral.

  This is known as the reverse charge procedure.

(c) **Errors on a VAT return and default interest**

Tutor's top tips

Again there are two separate requirements here. The first is explaining whether the error can be disclosed on the next return, which means applying the de minimis test to the amount of the error. Since the error is less than £10,000, the company's turnover figure is not required.

The second requirement is to explain whether default interest will be charged. If you have not learnt the rules here, it may be worth a guess!

- Tardy plc will be permitted to disclose the underpayment of VAT of £8,200 by entering this amount on its next VAT return as the net error is less than the limit of £10,000.

- Default interest is not charged where voluntary disclosure can be made by entering the underpayment on the next VAT return.

(d) **VAT penalties**

Tutor's top tips

This question covers the standard penalty for an incorrect return. The same penalty system applies to income tax, NICs, corporation tax and VAT and could be tested in relation to any of those taxes. It is therefore worthwhile learning the basic rules.

Here you are asked for the maximum amount of the penalty, which depends upon the taxpayer's behaviour and also by how much it could be reduced by an unprompted disclosure. Again, make sure you cover both points in your answer.

- Tardy plc has been careless in its incorrect treatment of the supply of services received, so the maximum amount of penalty will therefore be 30% of the VAT underpaid (£8,200 × 30% = £2,460).

- However, this penalty could be reduced to £0 as a result of the company's unprompted disclosure to HM Revenue and Customs.

Examiner's report

This question as a whole was generally not well answered. For the first requirement, many candidates wasted time by stating everything they knew about the default surcharge rather than confining their answer to the facts of the question – what penalties had been charged in respect of the previous defaults being irrelevant. For the second requirement, candidates often confused the VAT treatment of services received with that for imports or the acquisition of goods. In the fourth requirement, candidates often explained the full range of potential penalties despite being told that the underpayment had arisen due to carelessness.

ACCA marking scheme		Marks
(a)	Third default – 10% surcharge	1.0
	Default surcharge period extended	1.0
	Submit and pay on time for next four returns	1.0
		3.0
(b)	Earlier of service completion and payment date	1.0
	Declare output VAT on UK VAT return	1.0
	Reclaim input VAT on same return	1.0
		3.0
(c)	Can disclose on return as less than £10,000	1.0
	No default interest	1.0
		2.0
(d)	Careless therefore maximum penalty 30%	1.0
	Can be reduced to £0	1.0
		2.0
Total		**10.0**

279 GLACIER LTD

(a) **Output VAT for the quarter ended 31 March 2017**

	£
Sales	
VAT registered customers (£9,400 (£44,600 − £35,200) × 20%)	1,880
Additional contract	1,600
Non-VAT registered customers	
(£46,800 (£289,100 − £242,300) × 20/120)	7,800
Fuel scale charge (£408 × 20/120)	68
	———
	11,348
	———

Tutorial note

The basic tax point for a supply of services is the date when they are completed, but if a VAT invoice is issued or payment received before the basic tax point, then this becomes the actual tax point. Therefore the tax point for the contract is when the VAT invoice was issued on 1 March 2017.

(b) **Default surcharge implications**

Glacier Ltd was late in submitting VAT returns and paying the related VAT liability for two previous quarters. The company has not managed to revert to a clean default surcharge record by submitting four consecutive VAT returns on time.

The late payment of VAT for the quarter ended 31 March 2017 will therefore result in a surcharge of 5% of the VAT liability for that period, although this will not be collected if it is less than £400.

In addition, the surcharge period will be extended to 31 March 2018.

(c) **VAT invoices**

Glacier Ltd must issue a VAT invoice when it makes a standard rated supply to a VAT registered customer.

However, there is no requirement to do so if the supply is exempt or if the supply is to a non-VAT registered customer.

A VAT invoice should be issued within 30 days of the date when the supply is treated as being made.

280 SMART LTD *Walk in the footsteps of a top tutor*

Key answer tips

This question has four requirements covering various administrative aspects of VAT, including registration tests, due dates, tax points and the cash accounting scheme. It is not uncommon for a section C VAT question to be predominantly written and you need to be prepared for questions such as this.

In the answers the highlighted words are key phrases that markers are looking for.

(a) **VAT registration**

Tutor's top tips

This part of the question is testing knowledge of the future registration test. However, marks would also have been given for noting that the historic test was not relevant, as it would have resulted in a later registration date.

- Smart Ltd was liable to register for VAT from 1 November 2016 because this is the date when it signed the contract valued at £86,000.

- The company would therefore have known that its taxable supplies for the following 30-day period would have exceeded £83,000. Registration is required from the start of the 30-day period.

- Smart Ltd would have had to notify HM Revenue and Customs by 30 November 2016, being the end of the 30-day period.

(b) **Return submission and payment**

Tutor's top tips

Parts (b) and (c) of the question did not require any application to the scenario so could have been attempted before parts (a) and (d) if you felt more comfortable with these parts of the question.

- Smart Ltd will have to file its VAT returns online and pay the VAT which is due electronically.

- The deadline for filing the VAT return and paying any VAT which is due is one month and seven days after the end of each quarter (for example, on or before 7 March 2017 for the quarter ended 31 January 2017).

(c)   **Tax point**

- The basic tax point for services is the date when they are completed.

- Smart Ltd will have to account for output VAT at the time that payment is received if a customer pays before the basic tax point and before an invoice is issued (for example, if a deposit is paid).

(d)   **Advantages of cash accounting**

Tutor's top tips

Make sure you tailor your answer to the scenario; not being able to reclaim input VAT until the invoices are actually paid is normally stated as a disadvantage of cash accounting. However, this was not relevant here as Smart Ltd pays its invoices immediately.

- Output VAT will be accounted for 60 days later than at present, because the scheme will result in the tax point becoming the date when payment is received from customers.

- The recovery of input VAT on purchase invoices will not be affected because Smart Ltd pays these immediately after they are received.

- The scheme will provide automatic relief for an impairment loss should a customer default on the payment of a debt.

ACCA marking scheme		Marks
(a)	VAT registration	
	Liable from 1 November 2016	1.0
	Taxable supplies in next 30 days > £83,000	1.0
	Notify HMRC by 30 November 2016	1.0
		———
		3.0
		———
(b)	Submission and payment	
	File online/pay electronically	1.0
	File one month and 7 days after end of return period	1.0
		———
		2.0
		———
(c)	Tax point	
	BTP - Date completed	1.0
	Payment date if before BTP	1.0
		———
		2.0
		———
(d)	Cash accounting	
	Output VAT 60 days later	1.0
	Input VAT not affected	1.0
	Automatic bad debts relief	1.0
		———
		3.0
		———
Total		**10.0**
		———

281 ZIM *Walk in the footsteps of a top tutor*

Key answer tips

A classic VAT question covering the preparation of a VAT return and the flat rate scheme.

Part (a) requires the calculation of VAT payable by a sole trader for a year.

Part (b) considers why the flat rate scheme may be an option and requires knowledge of the conditions.

Part (c) requires a calculation to prove whether or not it would be advantageous to join the scheme.

The highlighted words in parts (b) and (c) are key phrases that markers are looking for.

Tutor's top tips

In this type of question, read the question carefully and find out whether the figures given are inclusive of VAT (as in this question) or exclusive of VAT.

(a) **Value added tax (VAT) – year ended 31 March 2017**

	£	£
Output VAT		
Sales – Standard rated (£115,200 × 20/120)		19,200
– Zero rated		0
Input VAT		
Impairment losses ((£780 + £660) × 20/120)	240	
Purchases – Standard rate (£43,200 × 20/120)	7,200	
– Zero rated	0	
Rent ((£1,200 × 13) × 20/120)	2,600	
Telephone (£2,600 × 60% × 20/120)	260	
Entertaining – UK customers	0	
– Overseas customers (£240 × 20/120)	40	
	———	(10,340)
VAT payable		8,860

Tutorial note

1   *Relief for impairment losses is given once six months have expired from the time the payment was due. Accordingly, relief can be claimed in respect of both impairment losses.*

2   *Rent is a continuous supply; therefore the tax point for the April 2017 rental invoice is the date of payment. Therefore, input VAT is recoverable in respect of all 13 rental payments in the year ended 31 March 2017.*

3   *An apportionment is made where a service such as the use of a telephone is partly for business purposes and partly for private purposes.*

4   *Input VAT on business entertainment is not recoverable unless it relates to the cost of entertaining overseas customers or staff.*

(b)   **Flat rate scheme – conditions**

Tutor's top tips

Make sure you memorise the conditions and thresholds for the various VAT schemes which provide easy marks as long as you have learnt them.

This requirement has two parts (joining and leaving the flat rate scheme), so be sure that you address both parts.

- Zim can join the flat rate scheme from 1 April 2017 because his taxable turnover (excluding VAT) for the next 12 months is not expected to exceed £150,000.

- He can continue to use the scheme until his total turnover (including VAT, but excluding sales of capital assets) for the previous year exceeds £230,000.

Tutorial note

It is also necessary to leave the flat scheme if total turnover is expected to exceed £230,000 during the following 30 days.

Although candidates are not expected to be aware of this point, equivalent marks were awarded if this was given instead of the previous year limit.

(c)   **Flat rate scheme – benefits**

Tutor's top tips

The notes underneath the requirement give a strong hint to recalculate the liability using the flat rate given. Remember to then conclude whether or not it would have been beneficial to have used the scheme.

- Using the flat rate scheme to calculate his VAT liability, Zim would have paid VAT of £15,120 (£126,000 × 12%) for the year ended 31 March 2017.

- It would therefore not have been beneficial to use the flat rate scheme as the additional cost of £6,260 (£15,120 − £8,860) for the year would appear to outweigh the advantage of simplified VAT administration.

Tutorial note

Under the flat rate scheme Zim would be required to pay the flat rate percentage of his VAT inclusive turnover (including zero rated supplies) with no deductions for input VAT.

ACCA marking scheme		Marks
(a)	Sales – standard rated	0.5
	Sales – zero rated	0.5
	Impairment losses	1.0
	Purchases – standard rated	0.5
	Purchases – zero rated	0.5
	Rent	1.0
	Telephone	1.0
	Entertaining – UK customers	0.5
	Entertaining – overseas customers	0.5
		────
		6.0
		────
(b)	Taxable turnover will not exceed £150,000	1.0
	Can continue until total turnover exceeds £230,000	1.0
		────
		2.0
		────
(c)	Liability under flat rate scheme	1.0
	Conclusion	1.0
		────
		2.0
		────
Total		**10.0**
		────

Section 11

SPECIMEN PAPER QUESTIONS

SECTION A – OBJECTIVE TEST (OT) QUESTIONS

ALL 15 QUESTIONS ARE COMPULSORY AND MUST BE ATTEMPTED

Please use the space provided on the inside cover of the Candidate Answer Booklet to indicate your chosen answer to each multiple-choice question.

Each question is worth 2 marks.

1   William is self-employed, and his tax adjusted trading profit for the year ended 5 April 2017 was £82,700. During the tax year 2016/17, William contributed £5,400 (gross) into a personal pension scheme.

   What amount of class 4 national insurance contributions (NIC) will William pay for the tax year 2016/17?

   A   £3,831

   B   £6,718

   C   £3,939

   D   £3,145

2   You are a trainee Chartered Certified Accountant and your firm has a client who has refused to disclose a chargeable gain to HM Revenue and Customs (HMRC).

   From an ethical viewpoint, which of the following actions could be expected of your firm?

   1   Reporting under the money laundering regulations.

   2   Advising the client to make disclosure.

   3   Informing HMRC of the non-disclosure.

   4   Warning the client that your firm will be reporting the non-disclosure.

   A   2 and 4 only

   B   1 and 2 only

   C   1 and 3 only

   D   1, 2, 3 and 4

3   Martin is self-employed, and for the year ended 5 April 2017 his trading profit was £109,400. During the tax year 2016/17, Martin made a gift aid donation of £800 (gross) to a national charity.

What amount of personal allowance will Martin be entitled to for the tax year 2016/17?

A   £11,000

B   £6,700

C   £6,300

D   £0

4   For the year ended 31 March 2017, Halo Ltd made a trading loss of £180,000.

Halo Ltd has owned 100% of the ordinary share capital of Shallow Ltd since it began trading on 1 July 2016. For the year ended 30 June 2017, Shallow Ltd will make a trading profit of £224,000.

Neither company has any other taxable profits or allowable losses.

What is the maximum amount of group relief which Shallow Ltd can claim from Halo Ltd in respect of the trading loss of £180,000 for the year ended 31 March 2017?

A   £180,000

B   £168,000

C   £45,000

D   £135,000

5   For the year ended 31 March 2016, Sizeable Ltd had taxable total profits of £820,000, and for the year ended 31 March 2017 had taxable total profits of £970,000. The profits accrue evenly throughout the year.

Sizeable Ltd has had one 51% group company for many years.

How will Sizeable Ltd pay its corporation tax liability for the year ended 31 March 2017?

A   Nine instalments of £16,400 and a balancing payment of £46,400

B   Four instalments of £48,500

C   Four instalments of £41,000 and a balancing payment of £30,000

D   One payment of £194,000

6   For the year ended 31 December 2016, Lateness Ltd had a corporation tax liability of £60,000, which it did not pay until 31 March 2018. Lateness Ltd is not a large company.

How much interest will Lateness Ltd be charged by HM Revenue and Customs (HMRC) in respect of the late payment of its corporation tax liability for the year ended 31 December 2016?

A   £900

B   £1,800

C   £300

D   £450

7   On 26 November 2016, Alice sold an antique table for £8,700. The antique table had been purchased on 16 May 2012 for £3,800.

What is Alice's chargeable gain in respect of the disposal of the antique table?

A   £4,500

B   £1,620

C   £4,900

D   £0

8   On 14 November 2016, Jane made a cash gift to a trust of £800,000 (after deducting all available exemptions). Jane paid the inheritance tax arising from this gift. Jane has not made any other lifetime gifts.

What amount of lifetime inheritance tax would have been payable in respect of Jane's gift to the trust?

A   £95,000

B   £190,000

C   £118,750

D   £200,000

9   During the tax year 2016/17, Mildred made the following cash gifts to her grandchildren:

1   £400 to Alfred.

2   £140 to Minnie.

3   A further £280 to Minnie.

4   £175 to Winifred.

Which of the gifts will be exempt from inheritance tax under the small gifts exemption?

A   (1), (2), (3) and (4)

B   (2), (3) and (4) only

C   (2) only

D   (4) only

10   For the quarter ended 31 March 2017, Zim had standard rated sales of £49,750 and standard rated expenses of £22,750. Both figures are exclusive of value added tax (VAT).

Zim uses the flat rate scheme to calculate the amount of VAT payable, with the relevant scheme percentage for her trade being 12%. The percentage reduction for the first year of VAT registration is not available.

How much VAT will Zim have to pay to HM Revenue and Customs (HMRC) for the quarter ended 31 March 2017?

A   £5,970

B   £3,888

C   £5,400

D   £7,164

11 **Which of the following assets will ALWAYS be exempt from capital gains tax?**

    1   A motor car suitable for private use.

    2   A chattel.

    3   A UK Government security (gilt).

    4   A house.

    A   (1) and (3)

    B   (2) and (3)

    C   (2) and (4)

    D   (1) and (4)

12 Winston has already invested £8,000 into a cash individual savings account (ISA) during the tax year 2016/17. He now wants to invest into a stocks and shares ISA.

What is the maximum possible amount which Winston can invest into a stocks and shares ISA for the tax year 2016/17?

    A   £15,240

    B   £7,240

    C   £0

    D   £7,000

13 Ming is self-employed.

How long must she retain the business and non-business records used in preparing her self-assessment tax return for the tax year 2016/17?

	Business records	Non-business records
A	31 January 2019	31 January 2019
B	31 January 2019	31 January 2023
C	31 January 2023	31 January 2023
D	31 January 2023	31 January 2019

14 Moon Ltd has had the following results:

Period	Profit/(loss)
	£
Year ended 31 December 2016	(105,000)
Four-month period ended 31 December 2015	43,000
Year ended 31 August 2015	96,000

The company does not have any other income.

How much of Moon Ltd's trading loss for the year ended 31 December 2016 can be relieved against its total profits of £96,000 for the year ended 31 August 2015?

A   £64,000

B   £96,000

C   £70,000

D   £62,000

15 Nigel has not previously been resident in the UK, being in the UK for less than 20 days each tax year. For the tax year 2016/17, he has three ties with the UK.

What is the maximum number of days which Nigel could spend in the UK during the tax year 2016/17 without being treated as resident in the UK for that year?

A   90 days

B   182 days

C   45 days

D   120 days

SECTION B – OT CASES

ALL THREE QUESTIONS ARE COMPULSORY AND MUST BE ATTEMPTED

The following scenario relates to questions 16–20.

Delroy and Grant

On 10 January 2017, Delroy made a gift of 25,000 £1 ordinary shares in Dub Ltd, an unquoted trading company, to his son, Grant. The market value of the shares on that date was £240,000. Delroy had subscribed for the 25,000 shares in Dub Ltd at par on 1 July 2006. Delroy and Grant have elected to hold over the gain as a gift of a business asset.

Grant sold the 25,000 shares in Dub Ltd on 18 March 2017 for £240,000.

Dub Ltd has a share capital of 100,000 £1 ordinary shares. Delroy was the sales director of the company from its incorporation on 1 July 2006 until 10 January 2017. Grant has never been an employee or a director of Dub Ltd.

For the tax year 2016/17, Delroy and Grant are both higher rate taxpayers. They have each made other disposals of assets during the tax year 2016/17, and therefore they have both already utilised their annual exempt amount for this year.

Marlon and Alvita

On 28 March 2017, Marlon sold a house for £497,000, which he had owned individually. The house had been purchased on 22 October 2001 for £152,600.

Throughout the period of ownership, the house was occupied by Marlon and his wife, Alvita, as their main residence. One-third of the house was always used exclusively for business purposes by the couple. Entrepreneurs' relief is not available in respect of this disposal.

For the tax year 2016/17, Marlon is a higher rate taxpayer, but Alvita did not have any taxable income. This will remain the case for the tax year 2017/18. Neither of them has made any other disposals of assets during the year.

16   What is Grant's capital gains tax (CGT) liability for the tax year 2016/17 in respect of the disposal of the shares in Dub Ltd?

    A   £43,000

    B   £21,500

    C   £0

    D   £40,780

17   What would the CGT implications have been if Delroy had instead sold the 25,000 shares in Dub Ltd himself for £240,000 on 10 January 2017, and then gifted the cash proceeds to Grant?

   1   Entrepreneurs' relief would have been available.

   2   The CGT liability would have been paid later.

   3   The cash gift would not have been a chargeable disposal.

   4   The cash gift would have qualified for holdover relief.

   A   (1) and (3)

   B   (2) and (3)

   C   (2) and (4)

   D   (1) and (4)

18   What is Marlon's chargeable gain for the tax year 2016/17?

   A   £229,600

   B   £0

   C   £114,800

   D   £344,400

19   What is the amount of CGT which could have been saved if Marlon had transferred 50% ownership of the house to Alvita prior to its disposal?

   A   £3,108

   B   £6,308

   C   £3,200

   D   £12,068

20   Why would it have been beneficial if Marlon had delayed the sale of the house until 6 April 2017?

   A   A lower rate of CGT would have been applicable

   B   Two annual exempt amounts would have been available

   C   Principal private residence relief would have been greater

   D   The CGT liability would have been paid later

The following scenario relates to questions 21–25.

You should assume that today's date is 15 March 2017.

Opal is aged 71, and has a chargeable estate for inheritance tax (IHT) purposes valued at £950,000.

She owns two properties, respectively valued at £374,000 and £442,000. The first property has an outstanding repayment mortgage of £160,000, and the second property has an outstanding endowment mortgage of £92,000.

Opal owes £22,400 in respect of a personal loan from a bank, and she has also verbally promised to pay legal fees of £4,600 incurred by her nephew. Opal expects the cost of her funeral to be £5,200, and this cost will be covered by the £6,000 which she has invested in an individual savings account (ISA).

Under the terms of her will, Opal has left all of her estate to her children. Opal's husband is still alive.

On 14 August 2006, Opal had made a gift of £100,000 to her daughter, and on 7 November 2016, she made a gift of £220,000 to her son. Both these figures are after deducting all available exemptions.

The nil rate band for the tax year 2006/07 is £285,000.

You should assume that both the value of Opal's estate and the nil rate band will remain unchanged for future years.

---

21   What is the net value for the two properties, and related mortgages, which will have been included in the calculation of Opal's chargeable estate of £950,000?

    A   £816,000

    B   £564,000

    C   £656,000

    D   £724,000

22   What is the total amount of deductions (ignoring mortgage debts) which will have been permitted in calculating Opal's chargeable estate of £950,000?

    A   £28,400

    B   £22,400

    C   £32,200

    D   £27,600

23   What amount of IHT will be payable in respect of Opal's chargeable estate valued at £950,000 were she to die on 20 March 2017?

    A   £250,000

    B   £338,000

    C   £378,000

    D   £335,600

24 **By how much would the IHT payable on Opal's death be reduced if she were to live for another seven years until 20 March 2024, compared to if she were to die on 20 March 2017?**

A   £88,000

B   £40,000

C   £128,000

D   £0

25 **Which of the following conditions must be met if Opal wants to make gifts out of her income, so that these gifts are exempt from IHT?**

1   The gifts cannot exceed 10% of income.

2   The gifts must be habitual.

3   Opal must have enough remaining income to maintain her normal standard of living.

4   Opal must make the gifts monthly or quarterly.

A   (3) and (4)

B   (1) and (4)

C   (2) and (3)

D   (1) and (2)

The following scenario relates to questions 26–30.

The following information is available in respect of Glacier Ltd's value added tax (VAT) for the quarter ended 31 March 2017:

(1)   Invoices were issued for sales of £44,600 to VAT registered customers. Of this figure, £35,200 was in respect of exempt sales and the balance in respect of standard rated sales. The standard rated sales figure is exclusive of VAT.

(2)   In addition to the above, on 1 March 2017 Glacier Ltd issued a VAT invoice for £8,000 plus VAT of £1,600 to a VAT registered customer in respect of a contract which will be completed on 15 April 2017. The customer paid for the contract in two instalments of £4,800 on 31 March 2017 and 30 April 2017.

(3)   The managing director of Glacier Ltd is provided with free fuel for private mileage driven in her company motor car. During the quarter ended 31 March 2017, the total cost of fuel for business and private mileage was £720, of which £270 was for private mileage. The relevant quarterly scale charge is £408. All of these figures are inclusive of VAT.

For the quarters ended 30 September 2015 and 30 June 2016, Glacier Ltd was one month late in submitting its VAT returns and in paying the related VAT liabilities. All of the company's other VAT returns have been submitted on time.

26 **What is the amount of output VAT payable by Glacier Ltd in respect of its sales for the quarter ended 31 March 2017?**

A   £2,680

B   £3,480

C   £10,520

D   £1,880

27   What output VAT and input VAT entries will Glacier Ltd include on its VAT return for the quarter ended 31 March 2017 in respect of the managing director's company motor car?

A   Output VAT of £68 and input VAT of £75

B   Output VAT of £0 and input VAT of £75

C   Output VAT of £0 and input VAT of £120

D   Output VAT of £68 and input VAT of £120

28   What surcharge penalty could Glacier Ltd be charged if the company is one month late in paying its VAT liability for the quarter ended 31 March 2017?

A   5% of the VAT liability

B   2% of the VAT liability

C   There will be no penalty

D   10% of the VAT liability

29   What is the minimum requirement which Glacier Ltd needs to meet in order to revert to a clean default surcharge record?

A   Submit four consecutive VAT returns on time

B   Submit any four VAT returns on time and also pay the related VAT liabilities on time

C   Pay four consecutive VAT liabilities on time

D   Submit four consecutive VAT returns on time and also pay the related VAT liabilities on time

30   In which circumstances will Glacier Ltd be required to issue a VAT invoice?

A   When a standard rated supply is made to any customer

B   When any type of supply is made to any customer

C   When a standard rated supply is made to a VAT registered customer

D   When any type of supply is made to a VAT registered customer

SECTION C – CONSTRUCTED RESPONSE (LONG QUESTIONS)

ALL THREE QUESTIONS ARE COMPULSORY AND MUST BE ATTEMPTED

1   **You should assume that today's date is 1 March 2016.**

Sarah is currently self-employed. If she continues to trade on a self-employed basis, her total income tax liability and national insurance contributions (NIC) for the tax year 2016/17 will be £12,631.

However, Sarah is considering incorporating her business on 6 April 2016. The forecast taxable total profits of the new limited company for the year ended 5 April 2017 will be £50,000 (before taking account of any director's remuneration). Sarah will pay herself gross director's remuneration of £30,000 and dividends of £10,000. The balance of the profits will remain undrawn within the new company.

Required:

Determine whether or not there will be an overall saving of tax and national insurance contributions (NIC) for the year ended 5 April 2017 if Sarah incorporates her business on 6 April 2016.

Notes:

1   **You are expected to calculate the income tax payable by Sarah, the class 1 NIC payable by Sarah and the new limited company, and the corporation tax liability of the new limited company for the year ended 5 April 2017.**

2   **You should assume that the rates of corporation tax remain unchanged.**

(10 marks)

2   On 6 April 2016, Simon commenced employment with Echo Ltd. On 1 January 2017, he commenced in partnership with Art running a small music venue, preparing accounts to 30 April. The following information is available for the tax year 2016/17:

Employment

(1)   During the tax year 2016/17, Simon was paid a gross annual salary of £23,700.

(2)   Throughout the tax year 2016/17, Echo Ltd provided Simon with living accommodation. The company had purchased the property in 2006 for £89,000, and it was valued at £143,000 on 6 April 2016. The annual value of the property is £4,600. The property was furnished by Echo Ltd during March 2016 at a cost of £9,400. The living accommodation is not job related.

(3)   On 1 December 2016, Echo Ltd provided Simon with an interest-free loan of £84,000, which he used to purchase a holiday cottage.

Partnership

(1)   The partnership's tax adjusted trading profit for the four-month period ended 30 April 2017 is £29,700. This figure is before taking account of capital allowances.

(2)   The only item of plant and machinery owned by the partnership is a motor car which cost £18,750 on 1 February 2017. The motor car has a CO_2 emission rate of 155 grams per kilometre. It is used by Art, and 40% of the mileage is for private journeys.

(3)   Profits are shared 40% to Simon and 60% to Art. This is after paying an annual salary of £6,000 to Art.

Property income

(1)   Simon owns a freehold house which is let out furnished. The property was let throughout the tax year 2016/17 at a monthly rent of £660.

(2)   During the tax year 2016/17, Simon paid council tax of £1,320 in respect of the property, and also spent £660 on replacement carpets.

Required:

(a)   Calculate Simon's taxable income for the tax year 2016/17.   **(13 marks)**

(b)   State TWO advantages for the partnership of choosing 30 April as its accounting date rather than 5 April.   **(2 marks)**

(Total: 15 marks)

3   (a)   You are a trainee accountant and your manager has asked you to correct a corporation tax computation which has been prepared by the managing director of Naive Ltd. The corporation tax computation is for the year ended 31 March 2017 and contains a significant number of errors:

Naive Ltd – Corporation tax computation for the year ended 31 March 2017

	£
Trading profit (W1)	372,900
Loan interest received (W2)	32,100
	405,000
Corporation tax (£405,000 at 20%)	81,000

Workings

(W1) Trading profit

	£
Profit before taxation	274,530
Depreciation	15,740
Donations to political parties	400
Qualifying charitable donations	900
Accountancy	2,300
Legal fees in connection with the issue of loan notes (the loan was used to finance the company's trading activities)	5,700
Entertaining suppliers	3,600
Entertaining employees	1,700
Gifts to customers (pens costing £40 each and displaying Naive Ltd's name)	920
Gifts to customers (food hampers costing £45 each and displaying Naive Ltd's name)	1,650
Capital allowances (W3)	65,460
	———
Trading profit	372,900
	———

(W2) Loan interest received

	£
Loan interest receivable	32,800
Accrued at 1 April 2016	10,600
Accrued at 31 March 2017	(11,300)
	———
Loan interest received	32,100
	———

The loan was made for non-trading purposes.

(W3) Capital allowances

	Main pool £	Motor car £	Special rate pool £	Allowances £
Tax written down value (TWDV) brought forward	12,400		13,600	
Additions				
Machinery	42,300			
Motor car [1]	13,800			
Motor car [2]		14,000		
	———			
	68,500			
Annual investment allowance (AIA)	(68,500)			68,500
Disposal proceeds			(9,300)	
			———	
			4,300	
Balancing allowance			(4,300)	(4,300)
			———	
Writing down allowance (WDA) – 18%		(2,520) × 50%		1,260
	———	———		
TWDV carried forward	0	11,480		
	———	———		———
Total allowances				65,460
				———

(1) Motor car [1] has a CO_2 emission rate of 110 grams per kilometre.

(2) Motor car [2] has a CO_2 emission rate of 155 grams per kilometre. This motor car is used by the sales manager and 50% of the mileage is for private journeys.

(3) All of the items included in the special rate pool at 1 April 2016 were sold for £9,300 during the year ended 31 March 2017. The original cost of these items was £16,200.

Required:

Prepare a revised version of Naive Ltd's corporation tax computation for the year ended 31 March 2017.

Note: Your calculations should commence with the profit before taxation figure of £274,530, and you should indicate by the use of zero (0) any items in the computation of the trading profit for which no adjustment is required.

(12 marks)

(b) The managing director of Naive Ltd understands that the company will have to file its self-assessment corporation tax returns online, and that the supporting accounts and tax computations will have to be filed using the inline eXtensible Business Reporting Language (iXBRL). The managing director is concerned about how the company will be able to produce documents in this format.

Required:

Explain the options available to Naive Ltd regarding the production of accounts and tax computations in the iXBRL format. **(3 marks)**

(Total: 15 marks)

Section 12

ANSWERS TO SPECIMEN PAPER QUESTIONS

SECTION A

1 C

(£34,940 (£43,000 − £8,060) at 9%) + (£39,700 (£82,700 − £ 43,000) at 2%) = £3,939

2 B

3 B

	£
Personal allowance	11,000
Restriction (£109,400 − £800 − £100,000 = £8,600/2)	(4,300)
Restricted personal allowance	6,700

4 D

Lower of:

£135,000 (£180,000 × 9/12)

£168,000 (£224,000 × 9/12)

5 B

(£970,000 at 20%)/4 = £48,500

6 A

£60,000 × 3% × 6/12 = £900 (period 1 October 2017 to 31 March 2018)

7 A

£2,700 (£8,700 − £6,000) × 5/3 = £4,500

This is less than £4,900 (£8,700 − £3,800).

8   C

£475,000 (£800,000 – £325,000) × 20/80 = £118,750

9   D

10   D

£49,750 × 120/100 at 12% = £7,164

11   A

12   B

£15,240 – £8,000 = £7,240

13   C

14   D

The maximum loss relief is greater of:

- Remaining loss: £62,000 (£105,000 – £43,000)

- Profits for 8 months ended 31.8.15: £64,000 (£96,000 × 8/12)

15   A

SECTION B

16   A

£215,000 (£240,000 – £25,000) at 20% = £43,000

Tutorial note

Grant's base cost in the shares is £25,000 being their market value at the date of the gift (£240,000) less the gain held over of £215,000 (£240,000 – £25,000).

17   A

18   C

£344,400 (£497,000 – £152,600) × 1/3 = £114,800

19   B

(£11,100 at 28%) + (£32,000 at 10% (28% – 18%)) = £6,308

Tutorial note

If half of the gain had been transferred to Alvin, his previously unused annual exempt amount would have reduced the gain by £11,100. In addition, as Alvin does not have any taxable income, £32,000 of the gain falling in his unused basic rate will be taxed at the lower rate of 18% rather than 28%. Remember that the higher capital gains tax rates of 18% and 28% apply to residential property.

20   D

21   C

£374,000 + £442,000 − £160,000 = £656,000

22   D

£22,400 + £5,200 = £27,600

23   B

£845,000 (£950,000 − (£325,000 − £220,000)) at 40% = £338,000

24   A

£220,000 at 40% = £88,000

Tutorial note

If Opal were to live until 20 March 2024 the PET on 7 November 2016 would no longer be chargeable and would result in an additional available nil rate band on death of £220,000.

25   C

26   B

(£9,400 (£44,600 − £35,200) × 20%) + £1,600 = £3,480

27   D

Output VAT £408 × 20/120 = £68

Input VAT £720 × 20/120 = £120

28 A

Second default during surcharge period.

29 D

30 C

SECTION C

1   SARAH

(1) **Sarah's income tax payable 2016/17:**

	£
Director's remuneration	30,000
Dividends	10,000
	40,000
Personal allowance	(11,000)
Taxable income	29,000

Income tax	£
£	
19,000 at 20%	3,800
5,000 at 0%	0
5,000 at 7.5%	375
29,000	
Income tax payable	4,175

(2) **National insurance contributions (NIC) 2016/17:**

	£
Employee class 1 (£21,940 (£30,000 – £8,060) at 12%)	2,633
Employer's class 1 (£21,888 (£30,000 – £8,112) at 13.8%)	3,021

(3) **Corporation tax liability of the new limited company for the year ended 5 April 2017:**

	£
Trading profit	50,000
Director's remuneration	(30,000)
Employer's class 1 NIC	(3,021)
Taxable total profits	16,979
Corporation tax (£16,979 at 20%)	3,396

(4) The total tax and NIC cost if Sarah incorporates her business is £13,225 (£4,175 + £2,633 + £3,021 + £3,396).

(5) Therefore, if Sarah incorporated her business there would be an overall increase in tax and NIC of £594 (13,225 – 12,631) compared to continuing on a self-employed basis.

ACCA marking scheme	
	Marks
Sarah's income tax payable	3.5
National insurance contributions	3.0
Corporation tax liability	2.0
Total tax and NIC cost	1.0
Increase	0.5
Total	**10.0**

2 SIMON

(a) **Simon – Taxable income 2016/17**

		£
Employment income		
Salary		23,700
Living accommodation	– Annual value	4,600
	– Additional benefit (W1)	2,040
	– Furniture (£9,400 × 20%)	1,880
Beneficial loan (£84,000 × 4/12 at 3%)		840
		33,060
Trading profit (W2)		8,220
Property income (W4)		5,940
Total income		47,220
Personal allowance		(11,000)
Taxable income		36,220

Workings

(W1) Living accommodation additional benefit

(1)   The benefit is based on the market value when first provided.

	£
Market value	143,000
Limit	(75,000)
	68,000

(2)   The additional benefit is therefore £2,040 (£68,000 at 3%).

Tutorial note

The property was purchased more than six years before first being provided, so the benefit is based on the market value when first provided.

(W2) Trading profit

(1)   Simon's share of the partnership's trading profit for the period ended 30 April 2017 is £10,960 calculated as follows:

	£
Trading profit	29,700
Capital allowances (W3)	(300)
	29,400
Salary paid to Art (£6,000 × 4/12)	(2,000)
	27,400
Profit share (£27,400 × 40%)	10,960

(2)   Simon's trading income assessment for 2016/17 is £8,220 (£10,960 × 3/4).

Tutorial note

Simon's assessment for 2016/17 is for the period 1 January 2017 to 5 April 2017.

(W3) Capital allowances

	Motor car		Allowances
	£		£
Addition	18,750		
WDA – 8% × 4/12	(500)	× 60%	300
	———		——
WDV carried forward	18,250		
	———		

Tutorial note

The partnership's motor car has CO$_2$ emissions over 130 grams per kilometre and therefore qualifies for writing down allowances at the rate of 8%.

(W4) Property income

	£	£
Rent receivable (£660 × 12)		7,920
Council tax	1,320	
Replacement carpets	660	
	———	
		(1,980)
		———
Property income		5,940
		———

Tutorial note

The initial cost of purchasing domestic items for use by the tenant, such as carpets, is not allowable, however, the cost of replacing such items is an allowable deduction.

(b) (1) The interval between earning profits and paying the related tax liability will be 11 months longer. This can be particularly beneficial where profits are rising.

(2) It will be possible to calculate taxable profits well in advance of the end of the tax year, making it much easier to implement tax planning and make pension contributions.

Marking scheme		Marks
(a)	**Calculate Simon's taxable income**	
	Employment income	5.0
	Trading profit	5.0
	Property income	2.5
	Personal allowance	0.5
		13.0
(b)	**Advantages of accounting date**	
	Two advantages	2.0
Total		**15.0**

3 NAIVE LTD

(a) **Naive Ltd – Corporation tax computation for the year ended 31 March 2017**

	£
Trading profit (W1)	248,340
Loan interest receivable	32,800
Total profits	281,140
Qualifying charitable donations	(900)
Taxable total profits	280,240
Corporation tax (£280,240 at 20%)	56,048

Workings

(W1) Trading profit for the year ended 31 March 2017

	£	£
Profit before taxation	274,530	
Depreciation	15,740	
Donations to political parties	400	
Qualifying charitable donations	900	
Accountancy	0	
Legal fees	0	
Entertaining suppliers	3,600	
Entertaining employees	0	
Gifts to customers – pens	0	
Gifts to customers – food hampers	1,650	
Capital allowances (W2)		48,480
	296,820	48,480
	(48,480)	
Trading profit	248,340	

Tutorial note

1   *The only exception to the non-deductibility of entertainment expenditure is when it is in respect of employees.*

2   *Gifts to customers are an allowable deduction if they cost less than £50 per recipient per year, are not of food, drink, tobacco or vouchers for exchangeable goods, and carry a conspicuous advertisement for the company making the gift.*

(W2) Capital allowances

		Main pool	Special rate pool	Allowances
	£	£	£	£
TWDV brought forward		12,400	13,600	
Additions qualifying for AIA				
Machinery	42,300			
AIA – 100%	(42,300)	0		42,300
Other additions				
Motor car [1]		13,800		
Motor car [2]			14,000	
Proceeds			(9,300)	
		26,200	18,300	
WDA – 18%		(4,716)		4,716
WDA – 8%			(1,464)	1,464
TWDV carried forward		21,484	16,836	
Total allowances				48,480

Tutorial note

1   *Motor car [1] has CO$_2$ emissions between 76 and 130 grams per kilometre and therefore qualifies for writing down allowances at the rate of 18%.*

2   *Motor car [2] has CO$_2$ emissions over 130 grams per kilometre and therefore qualifies for writing down allowances at the rate of 8%. The private use of the motor car is irrelevant, since such usage will be assessed on the employee as a benefit.*

(b)　(1)　If Naive Ltd has straightforward accounts, it could use the software provided by HM Revenue and Customs. This automatically produces accounts and tax computations in the iXBRL format.

(2)　Alternatively, other software which automatically produces iXBRL accounts and computations could be used.

(3)　A tagging service could be used to apply the appropriate tags to the accounts and tax computations, or Naive Ltd could use software to tag documents itself.

ACCA marking scheme		
		Marks
(a)	**Corporation tax computation**	
	Trading profit	5.0
	Capital allowances	5.0
	Loan interest	1.0
	Qualifying charitable donations	0.5
	Corporation tax	0.5
		12.0
(b)	**iXBRL**	
	HMRC software	1.0
	Other software	1.0
	Tagging service	1.0
		3.0
Total		**15.0**